A SMALL
4,000 OF T
QUO
THE NEW
DICTIONARY OF QUOTATIONS

"Man thinks. God laughs."　　　—Jewish Proverb

"The nation cannot afford to be materially rich and spiritually poor."　　　—John F. Kennedy

"The use of language is all we have to pit against death and silence."　　　—Joyce Carol Oates

"I know only two tunes: one is 'Yankee Doodle,' and the other isn't."　　　—Ulysses S. Grant

"Judicial decrees may not change the heart, but they can restrain the heartless."
　　　—Martin Luther King, Jr.

"In politics, if you want anything said, ask a man; if you want anything done, ask a woman."
　　　—Margaret Thatcher

"I used to be Snow White, but I drifted."
　　　—Mae West

"Love all, trust a few."　　　—Shakespeare

MARGARET MINER and HUGH RAWSON have collaborated as editors of *The American Heritage Dictionary of American Quotations*, *The Dictionary of Quotations from the Bible*, and *The Dictionary of Quotations from Shakespeare* and have written, contributed to, or edited a number of other books. They live in Roxbury, Connecticut.

Also by Margaret Miner and Hugh Rawson

*American Heritage Dictionary
of American Quotations*
A Dictionary of Quotations from Shakespeare
A Dictionary of Quotations from the Bible

By Margaret Miner

Allergies
(with Stuart Young, M.D.,
and Bruce Dobozin, M.D.)

By Hugh Rawson

Unwritten Laws
*Rawson's Dictionary of Euphemisms & Other
Doubletalk*
Devious Derivations
Wicked Words
An Investment in Knowledge
(with Hillier Krieghbaum)

THE NEW INTERNATIONAL DICTIONARY OF QUOTATIONS

THIRD EDITION

Selected and Annotated by
Margaret Miner
and
Hugh Rawson

A SIGNET BOOK

For
Nathaniel and Catherine

ACKNOWLEDGMENTS

We thank our excellent copy editors, Henry Price and Ronny Johnson. Our friends Bob Nadder, Ken Silverman, Pat Barrett, Bob Creamer, and David and Terry Vaughan helped in different ways, suggesting quotes as well as verifying them and their sources. For aid in tracking citations, we thank Inga-Britta Mills, Lee Seidler, John Peterson, Krishna Winston at Wesleyan University, Margrit Gillespie at The Taft School, Martin Gardner, Egon Schwarz at Washington University in St. Louis (who found the citation for a fine but little-known Rilke quotation), and Jack Zipes at the University of Minnesota. In verifying quotations, Stewart Brand, David Gergen, Clayton Rawson, Helen Stark at *The New Yorker*, and Victor K. McElheny were especially kind. At the Minor Memorial Library in Roxbury, Tim Beard, Susie Juram, and Betty Synnestvedt graciously coped with numerous questions. William Fuller greatly helped with the index.

Finally, we thank Arnold Dolin for suggesting that we undertake this project.

INTRODUCTION

The aim of *The New International Dictionary of Quotations* is to distill the most memorable words of the past with a view to the concerns of the present. The most memorable words are not necessarily the "best" words in a literary sense. Rather, they are the words that best encapsule the ideas, hopes, fears, loves, hates, that have been common to men and women throughout history. Thus, this dictionary is international in scope and it covers all periods, from ancient times to the present. Its bias, however, is toward the tried and the true—the familiar quotations that are on, or almost on, the tip of everyone's tongue, but whose exact wording, authorship, or source may have been forgotten.

To this end, *The New International Dictionary of Quotations* includes ample selections from the Bible, Shakespeare, Aesop, Burke, Carlyle, Churchill, Disraeli, Emerson, Euripides, Johnson, Pope, Shaw, Tennyson, and the works of other famous writers whose words have shaped the thoughts of everyone who has lived after them. At the same time, the dictionary also includes the observations of such luminaries as P. T. Barnum, Samuel Beckett, Leo Durocher, W. C. Fields, Arthur Miller, Satchel Paige, Dorothy Parker, and Mae West, who in their own highly quotable ways have contributed to the residual wisdom of the human race.

In sum, this dictionary of quotations differs from others that have been compiled by including relatively more quotes from well-known writers; relatively more prose compared to poetry; relatively more quotes from doers—politicians, entertainers, generals, athletes, and so on—as opposed to strictly literary figures; relatively more American material; and relatively more quotes from women, minority leaders, scientists, and others who have addressed topics of special importance to our times. Meanwhile, an attempt has been

made to weed out platitudes and other trite expressions that
do not bear repetition: nursery rhymes, lyrics from popular
songs whose currency depends largely on knowing the ac-
companying music; quotations that are so closely linked to
particular historic occasions that they are rarely used in
other contexts; and contemporary quotes and catch phrases
that have not yet been ratified by the test of time. Some
exceptions have been allowed to these rules, and any readers
who feel that their own favorite quotations have been un-
fairly excluded for whatever reason are invited to submit
them to the editors, in care of the publisher, and they will be
considered for inclusion when this dictionary is revised again.

Although not an encyclopedic work (several excellent examples of which already exist, including *Bartlett's Familiar
Quotations*, 16th edition, 1992; *The Oxford Dictionary of
Quotations*, 3rd edition, 1979; *The International Thesaurus
of Quotations,* Rhoda Thomas Tripp, 1970; and H. L. Mencken's *A New Dictionary of Quotations on Historical Principles*, 1942), *The New International Dictionary of Quotations*
should be a useful addition to most bookshelves. It brings
together in compact, easily accessible form the basic stock
of quotations that will satisfy most needs of most contemporary users of English. It should be of especial value to students and others seeking to track down references to
quotations they have read or to support their positions on
particular topics; to writers and speakers who wish to en-
hance their own words by drawing upon the best of the
rhetoric of the past; and, finally, to all lovers of language,
who will relish the riches here.

The New International Dictionary of Quotations is arranged to give readers at least two chances to find the quotes
they want—through the main text, which is organized by
subject, and through the author index. In the main text,
subjects are listed alphabetically, with the principal topics
printed in boldface capital letters along the left-hand margin
of the page. Thus:

ACCOMPLISHMENT

ACTION

ACTORS & ACTING

and so on, through to

YESTERDAY

YOUTH

ZEAL

Most subject categories also include references to related topics. These are printed in small cap letters along the right-hand margin of the text. For example:

ACCOMPLISHMENT   See also ACTIONS; DOING; GREATNESS; SUCCESS & FAME; WORK & WORKERS

Within the subject categories, quotations are arranged alphabetically by author, frequently beginning with that wise and prolific writer, ANONYMOUS. In cases of well-known works by unknown authors, or by groups of authors, such as the Bible, the Book of Common Prayer, and the Talmud, the titles are treated as though they are authors' names, and quotations from them are alphabetized accordingly.

All foreign quotations have been translated into English. Those from the Bible are from the Authorized, or King James Version unless specifically noted otherwise. Quotations are given in a foreign language as well as in English in instances where they are encountered frequently in their original form.

Following each quotation is the name of the author, the title of its source, and its date of publication or approximate time of composition or the death date of the author. In addition, many quotes are followed by notes from the editors. [These are printed in brackets, like this sentence.] The notes provide additional information on a variety of topics: earlier examples of a particular turn of phrase; use of similar expressions by later writers; the circumstances in which something was first said or written; the way a particular quote has been commonly mistranslated, misquoted, or "improved," and so on. The notes often cite additional sources for attributions and refer the reader to other subject categories.

Where the name of the author is known, the user of this dictionary may find the sought-for quotation even more quickly by consulting the index beginning on page 557. Here, names of authors (and titles of some works) are listed alphabetically in the same way as in the subject categories, along with key words, phrases, and page numbers for each of their quotations. Birth and death dates of authors also are given in the index.

Whether approaching the text via the subject categories or the author index, the user of this dictionary is likely to make many happy discoveries, including the fact that it is possible to drive home any point one wishes to make through the artful use of quotation. As Winston Churchill noted, "It is a good thing for an uneducated man to read books of quotations." (*Roving Commission* in *My Early Life*, 1930). Or as Ralph Waldo Emerson wrote in his *Journal* (May 1849): "I hate quotation. Tell me what you know." The same authority may even support both sides of the question: "Next to the originator of a good sentence is the first quoter of it." (Emerson, *Quotation and Originality* in *Letters and Social Aims*, 1876).

NOTE FOR
THE THIRD EDITION

No sooner had the first edition of *The New International Dictionary of Quotations* gone to press than we began to find additions and improvements that we wanted to make—a fate that befalls all creators of reference works. So we thank our publisher for giving us the opportunity to bring out a second edition and now a third, each version being larger, more up to date, and more detailed than the preceding one.

This third edition includes more than four hundred new quotes, as well as many dozens of new categories, new explanatory notes, and—new features for this edition—dates for citations and, under Tolstoy at FAMILY, a series of cross-references to famous first lines in both fiction and nonfiction.

Our son once irreverently asked, "If you covered the great quotations the first time, why do you need to add more?" Hours of watching television news had persuaded him that almost nothing memorable had been said in the preceding five years. Some of the additional quotes here are recent discoveries or rediscoveries. For example, any student who has wrestled with mathematics will appreciate the anonymous sixteenth-century lament "Multiplication is vexation, / Division is as bad; /The Rule of three doth puzzle me, /And Practice drives me mad." Another older quote that seems to us to deserve perpetuation is Cardinal Newman's supplication (from an 1834 sermon): "O Lord, support us all the day long, until the shadows lengthen and the evening comes, and the busy world is hushed, and the fever of life is over, and our work is done. Then in thy mercy grant us a safe lodging and a holy rest, and peace at the last."

Contemporary quotations tend to be less lyric, more to the point, and it is difficult to judge their longevity. However, the tendency to excuse errors and malfeasance knows no season, and no doubt all of us will continue to make use of the ubiquitous, evasive "mistakes were made" in some form or other. Therefore we included "Mistakes have been made" (Ulysses S. Grant, report to Congress, Dec. 5, 1876), and a note which reads in part: "This admission appears in an unprecedented apology that Grant appended to his final annual report to Congress. But Grant shed personal responsibility for the scandals that plagued his two terms as president by casting the apology in passive-evasive terms that later political leaders have found equally useful." We then list modern adaptations of the excuse by President Bill Clinton, Israeli Prime Minister Benjamin Netanyahu, and Pol Pot, former leader of Cambodia.

An example of a new quotation that gets directly to the point is certainly "Show me the money!" by Cameron Crowe, in the screenplay *Jerry McGuire*, 1996. Although this is hardly more succinct than the Uzbek proverb "A word said is a shot fired" (LANGUAGE & WORDS).

To return to one of the masters of not getting to the point, against President Clinton, we have included the notorious "It depends what the meaning of *is* is," with a note explaining the context. Only time will tell if this remark will find its place in the anthologies of memorable fin de siecle comments.

Finally, we would like to credit some of the sources that have been helpful to us: *Respectfully Quoted*, edited by Suzy Platt and published by the Library of Congress, 1989; *The Great Quotations*, edited by the late, wonderful George Seldes, 1960; *The Quotable Woman*, edited by Elaine Partnow, 2 vols., 1985; *The Quotable Lawyer*, edited by David Shrager and Elizabeth Frost, 1986; *The Oxford Dictionary of Modern Quotations*, edited by A. J. Augard, 1991; and *The Penguin Thesaurus of Quotations*, edited by M. J. Cohen, 1998.

A

ACCOMPLISHMENT

See also ACTION; DOING; GREATNESS; SUCCESS & FAME; WORK & WORKERS

Better is the end of a thing than the beginning thereof.
—BIBLE, *Ecclesiastes* 7:8

I have fought a good fight, I have finished my course, I have kept the faith.
—BIBLE, *II Timothy* 4:7

The reward of a thing well done is to have done it.
—RALPH WALDO EMERSON, *Nominalist and Realist* in *Essays: Second Series*, 1844

Each morning sees some task begin.
Each evening sees it close;
Something attempted, something done,
Has earned a night's repose.
—HENRY WADSWORTH LONGFELLOW, *The Village Blacksmith*, 1842

Death closes all: but something ere the end,
Some work of noble note, may yet be done,
Not unbecoming men that strove with gods.
—ALFRED, LORD TENNYSON, *Ulysses*, 1842

ACTION

See also BOLDNESS & INITIATIVE; DOING

We become just by performing just actions, temperate by performing temperate actions, brave by performing brave actions. —ARISTOTLE, *Nicomachean Ethics*, 4th cent. B.C.

He who desires but acts not breeds pestilence.
                                        —WILLIAM BLAKE,
                        The Marriage of Heaven and Hell, 1790–93

The world can only be grasped by action, not by contemplation. The hand is more important than the eye.
                        —JACOB BRONOWSKI, *The Ascent of Man*, 1973

Action is eloquence.   —SHAKESPEARE, *Coriolanus*, III, ii

ACTORS & ACTING   See ARTS: THEATER,
                               MOVIES, & ACTING

ADVERSITY   See TROUBLE

ADVERTISING   See also PUBLICITY &
                                PUBLIC RELATIONS

They all laughed when I sat down at the piano, but oh!,
when I began to play . . .
                        —JOHN CAPLES, legendary advertisement
                              for mail-order piano lessons, 1925

You can tell the ideals of a nation by its advertisements.
                        —NORMAN DOUGLAS, *South Wind*, 1917

We grew up founding our dreams on the infinite promise of
American advertising.
                        —ZELDA FITZGERALD, *Save Me the Waltz*, 1932

Promise, large promise, is the soul of an advertisement.
                        —SAMUEL JOHNSON, in *The Idler*, Jan. 20, 1759

The trade of advertising is now so near perfection that it is
not easy to propose any improvement.   —*Ibid.*

Half the money I spend on advertising is wasted, and the
trouble is, I don't know which half.
                        —WILLIAM HESKETH, LORD LEVERHULME,
                                          d. 1925, attributed
[Mr. Lever, as he was known before becoming a viscount,
founded Lever Brothers, which became the cornerstone of Uni-
lever. David Ogilvy, in *Confessions of an Advertising Man* (1964),

noted that American department store magnate John Wanamaker made the same complaint in the same words.]

Ads push the principle of noise all the way to the plateau of persuasion. They are quite in accord with the procedures of brainwashing.
—MARSHALL McLUHAN, *Understanding Media*, 1964

ADVICE   See also ARTS: CRITICISM & CRITICS; PRUDENCE & PRACTICAL WISDOM

There is nothing we receive with so much reluctance as advice.   —JOSEPH ADDISON, *The Spectator*, Oct. 12, 1712

Good but rarely came from good advice.
—LORD BYRON, *Don Juan*, 1819–24

Advice is seldom welcome; and those who want it the most always like it the least.   —EARL OF CHESTERFIELD, letter to his son, Jan. 29, 1748

Whatever advice you give, be brief.
—HORACE, *Art of Poetry*, c. 20–8 B.C.

When we ask advice, we are usually looking for an accomplice.   —MARQUIS DE LAGRANGE, d. 1876, *Pensées*

One gives nothing so freely as advice.
—LA ROCHEFOUCAULD, *Maxims*, 1678

People ask you for criticism, but they only want praise.
—W. SOMERSET MAUGHAM, *Of Human Bondage*, 1915

Many receive advice, few profit by it.
—PUBLILIUS SYRUS, *Moral Sayings*, 1st cent. B.C.

AESTHETICS   See ARTS: AESTHETICS

AFRICA   See NATIONS

AFRICAN AMERICANS   See RACES & PEOPLES

AFTERNOON   See NATURE: TIMES OF DAY

AGE & AGING   See also MIDDLE AGE &
MID-LIFE CRISIS; OLD THINGS,
OLD FRIENDS

Old men are always young enough to learn, with profit.
          —AESCHYLUS, *Agamemnon,* 5th cent. B.C.

To me, old age is always fifteen years older than I am.
          —BERNARD BARUCH, news reports
          on his 85th birthday, Aug. 20, 1955

When everything else physical and mental seems to diminish, the appreciation of beauty is on the increase.
          —BERNARD BERENSON, *Sunset and Twilight,* 1963

With the ancient is wisdom; and in length of days
understanding.   —BIBLE, *Job* 12:12

Grow old along with me!
The best is yet to be,
The last of life, for which the first was made.
          —ROBERT BROWNING, *Rabbi Ben Ezra,* 1864

So, we'll go no more a roving
So late into the night,
Though the heart be still as loving,
And the moon be still as bright.
          —LORD BYRON, *So, We'll Go
          No More a Roving,* 1817

"You are old, Father William," the young man said,
"And your hair has become very white;
And yet you incessantly stand on your head—
Do you think, at your age, it is right?"
          —LEWIS CARROLL,
          Alice's Adventures in Wonderland, 1865
[This is a parody of Robert Southey's pious poem of 1799, *The Old Man's Comforts and How He Gained Them,* which also begins, "You are old, Father William . . ." The young man then asks why William is so hale. The answer: "In the days of my youth, I remembered my God, / And he hath not forgotten my age."]

One keeps on forgetting old age up to the very brink of the grave.   —COLETTE, *My Mother and Illness*
in *My Mother's House,* 1922

Youth is a blunder; manhood a struggle; old age a regret.
—BENJAMIN DISRAELI, *Coningsby,*
or The New Generation, 1844

When a man fell into his anecdotage it was a sign for him to retire from the world.
—BENJAMIN DISRAELI, *Lothair,* 1870

I grow old . . . I grow old . . .
I shall wear the bottoms of my trousers rolled.
—T. S. ELIOT, *The Love Song*
of J. Alfred Prufrock, 1917

One aged man—one man—can't fill a house.
—ROBERT FROST, *An Old Man's*
Winter Night in *Mountain Interval,* 1923

To be seventy years young is sometimes far more cheerful and hopeful than to be forty years old.
—OLIVER WENDELL HOLMES, SR.,
letter to Julia Ward Howe on her
70th birthday, May 27, 1889

The riders in a race do not stop short when they reach the goal. There is a little finishing canter.
—OLIVER WENDELL HOLMES, JR.,
radio address on his 90th birthday, Mar. 8, 1931

Oh, to be seventy again! [At age 92, upon seeing a pretty, young woman]
—OLIVER WENDELL HOLMES, JR., attributed, 1933
[Also attributed to Georges Clemenceau.]

My only fear is that I may live too long. This would be a subject of dread to me.   —THOMAS JEFFERSON,
letter to Philip Mazzei, March 1801

Where are the songs of spring? Ay, where are they?
Think not of them, thou hast thy music too . . .
—JOHN KEATS, *To Autumn* in *Poems,* 1820

All, all are gone, the old familiar faces.
>   —CHARLES LAMB, *The Old Familiar Faces,* c. 1820

La viellesse est l'enfer des femmes.
Old age is woman's hell.
>   —NINON DE LENCLOS, *La Coquette vengée,* 1659

dance mehitabel dance
caper and shake a leg
what little blood is left
will fizz like wine in a keg.
>   —DON MARQUIS, *mehitabel dances
>   with boreas* in *archy and mehitabel,* 1927

Old age has its pleasures, which, though different, are not
less than the pleasures of youth.
>   —W. SOMERSET MAUGHAM, *The Summing Up,* 1938

Being seventy is not a sin.   —GOLDA MEIR, quoted by
>   David Reed, *Reader's Digest,* July 1971

The older I grow, the more I distrust the familiar doctrine
that age brings wisdom.
>   —H. L. MENCKEN, *Prejudices: Third Series,* 1922

How old would you be if you didn't know how old you was?
>   —SATCHEL PAIGE, attributed, c. 1950

Old age has a great sense of calm and freedom. When the
passions have relaxed their hold, you have escaped not from
one master but from many.
>   —PLATO, *The Republic,* 4th cent. B.C.

Darling, I am growing old,
Silver threads among the gold.
>   —EBEN EUGENE REXFORD,
>   *Silver Threads among the Gold,* 1873

For you and I are past our dancing days.
>   —SHAKESPEARE, *Romeo and Juliet,* I, v

Nobody loves life like him who is growing old.
>   —SOPHOCLES, *Acrisius,* 5th cent. B.C.

Being over seventy is like being engaged in a war. All our friends are going or gone and we survive amongst the dead and dying as on a battlefield.
—MURIEL SPARK, *Memento Mori,* 1959

There are so few who can grow old with a good grace.
—RICHARD STEELE, *The Spectator,* Jan. 1, 1711–12

Every man desires to live long, but no man would be old.
—JONATHAN SWIFT, *Thoughts on Various Subjects,* 1711

Old age is the most unexpected of all the things that can happen to a man.
—LEON TROTSKY, *Diary in Exile,* May 8, 1935

The tragedy of old age is not that one is old, but that one is young.
—OSCAR WILDE, *The Picture of Dorian Gray,* 1891

Oh, who could have foretold
That the heart grows old?
—W. B. YEATS, *A Song* in *The Wild Swans at Coole,* 1919

AGES   See FUTURE, THE; GENERATIONS; MODERN TIMES; PAST, THE; PRESENT, THE; TURBULENT TIMES

ALCOHOL & DRINKING   See also FOOD, WINE, & EATING; SIN, VICE, & NAUGHTINESS

If all be true that I do think,
There are five good reasons we should drink:
Good wine—a friend—or being dry—
Or lest we should be by and by—
Or any other reason why.
—HENRY ALDRICH, *Five Reasons for Drinking,* c. 1700

In vino veritas.
With wine comes truth.   —ANONYMOUS (PROVERB)
[Can be traced to Greek sources, including Alcaeus and Plato; the closest Latin source is Pliny.]

Drink no longer water, but use a little wine for thy stomach's sake and thine often infirmities.   —BIBLE, *I Timothy* 5:23

I have taken more good from alcohol than alcohol has taken from me.   —WINSTON CHURCHILL,
quoted by Quentin Reynolds,
By Quentin Reynolds, 1964

Bacchus ever fair and young,
Drinking joys did first ordain.
Bacchus's blessings are a treasure,
Drinking is the soldier's pleasure,
Rich the treasure,
Sweet the pleasure—
Sweet is pleasure after pain.
                    —JOHN DRYDEN, *Alexander's Feast*, 1697

Malt does more than Milton can
To justify God's ways to man.
                    —A. E. HOUSMAN, *A Shropshire Lad*, 1896
[The reference is to Milton's stated purpose in writing *Paradise Lost*; see Milton at PRAYERS.]

Tell me what brand Grant drinks so I can send some to all my generals.
  —ABRAHAM LINCOLN, to congressional delegation, 1863
[Lincoln told Chaplain John Eaton that he had made this answer while meeting with congressmen who had urged Grant's dismissal on grounds that he was a drunk. Eaton included the story in his memoir, *Grant, Lincoln, and the Freedman*, 1907.]

Better sleep with a sober cannibal than a drunken Christian.
                    —HERMAN MELVILLE, *Moby-Dick*, 1851

Candy
Is dandy
But liquor
Is quicker.   —OGDEN NASH, *Reflections on
Ice-Breaking* in *Hard Lines*, 1931

There's something about a Martini,
Ere the dining and dancing begin,
And to tell you the truth,
It is not the vermouth—
I think that perhaps it's the gin.
—OGDEN NASH, *A Drink with
Something in It* in *The Primrose Path,* 1935

Three highballs, and I think I'm St. Francis of Assisi.
—DOROTHY PARKER,
Just a Little One in *Laments for
the Living,* 1930
[See also Parker at SIN, VICE, & NAUGHTINESS.]

Water is best.   —PINDAR, *Olympian Odes,* 5th cent. B.C.

MACDUFF: What three things does drink especially provoke?
PORTER: Marry, Sir, nose-painting, sleep, and urine. Lechery,
sir, it provokes and unprovokes; it provokes the desire, but
it takes away the performance.
—SHAKESPEARE, *Macbeth,* II, iii
["Nose-painting" refers to the drunkard's characteristically
red nose.]

It's a long time between drinks.
—ROBERT LOUIS STEVENSON, *The Wrong Box,* 1889
[Quoting North Carolina Governor John Motley Morehead,
c. 1843]

You ought to get out of these wet clothes and into a dry
martini.   —MAE WEST, *Every Day's a Holiday,* 1937
[The remark is often attributed to Robert Benchley and occasionally to Alexander Woollcott. Benchley himself credited his
friend Charles Butterworth, who delivered the quip in the Mae
West movie. In the 1942 movie *The Major and the Minor,*
writers Billy Wilder and Charles Brackett gave Benchley the
line, "Why don't you get out of that wet coat and into a dry
martini?" He was addressing Ginger Rogers.]

Father, dear father, come home with me now;
The clock in the steeple strikes one;
You promised, dear father, that you would come home
As soon as your day's work was done.
—HENRY CLAY WORK, *Come Home, Father,*
temperance song, 1864

Though in silence, with blighted affection, I pine,
Yet the lips that touch liquor must never touch mine!
—GEORGE W. YOUNG, *The Lips That Touch
Liquor Must Never Touch Mine*, c. 1900

ALIENATION

See also DANGEROUS
PEOPLE; MADNESS

I have been a stranger in a strange land.
—BIBLE, *Exodus* 2:22, 11
[The same phrase was used by Sophocles in *Oedipus at Colonus*
in the 5th century B.C.]

I, a stranger and afraid
In a world I never made.
—A. E. HOUSMAN, *Last Poems*, 1922

He was outcast from life's feast.
—JAMES JOYCE, *A Painful Case* in *The Dubliners*, 1916

I would prefer not to.
—HERMAN MELVILLE, *Bartleby the Scrivener*, 1856
[The phrase with which Bartleby repeatedly rejects everything.]

AMBITION

See also BOLDNESS & INITIATIVE;
ELITE; GREATNESS;
PRIDE & VANITY

Aut Caesar, aut nihil.
Either Caesar or nothing.
—CESARE BORGIA, motto, c. 1500

Ah, but a man's reach should exceed his grasp,
Or what's a heaven for?
—ROBERT BROWNING, *Andrea del Sarto*, 1855

Hitch your wagon to a star.
—RALPH WALDO EMERSON,
Civilization in *Society and Solitude*, 1870

First say to yourself what you would be; and then do what
you have to do.   —EPICTETUS, *Discourses*, c. A.D. 100

Slight not what's near through aiming at what's far.
—EURIPIDES, *Rhesus,* 5th cent. B.C.

Nothing is so commonplace as to wish to be remarkable.
—OLIVER WENDELL HOLMES, SR.,
The Autocrat of the Breakfast-Table, 1860

All or nothing.   —HENRIK IBSEN, *Brand,* 1866

I would sooner fail than not be among the greatest.
—JOHN KEATS, letter to J. A. Hessey, Oct. 9, 1818

Most people would succeed in small things, if they were not
troubled by great ambitions.
—HENRY WADSWORTH LONGFELLOW,
Drift-Wood, 1857

Ambition . . .
The glorious fault of angels and of gods.
—ALEXANDER POPE, *Elegy to the
Memory of an Unfortunate Lady,* 1717

Fain would I climb, yet fear I to fall.
—SIR WALTER RALEIGH, attributed, c. 1585
[Legend has it that Raleigh scratched this on a window pane.
Queen Elizabeth I is said to have added underneath: "If thy
heart fails thee, climb not at all."]

The ripest peach is highest on the tree.
—JAMES WHITCOMB RILEY, d. 1916,
The Ripest Peach

Ambition, old as mankind, the immemorial weakness of the
strong.   —VITA SACKVILLE-WEST,
No Signposts in the Sea, 1961

Ambition should be made of sterner stuff.
—SHAKESPEARE, *Julius Caesar,* III, ii

Vaulting ambition, which o'erleaps itself
And falls on t'other [the other side].
—SHAKESPEARE, *Macbeth,* I, viii

AMERICA & AMERICANS   See also AMERICAN
                           HISTORY: MEMORABLE
                                      MOMENTS

God bless the USA, so large
So friendly, and so rich.
                    —W. H. AUDEN, *On the Circuit,* 1941

Westward the course of empire takes its way;
The four first acts already past,
A fifth shall close the drama with the day:
Time's noblest offspring is the last.
                    —GEORGE BERKELEY, *On the
                         Prospect of Planting Arts and
                         Learning in America,* 1752
[Bishop Berkeley's verse, written in 1752, was echoed a century
later by Arthur Hugh Clough in *Say Not the Struggle Nought
Availeth,* 1862: "In front the sun climbs slow, how slowly, / But
westward, look, the land is bright." See also John Soule's "Go
west, young man," in the section AMERICAN HISTORY:
MEMORABLE MOMENTS.]

They knew they were pilgrims.
                    —WILLIAM BRADFORD, *History of
                         the Plymouth Plantation,*
                                  written 1630–51

The chief business of the American people is business.
                    —CALVIN COOLIDGE, speech, Jan. 17, 1925
[See also Charles F. Wilson on General Motors and the U.S.,
at BUSINESS.]

America is a country of young men.
                    —RALPH WALDO EMERSON,
                         Old Age in *Society and Solitude,* 1870

There are no second acts in American lives.
                    —F. SCOTT FITZGERALD,
                         The Last Tycoon, Notes, 1941
[The novel was published a year after the author's death.]

The American system of rugged individualism.
                    —HERBERT HOOVER, speech, Oct. 22, 1928

If there is any fixed star in our constitutional constellation, it is that no official, high or petty, can prescribe what shall be orthodox in politics, nationalism, religion, or other matters of opinion or force citizens to confess by word or act their faith therein.
> —ROBERT H. JACKSON, Supreme Court
> ruling in *West Virginia Department of*
> *Education v. Barnette,* 1943

[The Court misspelled the name of the plaintiff, Walter Barnett.]

The spirit of this country is totally adverse to a large military force.
> —THOMAS JEFFERSON, letter to
> Chandler Price, Feb. 28, 1807

Indeed, I tremble for my country when I reflect that God is just.
> —THOMAS JEFFERSON, *Notes on*
> *the State of Virginia,* 1781–85

I am willing to love all mankind, except an American.
> —SAMUEL JOHNSON, in James Boswell,
> *Life of Johnson,* April 15, 1778

Americans are impatient with memory.
> —JAMAICA KINCAID, *Alien Soil* in
> *The New Yorker,* June 21, 1993

The essential American soul is hard, isolate, stoic, a killer.
> —D. H. LAWRENCE, *Cooper's Leatherstocking*
> *Novels* in *Studies in Classic*
> *American Literature,* 1922

This country, with its institutions, belongs to the people who inhabit it. Whenever they shall grow weary of the existing government, they can exercise their constitutional right of amending it, or their revolutionary right to dismember or overthrow it.
> —ABRAHAM LINCOLN, *First Inaugural*
> *Address,* Mar. 4, 1861

Thou, too, sail on, O Ship of State!
Sail on, O Union, strong and great!
Humanity with all its fears,
With all the hopes of future years,
Is hanging breathless on thy fate!
> —HENRY WADSWORTH LONGFELLOW,
> *The Building of the Ship,* 1849

We need Hawaii just as much and a good deal more than we did California. It is manifest destiny.
>   —WILLIAM McKINLEY, remark to his
>   presidential aide George Cortelyou, 1898

[Hawaii was annexed within the year. See also John L. O'Sullivan below.]

The men the American people admire most extravagantly are the most daring liars; the men they detest most violently are those who try to tell the truth.
>   —H. L. MENCKEN, quoted in Alistair Cooke,
>   ed., *The Vintage Mencken,* 1955

[For Mencken on the limited intelligence of the American people, see PEOPLE, THE.]

Of nothing [in the U.S.] are you allowed to get the real odor or savor. Everything is sterilized and wrapped in cellophane.
>   —HENRY MILLER, *Dr. Souchon: Surgeon-Painter*
>   in *The Air-Conditioned Nightmare,* 1945

Don't sell America short.
>   —J. P. MORGAN, popularized version of
>   one of his favorite sayings, 1890s

[Morgan's aphorism ran on the lines of "Don't be a bear on America." He was referring to a stock-market bear, who would bet on a stock price to drop, as opposed to a bull, who would expect a rise in price. This saying may have originated with J. P. Morgan's father, Junius Spenser Morgan.]

If when the chips are down the United States acts like a pitiful helpless giant, the forces of totalitarianism and anarchy will threaten free nations and free institutions throughout the world.
>   —RICHARD M. NIXON, speech, Apr. 30, 1970

Our manifest destiny is to overspread the continent allotted by Providence for the free development of our yearly multiplying millions. —JOHN L. O'SULLIVAN, *United States*
>   *Magazine,* July–Aug. 1845

In America, public opinion is the leader.
>   —FRANCES PERKINS, *People at Work,* 1934

You cannot conquer America.
> —WILLIAM PITT, EARL OF CHATHAM,
> speech, Nov. 18, 1777

All races and religions: that's America to me.
> —EARL ROBINSON, quoted in
> *The New York Times*, obituary, July 23, 1991

[Robinson was the author of the music for *Joe Hill,* the words coming from Alfred Hayes's poem about labor organizer Joe Hill, executed in 1915.]

We must be the great arsenal of democracy.
> —FRANKLIN D. ROOSEVELT,
> radio speech, Dec. 29, 1940

There can be no fifty-fifty Americanism in this country. There is room here for only hundred percent Americanism.
> —THEODORE ROOSEVELT, speech, July 19, 1918

Americans are suckers for good news.
> —ADLAI STEVENSON, speech, June 8, 1958

I know of no country, indeed, where the love of money has taken a stronger hold on the affections of men.
> —ALEXIS DE TOCQUEVILLE,
> *Democracy in America,* 1835–39

America is a land of wonders, in which everything is in constant motion and every change seems an improvement. . . . No natural boundary seems to be set to the efforts of man; and in his eyes, what is not yet done is only what he has not yet attempted to do.
> —*Ibid.*

The next Augustan age will dawn on the other side of the Atlantic.
> —HORACE WALPOLE, letter to
> Horace Mann, Nov. 24, 1774

The Constitution does not provide for first- and second-class citizens.
> —WENDELL WILLKIE, *An American Program,* 1944

For we must consider that we shall be as a city upon a hill.
The eyes of all people are upon us.
> —JOHN WINTHROP, *A Model of Christianity,*
> sermon on board the *Arbella,* en route
> to Massachusetts, 1630

[The allusion is to the Sermon on the Mount, *Matthew* 5:14:
"Ye are the light of the world. A city that is set on an hill
cannot be hid."]

America is God's crucible, the great melting pot.
> —ISRAEL ZANGWILL, *The Melting Pot,* 1908

[The image was not original to Zangwill. Michel Guillaume
Jean de Crèvecoeur reported in *Letters from an American
Farmer* (1782) that "Here individuals of all nations are melted
into a new race of men."]

AMERICAN HISTORY: MEMORABLE MOMENTS
See also AMERICA & AMERICANS;
MILITARY BATTLES; SCIENCE: DISCOVERY
& EXPLORATION; PATRIOTISM

What a glorious morning for America!
> —SAMUEL ADAMS, upon hearing the sound of
> guns at Lexington, Apr. 19, 1775, traditional attribution

Declare the United States the winner and begin de-
escalation.   —GEORGE AIKEN, speech to the
U.S. Senate, Oct. 19, 1966
[Sen. Aiken was advising Pres. Lyndon Johnson on how to end
the Vietnam War.]

Remember the Maine!   —ANONYMOUS, 1898
[Slogan popularized in Hearst and Pulitzer newspapers, leading
to the invasion of Cuba in the Spanish American War. The
U.S. battleship *Maine,* anchored in Havana harbor, was destroyed by an explosion of unknown origin on Feb. 15, 1898.
Of the 350 on board, 260 died. The U.S. held Spain responsible
and declared war against Spain in April. Cuba was liberated
from Spain but put under the tutelage of the U.S.]

Let us not be deceived—we are today in the midst of a cold
war.   —BERNARD BARUCH, speech, Apr. 16, 1947
[For Winston Churchill's "Iron Curtain" speech, see COM-
MUNISM.]

Bury my heart at Wounded Knee.
　　　—STEPHEN VINCENT BENÉT, *American Names*, 1927
[The last important battle in the Indian Wars was a massacre of two hundred Sioux warriors, women, and children at Wounded Knee Creek in South Dakota, Dec. 29, 1890.]

You shall not press down upon the brow of labor this crown of thorns. You shall not crucify mankind upon a cross of gold.　　　—WILLIAM JENNINGS BRYAN, speech,
　　　　　　　　　Democratic National Convention, July 8, 1896
[Bryan's impassioned speech so impressed delegates at the convention that it won him the presidential nomination although he was only age 36. Bryan supported the populist Free Silver movement, which essentially called for more available, more inflationary money, in opposition especially to Eastern financiers, who supported a tight, gold-based currency. Bryan had developed the "cross of gold" metaphor some years earlier. *Bartlett's* cites a similar passage from an 1894 speech in Congress.]

Read my lips: No new taxes.
　　　　　　　—GEORGE BUSH, presidential nomination
　　　　　　　　　acceptance speech, Aug. 18, 1988

Well, I think we ought to let him hang there. Let him twist slowly, slowly in the wind.
　　　　　　　—JOHN EHRLICHMAN, speaking to presidential
　　　　　　　　　counsel John Dean about F.B.I. head
　　　　　　　　　Patrick Gray, Mar. 6, 1973

In the councils of government, we must guard against the acquisition of unwarranted influence, whether sought or unsought, by the military-industrial complex. The potential for the disastrous rise of misplaced power exists and will persist.
　　　　　　　—DWIGHT D. EISENHOWER, presidential
　　　　　　　　　farewell speech, Jan. 17, 1961
[See also Eisenhower at MILITARY, THE.]

Here once the embattled farmers stood,
And fired the shot heard round the world.
　　　　　　　—RALPH WALDO EMERSON, *Hymn Sung
　　　　　　　at the Completion of the Battle Monument,*
　　　　　　　　　Concord, July 4, 1837

Damn the torpedoes! Captain Drayton, go ahead. Jouett, full speed! —DAVID FARRAGUT, Battle of
Mobile Bay, Aug. 5, 1864
[Usually shortened to "Damn the torpedoes! Full speed ahead." The Confederate torpedoes were what we call mines.]

Praise the Lord and pass the ammunition.
—HOWELL M. FORGY, chaplain on
the cruiser *New Orleans,* during the
attack on Pearl Harbor, Dec. 7, 1941

We must, indeed, all hang together or, most assuredly, we shall all hang separately.
—BENJAMIN FRANKLIN, at the signing of the
Declaration of Independence, July 4, 1776
[A late attribution, c. 1840.]

I would remind you that extremism in the defense of liberty is no vice. And let me remind you also that moderation in the pursuit of justice is no virtue!
—BARRY GOLDWATER, presidential nomination
acceptance speech, July 16, 1964

I propose to fight it out on this line if it takes all summer.
—ULYSSES S. GRANT, dispatch to
Washington, May 11, 1864

I only regret that I have but one life to lose for my country.
—NATHAN HALE, before being hanged
as a spy, Sept. 22, 1776
[The thought comes from Joseph Addison's play *Cato* (1713): "What a pity is it / That we can die but once to serve our country."]

As for me, give me liberty or give me death!
—PATRICK HENRY, speech, Mar. 23, 1775

We hold these truths to be self-evident; that all men are created equal; that they are endowed by their creator with certain unalienable rights; that among these are life, liberty, and the pursuit of happiness.
—THOMAS JEFFERSON, *Declaration of
Independence,* July 4, 1776

[Jefferson originally wrote "We hold these truths to be sacred and undeniable." Benjamin Franklin substituted "self-evident."]

Peace, commerce, and honest friendship with all nations—
entangling alliances with none.
> —THOMAS JEFFERSON, First Inaugural
> Address, Mar. 4, 1801

This administration . . . declares unconditional war on poverty in America.   —LYNDON B. JOHNSON, State of the
> Union address, Jan. 8, 1964

I have not yet begun to fight.
> —JOHN PAUL JONES, on the
> *Bonhomme Richard,* Sept. 23, 1779

Ich bin ein Berliner.
> —JOHN F. KENNEDY, speech, June 26, 1963

I have a dream today.   —MARTIN LUTHER KING, JR.,
> speech at the Lincoln Memorial,
> Aug. 28, 1963

[See also King at RACES & PEOPLES.]

Don't give up the ship.
> —JAMES LAWRENCE, June 1, 1813

[Commander Lawrence issued this order as his frigate, the *Chesapeake,* was being boarded by British sailors from H.M.S. *Shannon.* Reportedly, he said, "Tell the men to fire faster! Don't give up the ship!" He died of his wounds on June 4, continuing to call out this order in his last hours. The captain of the *Shannon,* too, was mortally wounded in the battle. Some credit the famous order to Oliver Hazard Perry, who signaled it by flag during the Battle of Lake Erie, Sept. 10, 1813.]

Give me your tired, your poor,
Your huddled masses yearning to breathe free.
> —EMMA LAZARUS, *The New Colossus:*
> *Inscription for the Statue of Liberty,* 1883

First in war, first in peace, first in the hearts of his countrymen.   —HENRY LEE, memorial address
> to Congress, Dec. 16, 1799, after the
> death of George Washington

A house divided against itself cannot stand. I believe this government cannot endure permanently half slave and half free.   —ABRAHAM LINCOLN, speech, June 16, 1858 [For the Biblical reference to a house divided, see CONFLICT.]

Fourscore and seven years ago our fathers brought forth on this continent, a new nation conceived in Liberty, and dedicated to the proposition that all men are created equal.
                              —ABRAHAM LINCOLN,
                         Address at Gettysburg, Nov. 19, 1863
[See also Lincoln at GOVERNMENT.]

With malice toward none, with charity for all, with firmness in the right, as God gives us to see the right, let us strive on to finish the work we are in, to bind up the nation's wounds.   —ABRAHAM LINCOLN, Second
                         Inaugural Address, Mar. 4, 1865

I shall return.   —DOUGLAS MacARTHUR, after
                         leaving the Philippines, Mar. 11, 1942

Old soldiers never die; they just fade away. And like the old soldier in that ballad, I now close my military career and just fade away, an old soldier who tried to do his duty as God gave him the sight to see that duty.
                         —DOUGLAS MacARTHUR, speech to
                    Congress after having been relieved of duty by
                         Pres. Harry S. Truman, Apr. 19, 1951

Nuts!   —ANTHONY McAULIFFE, refusing to
                    surrender at Bastogne in the Battle of
                         the Bulge, Dec. 22, 1944
[This is the reply publicized, reportedly a euphemism for a stronger term.]

All quiet along the Potomac.
                         —GEORGE B. McCLELLAN, in
                         dispatches to Washington, 1861

You won't have Nixon to kick around anymore, because, gentlemen, this is my last press conference.
                         —RICHARD M. NIXON, after losing the
                         California gubernatorial race, Nov. 5, 1962

I'm not a crook.
—RICHARD M. NIXON, press conference, Nov. 11, 1973

These are the times that try men's souls. The summer soldier and the sunshine patriot will, in this crisis, shrink from the service of their country.
—THOMAS PAINE, *The American Crisis*, No. I, Dec. 23, 1776

We have met the enemy, and they are ours.
—OLIVER HAZARD PERRY, dispatch, Battle of Lake Erie, Sept. 10, 1813
[For Walt Kelly's (Pogo's) version, see HUMANS & HUMAN NATURE.]

Don't fire until you see the whites of their eyes.
—ISRAEL PUTNAM, Battle of Bunker Hill, June 17, 1775
[Also attributed to William Prescott. This attribution is based on the report of militiaman Israel Potter, cited in Richard Wheeler's *The Voices of 1776*.]

I pledge you, I pledge myself, to a new deal for the American people.
—FRANKLIN D. ROOSEVELT, presidential nomination acceptance speech, July 2, 1932

The only thing we have to fear is fear itself.
—FRANKLIN D. ROOSEVELT, First Inaugural Address, Mar. 4, 1933
[Cf. Wellington's similar comment, under FEAR.]

To some generations much is given. Of others much is expected. This generation of Americans has a rendezvous with destiny.
—FRANKLIN D. ROOSEVELT, second presidential nomination acceptance speech, June 27, 1936

Yesterday, December 7, 1941—a date which will live in infamy—the United States of America was suddenly and deliberately attacked by naval and air forces of the Empire of Japan.
—FRANKLIN D. ROOSEVELT, speech to Congress, Dec. 8, 1941

A man who is good enough to shed his blood for his country is good enough to be given a square deal afterward.
                    —THEODORE ROOSEVELT, speech, July 4, 1903

Remember the Alamo!
                    —SIDNEY SHERMAN, battle cry, Apr. 21, 1836
[Col. Sherman's troops shouted this battle cry as they charged the Mexican army at San Jacinto, six weeks after the Mexicans had captured the Alamo in San Antonio, Texas, killing all its defendants.]

Hold out; relief is coming.
                    —WILLIAM TECUMSEH SHERMAN,
signal to Gen. John Murray Corse, Allatoona Pass, Oct. 5, 1864
[Usually quoted as "Hold the fort! for I am coming," which is the way it was rendered in an 1874 gospel song by Philip Paul Bliss.]

I will not accept if nominated, and will not serve if elected.
                    —WILLIAM TECUMSEH SHERMAN,
                    telegram to the Republican National Convention,
                                                    June 5, 1884

Go west, young man, go west.
                    —JOHN B. L. SOULE, editorial,
                    Terre Haute Express, 1851
[The saying was popularized by Horace Greeley, who reprinted Soule's editorial in *The New York Tribune.* In an editorial of his own, Greeley expanded Soule's advice to read: "Go west, young man, and grow up with the country."]

Lafayette, we are here.   —CHARLES E. STANTON,
                    at the grave of the Marquis de Lafayette,
                                            Paris, July 4, 1917
[Probably the best-remembered statement by an American in World War I. It is often attributed to Gen. John Pershing rather than Col. Stanton, with evidence for both attributions from people who were there.]

I'm going to fight hard. I'm going to give them hell.
                    —HARRY S. TRUMAN,
                    to Alben Barkley, Sept. 27, 1948
[Pres. Truman went on to beat Thomas E. Dewey.]

In the field of public education, the doctrine of "separate but equal" has no place. Separate educational facilities are inherently unequal. —EARL WARREN,
Brown v. Board of Education of Topeka,
May 17, 1954
[The unanimous ruling was supplemented by a unanimous implementation ruling the following year, when the Court ordered desegregation of schools to proceed "with all deliberate speed."]

It is our true policy to steer clear of permanent alliances with any portion of the foreign world.
—GEORGE WASHINGTON, *Farewell Address,*
published Sept. 19, 1796

The world must be made safe for democracy.
—WOODROW WILSON, speech, Apr. 2, 1917,
asking Congress for a declaration of war

This is the operative statement. The others are inoperative.
—RONALD ZIEGLER, White House
press conference, Apr. 17, 1973
[Ziegler was retracting numerous denials in previous months that the Administration had been involved in covering up the break-in at the Democratic Party headquarters in the Watergate Hotel.]

AMERICAN INDIANS   See RACES & PEOPLES

ANCIENT WORLD   See NATIONS

ANGER   See also HATE; VIOLENCE & FORCE

Whosoever shall say, Thou fool, shall be in danger of hell fire.   —BIBLE, *Matthew* 5:22

Be ye angry and sin not: let not the sun go down upon your wrath.   —BIBLE, *Ephesians* 4:26

Envy and wrath shorten the life.
—BIBLE, *Ecclesiasticus* 30:24

Speak when you are angry and you will make the best speech you will ever regret.
—AMBROSE BIERCE, *The Devil's Dictionary,* 1906

The tigers of wrath are wiser than the horses of instruction.
—WILLIAM BLAKE,
The Marriage of Heaven and Hell, 1790–93

I was angry with my friend:
I told my wrath, my wrath did end.
I was angry with my foe:
I told it not, my wrath did grow.   —WILLIAM BLAKE,
A Poison Tree in *Songs of Experience*, 1794

Anger makes dull men witty, but it keeps them poor.
—ELIZABETH I, quoted in Francis Bacon,
Apophthegms, 1624

Anger is a brief madness.
—HORACE, *Epistles*, Book I, 20 B.C.

When angry, count four; when very angry, swear.
—MARK TWAIN,
Pudd'nhead Wilson's Calendar in *Pudd'nhead Wilson*, 1894

Anger supplies arms.   —VIRGIL, *Aeneid*, c. 19 B.C.

ANIMALS   See NATURE: ANIMALS

ANSWERS   See QUESTIONS & ANSWERS

APPEARANCES   See also BEAUTY;
FASHION & CLOTHES;
STYLE

Appearances are often deceiving.
—AESOP, *The Wolf in Sheep's Clothing* from *Fables*,
6th cent. B.C.

Things are seldom what they seem,
Skim milk masquerades as cream.
—W. S. GILBERT, *H.M.S. Pinafore*, 1878

To establish oneself in the world, one has to do all one can
to appear established.
—LA ROCHEFOUCAULD, *Maxims*, 1678

The Lord prefers common-looking people. That is the reason he makes so many of them.
—ABRAHAM LINCOLN, Dec. 23, 1863
[Quoted by John Hay, *Letters of John Hay and Extracts from His Diary*, C. L. Hay, ed., 1908, reprint 1969. Lincoln recalled this comment from a dream in which he was in a crowd, and someone, recognizing him, had said, "He is a very common-looking man." The president responded with the above remark.]

Men should not care too much for good looks; neglect is becoming.   —OVID, *The Art of Love*, c. 2 B.C.

A fair exterior is a silent recommendation.
          —PUBLILIUS SYRUS, *Moral Sayings*, 1st cent. B.C.

All that glisters is not gold.
          —SHAKESPEARE, *The Merchant of Venice*, II, vii
[Shakespeare observed that this was a popular proverb. Earlier in *Merchant,* Shakespeare referred to the "goodly outside" of a falsehood; see DISHONESTY & LIES.]

It is only shallow people who do not judge by appearances. The true mystery of the world is the visible, not the invisible.
          —OSCAR WILDE, *The Picture of Dorian Gray,* 1891

APPEASEMENT VS. RESISTANCE
See also OBEDIENCE;
PACIFISM; PEACE; RESIGNATION;
REVOLUTION; SURVIVAL

Better Red than dead.
—ANONYMOUS, slogan of British ban-the-bomb movement,
from late 1950s
[Equally well known was the response, "Better dead than Red," which was also the title of a book by an Englishman, Stanley Reynolds.]

I believe it is peace for our time . . . peace with honor.
          —NEVILLE CHAMBERLAIN, speech, Sept. 30, 1938,
after the Munich Conference
[Less than a year later, Nazi forces invaded Poland. See also PEACE—quotes from Disraeli and the *Book of Common Prayer* for similar phrases.]

The name of peace is sweet and the thing itself is good, but between peace and slavery there is the greatest difference.
—CICERO, *Philippics*, 44–43 B.C.

'Tis better to have fought and lost,
Than never to have fought at all.
—ARTHUR HUGH CLOUGH, *Peschiera*, 1849

It is better to die on your feet than live on your knees! They shall not pass!
—DOLORES IBARRURI ("LA PASIONARIA"),
radio broadcast, July 18, 1936
[The last phrase—*"no pasarán"*—became the rallying cry of the Republicans in the Spanish Civil War. See also Nivelle's order under MILITARY BATTLES.]

If once you have paid him the Dane-geld
You never get rid of the Dane.   —RUDYARD KIPLING,
Dane-geld in *History of England*, 1911

Better that we should die fighting than be outraged and dishonored. . . . Better to die than to live in slavery.
—EMMELINE PANKHURST,
speech in Petrograd, Aug. 1917

There is a price which is too great to pay for peace, and that price can be put in one word. One cannot pay the price of self-respect.
—WOODROW WILSON, speech, Feb. 1, 1916

APRIL   See NATURE: SEASONS

ARCHITECTURE   See ARTS: ARCHITECTURE

ARMIES   See MILITARY, THE;
                          MILITARY BATTLES; WAR
ART & THE ARTS   See also LANGUAGE; STYLE
[and separate arts categories below]

Ars longa, vita brevis.
Art is long, life is short.   —ANONYMOUS
[This is the most common rendering of the concept expressed by Hippocrates—see under LIFE—and others. Longfellow put it thus: "Art is long, and Time is fleeting," *A Psalm of Life*, 1893.]

The object of art is to give life shape.
—JEAN ANOUILH, *The Rehearsal,* 1950

Il faut épater le bourgeois.
One must shock the bourgeois.
        —CHARLES BAUDELAIRE, d. 1867, attributed
[Also attributed to his contemporary Alexandre Privat d'An-glemont in the form, *"Je les ai épatés, les bourgeois*—"I shocked them, the bourgeois." *Épater* may also be translated as *to amaze* or *to flabbergast.*]

In everything that can be called art there is a quality of redemption.
—RAYMOND CHANDLER, *The Simple Art of Murder,* 1950

An artist will betray himself by some sort of sincerity.
        —G. K. CHESTERTON, *The Dagger with Wings* in
                The Incredulity of Father Brown, 1926

Art is a jealous mistress.   —RALPH WALDO EMERSON,
                Wealth in *The Conduct of Life,* 1860

Art without life is a poor affair.
                —HENRY JAMES, *The Art of Fiction,* 1888

It is art that *makes* life, makes interest, makes importance.
        —HENRY JAMES, letter to H. G. Wells, July 10, 1915

Is not a patron, my Lord, one who looks with unconcern on a man struggling for life in the water, and, when he has reached ground, encumbers him with help?
        —SAMUEL JOHNSON, letter to Lord Chesterfield,
                Feb. 7, 1755

Whenever I hear the word "culture," I release the safety catch on my Browning!   —HANNS JOHST, *Schlageter,* 1933
[Usually attributed to Hermann Goering thus: "When I hear anyone talk of culture, I reach for my revolver."]

Welcome O Life! I go to encounter for the millionth time the reality of experience and to forge in the smithy of my soul the uncreated conscience of my race.
                —JAMES JOYCE,
        A Portrait of the Artist as a Young Man, 1916

This nation cannot afford to be materially rich and spiritually poor.
> —JOHN F. KENNEDY, State of the Union address,
> Jan. 14, 1963
[Inscription on the Kennedy Center for the Performing Arts in Washington, D.C.]

To be an artist means never to avert one's eyes.
> —AKIRA KUROSAWA,
> quoted in *The New York Times* obituary, Sept. 7, 1998

Music is the universal language of mankind—poetry their universal pastime and delight.
> —HENRY WADSWORTH LONGFELLOW,
> *Outre-Mer; a Pilgrimage Beyond the Sea,* originally
> *The Schoolmaster,* c. 1832

Art is revolt against fate.
> —ANDRÉ MALRAUX, *The Voices of Silence,* 1951

Great artists have no country.
> —ALFRED DE MUSSET, *Lorenzaccio,* 1834

There seem to be two causes of the deterioration of the arts . . . wealth . . . and poverty. Wealth is the parent of luxury and indolence, and poverty of meanness and viciousness, and both of discontent.
> —PLATO, *The Republic,* 4th cent. B.C.

Only through art can we emerge from ourselves and know what another person sees.
> —MARCEL PROUST, *Maxims,* 1948

Fine art is that in which the hand, the head, and the heart of man go together.—JOHN RUSKIN, *The Two Paths,* 1859

All art is but imitation of nature.
> —SENECA, *Epistles,* 1st cent. A.D.

O! for a Muse of fire, that would ascend
The brightest heaven of invention!
> —SHAKESPEARE, Prologue, *Henry V*

The true artist will let his wife starve, his children go bare-
foot, his mother drudge for his living at seventy, sooner than
work at anything but his art.
—GEORGE BERNARD SHAW, *Man and Superman*, 1903

Art is a microscope which the artist fixes on the secrets of
his soul, and shows to people these secrets which are common to all.   —LEO TOLSTOY, *Diaries*, May 17, 1896

Mrs. Ballinger is one of the ladies who pursue Culture in
bands, as though it were dangerous to meet it alone.
—EDITH WHARTON, *Xingu*, 1916

All art is quite useless.
—OSCAR WILDE, *The Picture of Dorian Gray*, 1891

All art is at once surface and symbol. Those who go beneath
the surface do so at their peril.   —*Ibid.*

ARTS: AESTHETICS   See also ARTS: STYLE IN
WRITING & EXPRESSION;
BEAUTY; SIMPLICITY; STYLE

Tragedy is an imitation of an action that is serious, complete,
and of a certain magnitude, effecting through pity and fear
the proper purgation [katharsis] of these emotions.
—ARISTOTLE, *Poetics*, 4th cent. B.C.

That willing suspension of disbelief for the moment, which
constitutes poetic faith.
—SAMUEL TAYLOR COLERIDGE,
Biographia Literaria, 1817

The only way of expressing emotion in the form of art is by
finding an "objective correlative"; in other words, a set of
objects, a situation, a chain of events which shall be the
formula of that particular emotion.
—T. S. ELIOT, *Hamlet and His Problems*, 1919

Less is more. —LUDWIG MIES VAN DER ROHE, motto
[From Robert Browning—see SIMPLICITY. Contemporary ar-
chitect Robert Venturi counters, "Less is a bore." See also
Rostropovich at EXCESS, note to Mae West quote.]

All violent feelings . . . produce in us a falseness in all our impressions of external things, which I would generally characterize as the "Pathetic Fallacy."
—JOHN RUSKIN, *Modern Painters,* 1888

ARTS: ARCHITECTURE

La folie de bâtir.
Madness for building.   —ANONYMOUS (FRENCH)
[What the critic Brendan Gill described as "an irresistible impulse to go on building, beyond one's needs and whether one can pay for it or not," *The New Yorker,* Aug. 3, 1992.]

Architecture is inhabited sculpture.
—BRANCUSI, quoted by Igor Stravinsky and Robert Craft, *Themes and Episodes,* 1966

Une maison est une machine d'habiter.
A house is a machine for living in.
—LE CORBUSIER, *Vers une architecture,* 1923

I call architecture frozen music.
—GOETHE, letter to Johann Peter Eckermann, Mar. 23, 1829
[Goethe made the phrase famous; Friedrich von Schelling, however, used the "frozen music" metaphor earlier, in *Philosophie der Kunst,* 1809.]

One might regard architecture as history arrested in stone.
—A. L. ROWSE, *The Use of History,* 1946

When we build, let us think that we build forever.
—JOHN RUSKIN, *The Seven Lamps of Architecture,* 1849

The most beautiful house in the world is the one that you build for yourself.   —WITOLD RYBCZYNSKI, *The Most Beautiful House in the World,* 1989

Form ever follows function.
—LOUIS HENRI SULLIVAN, *The Tall Office Building Artistically Considered* in *Lippincott's Magazine,* Mar. 1896
["Form follows function" was the motto of the Bauhaus, the highly influential German school of architecture and art, closed by the Nazis in 1933.]

Si monumentum requiris circumspice.
If you seek a monument, look around.
                              —CHRISTOPHER WREN,
                        inscription in St. Paul's Cathedral,
                           London, written by his son
[Wren designed the cathedral and was buried there in 1723.]

The physician can bury his mistakes, but the architect can
only advise his client to plant vines.
           —FRANK LLOYD WRIGHT, in *The New York Times*,
                                          Oct. 4, 1953

ARTS: CRITICISM & CRITICS   See also INSULTS
                                    & PUT-DOWNS

Pleasure is by no means an infallible guide, but it is the least
fallible.   —W. H. AUDEN, *The Dyer's Hand*, 1962

Reviewers are usually people who would have been poets,
historians, biographers, if they could; they have tried their
talents at one or the other, and have failed; therefore they
turn critics.   —SAMUEL TAYLOR COLERIDGE,
                Lectures on Shakespeare and Milton, 1811–12

Be kind and considerate with your criticism. . . . It's just as
hard to write a bad book as it is to write a good book.
                   —MALCOLM COWLEY, quoted by Ken Kesey,
                          The New York Times, Dec. 31, 1989

A man is a critic when he cannot be an artist, in the same
way that a man becomes an informer when he cannot be a
soldier.   —GUSTAVE FLAUBERT,
                        letter to Louise Colet, Oct. 1846

A good critic is one who describes his adventures among
masterpieces.   —ANATOLE FRANCE,
                               La Vie littéraire, 1888

From now on art reporting will take the place of art criticism. Criticism has set itself up as a judge of art—a complete
perversion of the concept of "criticism." This dates from the
time of Jewish domination of art.
     —PAUL JOSEPH GOEBBELS, 1936, cited in Peter Adam,
                               Art of the Third Reich

A critic ought now and then to hesitate.
—IRVING HOWE, *A Critic's Notebook*, 1995

You *may* abuse a tragedy, though you cannot write one.
You may scold a carpenter who has made you a bad table,
though you cannot make a table. It is not your trade to
make tables. —SAMUEL JOHNSON, May 24, 1763,
quoted in James Boswell, *Life of Johnson*, 1791

I would rather be attacked than unnoticed. For the worst
thing you can do to an author is to be silent as to his works.
—SAMUEL JOHNSON, Mar. 26, 1779, *Ibid.*

Our American professors like their literature clear and cold
and pure and very dead. —SINCLAIR LEWIS,
Nobel Prize acceptance speech,
Dec. 12, 1930

I cried all the way to the bank [response to negative
reviews]. —LIBERACE, *Liberace: An Autobiography*, 1973

People who like this sort of thing will find this the sort of
thing they like.
—ABRAHAM LINCOLN, judgment on a book,
quoted in G. W. E. Russell,
Collections and Recollections, 1898
[Also credited to Max Beerbohm.]

Nature fits all her children with something to do,
He who would write and can't write, can surely review.
—JAMES RUSSELL LOWELL, *A Fable for Critics*, 1848

You puff the poets of other days,
The living you deplore.
Spare me the accolade: Your praise
Is not worth dying for. —MARTIAL,
Epigrams, 1st cent. A.D.

Nor in the critic let the man be lost.
—ALEXANDER POPE, *An Essay on Criticism*, 1711

Interpretation is the revenge of the intellect upon art.
—SUSAN SONTAG, *Against Interpretation*, title essay, 1966

The public is the only critic whose opinion is worth anything
at all.　　　　　　　　　　—MARK TWAIN, *A General Reply,*
　　　　　　　　　　　　　　in *The Galaxy* magazine, Nov. 1870

ARTS: MUSIC & DANCE

Music, the greatest good that mortals know,
And all of heaven we have here below.
　　　　　　—JOSEPH ADDISON, *A Song for St. Cecilia's Day*

The flute is not an instrument that has a good moral effect;
it is too exciting.　　　　—ARISTOTLE, *Politics,* 4th cent. B.C.

Whether angels play only Bach in praising God, I am not
sure. I am sure, however, that *en famille* they play Mozart.
　　　　　　—KARL BARTH, quoted in *The New York Times*
　　　　　　　　　　　　　　　　obituary, Dec. 11, 1968

A symphony is no joke.　—JOHANNES BRAHMS, d. 1897,
　　　　　　　　　　　　　　　　cited by Donal Henahan,
　　　　　　　　　　　　　　The New York Times, Mar. 17, 1985

The heart of the melody can never be put down on paper.
　　　　　　—PABLO CASALS, *Conversations,* 1975

Where there's music, there can be no evil.
　　　　　　—CERVANTES, *Don Quixote,* 1605–15

Opera . . . is one of the strangest inventions of Western
man. It could not have been foreseen by any logical process.
　　　　　　—SIR KENNETH CLARK, *Civilization,* 1970
[Regarding how operas end, see ENDINGS.]

Music has charms to soothe a savage breast,
To soften rocks, or bend a knotted oak.
　　　　　　—WILLIAM CONGREVE, *The Mourning Bride,* 1697
[Often misquoted as "to soothe a savage beast"—for obvious
reasons.]

Extraordinary how potent cheap music is.
　　　　　　—NOEL COWARD, *Private Lives,* 1930

[Dance:] The poetry of the foot.
　　　　　　—JOHN DRYDEN, *The Rival Ladies,* 1665

What passion cannot music raise and quell?
　　　—JOHN DRYDEN, *A Song for St. Cecilia's Day,* 1687

Dance is the loftiest, the most moving, the most beautiful of the arts, because it is no mere translation or abstraction from life; it is life itself. 　　　—HAVELOCK ELLIS,
The Dance of Life, 1923

One becomes . . . an athlete of God.
　　　—MARTHA GRAHAM, May 15, 1945
[More at GRACE.]

Dancing is just discovery, discovery, discovery.
　　　—MARTHA GRAHAM, interview,
The New York Times, Mar. 31, 1985

Dance is the hidden language of the soul. 　　　—*Ibid.*

I know only two tunes: one is *Yankee Doodle,* and the other isn't. 　　　—ULYSSES S. GRANT, attributed

When people hear good music, it makes them homesick for something they never had, and never will have.
　—EDGAR WATSON HOWE, *Country Town Sayings,* 1911

And the night shall be filled with music,
And the cares that infest the day
Shall fold their tents like the Arabs,
And as silently steal away.
　　　—HENRY WADSWORTH LONGFELLOW,
The Day Is Done, 1845

If the king loves music, there is little wrong in the land.
　　　—MENCIUS, *Discourses,* 3rd cent. B.C.

Come and trip it as ye go.
On the light fantastic toe. 　　　—JOHN MILTON,
L'Allegro, 1631

All art constantly aspires towards the condition of music.
　　　—WALTER PATER,
Giorgione in *Studies in the History of the Renaissance,* 1873

If music be the food of love, play on.
—SHAKESPEARE, *Twelfth Night,* I, i

I am never merry when I hear sweet music.
—SHAKESPEARE, *The Merchant of Venice,* V, i

Hell is full of musical amateurs.
—GEORGE BERNARD SHAW, *Man and Superman,* 1903

My soul is an enchanted boat,
Which, like a sleeping swan, doth float
Upon the silver waves of thy sweet singing.
—PERCY BYSSHE SHELLEY, *Prometheus Unbound,* 1819

Our sweetest songs are those that tell of saddest thoughts.
—PERCY BYSSHE SHELLEY, *To a Skylark,* 1819

If, as is nearly always the case, music appears to express something, this is only an illusion and not a reality.
—IGOR STRAVINSKY, *An Autobiography,* 1936

He was a fiddler, and consequently a rogue.
—JONATHAN SWIFT, letter to Stella, July 25, 1711
[In the Middle Ages, acrobats, jugglers, actors, and fiddlers wandered from town to town, and acquired a raffish reputation that to a degree has endured to our time.]

[Sign over a piano] Please do not shoot the pianist. He is doing his best.   —OSCAR WILDE,
Leadville (Col.) in *Personal Impressions of America,* 1883

O body swayed to music,
O brightening glance,
How can we know the dancer from the dance?
—W. B. YEATS, *Among School Children,* 1928

ARTS: PAINTING

One is never tired of painting, because you have to set down, not what you knew already, but what you have just discovered. There is a continual creation out of nothing going on.
—WILLIAM HAZLITT, *The Pleasure of Painting,* 1821

Art does not reproduce the visible; rather, it makes visible.
—PAUL KLEE, *Creative Credo,* 1920,
in *The Inward Vision,* 1958

All art worthy of the name is religious. Be it a creation of lines and colors, if it is not religious, it does not exist. If it is not religious, it is only a matter of documentary art, anecdotal art, which is no longer art.   —HENRI MATISSE,
d. 1954, quoted in Pierre Schneider, *Matisse,* 1984

With color one obtains an energy that seems to stem from witchcraft.   —HENRI MATISSE,
quoted by Michael Brenson,
The New York Times, May 26, 1985

I try to apply colors like words that shape poems, like notes that shape music.   —JOAN MIRÒ, d. 1983,
quoted in John Gruen, *Close-Up*

The painter who draws by practice and judgment of the eye without the use of reason is like the mirror which reproduces within itself all the objects which are set opposite to it without knowledge of the same.   —LEONARDO DA VINCI,
Notebooks, 1508–18

A picture is a model of reality.
—LUDWIG WITTGENSTEIN,
Tractatus logico-philosophicus, 1922

ARTS: PHOTOGRAPHY

There are things nobody would see if I didn't photograph them.   —DIANE ARBUS, in *Diane Arbus,* 1972

Stare. It is the way to educate your eye, and more.
—WALKER EVANS, c. 1940,
quoted in Belinda Rathbone, *Walker Evans,* 1995
[More at EDUCATION, entry and note.]

When we claim to "remember" our pasts, we are surely remembering our favorite snapshots, in which the long-faded past is given a distinct visual immortality.
—JOYCE CAROL OATES, in *Civilization* magazine,
Féb./Mar. 1997

ARTS: POETRY & POETS

You will never be alone with a poet in your pocket.
—JOHN ADAMS, letter to his son John Quincy Adams,
May 14, 1781

All poets are mad. —ROBERT BURTON,
The Anatomy of Melancholy, 1621–51

Poetry does not necessarily have to be beautiful to stick in
the depths of our memory. —COLETTE,
Under the Blue Lantern in *Earthly Paradise,* 1949

For that fine madness still he did retain
Which rightly should possess a poet's brain.
—MICHAEL DRAYTON,
To Henry Reynolds, of Poets and Poesy, 1627
[Drayton was speaking of Christopher Marlowe.]

Genuine poetry can communicate before it is understood.
—T. S. ELIOT, *Dante,* 1929

The world seems always to be waiting for its poet.
—RALPH WALDO EMERSON, *Journal,* Mar. 1845

The figure a poem makes. It begins in delight and ends in
wisdom. The figure is the same as for love.
—ROBERT FROST, Preface, *Collected Poems,* 1939

Writing free verse is like playing tennis with the net down.
—ROBERT FROST,
speech at Milton Academy in Massachusetts, May 17, 1935

The only thing that can save the world is the reclaiming of
the awareness of the world. That's what poetry does.
—ALLEN GINSBERG,
quoted in Helen Weaver, review of Ginsberg's *Collected Poems*
in *The Litchfield County Times,* May 31, 1985

If there's no money in poetry, neither is there poetry in
money. —ROBERT GRAVES, speech, Dec. 6, 1963

The poetical language of an age should be the current language heightened.   —GERARD MANLEY HOPKINS,
letter to Robert Bridges, Aug. 14, 1879

To be a mediocre poet, neither gods, nor men, nor booksellers have allowed.   —HORACE, *Art of Poetry,* c. 20–8 B.C.

To a poet nothing can be useless.
—SAMUEL JOHNSON, *Rasselas,* 1759

Poetry should surprise by a fine excess and not by singularity—it should strike the reader as a wording of his own highest thoughts, and appear almost a remembrance.
—JOHN KEATS, letter to John Taylor, Feb. 27, 1818

If poetry comes not as naturally as the leaves to a tree, it had better not come at all.   —*Ibid.*

When power narrows the areas of man's concern, poetry reminds him of the richness and diversity of his existence. When power corrupts, poetry cleanses.
—JOHN F. KENNEDY, speech, Oct. 26, 1963

A poem should not mean
But be.   —ARCHIBALD MacLEISH, *Ars Poetica,* 1926

Publishing a volume of poetry is like dropping a rose petal down the Grand Canyon and waiting for the echo.
—DON MARQUIS, *The Sun Dial,* column,
New York *Sun,* 1913–22

The subject of it [his book of poems] is war, and the pity
    of war.
The poetry is in the pity.
All a poet can do is warn.
—WILFRED OWEN, Preface, *Poems,* 1920

Chameleons feed on light and air:
Poets' food is love and fame.
—PERCY BYSSHE SHELLEY, *An Exhortation,* 1819

Poetry is the record of the best and happiest moments of the happiest and best minds.
—PERCY BYSSHE SHELLEY, *A Defense of Poetry,* 1821

Poets tell many lies.   —SOLON, fragment, 6th cent. B.C.
[For another less-than-flattering view of poets see the note at
Swift in the category NATURE: ANIMALS.]

The poet is the priest of the invisible.
                              —WALLACE STEVENS, d. 1955,
                              Adagia in *Opus Posthumous*, 1957

Poetry . . . is always unexpected, and always as faithful and
honest as dreams.   —ALICE WALKER,
                              We Have a Beautiful Mother, 1991

To have great poets, there must be great audiences, too.
                              —WALT WHITMAN, *Ventures,
                              On an Old Theme* in *Notes Left Over,
                              Complete Prose Works*, 1892

It is difficult
to get the news from poems
yet men die miserably every day
for lack
of what is found there.
                              —WILLIAM CARLOS WILLIAMS,
                              Asphodel, That Greeny Flower
                              in *A Journey to Love*, 1955

Poetry is the spontaneous overflow of powerful feelings: it
takes its origin from emotion recollected in tranquillity.
                              —WILLIAM WORDSWORTH,
                              Preface to 2nd Edition, *Lyrical Ballads*, 1820

We poets in our youth begin in gladness;
But thereof come in the end despondency and madness.
                              —WILLIAM WORDSWORTH,
                              Resolution and Independence, 1807

ARTS: STYLE IN WRITING & EXPRESSION
                              See also LANGUAGE & WORDS;
                              SIMPLICITY (Whitman); STYLE

The greatest thing in style is to have a command of
metaphor.   —ARISTOTLE, *Poetics*, 4th cent. B.C.

A good style must, first of all, be clear. It must be appropriate. —ARISTOTLE, *Rhetoric*, 4th cent. B.C.

A good style must have an air of novelty, at the same time concealing its art. —*Ibid.*

This is the sort of English up with which I will not put.
  —WINSTON CHURCHILL, attributed
[Comment in margin of a document. Churchill was objecting to a proofreader's excessive nicety in correcting a sentence that ended with a preposition. Quoted by Sir Ernest Gowers, *Plain Words*, 1948. In the same spirit, Raymond Chandler wrote, "When I split an infinitive, God damn it, I split it so it will stay split," letter to Edward Weeks, editor of the *Atlantic Monthly*, Jan. 18, 1947.]

It is when I struggle to be brief that I become obscure.
  —HORACE, *Art of Poetry*, c. 20–8 B.C.

Read over your compositions, and wherever you meet with a passage which you think is particularly fine, strike it out.
  —SAMUEL JOHNSON, quoting a college tutor,
  in James Boswell, *Life of Johnson*, entry for Apr. 30, 1773

For a man to write well, there are required three necessaries: to read the best authors, observe the best speakers, and much exercise of his own style. —BEN JONSON, *Timber;
  or Discoveries Made Upon Men and Matter*, c. 1635

Whatever is clearly expressed is well wrote.
  —MARY WORTLEY MONTAGU,
  letter to James Steuart, July 19, 1759

Verbal felicity is the fruit of art and diligence and refusing to be false. —MARIANNE MOORE,
  quoted by Louise Bogan, *College English*, Feb. 1953

I have made this letter longer than usual, because I lack the time to make it short. —PASCAL,
  Provincial Letters, 1656–57

True wit is nature to advantage dressed,
What oft was thought, but ne'er so well expressed.
  —ALEXANDER POPE, *Essay on Criticism*, 1711

Brevity is the soul of wit. —SHAKESPEARE, *Hamlet*, II, ii

Vigorous writing is concise. —WILLIAM STRUNK,
Elements of Style, 1918

Proper words in proper places make the true definition of
style. —JONATHAN SWIFT,
letter to a young clergyman, Jan. 9, 1720

The difference between the almost right word and the right
word is really a large matter—'tis the difference between
the lightning bug and the lightning. —MARK TWAIN,
letter to George Brinton, Oct. 15, 1888,
reprinted as *Reply to the Editor of
"The Art of Authorship,"* 1890

As to the adjective, when in doubt, strike it out.
—MARK TWAIN, *Pudd'nhead Wilson's Calendar*
in *Pudd'nhead Wilson*, 1894

Take eloquence and wring its neck. —PAUL VERLAINE,
L'art poétique in *Jadis et Naguère*, 1884

Style is the dress of thought. —SAMUEL WESLEY,
An Epistle to a Friend Concerning Poetry, 1700
[A half century later, on Nov. 24, 1749, the Earl of Chesterfield
wrote to his son, "Style is the dress of thoughts." See also
Johnson at LANGUAGE.]

ARTS: THEATER, MOVIES, & ACTING

You can't be boring. Life is boring. The weather is boring.
Actors must not be boring. —STELLA ADLER,
The New York Times, obituary, Dec. 22, 1992

A good actor does not make his entry before the theater is
built.
—JORGE LUIS BORGES & ADOLFO BIOY CASARES
Six Problems for Don Isidro Parodi, 1981

JOE GILLIS: You used to be in pictures. You used to be big.
NORMA DESMOND: I am big. It's the pictures that got small.
— CHARLES BRACKETT, BILLY WILDER,
& D. M. MARSHMAN, JR.,
screenplay, *Sunset Boulevard,* 1950
[Desmond's last line: "All right, Mr. DeMille, I'm ready for my close-up now."]

Dear Doctor, I have read your play,
Which is a good one in its way,—
Purges the eyes and moves the bowels,
And drenches handkerchiefs like towels. —LORD BYRON,
Epistle from Mr. Murray to Dr. Polidori, Aug. 21, 1817
[John Murray, the publisher, had asked Byron to write a "delicate declension" that he could use for rejecting the manuscript of a play submitted to him by the poet's physician, the vain and prickly Dr. John Polidori. These are the opening lines of the letter, first published in 1830.]

Never meddle with play actors, for they're a favored race.
— CERVANTES, *Don Quixote,* 1605–15
[The more common view was expressed by the English satirist Charles Churchill: "The strolling tribe; a despicable race," *Apology: Addressed to the Critical Reviewers,* 1761.]

If a gun is hanging on the wall in the first act, it must fire in the last. — ANTON CHEKHOV, d. 1904,
advice to a novice playwright,
quoted in John Gassner and Edward Quinn, eds.,
The Reader's Encyclopedia of World Drama, 1969

Photography is truth. And cinema is truth twenty-four times a second. — JEAN-LUC GODARD,
screenplay, *Le Petit Soldat,* 1960

GEORGE FRANJU: Movies should have a beginning, a middle, and an end.
GODARD: Certainly, but not necessarily in that order.
— JEAN-LUC GODARD, *Time* magazine, Sept. 14, 1981

There isn't anything on earth so obstinate and perverse as an audience. — AL JOLSON, d. 1950,
comment broadcast in *Vaudeville,*
PBS, Nov. 26, 1997

The words "Kiss Kiss Bang Bang," which I saw on an Italian movie poster, are perhaps the briefest statement imaginable of the basic appeal of movies. —PAULINE KAEL,
Kiss Kiss Bang Bang, 1968

Satire is what closes on Saturday night.
—GEORGE S. KAUFMAN, attributed, c. 1930,
in Howard Teichmann, *George S. Kaufman: An Intimate Portrait,* 1972
[See also Lady Mary Wortley Montagu on satire at ARTS: WRITING and James Thurber at HUMOR.]

The structure of a play is always the story of how the birds came home to roost. —ARTHUR MILLER,
The Shadows of the Gods in *Harper's Magazine,* Aug. 1958

Drama is action, sir, action and not confounded philosophy.
—LUIGI PIRANDELLO,
Six Characters in Search of an Author, 1921

The play's the thing
Wherein I'll catch the conscience of the king.
—SHAKESPEARE, *Hamlet,* II, ii

Speak the speech, I pray you, as I pronounced it to you, trippingly on the tongue. —*Ibid.,* III, ii

Suit the action to the word, the word to the action, with this special observance, that you o'erstep not the modesty of nature. —*Ibid.*

Hold as 'twere the mirror up to nature. —*Ibid.*

Exit, pursued by a bear.
—SHAKESPEARE, *The Winter's Tale,*
stage direction, III, iii

The bad end unhappily, the good unluckily. That is what tragedy means. —TOM STOPPARD,
Rosencrantz and Guildenstern Are Dead, 1967

We're *actors*—we're the opposite of people! —*Ibid.*

ARTS: WRITING   See also ARTS: POETRY & POETS;
ARTS: STYLE IN WRITING & EXPRESSION;
BOOKS & READING;
LANGUAGE & WORDS; STORIES

Of making many books, there is no end.
—BIBLE, *Ecclesiastes* 12:12
[Also translated as, "Writing books involves endless hard work," *The Jerusalem Bible*, 1966.]

Writing is nothing more than a guided dream.
—JORGE LUIS BORGES, Preface, *Dr. Brodie's Report*, 1972

Ideas are to literature what light is to painting.
—PAUL BOURGET, *La Physiologie de l'amour*, 1890

A well-written life is almost as rare as a well-spent one.
—THOMAS CARLYLE,
Richter in *Critical and Miscellaneous Essays*, 1827

A good novel tells us the truth about its hero; but a bad novel tells us the truth about its author.
—G. K. CHESTERTON, *Heretics*, 1905

My homely definitions of prose and poetry; that is, prose = words in their best order; poetry = the best words in the best order.   —SAMUEL TAYLOR COLERIDGE,
Table Talk, July 12, 1827

All writing comes by the grace of God.
—RALPH WALDO EMERSON,
Experience in *Essays: Second Series*, 1844

If a writer has to rob his mother, he will not hesitate; the *Ode on a Grecian Urn* is worth any number of old ladies.
—WILLIAM FAULKNER, quoted in *Writers at Work:
The Paris Review Interviews*, 1959

Madame Bovary, c'est moi.
I am Madame Bovary. —GUSTAVE FLAUBERT, d. 1880,
cited in René Descharnes, *Flaubert*, 1909

It is with noble sentiments that bad literature gets written.
—ANDRÉ GIDE, *Journal*, Sept. 2, 1940

Often you must turn your stylus to erase, if you hope to write anything worth a second reading.
—HORACE, *Satires*, 35–30 B.C.

Lexicographer, n. A writer of dictionaries, a harmless drudge. —SAMUEL JOHNSON, *Dictionary*, 1755

A man may write at any time, if he will set himself doggedly to it. —SAMUEL JOHNSON, March 1750,
quoted in James Boswell, *Life of Johnson*, 1791

No man but a blockhead ever wrote, except for money.
—SAMUEL JOHNSON, Apr. 5, 1776, *Ibid.*

An inveterate and incurable itch for writing besets many and grows old with their sick hearts.
—JUVENAL, *Satires*, c. A.D. 100

He writes nothing whose writings are not read.
—MARTIAL, *Epigrams*, 1st cent. A.D.

If you steal from one author it's plagiarism; if you steal from many it's research.
—WILSON MIZNER, attributed in John Burke,
Rogue's Progress, 1975

Satire should, like a polished razor keen,
Wound with a touch that's scarcely felt or seen.
—MARY WORTLEY MONTAGU,
To the Imitator of the First Satire of Horace, 1733
[See also George S. Kaufman on satire at ARTS: THEATER, MOVIES, & ACTING.]

If there's a book you really want to read but it hasn't been written yet, then you must write it. —TONI MORRISON
[This has been attributed to Ms. Morrison in *The New York Times*, and elsewhere; she told this book's editors that she does not remember the occasion on which she said it—just that it was in a speech.]

True ease in writing comes from art, not chance.
>—ALEXANDER POPE, *An Essay on Criticism*, 1711

Our passions shape our books, repose writes them in the intervals.
>—MARCEL PROUST,
>*Remembrance of Things Past:*
>*The Past Recaptured*, 1913–27

An honest tale speeds best being plainly told.
>—SHAKESPEARE, *Richard III*, IV, iv

Keep away from books and from men who get their ideas from books, and your own books will always be fresh.
>—GEORGE BERNARD SHAW,
>*Bernard Shaw's Letters to Siegfried Trebitsch*, 1986

Of all those arts in which the wise excel,
Nature's chief masterpiece is writing well.
>—JOHN SHEFFIELD, *Essay on Poetry*, 1682

There's nothing to writing. All you do is sit down at a typewriter and open a vein.
>—WALTER ("RED") SMITH in
>*Reader's Digest*, July 1982

A great writer is, so to speak, a second government in his country. And for that reason no regime has ever loved great writers, only minor ones.
>—ALEXANDER SOLZHENITSYN,
>*The First Circle*, 1964

Writing, when properly managed (as you may be sure, I think mine is), is but a different name for conversation.
>—LAURENCE STERNE, *Tristram Shandy*, 1759–67

Writing may be either the record of a deed or a deed. It is nobler when it is a deed.
>—HENRY DAVID THOREAU,
>*Journal*, Jan. 7, 1844

Three hours a day will produce as much as a man ought to write.
>—ANTHONY TROLLOPE, *An Autobiography*, 1883

There is no way of writing well and also of writing easily.
>—ANTHONY TROLLOPE, *Barchester Towers*, 1857

Being a great writer is not the same as writing great.
—JOHN UPDIKE, *The New Yorker,* May 20, 1985

Literature is a form of permanent insurrection.
—MARIO VARGAS LLOSA, *Literature Is Fire,* 1967

ASTRONOMY See SCIENCE: PHYSICS & COSMOLOGY

ATHEISM   See also GOD; FAITH; RELIGION;
SKEPTICISM

The fool hath said in his heart, There is no God.
—BIBLE, *Psalms* 14:1 & 53:1

I am an atheist still, thank God.   —LUIS BUÑUEL,
quoted in *Le Monde,* Dec. 16, 1959

There are no atheists in the foxholes.
—WILLIAM THOMAS CUMMINGS,
field sermon, Bataan, 1942
[Father Cummings died of dysentery two years later, while confined in a "hell ship" prison. Reportedly, he was reciting the words "give us this day" from the Lord's Prayer when he died.]

In spite of all the yearnings of men, no one can produce a single fact or reason to support the belief in God and in personal immortality.   —CLARENCE DARROW,
Sign magazine, May 1938

I believe that when I die I shall rot, and nothing of my ego will survive. . . . But I should scorn to shiver with terror at the thought of annihilation. Happiness is nonetheless true happiness because it must come to an end, nor do thought and love lose their value because they are not everlasting.
—BERTRAND RUSSELL, *What I Believe,* 1925
[Years later, a friend asked the elderly Russell what he would do if, after death, he discovered he was wrong and now stood before the Pearly Gates. Russell replied eagerly, "Why I should say, 'God, you gave us insufficient evidence!' " Anecdote courtesy of Roger Angell, *The New Yorker,* Nov. 9, 1992.]

My atheism . . . is true piety towards the universe and denies only gods fashioned by men in their own image, to be servants of their human interests.
—GEORGE SANTAYANA, *On My Friendly Critics* in *Soliloquies in England and Later Soliloquies,* 1922

An atheist is a man who has no invisible means of support.
—FULTON J. SHEEN, *Look* magazine, Dec. 14, 1955

AUTOMOBILES   See SCIENCE: TECHNOLOGY

AUTUMN   See NATURE: SEASONS

B

BABIES See CHILDREN & CHILDHOOD

BAD TIMES See MODERN TIMES;
TROUBLE; TURBULENT TIMES

BANKS See BUSINESS

BATTLES See MILITARY BATTLES

BEAUTY See also APPEARANCES; ART:
AESTHETICS; CHARM; GRACE; WOMEN,
BEAUTIFUL & HOMELY

Beauty is the gift of God.
 —ARISTOTLE, 4th cent. B.C., quoted in
 Diogenes Laërtius, *Lives of Eminent
 Philosophers,* 3rd cent. A.D.

What do I care if you are good?
Be beautiful! and be sad!
 —CHARLES BAUDELAIRE, *Madrigal triste*
 in *Nouvelles Fleurs du mal,* 1866–68

For beauty being the best of all we know
Sums up the unsearchable and secret aims
Of nature.
 —ROBERT BRIDGES, *The Growth of Love,* 1876

Think of all the beauty still left around you and be happy.
 —ANNE FRANK, *Diary of a Young Girl,*
 Mar. 7, 1944 (published 1952)

Beauty is in the eye of the beholder.
 —MARGARET HUNGERFORD, *Molly Bawn,* 1878

[David Hume, in *Of Tragedy* (*Essays,* 1741–42), put it: "Beauty in things exists in the mind which contemplates them."]

A thing of beauty is a joy for ever:
Its loveliness increases; it will never
Pass into nothingness.   —JOHN KEATS, *Endymion,* 1818

"Beauty is truth, truth beauty," —that is all
Ye know on earth, and all ye need to know.
     —JOHN KEATS, *Ode on a Grecian Urn* in *Poems,* 1820

Beauty is everlasting
And dust is for a time.
     —MARIANNE MOORE, *In Distrust of Merits,* 1941

Remember that the most beautiful things in the world are the most useless: peacocks and lilies, for instance.
     —JOHN RUSKIN, *The Stones of Venice,* 1851–53

It is amazing how complete is the delusion that beauty is goodness.   —LEO TOLSTOY, *The Kreutzer Sonata,* 1890

The superior gratification derived from the use and contemplation of costly and supposedly beautiful products is, commonly, in great measure, a gratification of our sense of costliness masquerading under the name of beauty.
     —THORSTEIN VEBLEN, *The Theory of
the Leisure Class,* 1899

The beauty of the world which is soon to perish, has two edges, one of laughter, one of anguish, cutting the heart asunder.   —VIRGINIA WOOLF, *A Room of One's Own,* 1929

BEGINNINGS

A good beginning makes a good ending.
     —ANONYMOUS (ENGLISH PROVERB)
[See also T. S. Eliot at FATE.]

A hard beginning maketh a good ending.
     —JOHN HEYWOOD, *Proverbs,* 1546

Who has begun has half done. Have the courage to be wise.
Begin!   —HORACE, *Epistles,* Book I, 20 B.C.
[Former New York City Mayor Ed Koch kept this motto on
his desk, with a different, freer translation: "Begin, be bold,
and venture to be wise." The Latin reads: *Dimindium facti qui
coepit habet. Sapere aude. Incipe!*]

A journey of a thousand miles must begin with a single step.
                    —LAO-TZU, *Tao Te Ching,* 6th cent. B.C.

Things are always at their best in their beginning.
                    —PASCAL, *Provincial Letters,* 1656–57

The beginning is the most important part of the work.
                    —PLATO, *The Republic,* 4th cent. B.C.

BELIEF   See FAITH; RELIGION

BETRAYAL

This night, before the cock crow, thou shalt deny me thrice.
                    —BIBLE, *Matthew* 26:34

Judas, betrayest thou the Son of man with a kiss?
                    —BIBLE, *Luke* 22:48

Et tu, Brute!   —SHAKESPEARE, *Julius Caesar,* III, i

This was the most unkindest cut of all.   —*Ibid.,* III, ii

Each man kills the thing he loves.
        —OSCAR WILDE, *The Ballad of Reading Gaol,* 1898
[For more, see CRIME.]

BIBLE   See RELIGION

BIRDS   See NATURE: ANIMALS

BOASTING

Big boast, small roast.
                    —ANONYMOUS (ENGLISH PROVERB)
[An early equivalent of "Where's the beef?", advertising slogan
for Wendy's restaurants, by Cliff Freeman, 1984.]

It ain't braggin' if you kin do it.
                    —DIZZY DEAN, d. 1974, attributed

Do you wish people to believe good of you? Don't speak
well of yourself.   —PASCAL, *Pensées,* 1670

BOATING   See SEAS & SHIPS, SAILING & BOATING

BODY, HUMAN   See also HEALTH; ILLNESS &
                    REMEDIES; WOMEN (Wollstonecraft)

The Spirit indeed is willing, but the flesh is weak.
                    —BIBLE, *Matthew* 26:41
[See also TEMPTATION.]

Your body is the temple of the Holy Ghost, which is in you,
which ye have of God, and ye are not your own.
                    —BIBLE, *I Corinthians* 6:19

Alas, after a certain age, every man is responsible for his
own face.   —ALBERT CAMUS, *The Fall,* 1956

The strongest, surest way to the soul is through the flesh.
              —MABEL DODGE, *Lorenzo in Taos,* 1932
[The Lorenzo in the title is writer D. H. Lawrence.]

Love's mysteries in souls do grow,
But yet the body is his book.
              —JOHN DONNE, *The Ecstasy,* c. 1591–1601

I see no objection to stoutness, in moderation.
                    —W. S. GILBERT, *Iolanthe,* 1882

The body says what words cannot.
                    —MARTHA GRAHAM, interview,
                    The New York Times, Mar. 31, 1985

I'm fat, but I'm thin inside. Has it ever struck you that
there's a thin man inside every fat man?
              —GEORGE ORWELL, *Coming Up for Air,* 1939
[Possibly originated by Cyril Connolly: "Imprisoned in every

fat man is a thin one wildly signaling to be let out," published
in his book of aphorisms, *The Unquiet Grave,* 1945.]

From a man's face, I can read his character; if I can see him
walk, I know his thoughts.
                                        —PETRONIUS, *Satyricon,* 1st cent. B.C.

O! that this too too solid flesh would melt,
Thaw and resolve itself into a dew.
                                        —SHAKESPEARE, *Hamlet,* I, ii

I have more flesh than another man, and therefore, more
frailty.   —SHAKESPEARE, *Henry IV, Part I,* III, iii

Our body is a machine for living. It is organized for that, it is
its nature. Let life go on in it unhindered and let it defend
itself; it will do more than if you paralyze it by encumbering
it with remedies.—LEO TOLSTOY, *War and Peace,* 1865–69

If anything is sacred the human body is sacred.
                                        —WALT WHITMAN, *I Sing the Body
                                        Electric* in *Leaves of Grass,* 1855

BOLDNESS & INITIATIVE   See also ACTION;
                                        AMBITION; COURAGE;
                                        DECISION; GREATNESS;
                                        OPPORTUNITY; REVOLUTION;
                                        SELF-CONFIDENCE;
                                        SELF-RELIANCE

Ask, and it shall be given you; seek, and ye shall find; knock,
and it shall be opened unto you.   —BIBLE, *Matthew* 7:7

Faint heart never won fair lady.
                                        —CERVANTES, *Don Quixote,* 1605–15
[Identified by Cervantes as "an old saying."]

He who seizes the right moment,
Is the right man.   —GOETHE, *Faust,* 1808–32

The first blow is half the battle. —OLIVER GOLDSMITH,
                                        She Stoops to Conquer, 1733

He either fears his fate too much,
Or his deserts are small,
That puts it not unto the touch
To win or lose it all. —JAMES GRAHAM (MARQUIS
OF MONTROSE), d. 1650,
My Dear and Only Love
[Sent in a message from Field-Marshal Montgomery to U.S. troops sailing toward Normandy on June 5, 1944. They landed the next morning, D-Day.]

Cruelties should be committed all at once.
—MACHIAVELLI, *The Prince*, 1532

Take calculated risks. That is quite different from being rash. —GEORGE S. PATTON, letter to his
son on D-Day, June 6, 1944

If it were done when 'tis done, then 'twere well
It were done quickly. —SHAKESPEARE, *Macbeth*, I, vii

Fortune sides with him who dares.
—VIRGIL, *Aeneid*, c. 19 B.C.

BOOKS & READING   See also ARTS: POETRY &
POETS; ARTS: WRITING;
CENSORSHIP; STORIES

Big book, big bore.
—CALLIMACHUS, *On Himself*, c. 270 B.C.
[Traditionally rendered: "Great book, great evil," but "evil" seems too strong a word, considering that the author worked many years at the great Library of Alexandria, though he never headed it as was once thought. The translation we have selected is by Peter Jay.]

Reading all the good books is like a conversation with the finest men of past centuries.
—RENÉ DESCARTES, *Discourse on Method*, 1637

Books are for nothing but to inspire.
—RALPH WALDO EMERSON,
The American Scholar, 1837

Read in order to live. —GUSTAVE FLAUBERT, letter to
Mlle. de Chantpie, June 1857

All good books are alike in that they are truer than if they
really happened and after you are finished reading one you
will feel that it all happened to you, and afterwards it all
belongs to you. —ERNEST HEMINGWAY,
Old Newsman Writes in *Esquire,* Dec. 1934

I cannot live without books.
—THOMAS JEFFERSON, letter to
John Adams, June 10, 1815

Literature is my utopia.
—HELEN KELLER, *The Story of My Life,* 1902

We shouldn't teach great books; we should teach a love of
reading. —B. F. SKINNER, quoted in Richard I. Evans,
B. F. Skinner: The Man and His Ideas, 1968

People say that life is the thing, but I prefer reading.
—LOGAN PEARSALL SMITH, *Afterthoughts,* 1931

For him that steals, or borrows and returns not, a book from
its owner, let it change into a serpent in his hand and rend
him. Let him be struck with palsy, and all his members
blasted. Let him languish in pain crying aloud for mercy,
and let there be no surcease to his agony until he sing in
dissolution. Let bookworms gnaw at his entrails in token of
the Worm that dieth not. And when at last he goes to his
final punishment, let the flames of Hell consume him for
ever. —ANONYMOUS, from the library of the
Monastery of San Pedro, founded A.D. 945, Barcelona, Spain,
cited in Alberto Manguel, *A History of Reading,* 1997

Literature . . . becomes the living memory of a nation.
—ALEXANDER SOLZHENITSYN,
Nobel Prize acceptance speech, 1972
[Solzhenitsyn had declined to go to Norway to accept the 1970
prize for fear that he would not be allowed back into the
U.S.S.R. The quote is from the address that he planned to
deliver at a special awards ceremony in Moscow two years
later. The text was published August 24 after it became clear
that Russian authorities would not allow a public ceremony

because they were afraid that it would inspire anti-government demonstrations.]

Reading is to the mind what exercise is to the body.
—RICHARD STEELE, *The Tatler*, Mar. 18, 1710

Books are good enough in their own way, but they are a mighty bloodless substitute for life.
—ROBERT LOUIS STEVENSON, *An Apology for Idlers* in *Virginibus Puerisque*, 1881

Books are the treasured wealth of the world and the fit inheritance of generations and nations.
—HENRY DAVID THOREAU, *Reading* in *Walden*, 1854

How many a man has dated a new era in his life from the reading of a book.   —*Ibid.*

A good book is the best of friends, the same today and forever.   —MARTIN E. TUPPER, *Of Reading* in *Proverbial Philosophy*, 1838–42

"Classic." A book which people praise and don't read.
—MARK TWAIN, *Pudd'nhead Wilson's New Calendar* in *Following the Equator*, 1897

There is no such thing as a moral or an immoral book. Books are well written, or badly written.
—OSCAR WILDE, *The Picture of Dorian Gray*, 1891

BORES & BOREDOM

Bore, n. A person who talks when you wish him to listen.
—AMBROSE BIERCE *The Devil's Dictionary*, 1906

Society is now one polished horde,
Formed of two mighty tribes, the *Bores* and *Bored*.
—LORD BYRON, *Don Juan*, 1819–24

Speeches measured by the hour die with the hour.
—THOMAS JEFFERSON, letter to David Harding, Apr. 20, 1824

Only one person in a thousand is a bore, and he is interesting because he is one person in a thousand.
—HAROLD NICOLSON, quoted by Nigel Nicolson,
Harold Nicolson: Diaries and Letters, 1930–1939, 1968

Gentlemen, you have just been listening to that Chinese sage, On Tu Long.
—WILL ROGERS, d. 1935, cited in Alex Ayres, ed.,
The Wit and Wisdom of Will Rogers, 1993

A healthy male adult bore consumes each year one and a half times his weight in other people's patience.
—JOHN UPDIKE, *Confessions of a Wild Bore*
in *Assorted Prose,* 1965

BOSTON   See CITIES

BRAGGING   See BOASTING

BRAVERY   See COURAGE

BROOKLYN   See CITIES (New York)

BROTHERHOOD   See EQUALITY; HUMANS &
              HUMAN NATURE; RACES & PEOPLES

BUSINESS   See also AMERICA & AMERICANS;
                      CAPITALISM; COMMITTEES &
                      CONFERENCES; ECONOMICS;
                      MONEY; NEGOTIATION;
                      WORK & WORKERS

Buying and selling is essentially antisocial.
—EDWARD BELLAMY, *Looking Backward,*
2000–1887, 1888

What is robbing a bank compared with founding a bank?
—BERTOLT BRECHT, *The Threepenny Opera,* 1928

It is better to lose opportunity than capital.
—SUSAN M. BYRNE, on *Wall St. Week in Review,*
television show, Feb. 15, 1985

Few people do business well who do nothing else.
                              —EARL OF CHESTERFIELD, letter
                                        to his son, Aug. 7, 1749

They [corporations] cannot commit treason, nor be out-
lawed, nor excommunicate, for they have no souls.
                    —EDWARD COKE, *The Case of Sutton's Hospital*
                         in *The Reports of Sir Edward Coke*, 1658
[See also Baron Thurlow below.]

No nation was ever ruined by trade.
                              —BENJAMIN FRANKLIN, *Thoughts
                                      on Commercial Subjects*

Ben, I just want to say one word to you. Just one word.
Plastics.   —BUCK HENRY & CALDER WILLINGHAM,
                                      screenplay, *The Graduate*, 1967
[Based on Charles Webb's 1963 novel.]

When a person with experience meets a person with money,
the person with experience will get the money. And the
person with the money will get some experience.
                    —LEONARD LAUDER, speech, Woman's Economic
                              Development Corporation, Feb. 1985

Trade is a social act.   —JOHN STUART MILL,
                                              On Liberty, 1859

He's a businessman. I'll make him an offer he can't refuse.
                              —MARIO PUZO, *The Godfather*, 1969
[The Godfather, Don Corleone, explaining his strategy for
dealing with a Hollywood producer.]

The customer is always right.—H. GORDON SELFRIDGE,
                                      slogan of his store in London
[Selfridge lived from 1857 to 1947. The saying was in popular
currency, and appears in Carl Sandburg's collection of folk sayings in *Smoke and Steel*, 1920.]

Corporations have neither bodies to be punished, nor souls
to be condemned, they therefore do as they like.
                              —EDWARD, FIRST BARON THURLOW,
                              attributed by Poynder, *Literary Extracts*, 1844
[See also Edward Coke above.]

No one on his deathbed ever said, "I wish I had spent more time on my business." —PAUL E. TSONGAS,
quoting a letter from a friend, 1983
[The thought was expressed in a variety of forms in the 1980s. Sen. Tsongas's friend wrote after the senator had announced on Jan. 12, 1983, that he would not finish his 1979–85 term as junior senator from Massachusetts. (He was being treated for cancer.) Anna Quindlen called this "the quote of the decade" in her column in *The New York Times,* Jan. 14, 1987.]

The public be damned! I'm working for my stockholders.
—WILLIAM HENRY VANDERBILT,
news reports, Oct. 2, 1882

For years I thought what was good for our country was good for General Motors and vice versa. The difference did not exist. —CHARLES E. WILSON, testimony,
Senate Armed Services Committee, Jan. 15, 1953
[Often misquoted as, "What is good for General Motors is good for the country." Mr. Wilson, chairman of General Motors, made the remark in hearings on his nomination to be Secretary of Defense. Wilson's comment is a qualified version of Calvin Coolidge's pronouncement that the business of America is business; see under AMERICA & AMERICANS.]

Most men are the servants of corporations.
—WOODROW WILSON, *The Old Order
Changeth* in *The New Freedom,* 1913
[The full sentence runs: "There was a time when corporations played a minor part in our business affairs, but now they play the chief part, and most men are the servants of corporations."]

C

CANADA   See NATIONS

CAPITALISM   See also BUSINESS; COMMUNISM;
                                    ECONOMICS; MONEY;
                           SELF-INTEREST; SOCIALISM;
                                    WORK & WORKERS

A market is a place set apart for men to deceive and get
the better of one another.   —ANACHARSIS,
                                  quoted in Diogenes Laërtius,
                    Lives of Eminent Philosophers, 3rd cent. A.D.

Laissez faire.
Let business go forward. No interference.
    —MARQUIS D'ARGENSON, *Mémoires*, 1736, Vol. 5
[The phrase is difficult to translate and has complicated origins:
The Concise Oxford Dictionary of Quotations notes that in
1751, when Jean Baptiste Colbert, France's minister of finance,
asked a group of commerce deputies what he could do to help
business, one of them replied, "*Laissez-nous faire,*" which may
be translated: "Let us get on with it." In 1758, in a speech, the
economist Vincent de Gournay urged, "*Laissez faire, laissez
passer,*" calling for free passage of goods and people; the
phrase was a favorite with him. François Quesnay also used
"*laissez passer . . . laissez faire*" with reference to commerce.]

What we call real estate—the solid ground to build a house
on—is the broad foundation on which nearly all the guilt of
this world rests.   —NATHANIEL HAWTHORNE,
                            The House of the Seven Gables, 1851

Capital has its rights, which are as worthy of protection as
any other rights.   —ABRAHAM LINCOLN, first annual
                             message to Congress, Dec. 3, 1861

[But see also his comments on labor under WORK & WORKERS.]

The forces of a capitalist society, if left unchecked, tend to make the rich richer and the poor poorer.
—JAWAHARLAL NEHRU, *Credo* in
The New York Times Magazine, Sept. 7, 1958

La propriété, c'est le vol.
Property is theft. —PIERRE-JOSEPH PROUDHON,
What Is Property?, 1840

The revolution eats its own. Capitalism recreates itself.
—MORDECAI RICHLER, *Cocksure,* 1968

Property is organized robbery.
—GEORGE BERNARD SHAW,
Preface, *Major Barbara,* 1907

Every individual . . . intends only his own gain, and he is in this, as in many other cases, led by an invisible hand to promote an end which was no part of his intention. By pursuing his own interest he frequently promotes that of the society more effectively than when he really intends to promote it. I have never known much good done by those who affected to trade for the public good.
—ADAM SMITH, *Wealth of Nations,* 1776

It is not from the benevolence of the butcher, the brewer, or the baker that we expect our dinner, but from their regard to their own self-interest. —*Ibid.*

Conspicuous consumption of valuable goods is a means of reputability to the gentleman of leisure.
—THORSTEIN VEBLEN, *The Theory
of the Leisure Class,* 1899

The trouble with the profit system has always been that it was highly unprofitable to most people.
—E. B. WHITE, *Control* in *One Man's Meat,* 1944

CARDS See GAMES

CARS See SCIENCE: TECHNOLOGY

CATS   See NATURE: ANIMALS

CAUTION   See PRUDENCE & PRACTICAL
                                                        WISDOM

CENSORSHIP   See also FREE SPEECH; PRESS, THE

Every suppressed or expunged word reverberates through
the earth from side to side.
                        —RALPH WALDO EMERSON, *Compensation*
                                        in *Essays: First Series,* 1841

Wherever they burn books, they will also, in the end, burn
people.   —HEINRICH HEINE, *Almansor,* 1820–21

As good almost kill a man as kill a good book: who kills a
man kills a reasonable creature, God's image; but he who
destroys a good book kills reason itself.
                        —JOHN MILTON, *Areopagitica,* 1644

Scenes of passion should not be introduced when not essential to the plot. In general, passion should be so treated that
these scenes do not stimulate the lower and baser element.
                        —THE MOTION PICTURE PRODUCERS
                               AND DISTRIBUTORS OF AMERICA,
                               INC., *Code for the Industry,* 1931

Sex perversion or any inference of it is forbidden. White
slavery shall not be treated. Miscegenation is forbidden. . . .
Scenes of actual childbirth, in fact or in silhouette, are never
to be represented.   —*Ibid.*

Assassination is the extreme form of censorship.
                        —GEORGE BERNARD SHAW,
                               The Limits of Toleration in *The Shewing
                               Up of Blanco Posnet,* 1911

We write frankly and freely but then we "modify" before
we print.   —MARK TWAIN, *Life on the Mississippi,* 1883
[Today, we call this "self-censorship."]

CEYLON   See NATIONS (Sri Lanka)

CHANCE   See LUCK

CHANGE
See also CONSISTENCY;
NEW THINGS; PROGRESS;
VARIETY

Nature's mighty law is change.
—ROBERT BURNS, *Let Not Women E'er Complain*, 1794

Change is inevitable in a progressive society. Change is constant.   —BENJAMIN DISRAELI, speech, Oct. 20, 1867

Unless one says goodbye to what one loves, and unless one travels to completely new territories, one can expect merely a long wearing away of oneself and an eventual extinction.
—JEAN DUBUFFET, quoted in
The New York Times, obituary, May 15, 1985

For the times they are a-changin'.
—BOB DYLAN, *The Times They Are A-Changin',* 1963

You can't step twice into the same river.
—HERACLITUS, *On the Universe,* c. 500 B.C.

Everything flows, nothing stays still.
—HERACLITUS, quoted in Plato,
Cratylus, 4th cent. B.C.

Nothing is permanent but change.
—HERACLITUS, quoted in Diogenes Laërtius,
Lives of Eminent Philosophers, 3rd cent. A.D.

Plus ça change, plus c'est la même chose.
The more things change, the more they remain the same.
—ALPHONSE KARR, *Les Guêpes,* Jan. 1849

It is not best to swap horses while crossing the river.
—ABRAHAM LINCOLN, remark, June 9, 1862

The wind of change is blowing through this Continent.
—HAROLD MACMILLAN, speech,
Cape Town, Feb. 3, 1960

[More of this is given at NATIONS (Africa).]

The basic fact of today is the tremendous pace of change in human life.   —JAWAHARLAL NEHRU, *Credo* in
The New York Times Magazine, Sept. 7, 1958

The old order changeth, yielding place to new,
And God fulfills Himself in many ways,
Lest one good custom should corrupt the world.
                    —ALFRED, LORD TENNYSON, *The Passing of
Arthur* in *Idylls of the King,* 1869

CHARITY   See CHARITY: PHILANTHROPY;
                    LOVE & CHARITY: BIBLICAL
                    REFERENCES

CHARITY: PHILANTHROPY

All that is not given is lost.
                    —ANONYMOUS (INDIAN PROVERB),
                    associated with Calcutta

The living need charity more than the dead.
        —GEORGE ARNOLD, *The Jolly Old Pedagogue,* 1866

Cast thy bread upon the waters.   —BIBLE, *Ecclesiastes* 11:1

Take heed that ye do not your alms before men, to be seen of them: otherwise you have no reward of your Father which is in heaven. Therefore when thou doest thine alms, do not sound a trumpet before thee, as the hypocrites do in the synagogues and in the streets, that they may have glory of men. Verily, I say unto you, they have their reward.
   But when thou doest alms, let not thy left hand know what thy right hand doeth.   —BIBLE, *Matthew* 6:1–3

Jesus said unto him, If thou wilt be perfect, go and sell that thou hast, and give to the poor, and thou shalt have treasure in heaven.   —*Ibid.* 19:21

I was an hungred, and ye gave me meat: I was thirsty, and ye gave me drink: I was a stranger, and ye took me in:
   Naked, and ye clothed me: I was sick, and ye visited me: I was in prison, and ye came unto me.   —*Ibid.* 25:35, 36

It is more blessed to give than to receive.
—BIBLE, *Acts* 20:35

God loveth a cheerful giver.   —BIBLE, *II Corinthians* 9:7

He is rich who hath enough to be charitable.
—SIR THOMAS BROWNE, *Religio medici,* 1643

Philanthropy is commendable, but it must not cause the philanthropist to overlook the circumstances of economic injustice which make philanthropy necessary.
—MARTIN LUTHER KING, JR., *Strength to Love,* 1963

He gives twice who gives promptly.
—PUBLILIUS SYRUS, *Moral Sayings,* 1st cent. B.C.
[Also, Cervantes in *Don Quixote,* 1605–15: "He that gives quickly gives twice."]

Give all thou can'st; high Heaven rejects the lore
Of nicely calculated less or more.
—WILLIAM WORDSWORTH, *Sonnet 43,*
Inside of King's College Chapel in
Ecclesiastic Sonnets, 1822

CHARM   See also BEAUTY; GRACE

Charm: the quality in others that makes us more satisfied with ourselves.
—HENRI-FRÉDÉRIC AMIEL, *Journal intime,* 1883

It's a sort of bloom on a woman. If you have it, you don't need to have anything else; and if you don't have it, it doesn't much matter what else you have.
—J. M. BARRIE, *What Every Woman Knows,* 1908

Charm is a way of getting the answer yes without ever having asked a clear question.
—ALBERT CAMUS, *The Fall,* 1956

All charming people have something to conceal, usually their total dependence on the appreciation of others.
—CYRIL CONNOLLY, *Enemies of Promise,* 1938

He had that nameless charm, with a strong magnetism, which can only be called "It."   —ELINOR GLYN, *It*, 1927
[The movie made from Glyn's 1927 novel starred Clara Bow, the "it" girl. The term probably had been around for a while. "It" appears in Kipling's *Traffic and Discoveries* (1904): " 'Tisn't beauty, so to speak, nor good talk, necessarily. It's just It. Some women'll stay in a man's memory if they once walk down a street."]

All charming people, I fancy, are spoiled. It is the secret of their attraction.
          —OSCAR WILDE, *The Portrait of Mr. W. H.*, 1901

CHICAGO   See CITIES

CHILDREN & CHILDHOOD   See also EDUCATION;
                                 INNOCENCE; FAMILY;
                            PARENTS & PARENTHOOD;
                                             YOUTH

Out of the mouth of babes and sucklings hast thou ordained strength.   —BIBLE, *Psalms* 8:2

A little child shall lead them.   —BIBLE, *Isaiah* 11:6
[The entire verse is given under PEACE.]

But whoso shall offend one of these little ones which believe in me, it were better for him that a millstone were hanged about his neck, and that he were drowned in the depth of the sea.   —BIBLE, *Matthew* 18:6

Suffer the little children to come unto me, and forbid them not: for of such is the kingdom of God.
                            —BIBLE, *Mark* 10:14

When I was a child, I spake as a child, I understood as a child, I thought as a child: but when I became a man, I put away childish things.   —BIBLE, *I Corinthians* 9:11

There is no finer investment for any community than putting milk into babies.
     —WINSTON CHURCHILL, radio address, Mar. 21, 1943

Every baby born into the world is a finer one than the last.
—CHARLES DICKENS, *Nicholas Nickleby,* 1838–39

We find delight in the beauty and happiness of children that makes the heart too big for the body.
—RALPH WALDO EMERSON, *The Conduct of Life,* 1860

We can't form our children on our own concepts; we must take them and love them as God gives them to us.
—GOETHE, *Hermann und Dorothea,* 1797

There is always one moment in childhood when the door opens and lets the future in.
—GRAHAM GREENE, *The Power and the Glory,* 1940

Children need models more than they need critics.
—JOSEPH JOUBERT, *Pensées,* 1842

Between the dark and the daylight,
When the night is beginning to lower,
Comes a pause in the day's occupations,
That is known as the Children's Hour.
—HENRY WADSWORTH LONGFELLOW,
The Children's Hour, 1860
[This poem is also the source of "the patter of little feet" in the lines "I hear in the chamber above me/ The patter of little feet."]

There was a little girl
Who had a little curl
Right in the middle of her forehead;
And when she was good
She was very, very good,
But when she was bad she was horrid.
—HENRY WADSWORTH LONGFELLOW,
There Was a Little Girl, c. 1850, in
B. R. Tucker-Machetta, *The Home Life of
Henry W. Longfellow,* 1882
[A lullaby for his second daughter.]

The happy childhood is hardly worth your while.
—FRANK McCOURT, *Angela's Ashes,* 1996

Childhood is the kingdom where nobody dies.
>—EDNA ST. VINCENT MILLAY, title of
>poem in *Wine from these Grapes,* 1934

Children's games are hardly games. Children are never more serious than when they play.
>—MONTAIGNE, *Essays,* 1580–88

Of all the animals, the boy is the most unmanageable.
>—PLATO, *Theaetetus,* 4th cent. B.C.

But soon a milder age will follow. An age of truer wisdom. Then the careful state will spare her children.
>—J.C.F. VON SCHILLER, *Don Carlos,* 1787

A child should always say what's true
And speak when he is spoken to,
And behave mannerly at table:
At least as far as he is able.
>—ROBERT LOUIS STEVENSON,
>*A Child's Garden of Verses,* 1885

A baby is an inestimable blessing and bother.
>—MARK TWAIN, letter to Annie Webster, Sept. 1, 1876

Our birth is but a sleep and a forgetting:
The soul that rises with us, our life's Star,
Hath had elsewhere its setting,
And cometh from afar:
Not in entire forgetfulness,
And not in utter nakedness,
But trailing clouds of glory do we come
From God, who is our home:
Heaven lies about us in our infancy!
>—WILLIAM WORDSWORTH, *Ode, Intimations
>of Immortality from Recollections
>of Early Childhood,* 1807

The child is father of the man.
>—WILLIAM WORDSWORTH, *My Heart Leaps Up,* 1807

CHINA   See NATIONS

CHRIST   See CHRISTMAS; JESUS

CHRISTMAS See also JESUS

I'm dreaming of a white Christmas.
—IRVING BERLIN, *White Christmas,*
song in *Holiday Inn,* 1942

And she brought forth her first-born son, and wrapped him
in swaddling clothes, and laid him in a manger; because
there was no room for them in the inn. —BIBLE, *Luke* 2:7

Glory to God in the highest, and on earth peace, good will
toward men. —*Ibid.* 2:14

O little town of Bethlehem
How still we see thee lie!
Above thy deep and dreamless sleep
The silent stars go by.
—PHILLIPS BROOKS, *O Little Town of Bethlehem,* 1868

Yes, Virginia, there is a Santa Claus. He exists as certainly
as love and generosity and devotion exist.
—FRANCIS P. CHURCH, *The Sun,*
editorial, Sept. 21, 1897
[Virginia O'Hanlon of Manhattan had written, "Dear Editor,
I am eight years old. Some of my little friends say there is no
Santa Claus. Papa says, 'If you see it in *The Sun,* it's so.' Please
tell me the truth; is there a Santa Claus?" Church wrote an
unsigned five-paragraph editorial reply. After his death in 1906,
the paper made an exception to its rule of editorial anonymity
to reveal that Church was the author.]

"Bah," said Scrooge. "Humbug!"
—CHARLES DICKENS, *A Christmas Carol,* 1843

"God bless us every one!" said Tiny Tim, the last of all.
—*Ibid.*

A cold coming we had of it,
Just the worst time of the year.
—T. S. ELIOT, *Journey of the Magi,* 1927
[Cf. Lancelot Andrewes, *Of the Nativity,* 1622: "A cold coming
they had of it at this time of the year; just the worst time of
the year to take a journey, and specially a long journey, in."]

I heard the bells on Christmas Day,
Their old familiar carols play,
And wild and sweet
The words repeat
Of peace on earth, good-will to men!
      —HENRY WADSWORTH LONGFELLOW,
        Christmas Bells in *Flower-de-Luce*, 1867

It was the winter wild
While the Heaven-born child
All meanly wrapt in the rude manger lies.
      —JOHN MILTON, *On the Morning*
        of Christ's Nativity, 1629

'Twas the night before Christmas, when all through the
  house
Not a creature was stirring, not even a mouse;
The stockings were hung by the chimney with care,
In hopes that St. Nicholas soon would be there.
The children were nestled all snug in their beds,
While visions of sugar-plums danced in their heads.
      —CLEMENT C. MOORE, *The Night Before Christmas*
        in the *Troy Sentinal*, Dec. 23, 1823
[Dr. Moore, a distinguished classical scholar, wrote this poem
in 1822 as a Christmas present for his daughter, who was seri-
ously ill.]

Now, *Dasher!* now, *Dancer!* now, *Prancer* and *Vixen!*
On, *Comet!* on, *Cupid!* on, *Donner* and *Blitzen!*   —*Ibid.*

He had a broad face and a little round belly,
That shook when he laughed, like a bowlful of jelly.—*Ibid.*

But I heard him exclaim, ere he drove out of sight,
"Happy Christmas to all and to all a good night!"   —*Ibid.*

Heap on more wood! the wind is chill,
But let it whistle as it will,
We'll keep our Christmas merry still.
      —SIR WALTER SCOTT, *Marmion*, 1808

It came upon the midnight clear,
That glorious song of old,
From angels bending near the earth
To touch their harps of gold;
"Peace on the earth, good will to men
From Heaven's all-gracious King"—
The world in solemn stillness lay
To hear the angels sing.
 —EDMUND HAMILTON SEARS, *Christmas Carol,* 1850

The time draws near the birth of Christ;
The moon is hid; the night is still;
The Christmas bells from hill to hill
Answer each other in the mist.
  —ALFRED, LORD TENNYSON, *In Memoriam,* 1850

At Christmas play, and make good cheer,
For Christmas comes but once a year.
   —THOMAS TUSSER, *The Farmer's Daily Diet* in
    Five Hundred Points of Good Husbandry, 1557

CHURCH   See RELIGION

CINCINNATI   See CITIES

CITIES

Omnis civitas corpus est.
Every city is a living body.
   —ST. AUGUSTINE, *City of God,* A.D. 415
[Plutarch expressed a similar idea: "A city, like a living thing,
is a united and continuous whole," *Morals,* c. A.D. 100.]

The first requisite to happiness is to be born in a famous
city. —EURIPIDES, *On Alcibiades,* fragment, 5th cent. B.C.

When we get piled upon one another in large cities, as in
Europe, we shall become as corrupt as Europe.
    —THOMAS JEFFERSON, letter to
     James Madison, Dec. 20, 1787

All cities are mad: but the madness is gallant. All cities are beautiful: but the beauty is grim.
> —CHRISTOPHER MORLEY, *Where the Blue Begins*, 1922

Any ordinary city is in fact two cities, one the city of the poor and the other the city of the rich, each at war with the other.   —PLATO, *The Republic*, 4th cent. B.C.

Cities are the abyss of the human species.
> —JEAN JACQUES ROUSSEAU, *Émile*, 1762

What is the city but the people?
> —SHAKESPEARE, *Coriolanus*, III, i

The City is of night; perchance of death,
But certainly of night.
> —JAMES THOMSON, *The City of Dreadful Night*, 1874

Boston

And this is good old Boston,
The home of the bean and the cod,
Where the Lowells talk to the Cabots
And the Cabots talk only to God.
> —JOHN COLLINS BOSSIDY, toast at Holy Cross alumni dinner, 1910

Carthage

Carthago delenda est.
Carthage must be destroyed.
> —CATO THE ELDER, in speeches after the Second Punic War (218–201 B.C.), quoted in Plutarch's *Parallel Lives*, c. A.D. 100

Chicago

The city that works.   —ANONYMOUS, saying, described as "recently traditional" in *The Economist*, Mar. 3–9, 1979

Chicago is the product of modern capitalism, and, like other great commercial centers, is unfit for human habitation.
—EUGENE DEBS, 1908, quoted in
Kevin Tierney, *Darrow,* 1979

Hog butcher for the world,
Tool maker, stacker of wheat,
Player with railroads and the nation's freight handler;
Stormy, husky, brawling,
City of the big shoulders.
—CARL SANDBURG, *Chicago,* 1916

Cincinnati

The Queen of the West.
—HENRY WADSWORTH LONGFELLOW,
Catawba Wine, 1854
[The nickname dates from the 1830s, and was validated when used in this poem, which was essentially a thank-you note for a gift of wine.]

Jerusalem

Ten measures of beauty came into the world; Jerusalem received nine measures, and the rest of the world one.
—ANONYMOUS (HEBREW PROVERB)

London

By seeing London, I have seen as much of life as the world can show.   —SAMUEL JOHNSON,
quoted by James Boswell,
*The Journal of a Tour to the Hebrides with
Samuel Johnson, LL.D.,* 1785

Hell is a city much like London.
—PERCY BYSSHE SHELLEY, *Peter Bell the Third,* 1819
[More at HELL.]

Los Angeles

Nineteen suburbs in search of a metropolis.
—ALDOUS HUXLEY, *Americana,* 1925
[Attributed to others, too, in various forms.]

It's redundant to die in L.A.
> —TRUMAN CAPOTE, 1975, quoted in Jay
> Presson Allen's play *Tru*, 1989

If you tip the whole country sideways, Los Angeles is the place where everything will fall.
> —FRANK LLOYD WRIGHT, d. 1959, attributed

Mandalay

On the road to Mandalay,
Where the flyin'-fishes play,
An' the dawn comes up like thunder outer China 'crost the
Bay!
> —RUDYARD KIPLING, *Mandalay* in
> *Barrack-Room Ballads*, 1892

Miami

Miami is where neon goes to die.
> —LENNY BRUCE, d. 1966, quoted by
> Barbara Gordon, *Saturday Review*,
> May 20, 1972

Naples

Vedi Napoli e poi muori.
See Naples and die.
> —ANONYMOUS (ITALIAN PROVERB)

New York

They [New Yorkers] talk very loud, very fast, and all together.   —JOHN ADAMS, July 23, 1774, *The Diary*, 1850

Ford to City: Drop Dead.
> —*NEW YORK DAILY NEWS* headline, Oct. 30, 1975

[Pres. Gerald Ford had pledged to veto any bill that would provide bailout funds for the nearly bankrupt New York City. According to columnist Jimmy Breslin, the reporters who came up with this line were William Brink and Michael O'Neill.]

New York, New York—a helluva town,
The Bronx is up but the Battery's down.
> —BETTY COMDEN & ADOLPH GREEN,
> *New York, New York,* 1945

[The authors paid obeisance to the Hollywood Production Code by changing "helluva town" to "wonderful town" in the 1949 film *On the Town.*]

It couldn't have happened anywhere but in little old New York.
> —O. HENRY, *A Little Local Color* in *Whirligigs,* 1910

O sweep of stars over Harlem streets,
O little breath of oblivion that is night.
A city building to a mother's song,
A city dreaming to a lullaby.
> —LANGSTON HUGHES, d. 1967, *Stars* in *From My People*

[Re New York:] There is no greenery. It is enough to make a stone sad.
> —NIKITA KHRUSHCHEV, d. 1971, cited by
> Bruce Weber, *The New York Times,*
> June 21, 1992

My own Manhattan, with spires and the sparkling and hurrying tides, and the ships.
> —WALT WHITMAN, *When Lilacs Last in the Dooryard Bloom'd,* 1865–66

Only the Dead Know Brooklyn.
> —THOMAS WOLFE, story title in
> *The Web and the Rock,* 1939

Oakland

What was the use of my having come from Oakland. . . . there is no there there.
> —GERTRUDE STEIN, *Everybody's Autobiography,* 1937

Paris

Good Americans when they die go to Paris.
> —THOMAS GOLD APPLETON, saying, c. 1850

The last time I saw Paris, her heart was warm and gay,
I heard the laughter of her heart in every street cafe.
—OSCAR HAMMERSTEIN II,
The Last Time I Saw Paris, 1940

If you are lucky enough to have lived in Paris as a young
man, then wherever you go for the rest of your life, it stays
with you, for Paris is a moveable feast.
—ERNEST HEMINGWAY, *epigraph, A Moveable
Feast,* 1964
[For another appreciation of Paris, see Henry IV at EX-
PEDIENCY.]

Petra

Match me such a marvel save in Eastern clime,
A rose-red city "half as old as time."
—JOHN WILLIAM BURGON, *Petra,* 1845

Philadelphia

On the whole I'd rather be in Philadelphia.
—W. C. FIELDS, epitaph
[Fields was born in Philadelphia, and numerous other jibes at
the place are attributed to him, including: "I went to Philadelphia one Sunday. The place was closed."]

Pittsburgh

[Re Pittsburgh:] Hell with the lid taken off.
—JAMES PARTON, article in *Atlantic Monthly,* 1868

Rome

Everyone soon or late comes round by Rome.
—ROBERT BROWNING, *The Ring and
the Book,* 1868–69
[A variant on the ancient adage, "All roads lead to Rome."]

At Rome, all things can be had at a price.
—JUVENAL, *Satires,* c. A.D. 100

San Francisco

The miner's came in forty-nine,
The whores in fifty-one;
And when they got together
They produced the native son.
—ANONYMOUS, song, c. 1852

San Francisco is a mad city—inhabited for the most part by perfectly insane people whose women are of a remarkable beauty. —RUDYARD KIPLING, *American Notes*, 1891

Washington, D.C.

If you want a friend in Washington, go buy a dog.
—ANONYMOUS, 20th cent., sometimes
attributed to Harry S. Truman

Washington is a city of southern efficiency and northern charm. —JOHN F. KENNEDY, comment to trustees and
advisory committee of the national cultural
center, Nov. 14, 1961

CIVIL SERVANTS See GOVERNMENT

CIVILIZATION See also MODERN TIMES; PROGRESS

The three great elements of modern civilization, Gunpowder, Printing, and the Protestant Religion.
—THOMAS CARLYLE, *The State of German
Literature* in *Critical and
Miscellaneous Essays*, 1827

Increased means and increased leisure are the two civilizers of man. —BENJAMIN DISRAELI, speech, Apr. 3, 1872

Civilized men arrive in the Pacific, armed with alcohol, syphilis, trousers, and the Bible.
—HAVELOCK ELLIS, *The Dance of Life*, 1923

We think our civilization near its meridian, but we are yet only at the cock-crowing and the morning star.
—RALPH WALDO EMERSON, *Politics*
in *Essays: Second Series*, 1844

The resources of civilization are not yet exhausted.
    —W. E. GLADSTONE, speech, May 7, 1877

What man calls civilization always results in deserts.
    —DON MARQUIS, *what the ants are*
    saying in *archy does his part,* 1935

Our civilization depends largely on paper.
    —PLINY, *Natural History,* A.D. 77

Civilization is the progress toward a society of privacy.
    —AYN RAND, *The Fountainhead,* 1943

You can't say civilization don't advance . . . in every war
they kill you in a new way.
    —WILL ROGERS, *The New York Times,* Dec. 23, 1929

The civilized man has the habits of the house. His house is
a prison.
    —HENRY DAVID THOREAU, *Journal,* Apr. 26, 1841

Civilization advances by extending the number of important
operations which we can perform without thinking about
them.   —ALFRED NORTH WHITEHEAD,
    An Introduction to Mathematics, 1911

CLEANLINESS

[Re not doing housework:] After the first four years, the
dirt doesn't get any worse.
    —QUENTIN CRISP, *The Naked Civil Servant,* 1968

"Cleanliness is indeed next to godliness."
    —JOHN WESLEY, *On Dress,*
    sermon 93 in *Works,* 1771–74
[Wesley put the phrase within quotation marks, apparently because the thought appears in similar form in the Talmud.]

CLERGY   See GOD; RELIGION

CLOTHES   See FASHION & CLOTHES

COMEDY   See HUMOR

COMMITTEES & CONFERENCES

No grand idea was ever born in a conference, but a lot of foolish ideas have died there.
—F. SCOTT FITZGERALD, *The Crack-up,* 1945

Could *Hamlet* have been written by a committee, or the *Mona Lisa* painted by a club? Could the New Testament have been composed as a conference report? Creative ideas do not spring from groups. They spring from individuals. The divine spark leaps from God to the finger of Adam.
—A. WHITNEY GRISWOLD, speech, 1957
[Griswold was president of Yale University.]

A committee is an animal with four back legs.
—JOHN LE CARRÉ, *Tinker Tailor Soldier Spy,* 1974

COMMUNICATION See CONVERSATION;
LANGUAGE & WORDS (Pierson);
MEDIA; TALK

COMMUNISM See also CAPITALISM;
ECONOMICS; REVOLUTION;
SOCIALISM

That which is common to the greatest number has the least care bestowed upon it.
—ARISTOTLE, *Politics,* 4th cent. B.C.

From Stettin in the Baltic to Trieste in the Adriatic, an iron curtain has descended across the Continent.
—WINSTON CHURCHILL, speech, Mar. 5, 1946
[Churchill made the phrase famous. *Bartlett's,* however, notes several earlier uses, including one by Queen Elizabeth of Belgium in 1914, referring to Germany. *The Penguin Dictionary of Quotations* cites an article by St. Vincent Troubridge in 1945, stating, "There is an iron curtain across Europe." William Safire, in his dictionary of political terms, points out that the phrase has a theatrical origin, an iron curtain having been used in theaters since the 18th century to retard fires. He believes the metaphor was used in the political sense as early as 1819, and notes that Goebbels, in 1945, employed it with specific reference to Russia.]

What is a communist? One who hath yearnings
For equal division of unequal earnings.
—EBENEZER ELLIOTT, *Epigram* in *Poetical Works,* 1846

[Communism] has never come to power in a country that
was not disrupted by war or internal corruption or both.
—JOHN F. KENNEDY, speech, July 3, 1963

We Communists are like seeds and the people are the soil.
Wherever we go, we must unite with the people, take root
and blossom among them.
—MAO ZEDUNG, *Quotations from
Chairman Mao Zedung,* 1966

A specter is haunting Europe—the specter of Communism.
—KARL MARX, *Manifesto of the Communist Party,* 1848

From each according to his abilities, and to each according
to his needs.
—KARL MARX, *Critique of the Gotha Program,* 1875

Property is the exploitation of the weak by the strong. Com-
munism is the exploitation of the strong by the weak.
—PIERRE-JOSEPH PROUDHON,
What Is Property?, 1840

The economy of Communism is an economy which grows
in an atmosphere of misery and want.
—ELEANOR ROOSEVELT, *My Day,*
syndicated column, Feb. 12, 1947

Communism is the corruption of a dream of justice.
—ADLAI STEVENSON, speech, Urbana, Ill., 1951

COMPARISONS

Comparisons are odious.   —JOHN FORTESCUE,
De Laudibus Legum Angliae, 1471
[*Bartlett's* gives this as the earliest use, noting that the phrase
was common in the 15th century; and it appears often there-
after. Shakespeare wrote "Comparisons are odorous," *Much
Ado About Nothing,* III, v.]

Nothing is good or bad by comparison.
> —Thomas Fuller, *Gnomologia*, 1732

COMPASSION & PITY
See also FORGIVENESS & MERCY

One cannot weep for the entire world. It is beyond human strength. One must choose.
> —JEAN ANOUILH, *Cecile*, 1949

To him that is afflicted pity should be showed from his friend.
> —BIBLE, *Job* 6:14

Human it is to have compassion on the unhappy.
> —BOCCACCIO, opening line of the *Decameron*, 1351–53

[See Tolstoy at FAMILY for other famous openings.]

More helpful than all wisdom is one draught of simple human pity that will not forsake us.
> —GEORGE ELIOT, *The Mill on the Floss*, 1860

The poetry is in the pity.
> —WILFRED OWEN, Preface, *Poems*, 1920

[More at ARTS: POETRY & POETS.]

No beast so fierce but knows some touch of pity.
> —SHAKESPEARE, *Richard III*, I, ii

Pity is the virtue of the law.
> —SHAKESPEARE, *Timon of Athens*, III, v

CONFIDENCE
See BOLDNESS & INITIATIVE; SELF-CONFIDENCE

CONFLICT
See also TROUBLE; TURBULENT TIMES; UNITY & LOYALTY; WAR

Every kingdom divided against itself is brought to desolation; and every city or house divided against itself, shall not stand.
> —BIBLE, *Matthew* 12:25

[Mark 3:25 reads: "If a house be divided against itself, that house cannot stand." For Lincoln's use of the thought, see under AMERICAN HISTORY: MEMORABLE MOMENTS.]

When one prefers one's own children to the children of others, war is near.

—MAHABHARATA, c. 200 B.C.–A.D. 200

CONSCIENCE   See also ETHICS & MORALITY

Conscience is the perfect interpreter of life.

—KARL BARTH, *The Word of God
and the Word of Man,* 1957

I cannot and will not cut my conscience to suit this year's fashions.   —LILLIAN HELLMAN, letter to the chairman
of the House Committee on Un-American
Activities, May 19, 1952

Conscience is the inner voice that warns us somebody may be looking.

—H. L. MENCKEN, *A Mencken Chrestomathy,* 1949

CONSISTENCY   See also CHANGE

Consistency requires you to be as ignorant today as you were a year ago.

—BERNARD BERENSON, *Notebook,* 1892

A foolish consistency is the hobgoblin of little minds, adored by little statesmen and philosophers and divines.

—RALPH WALDO EMERSON, *Self-Reliance*
in *Essays: First Series,* 1841

Do I contradict myself?
Very well then I contradict myself,
(I am large, I contain multitudes.)

—WALT WHITMAN, *Song of Myself*
in *Leaves of Grass,* 1855

CONVERSATION   See also TALK

"The time has come," the Walrus said, "To talk of many
    things:
Of shoes—and ships—and sealing wax—
Of cabbages—and kings—
And why the sea is boiling hot—
And whether pigs have wings."

—LEWIS CARROLL, *Through the Looking-Glass,* 1872

In the room the women come and go
Talking of Michelangelo.
   —T. S. ELIOT, *The Love Song of J. Alfred Prufrock,* 1917

If you can't say anything good about someone, sit right here
by me.   —ALICE ROOSEVELT LONGWORTH,
saying, quoted in *The New York Times,*
obituary, 1979

We do not talk—we bludgeon one another with facts and
theories gleaned from cursory readings of newspapers, mag-
azines, and digests.   —HENRY MILLER, *The Shadows* in
The Air-Conditioned Nightmare, 1945

The more the pleasures of the body fade away, the greater
to me is the pleasure and charm of conversation.
    —PLATO, *The Republic,* 4th cent. B.C.

Teas,
Where small talk dies in agonies.
   —PERCY BYSSHE SHELLEY, *Peter Bell the Third,* 1819

In few people is discretion stronger than the desire to tell a
good story.—MURASAKI SHIKIBU, *The Tale of Genji,* 1001–15

I cannot hold with those who wish to put down the insignificant chatter of the world.
   —ANTHONY TROLLOPE, *Framley Parsonage,* 1861

COUNTRY, ONE'S OWN   See PATRIOTISM

COUNTRY, THE   See also NATURE

Nothing ages a woman like living in the country.
   —COLETTE, *On Tour* in *Music Hall Sidelights,* 1913

It is my belief, Watson, founded upon my experience, that
the lowest and vilest alleys in London do not present a more
dreadful record of sin than does the smiling and beautiful
countryside.   —A. CONAN DOYLE, *The Adventure of the
Copper Beeches* in *The Adventures
of Sherlock Holmes,* 1892

When I am in the country I wish to vegetate like the country. —WILLIAM HAZLITT, *On Going a Journey* in *Table Talk*, 1821–22

I have no relish for the country; it is a kind of healthy grave. —SYDNEY SMITH, letter to Miss G. Harcourt, 1838

Anybody can be good in the country. —OSCAR WILDE, *The Picture of Dorian Gray*, 1891

COURAGE   See also BOLDNESS & INITIATIVE; FEAR; HEROES

Often the test of courage is not to die but to live. —VITTORIO ALFIERI, *Oreste*, 1778

Until the day of his death, no man can be sure of his courage. —JEAN ANOUILH, *Becket*, 1959

Courage is almost a contradiction in terms. It means a strong desire to live taking the form of a readiness to die. —G. K. CHESTERTON, *Orthodoxy*, 1908

Tender-handed stroke a nettle,
And it stings you for your pains;
Grasp it like a man of mettle,
And it soft as silk remains. —AARON HILL, *Verses Written on a Window in Scotland*, 1794

One man with courage makes a majority. —ANDREW JACKSON, d. 1845, saying [For a majority consisting of one man with God, see under Knox at GOD. See also Coolidge at LAW.]

Cowards die many times before their deaths;
The valiant never taste of death but once. —SHAKESPEARE, *Julius Caesar*, II, ii

But screw your courage to the sticking place
And we'll not fail. —SHAKESPEARE, *Macbeth*, I, vii

Courage is resistance to fear, mastery of fear—not absence
of fear.   —MARK TWAIN, *Pudd'nhead Wilson's
Calendar* in *Pudd'nhead Wilson,* 1894

CRAFTINESS   See also DISHONESTY & LIES

To make a living, craftiness is better than learnedness.
                            —PIERRE-AUGUSTIN DE
BEAUMARCHAIS, *The Marriage of
Figaro,* 1784

Let not thy left hand know what thy right hand doeth.
                            —BIBLE, *Matthew* 6:3
[For the context, see CHARITY: PHILANTHROPY.]

Make to yourselves friends of the mammon of unrigh-
teousness.   —BIBLE, *Luke* 16:9

Open not thine heart to every man, lest he requite thee with
a shrewd turn.   —BIBLE, *Ecclesiasticus* 8:19

Will you walk into my parlor? said the Spider to the Fly.
'Tis the prettiest little parlor that ever you did spy.
                —MARY HOWITT, *The Spider and the Fly,* 1844

Never fight fair with a stranger, boy. You'll never get out
of the jungle that way.
                —ARTHUR MILLER, *Death of a Salesman,* 1949

The fox knows many tricks, but the hedgehog's trick is the
best of all.   —PIGRES, 6th cent. B.C., attributed by
Zenobius, *Compendium Proverbium,*
2nd cent. A.D.
[A different version of this, attributed to Archilochus, is given
under WISDOM.]

I know a trick worth two of that.
                —SHAKESPEARE, *Henry IV, Part I,* II, i

Friends, Romans, countrymen, lend me your ears;
I come to bury Caesar, not to praise him.
                —SHAKESPEARE, *Julius Caesar,* III, ii

CREATION, DIVINE   See also NATURE; SCIENCE:
PHYSICS & COSMOLOGY;
UNIVERSE

All things bright and beautiful
All creatures great and small,
All things wise and wonderful,
The Lord God made them all.
                    —CECIL FRANCES ALEXANDER, hymn,
                        All Things Bright and Beautiful, 1848

In the beginning God created the heaven and the earth.
    And the earth was without form, and void; and darkness
was upon the face of the deep. And the spirit of God moved
upon the face of the waters.
    And God said, Let there be light: and there was light.
                    —BIBLE, *Genesis* 1:1–4

We made from water every living thing.
                    —KORAN, c. 610–632

Nothing can be created out of nothing.   —LUCRETIUS,
                        On the Nature of Things, c. 57 B.C.

CRIME   See also DANGEROUS PEOPLE;
EVIDENCE; EVIL; GUILT; PUNISHMENT;
VIOLENCE & FORCE

Murder will out.   —ANONYMOUS (PROVERB)
[The idea has been expressed by many writers, including Chaucer, John Webster, Shakespeare, and Emerson; see their quotes
below.]

Le mauvais goût mène au crime.
Poor taste leads to crime.
                    —ANONYMOUS (FRENCH PROVERB),
                        quoted by A. Conan Doyle in
                        The Sign of Four, 1890

And the Lord set a mark upon Cain.
                    —BIBLE, *Genesis* 4:15

These, having not the law, are a law unto themselves.
                    —BIBLE, *Romans* 2:14

The soul of a murderer is blind.   —ALBERT CAMUS,
                                                The Plague, 1947

Murder will out, certain, it will not fail.
                    —GEOFFREY CHAUCER, *The Prioress's Tale*
                          in *The Canterbury Tales,* 1387–1400
[One of many expressions of this proverbial concept; see the
first entry in this section.]

If once a man indulges himself in murder, very soon, he
comes to think little of robbing; and from robbing he comes
next to drinking and Sabbath-breaking, and from that to
incivility and procrastination. —THOMAS DE QUINCEY,
              Murder Considered as One of the Fine Arts, 1827

It's a wicked world, and when a clever man turns his brains
to crime, it is the worst of all.   —A. CONAN DOYLE,
                            The Adventure of the Speckled Band
                        in *The Adventures of Sherlock Holmes,* 1892

Any man might do a girl in
Any man has to, needs to wants to
Once in a lifetime, do a girl in.   —T. S. ELIOT,
                                          Sweeney Agonistes, 1932
[Dickens, in *Our Mutual Friend,* 1864–65, similarly commented
on the universality of homicidal feelings: "If a murder, anybody
might have done it. Burglary or pocket-picking wanted 'prentice-
ship. Not so murder. We were all of us up to that."]

Character is always known. Thefts never enrich; alms never
impoverish; murder will speak out of stone walls.
              —RALPH WALDO EMERSON, commencement
                        address, Harvard Divinity School, 1838
[The concept that even stones will testify against atrocities appears in the Bible in *Habakkuk* 2:11, "The stone shall cry out
of the wall"; and in *Luke* 19:40. Shakespeare used the image
twice in *Macbeth*: "The very stones prate of my whereabout,"
II, i; and "Blood will have blood./ Stones have been known to
move and trees to speak," III, iv.]

Round up the usual suspects.
                    —JULIUS EPSTEIN, PHILIP EPSTEIN, and
                        HOWARD KOCH, screenplay,
                                          Casablanca, 1942

Cherchez la femme.
Find the woman.   —JOSEPH FOUCHÉ, attributed
[Also used by Alexandre Dumas in *The Mohicans of Paris*,
1854–55, one of the first collections of detective stories: "There
is a woman in every case; as soon as they bring me a report, I
say, 'Look for the woman.' " Fouché, by the way, was Napoleon's feared minister of justice.]

I've got a little list—I've got a little list.
Of society offenders who might well be underground,
And who never would be missed—who never would be
  missed.   —W. S. GILBERT, *The Mikado*, 1885

The policeman's lot is not a happy one.
            —W. S. GILBERT, *The Pirates of Penzance*, 1879

It was beautiful and simple, as all truly great swindles are.
            —O. HENRY, *The Octopus Marooned* in
                        The Gentle Grafter, 1908

We never sleep.   —ALLAN PINKERTON, motto of the
                        Pinkerton Agency, c. 1855
[The Pinkerton Agency was known as "the Eye," which is apparently the origin of the phrase "private eye," meaning
detective.]

I don't know what it says about human nature, but there
are few activities more stimulating than planning a crime.
            —ROBERT PLUNKETT, book review,
                        The New York Times, Oct. 6, 1991

Crime, like virtue, has its degrees. —RACINE, *Phèdre*, 1677

Successful and fortunate crime is called virtue.
            —SENECA, *Hercules Furens*, 1st cent. A.D.

Murder most foul, as in the best it is,
But this most foul, strange, and unnatural.
                        —SHAKESPEARE, *Hamlet*, I, v

Murder, though it have no tongue, will speak. —*Ibid.*, II, ii
[Similarly, Shakespeare wrote, "Truth will come to light; mur-
der cannot be hid long," *The Merchant of Venice* II, ii; and in
Richard III, a murderer concludes "This will out," I, iv. See

also the quotes from Emerson, above, and John Webster, below.]

Yet who would have thought the old man to have had so much blood in him?　　—SHAKESPEARE, *Macbeth,* V, i

The robbed that smiles steals something from the thief.
　　　　　　　　　　　—SHAKESPEARE, *Othello* I, iii

He who bears the brand of Cain shall rule the earth.
　　　　　　　　　　—GEORGE BERNARD SHAW,
　　　　　　　　　　　　Back to Methuselah, 1921

People of the same trade seldom meet together, even for merriment and diversion, but the conversation ends in a conspiracy against the public, or in some contrivance to raise prices.　　—ADAM SMITH, *Wealth of Nations,* 1776

Why do you rob banks?
Because that's where the money is.
　　　　　　　　　　—WILLIE SUTTON, attributed
[A famous line, but Mr. Sutton, a notorious bank robber, disclaimed it, crediting a reporter with making it up. Neverthless, he—or his publisher—couldn't resist adopting it for the title of his 1976 autobiography, *Where the Money Was.*]

The rich rob the poor and the poor rob one another.
　　　　　　　　　　—SOJOURNER TRUTH, d. 1883, saying

Other sins only speak; murder shrieks out.
　　　　　　—JOHN WEBSTER, *The Duchess of Malfi,* 1623

Yet each man kills the thing he loves
. . . . The coward does it with a kiss,
The brave man with a sword.
　　　　—OSCAR WILDE, *The Ballad of Reading Gaol,* 1898

CRISIS　　　　　　See MIDDLE AGE & MID-LIFE
　　　　　　　　　　CRISIS; RUIN; TROUBLE;
　　　　　　　　　　TURBULENT TIMES

CRITICISM　　　　　　See ADVICE; ARTS:
　　　　　　　　　　CRITICISM & CRITICS

CULTURE   See ARTS entries; CIVILIZATION;
                                                    EDUCATION

CUSTOM   See also HABIT; MANNERS

Custom reconciles us to everything.
> —EDMUND BURKE, *On the
> Sublime and Beautiful*, 1756

Custom, then, is the great guide of human life.
> —DAVID HUME, *An Enquiry
> Concerning Human Understanding*, 1743

Custom is king over all.—PINDAR, fragment, 5th cent. B.C.

It is a custom
More honored in the breach than the observance.
> —SHAKESPEARE, *Hamlet*, I, iv

[The custom was the Danish habit of draining a goblet of wine
with each toast.]

D

DANCE See ARTS: MUSIC & DANCE

DANGER See also DANGEROUS PEOPLE; EVIL;
RUIN; TROUBLE; TURBULENT TIMES

Dangers by being despised grow great.
—EDMUND BURKE, speech on the
Petition of the Unitarians, May 11, 1792

'Twas brillig, and the slithy toves
Did gyre and gimble in the wabe;
All mimsy were the borogoves,
And the mome raths outgrabe.
Beware the Jabberwock, my son!
The jaws that bite, the claws that catch!
Beware the Jubjub bird, and shun
The frumious Bandersnatch! —LEWIS CARROLL,
Jabberwocky in *Through the Looking-Glass,* 1872

Nothing in life is so exhilarating as to be shot at without
result. —WINSTON CHURCHILL, *The Story of
the Malakand Field Force,* 1898
[Often misquoted as: ". . . shot at and missed." U.S. Pres.
Ronald Reagan, in 1981, after being wounded in an assassination attempt, offered a close variant on Churchill's observation:
"There is no more exhilarating feeling than being shot at without result."]

To vanquish without danger is to triumph without glory.
—PIERRE CORNEILLE, *Le Cid,* 1636

Wisdom consists in being able to distinguish among dangers
and make a choice of the least harmful.
—MACHIAVELLI, *The Prince,* 1532

Believe me, the secret of the greatest fruitfulness and the greatest enjoyment of existence is: to *live dangerously!*"
—FRIEDRICH NIETZSCHE, *The Joyful Wisdom,* 1882

Beware the ides of March.
—SHAKESPEARE, *Julius Caesar,* I, ii

A snake lurks in the grass.   —VIRGIL, *Eclogues,* c. 37 B.C.

Everything is dangerous, my dear fellow. If it wasn't so, life wouldn't be worth living.
—OSCAR WILDE, *The Importance of Being Earnest,* 1895

DANGEROUS PEOPLE   See also CRIME;
                               DANGER; EVIL; POWER

He stood a stranger in this breathing world,
An erring spirit from another hurled;
A thing of dark imaginings.   —LORD BYRON, *Lara,* 1814

People who make no noise are dangerous.
—LA FONTAINE, *Fables,* 1668

Mad, bad, and dangerous to know.
—LADY CAROLINE LAMB, referring to
Lord Byron, *Journal,* Mar. 1812

Yond Cassius has a lean and hungry look;
He thinks too much: such men are dangerous.
—SHAKESPEARE, *Julius Caesar,* I, ii

DAY   See NATURE: TIMES OF DAY

DEATH   See also EPITAPHS; IMMORTALITY;
                     LAST JUDGMENT & THE
                     HEREAFTER; SUICIDE

People who die are not buried in a field, they are buried in the heart.   —ANONYMOUS (RWANDAN ADAGE)
[Quoted by Ephrem Karangwa, mayor of Taba, Rwanda, in *The New York Times,* Sept. 27, 1996.]

Man goeth to his long home, and the mourners go about the streets.   —BIBLE, *Ecclesiastes* 12:5

O death, where is thy sting? O grave, where is thy victory?
                                    —BIBLE, *I Corinthians* 15:55

And I looked, and behold a pale horse: and his name that
sat on him was Death.   —BIBLE, *Revelation* 6:8

The truth of this world is death.
                        —CÉLINE, *Journey to the End of the Night*, 1936

Because I could not stop for Death
He kindly stopped for me
The Carriage held but just Ourselves
And Immortality!   —EMILY DICKINSON,
                                            poem no. 712, c. 1863

Death be not proud, though some have called thee
Mighty and dreadful, for, thou art not so,
For, those, whom thou think'st thou dost overthrow,
Die not, poor death, nor yet can'st thou kill me.
                        —JOHN DONNE, *Death Be Not Proud*
                                in *Holy Sonnets*, c. 1617–19

Never send to know for whom the bell tolls. It tolls for thee.
                        —JOHN DONNE, *Devotions Upon
                            Emergent Occasions, XVII*, 1624
[More at HUMANS & HUMAN NATURE.]

Death is nothing to us, since when we are, death has not
come, and when death has come, we are not.
                        —EPICURUS, quoted in Diogenes Laërtius,
                            Lives of Eminent Philosophers,
                                    3rd cent. A.D.

It hath often been said that it is not death but dying that is
terrible.   —HENRY FIELDING, *Amelia*, 1751

Let us cross over the river and rest under the shade of the
trees.   —THOMAS "STONEWALL" JACKSON,
                                dying words, May 10, 1863
[He had been shot inadvertently by his own men.]

Depend upon it, Sir, when a man knows he is to be hanged in a fortnight, it concentrates his mind wonderfully.
> —SAMUEL JOHNSON, Sept. 19, 177, quoted in James Boswell, *Life of Johnson,* 1791

The only religious way to think of death is as part and parcel of life. —THOMAS MANN, *The Magic Mountain,* 1924

Whom the Gods love dies young.
> —MENANDER, *The Double Deceiver,* 4th cent. B.C.

[Expressed by many other writers, including Wordsworth, see below.]

Life is a great surprise. I do not see why death should not be an even greater one.
> —VLADIMIR NABOKOV, *Pale Fire,* 1962

It costs me never a stab nor squirm
To tread by chance upon a worm.
"Aha, my little dear," I say,
"Your clan will pay me back one day."
> —DOROTHY PARKER, *Thoughts for a Sunshiny Morning* in *Sunset Gun,* 1928

He hath joined the great majority.
> —PETRONIUS, *Satyricon,* 1st cent. A.D.

Dying
Is an art, like everything else. —SYLVIA PLATH, *Lady Lazarus,* 1962–63

Je vais quérir un grand peutêtre. . . . Tirez le rideau, la farce est jouée.
I am going to seek a great perhaps. . . . Pull down the curtain, the farce is ended.
> —RABELAIS, last words, Apr. 9, 1553

[Both words and date are according to tradition—and tradition only. Note similar last words in Leoncavallo's 1892 opera, *I Pagliacci,* "*La commedia è finita*"—"The comedy is ended."]

So little done, so much to do. —CECIL RHODES, dying words, Mar. 26, 1902

[Rhodes, a mining magnate and the leading British imperialist in South Africa, established the Rhodes Scholarships at Oxford University.]

When I am dead, my dearest,
Sing no sad songs for me. —CHRISTINA G. ROSSETTI,
Song, 1862

Death is an evil; the gods have so judged; had it been good,
they would die. —SAPPHO, fragment, 7th cent. B.C.

There is no death. Only a change of worlds.
—SEATTLE, c. 1854, in Joseph Epes
Brown, *The Spiritual Legacy of the
American Indian,* 1964

I have a rendezvous with Death
At some disputed barricade. —ALAN SEEGER, *I Have a
Rendezvous with Death,* 1916

All that live must die,
Passing through nature to eternity.
—SHAKESPEARE, *Hamlet,* I, ii

Alas! poor Yorick. I knew him, Horatio. —*Ibid.,* V, i

A man can die but once. We owe God a death.
—SHAKESPEARE, *Henry IV, Part II,* III, ii

Men must endure
Their going hence even as their coming hither.
—SHAKESPEARE, *King Lear,* V, ii

Nothing in his life
Became him like the leaving it. —SHAKESPEARE,
Macbeth, I, iv

How oft when men are at the point of death
Have they been merry! —SHAKESPEARE,
Romeo and Juliet, V, iii

He that dies pays all debts. —SHAKESPEARE,
The Tempest, III, ii

Death is the veil which those who live call life:
They sleep, and it is lifted.
—PERCY BYSSHE SHELLEY,
Prometheus Unbound, 1819

A single death is a tragedy, a million deaths is a statistic.
—JOSEPH STALIN, attributed
[George Seldes's *The Great Quotations* is the only source we
know to offer even a secondary citation for this famous remark.
The attribution he cited is from Anne Fremantle, *The New
York Times Book Review,* Sept. 28, 1958.]

Home is the sailor, home from the sea,
And the hunter home from the hill.
—ROBERT LOUIS STEVENSON,
Requiem in *Underwoods,* 1887
[More at EPITAPHS.]

If this is dying, then I don't think much of it.
—LYTTON STRACHEY, last words,
Jan. 11, 1932, cited in Michael Holroyd,
Lytton Strachey, 1968

Sunset and evening star,
And one clear call for me!
And may there be no moaning of the bar,
When I put out to sea.   —ALFRED, LORD TENNYSON,
Crossing the Bar, 1889

He seems so near and yet so far.
—ALFRED, LORD TENNYSON, *In Memoriam,* 1850

And a day less or more
At sea or shore,
We die—does it matter when?
—ALFRED, LORD TENNYSON, *The Revenge,* 1880

Man comes and tills the field and lies beneath,
And after many a summer dies the swan.
—ALFRED, LORD TENNYSON, *Tithonus,* 1860

Do not go gentle into that good night,
Old age should burn and rave at close of day;
Rage, rage against the dying of the light.
　　　　　　　　　—DYLAN THOMAS, *Do Not Go*
　　　　　　　　　Gentle into That Good Night, 1952

Death is not an event in life; we do not experience death.
　　　　　　　　　—LUDWIG WITTGENSTEIN,
　　　　　　　　　Tractatus logico-philosophicus, 1922
[Diderot, in *Rameau's Nephew*, 1762, said it thus: "The dead
do not hear the bells tolling."]

The good die first,
And they whose hearts are dry as summer dust
Burn to the socket. 　　　　—WILLIAM WORDSWORTH,
　　　　　　　　　　　　　The Excursion, 1814

DECEPTION　See CRAFTINESS; DISHONESTY & LIES

DECISION　　　　　See also BOLDNESS & INITIATIVE;
　　　　　　　　　DECISION, MOMENT OF; INDECISION

The rarest gift that God bestows on man is the capacity for
decision. 　　　　—DEAN ACHESON, speech, Apr. 13, 1965

In bad times, you make only bad decisions.
　　　　　　　　　—ANONYMOUS (SANSKRIT PROVERB)

Two roads diverged in a wood, and I,
I took the one less traveled by.
　　　　　　　　　—ROBERT FROST, *The Road Not Taken*, 1916
[More at REGRET, along with T. S. Eliot's "door we never
opened." See also Yogi Berra on what to do at a fork in the
road in the note to his quote at ENDINGS.]

DECISION, MOMENT OF

The decisive moment in a man's life is when he decides to
confront death. 　　　　—CHE GUEVARA, d. 1967, quoted in
　　　　　　　　Jorge G. Castañeda, *Compañero: The Life*
　　　　　　　　and Death of Che Guevara, 1997

The die is cast. —JULIUS CAESAR, on crossing the
Rubicon, 49 B.C., quoted in Plutarch, *Life
of Caesar* in *Parallel Lives*, c. A.D. 100
[The phrase was proverbial even in Caesar's time.]

Once to every man and nation comes the moment to decide,
In the strife of Truth with Falsehood, for the good or evil
side. —JAMES RUSSELL LOWELL,
The Present Crisis, 1844

There is a tide in the affairs of men. —SHAKESPEARE,
Julius Caesar, IV, iii

[More at OPPORTUNITY.]

DEEDS See ACTION; DOING

DEFEAT See WINNING & LOSING,
VICTORY & DEFEAT

DELAY See INDECISION; PROCRASTINATION

DEMOCRACY See also AMERICA & AMERICANS;
AMERICAN HISTORY: MEMORABLE
MOMENTS; EQUALITY; FREEDOM;
PEOPLE, THE; RIGHTS

Democracy is the worst form of government except all those
other forms that have been tried from time to time.
—WINSTON CHURCHILL, speech,
House of Commons, Nov. 11, 1947

The ballot is stronger than the bullet.
—ABRAHAM LINCOLN, speech, May 19, 1856

Under democracy, one party always devotes its chief efforts
to trying to prove that the other is unfit to rule—and both
commonly succeed and are right.
—H. L. MENCKEN, *Minority Report:
H. L. Mencken's Notebooks*, 1956

The blind lead the blind. It's the democratic way.
—HENRY MILLER,
With Edgard Varèse in the Gobi Desert in
*The Air-Conditioned
Nightmare,* 1945

Democracy and socialism are means to an end, not the end
itself.   —JAWAHARLAL NEHRU, *Credo* in *The New
York Times Magazine,* Sept. 7, 1958

Democracy . . . is a charming form of government, full of
variety and disorder. It dispenses a sort of equality to
equals and unequals alike.
—PLATO, *The Republic,* 4th cent. B.C.

Democracy passes into despotism.   —*Ibid.*

Democracy substitutes election by the incompetent many for
appointment by the corrupt few.
—GEORGE BERNARD SHAW,
Man and Superman, 1903

DEPRESSION See DESPAIR, DEPRESSION, & MISERY

DEPRESSION, ECONOMIC   See ECONOMICS

DESPAIR, DEPRESSION, & MISERY
See also EPITAPHS (Keats);
SORROW, SADNESS, &
SUFFERING; SUICIDE; TROUBLE

My days are swifter than a weaver's shuttle, and are spent
without hope.   —BIBLE, *Job* 5:7

My God, my God, why hast Thou forsaken me?
—BIBLE, *Psalms* 22:1; *Matthew* 27:46; *Mark* 15:34

Vanity of vanities, saith the preacher, vanity of vanities: all
is vanity.   —BIBLE, *Ecclesiastes* 1:2

I write of melancholy, by being busy to avoid melancholy.
　　　　　　　　—ROBERT BURTON, *The Anatomy of*
　　　　　　　　　　　　　　　Melancholy, 1621–51
[Moods that we would probably associate with "depression"
were in the past commonly called "melancholy." Burton's more
general cure for melancholy is given at WORK.]

In the real dark night of the soul it is always three o'clock
in the morning. 　　　—F. SCOTT FITZGERALD, *The Hours*
　　　　　　　　　　　　　　in *The Crack-Up,* 1936
[The allusion is to St. John of the Cross; see under MYSTICISM.]

And nothing to look backward to with pride;
And nothing to look forward to with hope.
　　　—ROBERT FROST, *The Death of the Hired Man,* 1914

When I survey my past life, I discover nothing but a barren
waste of time, with disorders of the mind very near to
madness. 　　　　　　　　　　　—SAMUEL JOHNSON,
　　　　　　　　　　　　　　Prayers and Meditations, 1777

O! what a rogue and peasant slave am I.
　　　　　　　　　　　—SHAKESPEARE, *Hamlet,* II, ii

Tomorrow, and tomorrow, and tomorrow,
Creeps in this petty pace from day to day,
To the last syllable of recorded time.
　　　　　　　　　　　—SHAKESPEARE, *Macbeth,* V, v

I was much further out than you thought
And not waving but drowning. 　　　—STEVIE SMITH,
　　　　　　　　　　　　Not Waving but Drowning, 1957

DESPOTS　　　　See TYRANNY & TOTALITARIANISM

DESTINY　　　　　　　　　　　　　　See FATE

DETAILS & OTHER SMALL THINGS

The devil is in the details.
　　　　　　　　—ANONYMOUS (GERMAN PROVERB)
[This is an old saying, and may not be German in its ultimate
origin. A major variant is "God is in the details," used by Mies

van der Rohe with reference to architecture, but probably also coming from a much earlier source.]

He that contemneth small things shall fall by little and little.
　　　　　　　　　　　　　—BIBLE, *Ecclesiasticus* 19:1

Little drops of water,
Little grains of sand,
Make the mighty ocean
And the pleasant land.

So the little minutes,
Humble though they be,
Make the mighty ages
Of eternity.
. . .
Little deeds of kindness,
Little words of love,
Help to make earth happy
Like the heaven above.　　　　　　　　—JULIA CARNEY,
　　　　　　　　　　　　　　　　　　Little Things, 1845

Little things affect little minds.
　　　　　　　　　—BENJAMIN DISRAELI, *Sybil,* 1845

I neglect God and his Angels for the noise of a fly, for the rattling of a coach, for the whining of a door.
　　　　　　　　—JOHN DONNE, sermon, Dec. 12, 1626

It has long been an axiom of mine that the little things are infinitely the most important.　　　—A. CONAN DOYLE,
　　　　　　　　　　　　　　　A Case of Identity in
　　　　　　　　The Adventures of Sherlock Holmes, 1892

Large streams from little fountains flow,
Tall oaks from little acorns grow.
　　　　　　—DAVID EVERETT, *Lines written for a school
　　　　　　　declamation,* New Ipswich, N.H., 1791
[Drawn from proverbial comment on acorns and oaks—and appropriate in the context, the student orator being just seven years old.]

A little neglect may breed great mischief . . . for the want of a nail the shoe was lost; for the want of a shoe the horse was lost; and for the want of a horse the rider was lost.
—BENJAMIN FRANKLIN,
Poor Richard's Almanac, June 1758

It takes five hundred small details to add up to one favorable impression.   —CARY GRANT, d. 1986, quoted in Graham McCann, *Cary Grant: A Life Apart,* 1997

The Lord made small things as well as big ones, and everything man looks at closely is full of wonder.
—JAKOB GRIMM, d. 1863, letter to friends

Men who love wisdom should acquaint themselves with a great many particulars.   —HERACLITUS,
fragment, c. 500 B.C.

A trifle consoles us because a trifle distresses us.
—PASCAL, *Pensées,* 1670

Small Is Beautiful. —E. F. SCHUMACHER, book title, 1973

Our life is frittered away by detail. . . . Simplify, Simplify.
—HENRY DAVID THOREAU, *Where I Lived and What I Lived For* in *Walden,* 1854

DETECTIVES & DETECTION   See CRIME

DEVIL   See also RELIGION (Shakespeare)

How art thou fallen from heaven, O Lucifer, son of the morning!   —BIBLE, *Isaiah* 14:12

An apology for the Devil: It must be remembered that we have only heard one side of the case. God has written all the books.   —SAMUEL BUTLER, *Higgledy-Piggledy* in *Notebooks,* 1912

Wherever God erects a house of prayer,
The Devil always builds a chapel there,
And 'twill be found upon examination,
The latter has the largest congregation.
—DANIEL DEFOE, *The True-Born Englishman,* 1701

If the devil does not exist, and man has therefore created him, he has created him in his own image and likeness.
—FEODOR DOSTOEVSKI, *The Brothers Karamazov*, 1879–80

Why should the devil have all the good tunes?
—ROWLAND HILL, *Sermons*, c. 1800.

. . . The devil hath power
T'assume a pleasing shape. —SHAKESPEARE,
Hamlet, II, ii
[See DISHONESTY & LIES for Shakespeare on "the goodly outside" of falsehood.]

The prince of darkness is a gentleman. —SHAKESPEARE,
King Lear, III, iv
[Also, Percy Bysshe Shelley, "Sometimes / The Devil is a gentleman," *Peter Bell the Third*, 1819.]

The devil is an angel too. —MIGUEL DE UNAMUNO,
Two Mothers, c. 1913

DIFFERENCES See INDIVIDUALITY; VARIETY

DIPLOMACY See also NATIONS; NEGOTIATION

Diplomacy is to do and say
The nastiest thing in the nicest way.
—ISAAC GOLDBERG, *The Reflex*, Oct. 1927

An ambassador is an honest man sent to lie abroad for the good of his country.
—SIR HENRY WOTTON, inscribed in the album of Christopher Fleckmore, 1604, in Izaak Walton, *Reliquiae Wottonianae*, 1651

All diplomacy is a continuation of war by other means.
—ZHOU EN-LAI, quoted by Edgar Snow, *Saturday Evening Post*, Mar. 27, 1954
[The unstated reference is to von Clausewitz's famous observation on war and diplomacy; see under WAR.]

DISCOVERY See SCIENCE: DISCOVERY & EXPLORATION

DISHONESTY & LIES   See also CRAFTINESS; CRIME;
HYPOCRISY PEOPLE,
THE (Adolf Hitler)

A lie can be half-way around the world before the truth has
got its boots on.   —ANONYMOUS (PROVERB)

Sin has many tools, but a lie is the handle which fits them
all.   —OLIVER WENDELL HOLMES, SR.,
The Autocrat of the Breakfast-Table, 1858

Unless a man feels he has a good enough memory, he should
never venture to lie.   —MONTAIGNE, *Essays*, 1580–88

A lie is an abomination unto the Lord and an ever present
help in time of need.   —JOHN A. TYLER MORGAN,
comment in the U.S. Senate, c. 1890
[Sen. Morgan of Alabama was an ardent supporter of a Nicaraguan
(not Panamanian) canal; he is quoted in David McCullough's *The
Path Between the Seas* (1977). Decades later, two-time Democratic presidential candidate Adlai Stevenson made essentially
the same remark in a speech in Springfield, Ill., Jan. 1951.]

White lies always introduce others of a darker complexion.
—WILLIAM PALEY, *The Principles of
Moral and Political Philosophy*, 1785

O, what a tangled web we weave,
When first we practice to deceive!
—SIR WALTER SCOTT, *Marmion*, 1808

Lord, Lord, how this world is given to lying!
—SHAKESPEARE, *Henry IV, Part I*, V, iv

O, what a goodly outside falsehood hath!
—SHAKESPEARE, *The Merchant of Venice*, I, iii

Don't lie if you don't have to.
—LEO SZILARD, *Science*, no. 176, 1972
[Szilard, a brilliant Hungarian-American physicist, played a key
role in the development of the atomic bomb. He later opposed
the nuclear arms race.]

DOCTORS & THE PRACTICE OF MEDICINE

See also ILLNESS
& REMEDIES; SCIENCE:
PSYCHOLOGY

Physicians of the Utmost Fame
Were called at once; but when they came
They answered, as they took their Fees,
"There is no cure for this disease."
> —HILAIRE BELLOC, *Henry King* in
> *Cautionary Tales,* 1907

Physician, heal thyself. —BIBLE, *Luke* 4:23

Honour a physician with the honour due unto him for the
uses which you may have of him: for the Lord hath created
him. —BIBLE, *Ecclesiasticus* 38:1

The most high hath created medicines out of the earth, and
a wise man will not abhor them. —*Ibid.* 38:4

Surgeons must be very careful
When they take the knife!
Underneath their fine incisions
Stirs the culprit—*life*! —EMILY DICKINSON,
poem no. 108, c. 1859

Every physician almost hath his favorite disease.
> —HENRY FIELDING, *Tom Jones,* 1749

God heals and the doctor takes the fees.
> —BENJAMIN FRANKLIN,
> *Poor Richard's Almanac,* 1736

The life so short, the craft so long to learn.
> —HIPPOCRATES, *Aphorisms,* c. 400 B.C.

[See also the first quote at ART & THE ARTS.]

For extreme illnesses, extreme treatments are most fitting.
> —*Ibid.*

[See also Guy Fawkes and Shakespeare at REVOLUTION.]

I often say a great doctor kills more people than a great
general. —G. W. LEIBNIZ, attributed

One of the first duties of the physician is to educate the masses not to take medicine.
—WILLIAM OSLER, d. 1919, quoted in
Aphorisms from His Bedside Teachings, 1961

Physicians acquire their knowledge from our dangers, making experiments at the cost of our lives.
—PLINY, *Natural History,* A.D. 77

Who shall decide when doctors disagree?
—ALEXANDER POPE, *To Lord
Bathurst* in *Moral Essays,* 1732

Cured yesterday of my disease,
I died last night of the physician.   —MATTHEW PRIOR,
The Remedy Worse Than the Disease, 1714

Consider the deference which is everywhere paid to a doctor's opinion. Nothing more strikingly betrays the credulity of mankind than medicine. —HENRY DAVID THOREAU,
A Week on the Concord and Merrimack Rivers, 1849

Ah, well, then, I suppose I shall have to die beyond my means.   —OSCAR WILDE, c. Oct. 1900
[Wilde's reponse upon hearing the cost of a proposed operation, cited in R. H. Shepherd, *Life of Oscar Wilde,* 1906. Frequently quoted but perhaps an improved version of references by Wilde to living beyond his means.]

DOGS   See NATURE: ANIMALS

DOING   See also ACCOMPLISHMENT; ACTION;
EFFORT; PERSEVERANCE & ENDURANCE;
VIRTUE; WORK & WORKERS

Whatsoever thy hand findeth to do, do it with thy might; for there is no work, nor device, nor knowledge, nor wisdom, in the grave, whither thou goest.   —BIBLE, *Ecclesiastes* 9:10

Be ye doers of the word and not hearers only.
—BIBLE, *James I* 1:22

It is better to light one candle than to curse the darkness.
—CHRISTOPHER SOCIETY, Motto
[At VIRTUE, see Adlai Stevenson for his use of this idea with reference to Eleanor Roosevelt.]

I leave this rule for others when I'm dead,
Be always sure you're right—then go ahead.
—DAVID CROCKETT, his motto from the War
of 1812, cited in his *Narrative of the
Life of David Crockett*, 1834

Our deeds determine us, as much as we determine our deeds.
—GEORGE ELIOT, *Adam Bede*, 1859

Let's meet and either do or die.
—JOHN FLETCHER,
The Island Princess, 1647

Do noble things, do not dream them all day long.
—CHARLES KINGSLEY, *A Farewell*, 1856
[More of this at VIRTUE.]

Watch what we do, not what we say.
—JOHN MITCHELL, remark, July 1969
[This is the usual rendering; in *Respectfully Quoted*, published by the Library of Congress, the line is: "You will be better advised to watch what we do instead of what we say." Attorney General Mitchell was referring to the Nixon administration's approach to civil rights. Mitchell later went to jail for his role in the Watergate scandal.]

Men are all alike in their promises. It is only in their deeds that they differ.
—MOLIÈRE, *The Miser*, 1668

Saying is one thing and doing is another.
—MONTAIGNE, *Essays*, 1580–88

Our nature lies in movement; complete rest is death.
—PASCAL, *Pensées*, 1670

No one knows what he can do till he tries.
—PUBLILIUS SYRUS, *Moral Sayings*, 1st cent. B.C.

One must learn by doing the thing; though you think you know it, you have no certainty until you try.

—SOPHOCLES, *Trachiniae,* 5th cent. B.C.

[See also the entry at EDUCATION under Anonymous (Proverb).]

DOUBT   See SKEPTICISM

DRAMA   See ARTS: THEATER, MOVIES,
                                                  & ACTING

DREAMERS & DREAMS   See AMBITION; SCIENCE:
              PSYCHOLOGY; SLEEP & DREAMS;
                             VISION & VISIONARIES

DRINKING   See ALCOHOL & DRINKING;
                            FOOD, WINE, & EATING

DUTY   See RESPONSIBILITY

E

EARTH See CREATION, DIVINE; ENVIRONMENT; NATURE; SCIENCE

EAST, THE See NATIONS

EATING See FOOD, WINE, & EATING

ECONOMICS See also BUSINESS; CAPITALISM; COMMUNISM; MONEY; SOCIALISM; TAXES; WORK & WORKERS

There's no such thing as a free lunch. —ANONYMOUS
[The saying goes back to the 19th century, when bars offered "free" sandwiches and snacks to attract customers—but of course you had to buy a drink to get the food. In 1934, New York Mayor Fiorello La Guardia gave us *"È finite la cuccagna!"* —"The free lunch is over!" (quoted in Robert A. Caro, *The Power Broker*, 1974). The phrase was taken up by political conservatives, and is most often associated with economist Milton Friedman. In the form "TANSTAAFL" (acronym of "There ain't no such thing as a free lunch") the saying was used in one of Robert Heinlein's bestsellers, *The Moon Is a Harsh Mistress*, 1968.]

Recession is when your neighbor loses his job; depression is when you lose yours. —ANONYMOUS
[Sometimes attributed to Harry S. Truman.]

You shall not crucify mankind upon a cross of gold.
    —WILLIAM JENNINGS BRYAN, July 8, 1896
[More at AMERICAN HISTORY: MEMORABLE MOMENTS.]

Voodoo economics. —GEORGE BUSH, speech, Apr. 1980
[In the Republican presidential primary in Pennsylvania, contender George Bush used this neat phrase to describe the "supply side" economic theory espoused by his opponent, Ronald Reagan. According to this theory, a tax cut would increase government revenues by stimulating the economy. After Bush became Reagan's running mate, he remarked, "God, I wish I hadn't said that."]

[Economics:] What we might call, by way of eminence, the Dismal Science.
—THOMAS CARLYLE,
Occasional Discourse on the
Negro Question in *Fraser's Magazine,*
Dec. 1849
[Following modern practice; we have used *Negro* in this citation in place of the so-called "N-word," originally used by Carlyle and commonly employed by other educated, even liberal-minded Britons long after it had become taboo among their American counterparts.]

A national debt, if it is not excessive, will be to us a national blessing.
—ALEXANDER HAMILTON, letter to
Robert Morris, Apr. 30, 1781

We must not let our rulers load us with perpetual debt.
—THOMAS JEFFERSON, letter to
Samuel Kercheval, July 12, 1816

Practical men, who believe themselves to be quite exempt from any intellectual influences, are usually the slaves of some defunct economist.
—JOHN MAYNARD KEYNES, *The General Theory*
of Employment, Interest, and Money, 1936
[A propos, Richard Nixon is reported to have said in 1971, "We are all Keynesians now."]

Political institutions are a superstructure resting on an economic foundation.
—V. I. LENIN, *The Three Sources and Three*
Constituent Parts of Marxism, 1913

We have heard it said that five percent is the natural interest of money.
—THOMAS BABINGTON MACAULAY,
Southey's Colloquies on Society, 1830

He is well paid that is well satisfied.   —SHAKESPEARE,
The Merchant of Venice, IV, i

The Forgotten Man.   —WILLIAM GRAHAM SUMNER,
speech title, 1885
["The forgotten man," wrote Sumner, "works and votes—generally he prays—but his chief business in life is to pay." Franklin D. Roosevelt used the image of the forgotten man in 1932; see POVERTY & HUNGER.]

The truth is we are all caught in a great economic system which is heartless.   —WOODROW WILSON,
The New Freedom, 1913

EDUCATION & LEARNING   See also ELITE, THE
(Auden); SCIENCE

They know enough who know how to learn.
—HENRY ADAMS, *The
Education of Henry Adams*, 1907

A teacher affects eternity; he can never tell where his influence stops.   —*Ibid.*

Learn by doing.   —ANONYMOUS (PROVERB)
[An ancient proverb, in modern times associated with the educational views of John Dewey. In the *Nicomachean Ethics,* Aristotle wrote in the fourth century B.C., "For the things we have to learn before we can do them, we learn by doing them." See also Sophocles at DOING.]

It takes an entire village to raise a child.
—ANONYMOUS (AFRICAN PROVERB)

What I know, that you ought to know but do not know, makes me powerful.
—ANONYMOUS, saying of a tribal elder of
Ghana, cited in *The New York Times,*
Feb. 12, 1993

Education is the best provision for old age.
—ARISTOTLE, 4th cent. B.C., quoted in
Diogenes Laërtius, *Lives of Eminent
Philosophers*, 3rd cent. A.D.

Knowledge itself is power.　　　　　—FRANCIS BACON,
　　　　　　Of Heresies in *Meditations Sacrae,* 1597

First come I: My name is Jowett.
There's no knowledge but I know it.
I am Master of this college.
What I don't know isn't knowledge.　—H. C. BEECHING,
　　　　　　The Masque of Balliol, late 1870s
[Benjamin Jowett, a great Plato ⁀holar, was Master at Balliol
College, Oxford University, from 1870–93. For a quote from
him, see under GOD.]

My people are destroyed for lack of knowledge.
　　　　　　　　　　—BIBLE, *Hosea* 4:6

If you think education is expensive, try ignorance.
　　　　　　　　—DEREK BOK, attributed
[The saying was widely used in the 1980s and appeared on
bumper stickers. It is not clear whether it was original with Mr.
Bok, then president of Harvard University.]

A Master of Art
Is not worth a Fart.　　　　　—ANDREW BOORDE,
　　*Scogin's Jest: Full of Witty Mirth and Pleasant Shifts . . .
　　　　Being a Preservative Against Melancholy,* 1796
[John Scogan, or Scogin, Edward IV's court fool, flourished
around 1480. The oldest extant edition of his jests is dated
1626.]

What I want is Facts. Teach these boys and girls nothing
but Facts. Facts alone are wanted in life. Plant nothing else,
and root out everything else.　　—CHARLES DICKENS,
　　　　　　　　　　Hard Times, 1854

The foundation of every state is the education of its youth.
　　　　　—DIOGENES ("THE CYNIC"), quoted in
　　　　　　Diogenes Laërtius, *Lives of Eminent
　　　　　　Philosophers,* 3rd cent. A.D.

Only the educated are free.
　　　　　　—EPICTETUS, *Discourses,* c. 100 A.D.

Die knowing something. You are not here for long.
                    —WALKER EVANS, c. 1940, quoted in
                       Belinda Rathbone, *Walker Evans*, 1995
[Evans was one of America's great photographers, most remembered for his portraits of Alabama tenant farmers in the
Depression. This exhortation begins, "Stare. It is the way to
educate your eye, and more. Stare, pry, listen, eavesdrop. Die
knowing something . . . (etc.)."]

Education, c'est délivrance.
Education is freedom.
                              —ANDRÉ GIDE,
                                Journals, tr. 1948–51

I find no other pleasure than learning.   —INIGO JONES,
                                Notebooks, Rome, 1614

I find that the three major administrative problems on cam-
pus are sex for the students, athletics for the alumni, and
parking for the faculty.
                    —CLARK KERR, speech at the University
                              of Washington, reported in *Time*,
                                                    Nov. 17, 1958
[Mr. Kerr had recently taken the helm at the University of
California.]

Education . . . is the great equalizer of the conditions of
men,—the balance wheel of society.
                    —HORACE MANN, *Report as Secretary of the
                          Massachusetts Board of Education*, 1848

If by being overstudious, we impair our health and spoil our
good humor, let us give it up.   —MONTAIGNE,
                                        Essays, 1580–88

The direction in which education starts a man will determine
his future life.   —PLATO, *The Republic*, 4th cent. B.C.
[Plato also advised, "Let early education be a sort of amuse-
ment; you will then be better able to find out the natural
bent," *Ibid.*]

A little learning is a dangerous thing.
          —ALEXANDER POPE, *An Essay on Criticism*, 1711

'Tis education forms the common mind,
Just as the twig is bent, the tree's inclined.
> —ALEXANDER POPE, *To Lord Cobham*
> in *Moral Essays*, 1734

In an examination those who do not wish to know ask questions of those who cannot tell.
> —SIR WALTER A. RALEIGH, *Some Thoughts on*
> *Examinations* in *Laughter from a Cloud*, 1923

You can't expect a boy to be depraved until he has been to a good school.
> —SAKI, *Baker's Dozen*, in *The Works of Saki*, 1921

The vanity of teaching often tempteth a man to forget he is a blockhead.   —GEORGE SAVILE, *Maxims*, 1750

Then the whining schoolboy, with his satchel
And shining morning face, creeping like snail
Unwillingly to school.   —SHAKESPEARE,
> *As You Like It*, II, vii

[From the "seven ages of man" speech. William Blake also sympathized with reluctant young scholars: "But to go to school in a summer morn, / Oh, it drives all joy away! / Under a cruel eye outworn, / The little ones spend the day— / In sighing and dismay," *The School Boy* in *Songs of Experience*, 1794.]

There is . . . nothing on earth intended for innocent people so horrible as a school.   —GEORGE BERNARD SHAW,
> *Parents and Children*, 1914

He who can, does. He who cannot, teaches.
> —GEORGE BERNARD SHAW,
> *Man and Superman*, 1903

Education is what survives when what has been learnt has been forgotten.   —B. F. SKINNER, *Scientist*, May 21, 1964

I was moving among two groups . . . who had almost ceased to communicate at all, who in intellectual, moral, and psychological climate had so little in common that . . . one might have crossed the ocean.
> —C. P. SNOW, *The Two Cultures and*
> *the Scientific Revolution*, 1959

[C. P. Snow in his famous 1959 "two cultures" Rede Lecture highlighted the chasm between the communities of science and of arts and humanities. He described being among people who complained of "the illiteracy of scientists," but who could not themselves describe the second law of thermodynamics.]

Education has for its object the formation of character.
—HERBERT SPENCER, *Social Statics,* 1850

What does education often do? It makes a straight-cut ditch of a free, meandering brook.
—HENRY DAVID THOREAU, *Journal,* 1850

Education . . . has produced a vast population able to read but unable to distinguish what is worth reading.
—G. M. TREVELYAN, *English Social History,* 1942

Training is everything. The peach was once a bitter almond; cauliflower is nothing but cabbage with a college education.
—MARK TWAIN, *Pudd'nhead Wilson's Calendar*
in *Pudd'nhead Wilson,* 1894

Soap and education are not as sudden as a massacre, but they are more deadly in the long run.
—MARK TWAIN, *The Facts Concerning the Recent
Resignation* in *Sketches New and Old,* 1867

The founding fathers in their wisdom decided that children were an unnatural strain on parents. So they provided jails called schools, equipped with torture called education.
—JOHN UPDIKE, *The Centaur,* 1963

Separate educational facilities are inherently unequal.
—EARL WARREN, *Brown v. Board of
Education of Topeka,* May 17, 1954
[More at AMERICAN HISTORY: MEMORABLE MOMENTS.]

Human history becomes more and more a race between education and catastrophe.
—H. G. WELLS, *The Outline of History,* 1920

EFFORT
See also ACTION; DOING;
PERSEVERANCE & ENDURANCE;
WORK & WORKERS

It takes all the running you can do to keep in the same place.
—LEWIS CARROLL, *Through the Looking-Glass*, 1872

Much effort, much prosperity.
—EURIPIDES, *The Suppliant Women*, 420 B.C.

There are no gains without pains.
—BENJAMIN FRANKLIN,
Poor Richard's Almanac, 1745

Striving to do better, oft we mar what's well.
—SHAKESPEARE, *King Lear*, I, iv

To strive, to seek, to find, and not to yield.
—ALFRED, LORD TENNYSON, *Ulysses*, 1842
[Inscribed on the cross in Antarctica as a memorial to Robert Scott and his team, who died there in 1912.]

ELITE, THE
See also GENIUS; GREATNESS; HIGH
POSITION: RULERS & LEADERS

To the man-in-the-street, who, I'm sorry to say,
Is a keen observer of life,
The word "Intellectual" suggests straight away
A man who's untrue to his wife.
—W. H. AUDEN, *New Year Letter*, 1961

Like many of the Upper Class
He liked the sound of broken glass.
—HILAIRE BELLOC, *About John*
in *New Cautionary Tales*, 1930
[Cf. Evelyn Waugh, Prelude, *Decline and Fall*, 1928: "the sound of English county families baying for broken glass."]

For many are called, but few are chosen.
—BIBLE, *Matthew* 22:14

What is aristocracy? A corporation of the best, of the bravest.
—THOMAS CARLYLE, *Chartism*, 1839

[A similar phrase, "the best and the brightest," was used as the title of a 1969 book by David Halberstam about the Vietnam War. The phrase derives from an 1811 hymn by Bishop Reginald Heber: "Brightest and best of the sons of the morning, / Dawn on our darkness and lend us thine aid!" In 1822, the poet Percy Bysshe Shelley wrote, "Best and brightest, come away" in *To Jane: An Invitation*.]

The stately homes of England!   —FELICIA HEMANS,
The Homes of England, 1827
[More at NATIONS, (England).]

The minority is always right.   —HENRIK IBSEN,
An Enemy of the People, 1882

I agree with you that there is a natural aristocracy among men. The grounds of this are virtue and talent.
—THOMAS JEFFERSON, letter to
John Adams, Oct. 28, 1813

I don't want to belong to any club that would accept me as a member.   —GROUCHO MARX, attributed
[Groucho wrote in *Groucho and Me*, 1959, that this was how he resigned from the Delaney Club. His brother Zeppo and his son Arthur said that the resignation was from the Friars Club.]

What men value in this world is not rights but privileges.
—H. L. MENCKEN, *Minority Report:
H. L. Mencken's Notebooks*, 1956

We few, we happy few, we band of brothers.
—SHAKESPEARE, *Henry V*, IV, iii

As a rule, provincial governors seem to think that there are no reputable families in the land except those of other provincial governors.   —MURASAKI SHIKIBU,
The Tale of Genji, 1001–15

To consider oneself different from ordinary men is wrong, but it is right to hope that one will not remain like ordinary men.   —YOSHIDA SHOIN, d. 1859, *Yoshida Shoin Zenshu*

The difficult we do immediately. The impossible takes a little longer.   —U. S. ARMY SERVICE FORCES,
motto, World War II

EMOTIONS   See also ANGER; DESPAIR, DEPRESSION,
MISERY; ENTHUSIASM, ENERGY, ZEAL;
GUILT; HAPPINESS; HATE; HEART; LOVE;
SORROW, SADNESS, & SUFFERING

It is not a good time out in the world for emotions anymore.
—RAINER WERNER FASSBINDER,
screenplay, *The Marriage of Maria Braun*,
1978

Sturm und drang.
Storm and stress.
—FRIEDRICH MAXIMILIAN VON KLINGER,
from title of play, *Die Wirrwarr; oder,
Sturm und Drang,* 1776
[The phrase describes a revolutionary movement in German
literature from about 1770 to 1784. Goethe was the dominant
figure in this approach, which focused on intense emotions and
love of nature.]

I have something more to do than feel.
—CHARLES LAMB, letter to Coleridge, 1796
[A great line but a strange context: the letter was written just
after the death of Lamb's mother. Lamb also wrote to Robert
Southey in 1815, "Anything awful makes me laugh. I misbe-
haved once at a funeral."]

You are not wood, you are not stones, but men.
—SHAKESPEARE, *Julius Caesar,* III, ii

ENDINGS   See also ACCOMPLISHMENT;
BEGINNINGS; PATIENCE (Bible)

The opera ain't over till the fat lady sings.
—ANONYMOUS
[This was popularized in the late 1970s by coach Dick Motta
of the Chicago Bulls. In a column in *The New York Times
Magazine,* Feb. 15, 1987, William Safire traced it to a remark
by the sportswriter Dan Cook in 1975, but it is probably a folk
adage. *Southern Words and Sayings,* edited by Fabia R. Smith

and Charles R. Smith, includes this version: "Church ain't out until the fat lady sings."]

It ain't over till it's over.

        —YOGI BERRA, saying, attributed
[*Bartlett's* says that Berra was referring to the 1973 National League pennant race. He was managing the Mets, who finally prevailed. The remark exists in a variety of forms, including "The game isn't over till it's over"; see also SPORTS (Anonymous).

Numerous other catchy comments are attributed to Berra—many being malapropisms, perhaps reflecting the complex thought and speech patterns of Casey Stengel, who managed the Yankees, where Berra played catcher. Among the best Berra-isms are:

"You can observe a lot by watching" (remark by Berra at a press conference introducing him as the new manager of the Yankees, Oct. 24, 1963).

"If you come to a fork in the road, take it." He used this in accepting an honorary degree from Montclair State University in New Jersey, as reported in *The New York Times,* May 17, 1996; but the attribution may precede this occasion.

"It's like *déja vu* all over again."

"The future ain't what it used to be."

"Nobody ever goes there anymore. It's too crowded." Reportedly, said by Berra, but as Ralph Keyes pointed out in *Nice Guys Finish Seventh,* the same line appears in a 1943 *New Yorker* short story by John McNulty.

"Anybody who is popular is bound to be disliked."

"You have got to be very careful if you don't know where you are going, because you might not get there."

"You can't win all the time. There are guys out there who are better than you." But not many were better than Berra; he earned ten World Series rings.]

La commedia è finita.
The comedy is finished. —RUGGIERO LEONCAVALLO,
                last words in the opera *I Pagliacci*
                (The Clowns), 1892

In my end is my beginning.

        —MARY QUEEN OF SCOTS, motto
[Also used by T. S. Eliot to close *East Coker*; see FATE. Mary's end came by beheading at Fotheringay Castle, Feb. 8, 1587.]

The end crowns all.   —SHAKESPEARE,
                                          Troilus and Cressida, IV, v
[The next two lines are: "And that old common arbitrator,
Time, / Will one day end it.")

ENDS & MEANS   See also ETHICS & MORALITY;
                              EXPEDIENCY; SELF-INTEREST

Whoever wills the end, wills also . . . the means.
                    —IMMANUEL KANT, *Fundamental Principles
                         of the Metaphysic of Morals*, 1785

If the ends don't justify the means, what does?
                    —ROBERT MOSES, d. 1981, saying

The end must justify the means.
                    —MATTHEW PRIOR, *Hans Carvel*, 1700

To do a great right do a little wrong.   —SHAKESPEARE,
                              The Merchant of Venice, IV, i
[Bassanio pleading that the pound-of-flesh contract be broken.]

The end excuses any evil.   —SOPHOCLES,
                              Electra, 5th cent. B.C.
[Ends and means were specifically coupled by St. Jerome
(c. 342–420), who referred to "The line often adopted by strong
men . . . of justifying the means by the end," letter 48. See
also the Theodore Roosevelt quote at EVIL.]

The end may justify the means as long as there is something
that justifies the end.   —LEON TROTSKY, d. 1940,
                         quoted in A. Pozzolini, *Antonio Gramsci:
                    An Introduction to His Thought*, Preface, 1970

ENDURANCE   See PERSEVERANCE & ENDURANCE;
                              PATIENCE; SURVIVAL

ENEMIES   See also FORGIVENESS & MERCY;
                              PATIENCE (Anonymous,
                              Indian Proverb)

We often give our enemies the means of our own
destruction.   —AESOP, *Fables*, 6th cent. B.C.

He who has a thousand friends has not a friend to spare,
And he who has one enemy will meet him everywhere.
—ALI IBN-ABI-TALIB,
A Hundred Sayings, 7th cent. B.C.
[Ali, son-in-law of Muhammad and 4th Caliph, was murdered in 661. Called "the Lion of God," Ali and his son Husein are the great saints of the Shiite branch of Islam.]

Friends come and go, but enemies accumulate.
—ANONYMOUS, saying in government circles, cited by
Peggy Noonan, *Charlie Rose Show,* Jan. 6, 1994

Pay attention to your foes, for they are the first to discover your mistakes.
—ANTISTHENES, quoted in Diogenes Laërtius,
Lives of Eminent Philosophers, 3rd cent. A.D.

Love your enemies.
—BIBLE, *Matthew* 5:44

Yet every man is his greatest enemy, and, as it were, his own executioner.
—THOMAS BROWNE,
Religio Medici, 1643
[For Walt Kelly's version, "the enemy . . . is us," see under HUMANS & HUMAN NATURE.]

You shall judge of a man by his foes as well as by his friends.
—JOSEPH CONRAD, *Lord Jim,* 1900

There is no little enemy.
—BENJAMIN FRANKLIN, *Poor Richard's Almanac,* Sept. 1733

If you have no enemies, it is a sign fortune has forgot you.
—THOMAS FULLER, *Gnomologia,* 1732

He who forgiveth, and is reconciled unto his enemy, shall receive his reward from God.
—KORAN, c. 610–632

Keep your friends close, but your enemies closer.
—MARIO PUZO, *The Godfather,* 1969

He makes no friend who never made a foe.
—ALFRED, LORD TENNYSON, *Lancelot and Elaine* in *Idylls of the King,* 1859–85

A man cannot be too careful in the choice of his enemies.
　　　　　—OSCAR WILDE, *The Picture of Dorian Gray,* 1891

ENERGY　　　　　See ENTHUSIASM, ENERGY, & ZEAL

ENGLAND　　　　　　　　　　See NATIONS

ENTHUSIASM, ENERGY, & ZEAL

My zeal hath consumed me.　　　　—BIBLE, *Psalms* 50:2

Energy is eternal delight.　　　　—WILLIAM BLAKE,
　　　　　The Marriage of Heaven and Hell, 1790–93

The greatest dangers to liberty lurk in insidious encroach-
ment by men of zeal, well-meaning but without understanding.　　　　　—LOUIS D. BRANDEIS, *Olmstead v.
　　　　　the United States,* 1928

Only passions, great passions, can elevate the soul to great
things.　　　　　—DENIS DIDEROT, *Discours sur la
　　　　　poésie dramatique,* 1773–78

Nothing great was ever achieved without enthusiasm.
　　　　　—RALPH WALDO EMERSON, *Circles*
　　　　　in *Essays: First Series,* 1841
[See also Hegel, below.]

Zeal is fit only for wise men, but is found mostly in fools.
　　　　　—THOMAS FULLER, *Gnomologia,* 1732

Nothing great in the world has been accomplished without
passion.　　　　　—HEGEL, *Philosophy of History,* 1832

Fanaticism consists in redoubling your efforts when you
have forgotten your aim.
　　　　　—GEORGE SANTAYANA, *The Life of
　　　　　Reason: Reason in Common Sense,* 1905–06

Enthusiasm signifies God in us.
　　　　　—MME. DE STAËL, *De l'Allemagne,* 1810
[She explains that this is the sense of the word in Greek.]

Pas trop de zèle.
Not too much enthusiasm.
> —CHARLES-MAURICE DE TALLEYRAND,
> d. 1838, attributed by several writers, including
> C. A. Saint-Beuve, *Portrait des Femmes*, 1858

ENVIRONMENT

See also FUTURE;
NATURE; POPULATION

A culture is no better than its woods.
> —W. H. AUDEN, *Bucolics* in *Shield of Achilles*, 1955

[More at MODERN TIMES.]

Over increasingly large areas of the United States, spring now comes unheralded by the return of the birds, and the early mornings are strangely silent where once they were filled with the beauty of bird song.
> —RACHEL CARSON,
> *Silent Spring*, 1962

[Startling and controversial when published, *Silent Spring* issued in a new era of environmental awareness and activism. Its first effect was to limit the use of the popular pesticide DDT. Another famous passage, still often cited today, is: "For the first time in the history of the world, every human being is now subjected to contact with dangerous chemicals from the moment of conception until death."]

Forests keep disappearing, rivers dry up, wild life's become extinct, the climate's ruined, and the land grows poorer and uglier every day.
> —ANTON CHEKHOV, *Uncle Vanya*, 1899

[The sentences preceding this statement read: "Man has been endowed with reason, with the power to create, so that he can add to what he's been given. But up to now, he hasn't been a creator, only a destroyer."]

We are the children of our landscape.
> —LAWRENCE DURRELL, *Justine*, 1957

I am a passenger on the spaceship Earth.
> —R. BUCKMINSTER FULLER, *Operating
> Manual for Spaceship Earth*, 1969

What would the world be once bereft
Of wet and wildness? Let them be left,
O let them be left, wildness and wet;
Long live the weeds and the wilderness yet.
> —GERARD MANLEY HOPKINS,
> *Inversnaid* in *Poems,* 1918

We have forgotten how to be good guests, how to walk
lightly on the earth as its other creatures do.
> —BARBARA WARD JACKSON and
> RENÉ DUBOS, *Only One Earth* (report
> of the United Nations Stockholm Conference on
> the Human Environment), 1972

The earth is given as a common stock for man to labor and
live on.
> —THOMAS JEFFERSON, letter to
> Rev. James Madison, Oct. 28, 1785

The supreme reality of our time is . . . the vulnerability of
our planet. —JOHN F. KENNEDY, speech, June 28, 1963

Conservation is a state of harmony between men and land.
> —ALDO LEOPOLD, *A Sand County Almanac,* 1949

Pity the Meek, for they shall inherit the earth.
> —DON MARQUIS, d. 1937, quoted in Frederick B. Wilcox,
> *A Little Book of Aphorisms,* 1947

In God's wilderness lies the hope of the world.
> —JOHN MUIR, note from Alaska, 1890
[See also Muir at NATURE.]

The nation that destroys its soil destroys itself.
> —FRANKLIN D. ROOSEVELT, letter to
> state governors, Feb. 26, 1937

In wildness is the preservation of the world.
> —HENRY DAVID THOREAU, *Walking,* 1862

We must make our garden grow.
> —VOLTAIRE, *Candide,* 1759
[The conclusion of Part One of *Candide.* Used by British Prime
Minister John Major at the 1992 international conference on the

environment, held in Brazil. A more literal translation is, "We must cultivate our garden." Sometimes "garden" is pluralized.]

EPITAPHS   See also DEATH; HAPPINESS (Thucydides);
   LIFE (John Gay); NATURE: ANIMALS (Byron)

Sit tibi terra levis.
May the earth lie light upon thee.   —ANONYMOUS
[This common Roman epitaph was often abbreviated S.T.T.L.]

Behold and see as you pass by
As you are now, so once was I;
As I am now, so you will be—
Prepare for death and follow me.
                         —ANONYMOUS, from the tomb of
                             Edward, the Black Prince, 1376
[Also commonly used on Colonial American gravestones.]

Bury me standing. I've been on my knees all my life.
                    —ANONYMOUS (GYPSY PROVERB)

Earth receive an honored guest;
William Yeats is laid to rest.
          —W. H. AUDEN, *In Memory of W. B. Yeats,* 1940

Epitaph, n. An inscription on a tomb showing that virtues acquired by death have a retroactive effect.
          —AMBROSE BIERCE, *The Devil's Dictionary,* 1906
[The founder of *The Argonaut* magazine, Frank Pixley, fired Bierce from the staff, and reportedly thereafter the two men amused themselves writing epitaphs for each other. One composed by Bierce was: "Here lies Frank Pixley—as usual."]

Here Skugg
Lies snug
As a bug
In a rug.   —BENJAMIN FRANKLIN, letter to
                          Georgiana Shipley, Sept. 26, 1772
[Skugg was Miss Shipley's pet squirrel.]

I had a lover's quarrel with the world.
                    —ROBERT FROST, *The Lesson for Today,*
                     read at Harvard University, June 20, 1941
[The full statement is: "And were an epitaph to be my story, /

I'd have a short one ready for my own. / I would have written of me on my stone: / I had a lover's quarrel with the world."]

Born 1711. Died 1776. Leaving it to posterity to add the rest.   —DAVID HUME, written by himself, 1775

In lapidary inscriptions a man is not upon oath.
                    —SAMUEL JOHNSON, Apr. 18, 1775, quoted in
                    James Boswell, *Life of Johnson,* 1791

Here lies one whose name was writ in water.
                    —JOHN KEATS, epitaph for himself, 1821

By and by
God caught his eye.
                    —DAVID McCORD, *Remainders,* epitaph for a
                    waiter in *Bay Window Ballads,* 1935

This be the verse you grave for me:
Here he lies where he longed to be;
Home is the sailor, home from the sea,
And the hunter home from the hill.
                    —ROBERT LOUIS STEVENSON,
                    Requiem in *Underwoods,* 1887
[The opening lines of the passage form a separate epitaph: "Under the wide and starry sky, / Dig the grave and let me lie. / Glad did I live and gladly die." Stevenson died at age 44 in 1894.]

Warm summer sun, shine kindly here;
Warm southern wind, blow softly here;
Green sod above, lie light, lie light—
Good night, dear heart, good night, good night.
                    —MARK TWAIN, verses on gravestone of
                    daughter Susy, Elmira, N.Y., 1896
[Commonly credited to Twain, the verse actually is his adaptation of lines written some ten years earlier by an Australian, Robert Richardson. Twain merely changed Richardson's original "northern wind," fitting for Australia, to "southern wind," more appropriate to the northern hemisphere. When Twain learned that the lines were being attributed to him, he had Richardson's name added to the monument, but the verse has remained popularly associated with Twain.]

EQUALITY   See also RACES & PEOPLES

When Adam delved and Eve span,
Who was then a gentleman?
    —JOHN BALL, sermon at Blackheath, June 12, 1381,
               at the height of Wat Tyler's Rebellion
[From an earlier poem by Richard Rolle. The uprising of the peasants was put down quickly and their leaders killed. Ball was executed before King Richard II on July 15.]

Have we not all one father? hath not one God created us?
    —BIBLE, *Malachi* 2:10

A man's a man for a'that!   —ROBERT BURNS,
    For a'that and a'that, 1790

Everyone has won, and *all* must have prizes!
    —LEWIS CARROLL, *Alice's Adventures in
        Wonderland,* 1865
[The Dodo is speaking. The contest was a footrace.]

All men are created equal.   —THOMAS JEFFERSON,
    Declaration of Independence, 1776
[More at AMERICAN HISTORY: MEMORABLE MOMENTS.]

There is no king who has not had a slave among his ancestors, and no slave who has not had a king among his.
    —HELEN KELLER, *The Story of My Life,* 1902

The boundaries of democracy have to be widened so as to include economic equality also. This is the great revolution through which we are all passing.
    —JAWAHARLAL NEHRU,
    Glimpses of World History, 1939

All animals are equal, but some animals are more equal than others.   —GEORGE ORWELL, *Animal Farm,* 1945

ERAS   See FUTURE, THE; GENERATIONS;
MODERN TIMES; PAST, THE; PRESENT, THE;
TURBULENT TIMES

ERROR   See FAILINGS; MISTAKES

ESCAPE

See also TRAVEL

Oh that I had wings like a dove! for then I would fly away,
and be at rest. —BIBLE, *Psalms* 55:6

listen: there's a hell
of a good universe next door: let's go.
—E. E. CUMMINGS, *One Times One*, 1944

O! for a horse with wings! —SHAKESPEARE,
Cymbeline, III, iii

Let us rise up and part; she will not know.
Let us go seaward as the great winds go,
Full of blown sand and foam.
—ALGERNON CHARLES SWINBURNE,
A Leave-taking, 1866

I will arise and go now, and go to Innisfree,
And a small cabin build there, of clay and wattles made:
Nine bean-rows will I have there, a hive for the honeybee,
And live alone in the bee-loud glade.
—WILLIAM BUTLER YEATS, *The Lake Isle of
Innisfree* in *The Rose*, 1893

ESTHETICS

See ARTS: AESTHETICS

ETHICS & MORALITY
See also CONSCIENCE; ENDS & MEANS;
EVIL; PHILOSOPHY; VIRTUE

It is easier to fight for one's principles than to live up to
them. —ALFRED ADLER, quoted in Phyllis Bottome,
Alfred Adler, 1939

No morality can be founded on authority, even if the authority were divine. —A. J. AYER, d. 1989, *Essay on Humanism*

All good moral philosophy is but the handmaid to religion.
—FRANCIS BACON,
The Advancement of Learning, 1605

Expedients are for the hour, but principles are for the ages.
—HENRY WARD BEECHER, *Proverbs from
Plymouth Pulpit*, 1887

The greatest happiness of the greatest number is the foundation of morals and legislation. —JEREMY BENTHAM,
The Commonplace Book, 1832
[The thought is irredeemably associated with Bentham and his doctrine of utilitarianism, but he himself noted in *The Commonplace Book*, published shortly after his death, that this "sacred truth" had been articulated earlier by others. His ultimate source may have been the Scottish philosopher Francis Hutcheson, who declared in his *Enquiry Concerning Moral Good and Evil* (1725): "That action is best which procures the greatest happiness for the greatest number."]

No actions are bad in themselves—even murder can be justified. —DIETRICH BONHOEFFER,
No Rusty Swords, tr. 1965
[Bonhoeffer, a German theologian, was imprisoned and later hanged for taking part in the 1944 plot to assassinate Hitler.]

The world has achieved brilliance without conscience. Ours is a world of nuclear giants and ethical infants.
—GEN. OMAR BRADLEY, speech, Armistice Day, 1948

It doesn't matter what you do, as long as you don't do it in public and frighten the horses.
—MRS. PATRICK CAMPBELL, d. 1940,
traditional attribution

"Do the duty which lies nearest thee," which thou knowest to be a duty! Thy second duty will already have become clearer. —THOMAS CARLYLE, *Sartor Resartus*, 1833–34

The number of people in possession of any criteria for discriminating between good and evil is very small.
—T. S. ELIOT, Virginia lectures, 1933

Rise above principle and do what's right.
—WALTER HELLER,
Congressional testimony, May 7, 1985
[Heller had headed the Council of Economic Advisers.]

I know only that what is moral is what you feel good after and what is immoral is what you feel bad after.
—ERNEST HEMINGWAY, *Death in the Afternoon,* 1932

If he does really think that there is no distinction between virtue and vice, why, Sir, when he leaves our houses, let us count our spoons.
—SAMUEL JOHNSON, July 14, 1763, quoted in James Boswell, *Life of Johnson,* 1791
[The quote refers to James Macpherson, the Scotsman who wrote *The Poems of Ossian* and tried to pass it off as a translation of ancient Gaelic poetry. For another occasion on which to count spoons, see Emerson under SELF-RIGHTEOUSNESS.]

Morality is not properly the doctrine of how we may make ourselves happy, but how we may make ourselves worthy of happiness.
—IMMANUEL KANT, *Critique of Practical Reason,* 1781

Act only on that maxim which you can at the same time wish that it should become a universal law [definition of the categorical imperative].
—IMMANUEL KANT, *Fundamental Principles of the Metaphysic of Morals,* 1785

Morality is the herd instinct in the individual.
—FRIEDRICH NIETZSCHE, *The Joyful Wisdom,* 1882

My country is the world, and my religion is to do good.
—THOMAS PAINE, *The Rights of Man,* 1791

As soon as one is unhappy, one becomes moral.
—MARCEL PROUST, *Remembrance of Things Past: Within a Budding Grove,* 1913–27

Ethical metaphysics is fundamentally an attempt, however disguised, to give legislative force to our own wishes.
—BERTRAND RUSSELL, *On Scientific Method in Philosophy* in *Mysticism and Logic,* 1917

No one can be perfectly free till all are free; no one can be perfectly moral till all are moral; no one can be perfectly happy till all are happy. —HERBERT SPENCER, *Social Statics,* 1850

One impulse from a vernal wood
May teach you more of man,
Of moral evil and of good,
Than all the sages can.

—WILLIAM WORDSWORTH,
The Tables Turned, 1798

EUROPE   See NATIONS

EVENING   See NATURE: TIMES OF DAY

EVIDENCE   See also CRIME; GUILT; SCIENCE

You should not decide until you have heard what both have to say.   —ARISTOPHANES, *The Wasps,* 422 B.C.

Hear the other side.   —ST. AUGUSTINE, d. A.D. 430,
De Duabus Animabus Contra Manicheos

By their fruits you shall know them.—BIBLE, *Matthew* 7:20

Out of thine own mouth will I judge thee.
—BIBLE, *Luke* 19:22

Oaths are but words, and words but wind.
—SAMUEL BUTLER, *Hudibras,* 1663

"Is there any point to which you wish to draw my attention?"
"To the curious incident of the dog in the night-time."
"The dog did nothing in the night-time."
"That was the curious incident," remarked Holmes.
—A. CONAN DOYLE, *Silver Blaze* in
The Memoirs of Sherlock Holmes, 1894

The absence of evidence is not evidence of absence.
> —MICHAEL PAPAGIANNIS, quoted in
> C.D.B. Bryan, *Close Encounters of the Fourth
> Kind: Alien Abductions, UFOs, and the Conference
> at M.I.T.,* 1995

If it walks like a duck, and quacks like a duck, then it just may be a duck.   —WALTER REUTHER, d. 1970,
> attributed by William Safire,
> *Safire's Political Dictionary,* 1993

The most savage controversies are about those matters as to which there is no good evidence either way.
> —BERTRAND RUSSELL,
> *An Outline of Intellectual Rubbish,* 1950

Things seen are mightier than things heard.
> —ALFRED, LORD TENNYSON, *Enoch Arden,* 1864

[The notion can be traced as far back as Herodotus in the fifth century B.C.: "We are less convinced by what we hear than by what we see."]

Some circumstantial evidence is very strong, as when you find a trout in the milk.   —HENRY DAVID THOREAU,
> *Journal,* Nov. 11, 1850

[A common consumer fraud in Thoreau's day was watering milk.]

EVIL   See also CRIME; DANGEROUS PEOPLE;
ENDS & MEANS; HELL; SIN, VICE, &
NAUGHTINESS; TEMPTATION; TROUBLE;
VIOLENCE & FORCE

The fearsome . . . *banality of evil.*   —HANNAH ARENDT,
> *Eichmann in Jerusalem,* 1963

[Nazi Adolf Eichmann, who had more the manner of a bureaucrat than obvious demon, personified for Arendt the institutionalization of evil. Just before his trial for war crimes, he remarked, "To sum it all up, I must say I regret nothing." Arendt wrote: "It was as though in those last minutes he was summing up the lessons that this long course in human wickedness had taught us—the lesson of the fearsome, word-and-thought-defying *banality of evil.*"]

Evil is unspectacular and always human
And shares our bed and eats at our own table.
—W. H. AUDEN, *Herman Melville* in
Collected Poetry, 1945

I had rather be a doorkeeper in the house of my God, than to dwell in the tents of wickedness.   —BIBLE, *Psalms* 84:10

For wide is the gate, and broad is the way, that leadeth to destruction.   —BIBLE, *Matthew* 7:13

Men loved darkness rather than light, because their deeds were evil.   —BIBLE, *John* 3:19

For the wages of sin is death.   —BIBLE, *Romans* 6:23

Be not overcome of evil, but overcome evil of good.
—BIBLE, *Romans* 12:21

He that toucheth pitch shall be defiled therewith.
—BIBLE, *Ecclesiasticus* 13:1

The only thing necessary for the triumph of evil is for good men to do nothing. —EDMUND BURKE, d. 1797, attributed [Pres. John F. Kennedy attributed this to Burke, but the sentence has not been found in his writings. For the passage that is probably the basis of this attribution, see Burke at UNITY & LOYALTY. For an American version see Martin Luther King, Jr., below.]

The evil that is in the world almost always comes of ignorance, and good intentions may do as much harm as malevolence if they lack understanding.
—ALBERT CAMUS, *The Plague,* 1947

Pity the criminal all you like, but don't call evil good.
—FEODOR DOSTOEVSKI, *Crime and Punishment,* 1866

There is a capacity of virtue in us, and there is a capacity of vice to make your blood creep.
—RALPH WALDO EMERSON, *Journal,* 1831

Sin is whatever obscures the soul.   —ANDRÉ GIDE,
La Symphonie pastorale, 1919

Wickedness is always easier than virtue; for it takes the short cut to everything. —SAMUEL JOHNSON, Sept. 17, 1773, quoted by James Boswell, *Journal of a Tour to the Hebrides*, 1785

No one becomes depraved all at once.
—JUVENAL, *Satires*, c. A.D. 100

He who accepts evil without protesting against it is really cooperating with it. —MARTIN LUTHER KING, JR., *Stride Toward Freedom*, 1958

Surely God wrongs not men, but themselves men wrong.
—KORAN, c. 610–632

Destruction never comes with weapon in hand. It comes on tiptoe, seeing good in bad and bad in good.
—MAHABHARATA, c. 200 B.C.–A.D. 200

A man does not sin by commission only, but often by omission. —MARCUS AURELIUS, *Meditations*, 2nd cent. A.D.

Nothing is evil which is according to nature. —*Ibid.*

It is a sin to believe evil of others, but it is seldom a mistake.
—H. L. MENCKEN, *A Mencken Chrestomathy*, 1949

So farewell hope, and with hope farewell fear,
Farewell remorse: all good to me is lost;
Evil be thou my Good.
—JOHN MILTON, *Paradise Lost*, 1667

Whoever fights monsters should see to it that in the process he does not become a monster. And when you look long into an abyss, the abyss also looks into you.
—FRIEDRICH NIETZSCHE, *Beyond Good and Evil*, 1885–86

All human evil comes from this: a man's being unable to sit still in a room. —PASCAL, *Pensées*, 1670

No man is justified in doing evil on the ground of expediency. —THEODORE ROOSEVELT, *The Strenuous Life*, title essay, 1900

The evil that men do lives after them,
The good is oft interrèd with their bones.
—SHAKESPEARE, *Julius Caesar*, III, ii

If one good deed in all my life I did,
I do repent it from my very soul.
—SHAKESPEARE, *Titus Andronicus,* V, iii

All spirits are enslaved that serve things evil.
—PERCY BYSSHE SHELLEY,
Prometheus Unbound, 1819

Between two evils, I always like to take the one I've never tried before. —MAE WEST, *Klondike Annie,* 1936

No man chooses evil because it is evil; he only mistakes it for happiness, the good he seeks.
—MARY WOLLSTONECRAFT,
A Vindication of the Rights of Man, 1790

EVOLUTION   See SCIENCE: BIOLOGY

EXCELLENCE   See AMBITION; ELITE, THE;
                            GRACE; GREATNESS

EXCESS   See also HEDONISM

Drinking when we are not thirsty and making love at any time, madame: that is all there is to distinguish us from the other animals.
—PIERRE-AUGUSTIN DE BEAUMARCHAIS,
The Marriage of Figaro, 1784

The road of excess leads to the palace of wisdom.
—WILLIAM BLAKE, *The Marriage of
Heaven and Hell,* 1790–93

Those who have great passions find themselves all their lives both happy and unhappy at being cured of them.
—LA ROCHEFOUCAULD, *Maxims,* 1678

Excess on occasion is exhilarating. It prevents moderation from acquiring the deadening effect of habit.
　　—W. SOMERSET MAUGHAM, *The Summing Up,* 1938

My candle burns at both ends;
It will not last the night;
But ah, my foes, and oh my friends—
It gives a lovely light!
　　　　　　—EDNA ST. VINCENT MILLAY,
　　　　　　First Fig in *A Few Figs from Thistles,* 1920

Can one desire too much of a good thing?
　　　　　—SHAKESPEARE, *As You Like It,* IV, i

To gild refinèd gold, to paint the lily,
To throw a perfume on the violet,
To smooth the ice, or add another hue
Unto the rainbow, or with taper light
To seek the beauteous eye of heaven to garnish,
Is wasteful and ridiculous excess.
　　　　　　　—SHAKESPEARE, *King John,* IV, ii
[This is the source of the popular phrase "to gild the lily."]

These violent delights have violent ends.
　　　　　—SHAKESPEARE, *Romeo and Juliet,* II, vi

Nothing to excess.　　　　—SOLON, 6th cent. B.C., quoted in
　　　　Diogenes Laërtius, *Lives of Eminent Philosophers,*
　　　　　　　　　　　　　　3rd cent. A.D.

Too much of a good thing can be wonderful.
　　　　　—MAE WEST, quoted in Joseph Weintraub, ed.,
　　　　　　The Wit and Wisdom of Mae West, 1967
[Or as cellist Mstislav Rostropovich puts it, "More is, more," quoted in the Kennedy Center Honors Performance, Dec. 30, 1992.]

Nothing succeeds like excess.　　　—OSCAR WILDE,
　　　　　　A Woman of No Importance, 1893
[A play on "Nothing succeeds like success"; see Dumas at SUCCESS.]

Never . . . murder a man who is committing suicide.
　　—WOODROW WILSON, letter to Bernard Baruch, 1916

EXCUSES & EXPLANATIONS   See also MISTAKES
(U. S. Grant)

Qui s'excuse, s'accuse.
Who excuses himself, accuses himself.
—ANONYMOUS (PROVERB)

It's not how you win or lose, it's how you place the blame.
—ANONYMOUS
[Baseball slugger Ralph Kiner quoted this saying while broad-
casting a Mets game c. 1990. It's a variation, of course, of "It's
not how you win or lose, it's how you play the game"; see
Grantland Rice at WINNING & LOSING, VICTORY &
DEFEAT.]

Never complain, never explain.
—HENRY FORD II, d. 1987
[*The New York Times* obituary for Ford (Sept. 30, 1987) cred-
ited him with this remark, uttered after he was arrested for
drunk driving; it is also the title of Victor Lasky's biography
of Ford. In the same vein, former Secretary of State Dean
Acheson observed, "How vulnerable are those who explain,"
Time magazine, June 26, 1964. In England, Admiral of the
Fleet John Arbuthnot Baron Fisher wrote in a letter to the
London *Times,* Sept. 5, 1919: "(It's only d——d fools who
argue!) Never contradict. Never explain. Never apologize.
(Those are the secrets of a happy life!)" The earliest attribution
is to the English Prime Minister Benjamin Disraeli in John
Morley's *The Life of William Gladstone,* 1903.]

Bad excuses are worse than none.   —THOMAS FULLER,
Gnomologia, 1732

Several excuses are always less convincing than one.
—ALDOUS HUXLEY, *Point Counter Point,* 1928

[On being observed by his wife kissing a chorus girl] I wasn't
kissing her, I was whispering into her mouth.
—CHICO MARX, attributed

And oftentimes excusing of a fault
Doth make the fault the worse by the excuse.
—SHAKESPEARE, *King John,* IV, ii

I am a man
More sinned against than sinning.   —SHAKESPEARE,
King Lear, III, ii

Two wrongs don't make a right, but they make a good
excuse.   —THOMAS SZASZ, *Social Relations* in
The Second Sin, 1973

EXERCISE   See PHYSICAL FITNESS; SPORTS

EXPEDIENCY   See also ENDS & MEANS;
NECESSITY; SELF-INTEREST

In practice, such trifles as contradictions in principle are easily set aside; the faculty of ignoring them makes the practical
man.   —HENRY ADAMS, *The Education
of Henry Adams*, 1907
[But see Theodore Roosevelt at EVIL.]

And this is the law I will maintain,
Until my dying day, Sir,
That whatsoever king shall reign,
I'll still be the Vicar of Bray, Sir.

—ANONYMOUS, c. 1700
[This verse from a song attributed to an anonymous British
dragoon serving under George I celebrates a supposed Vicar
of Bray from the time of Charles II and George I. But the
legend is older and more likely is based on the career of Simon
Aleyn, who was sufficiently flexible in religion to hold on to
his office from ca. 1540–88, through the alternating changes in
England's state creed in the reigns of Henry VIII, Edward VI,
Mary I, and Elizabeth I. See also Henry IV, below.]

We do what we must, and call it by the best names.
—RALPH WALDO EMERSON, *Considerations
By the Way* in *The Conduct of Life,* 1860

Paris is well worth a Mass.   —HENRY IV, attributed, 1593
[Henry of Navarre, a politic survivor in a period of fierce religious wars, became Henry IV of France. Tradition holds that
he made this remark when, by abjuring Protestantism for the
second time in his career, he effected reconciliation with the
Catholic forces in control of Paris. He was welcomed into Paris
in 1594, ruling until 1610. A skilled and popular king, he

wanted every peasant family to have a chicken in the pot for Sunday dinner; see FOOD, WINE, & EATING.]

Policy sits above conscience. —SHAKESPEARE,
Timon of Athens, III, ii

In every sort of danger, there are various ways of winning through, if one is ready to do and say anything whatever.
—SOCRATES, 5th cent. B.C., quoted in
Plato, *Apology,* 4th cent. B.C.

Custom adapts itself to expediency. —TACITUS, *Annals,*
c. A.D. 115–17

EXPERIENCE
See also DOING; LIFE

All experience is an arch to build up. —HENRY ADAMS,
The Education of Henry Adams, 1907
[Tennyson saw experience as an arch to see through: "Yet all experience is an arch wherethrough / Gleams that untravelled world whose margin fades / For ever and for ever when I move," *Ulysses,* 1842.]

Experience keeps a dear school, yet fools will learn in no other. —BENJAMIN FRANKLIN, *Poor
Richard's Almanac,* Dec. 1743

Experience gives us the tests first and the lessons later.
—NAOMI JUDD, public radio interview,
Weekend Edition, 1994
[Attributed to others as well.]

A man should have the fine point of his soul taken off to become fit for this world. —JOHN KEATS,
letter to J. H. Reynolds, Nov. 22, 1817

No man's knowledge here can go beyond his experience.
—JOHN LOCKE, *Essay Concerning
Human Understanding,* 1690

One thorn of experience is worth a whole wilderness of warning. —JAMES RUSSELL LOWELL, *Shakespeare
Once More* in *Among My Books,* 1870

The journey not the arrival matters.
                                    —MONTAIGNE,
                                       Essays, 1580–88

I've been things, and seen places.
                                    —MAE WEST,
                                       I'm No Angel, 1933

Experience is the name everyone gives to their mistakes.
    —OSCAR WILDE, *Lady Windermere's Fan,* 1892
[The originator of this thought is uncertain. Several different
attributions have been offered. It may be a Jewish folk saying.]

EXPERTS   See also DOCTORS & THE PRACTICE
                         OF MEDICINE; LAWYERS

Professionals built the *Titanic*—amateurs the ark.
    —ANONYMOUS, cited by Frank S. Pepper, *Handbook
            of 20th Century Quotes,* source: BBC radio,
                      The News Quiz, Oct. 27, 1979

An expert is one who knows more and more about less and
less.   —NICHOLAS MURRAY BUTLER, attributed,
                  commencement speech, Columbia University
[Butler served as Columbia's president from 1901 to 1945.]

An expert is someone who knows some of the worst mistakes that can be made in his subject and how to avoid
them.
    —WERNER HEISENBERG, *Physics and Beyond,* 1969

An expert is someone who borrows your watch to tell you
what time it is, and then keeps the watch.
                                    —JOHN RAUCH, saying
[Rauch is a partner in the architectural firm of Venturi, Scott-
Brown and Associates.]

EXPLORATION   See SCIENCE: DISCOVERY &
                             EXPLORATION; TRAVEL

F

FACE   See BODY, HUMAN

FACTS   See also TRUTH

Facts are better than dreams.   —WINSTON CHURCHILL,
Second World War, 1948

In this life we want nothing but facts, Sir; nothing but facts.
—CHARLES DICKENS, *Hard Times*, 1854
[For more of Gradgrind's philosophy, see EDUCATION.]

A little fact is worth a whole limbo of dreams.
—RALPH WALDO EMERSON, *The Superlative*, 1847

Her taste exact
For faultless fact
Amounts to a disease.
—W. S. GILBERT, *The Mikado*, 1885

The smallest fact is a window through which the infinite may
be seen.   —ALDOUS HUXLEY, d. 1963, cited in Richard
Norton Smith, *Thomas E. Dewey*, 1982

The vocation of mankind is to create facts.
—EMMANUEL MOUNIER, May 1933
[Cited by William Pfaff, *New Yorker* article on André Malraux,
July 9, 1990. Mounier was a French Catholic writer and editor.]

Learn, compare, collect the facts!
—IVAN PETROVICH PAVLOV, *Bequest to the
Academic Youth of Soviet Russia*, Feb. 27, 1936

The facts are to blame my friend. We are all imprisoned by facts.

> —LUIGI PIRANDELLO, *The Rules of the Game,* 1918

Mere fact will never stop an Englishman.

> —GEORGE BERNARD SHAW, speech, Oct. 28, 1930

Let us not underrate the value of a fact; it will one day flower into a truth.

> —HENRY DAVID THOREAU, *Excursions,* 1863

You Could Look It Up.   —JAMES THURBER, story title,
> *The Saturday Evening Post,* 1941

[The phrase was a favorite expression of baseball manager Casey Stengel, but probably originated with Thurber's story about a manager who sends a midget up to bat. In 1951, Bill Veeck, owner of the St. Louis Browns, actually tried this maneuver.]

Get your facts first, and then you can distort them as much as you please.   —MARK TWAIN, quoted in
> Rudyard Kipling, *From Sea to Sea,* 1899

FAILINGS   See also MEDIOCRITY; MISTAKES

No rose without a thorn.

> —ANONYMOUS (FRENCH PROVERB)

Thou art weighed in the balances, and art found wanting.

> —BIBLE, *Daniel* 5:27

She had
A heart—how shall I say?—too soon made glad,
Too easily impressed

> —ROBERT BROWNING,
> *My Last Duchess,* 1842

The greatest of faults, I should say, is to be conscious of none.   —THOMAS CARLYLE, *On Heroes and*
> *Hero-Worship: The Hero as Prophet,* 1841

Sometimes even excellent Homer nods.

> —HORACE, *Art of Poetry,* c. 20–8 B.C.

Ignorance, pure ignorance.
>—SAMUEL JOHNSON, explaining in 1762 why in his
>*Dictionary* he had defined *pastern* as the knee of
>a horse, quoted in James Boswell,
>*Life of Johnson,* 1791

All men are liable to error; and most men are, in many points, by passion or interest, under temptation to it.
>—JOHN LOCKE, *Essay Concerning Human
>Understanding,* 1690

He's liked, but he's not well liked.
>—ARTHUR MILLER, *Death of a Salesman,* 1949

His only fault is that he has none.
>—PLINY THE YOUNGER, *Book IX,
>Letter 26,* A.D. 108–09

[Not a lovable feature according to William Hazlitt: "It is well that there is no one without a fault; for he would not have a friend in the world," *Characteristics,* c. 1821.]

O saisons, O chateaux
Quelle âme est sans defauts?
O seasons, O chateaux,
What soul is without flaws?
>—ARTHUR RIMBAUD, *A Season in Hell,* 1873

He wants the natural touch.
>—SHAKESPEARE, *Macbeth,* IV, ii

They say best men are molded out of faults:
And, for the most, become much more the better
For being a little bad.
>—SHAKESPEARE, *Measure for Measure,* V, i

But men are men, the best sometimes forget.
>—SHAKESPEARE, *Othello,* II, iii

[On confessing one's small faults, and hiding the large, see La Rochefoucauld at HONESTY & SINCERITY.]

FAILURE   See HAVES & HAVE-NOTS; RUIN;
WINNING & LOSING, VICTORY &
DEFEAT

FAIRNESS   See EVIDENCE; JUSTICE

FAITH   See also ATHEISM; GOD; RELIGION;
                                             SKEPTICISM

Unless you believe, you shall not understand.
                     —BIBLE, *Isaiah* 7:9 (Septuagint Version)
[A favorite saying of St. Augustine, who formulated it in several ways, including: "Understanding is the reward of faith"
and "We believe in order to know," *Joannis evangelium tractatus*. St. Anselm put it: *Credo ut intelligam*, "I believe in order that I may understand," *Proslogion*. He summed up his intellectual mission with the motto, "Faith seeking understanding."]

For by grace are ye saved through faith; and that not of yourselves; it is the gift of God.   —BIBLE, *Ephesians* 2:8

Faith without works is dead.   —BIBLE, *James* 2:20

You can do very little with faith, but you can do nothing without it.
     —SAMUEL BUTLER, *Rebelliousness* in *Notebooks*, 1912

"Well, now that we have seen each other," said the Unicorn, "if you believe in me, I'll believe in you. Is that a bargain?"
     —LEWIS CARROLL, *Through the Looking-Glass*, 1872

Faith in a holy cause is to a considerable extent a substitute for the lost faith in ourselves.
                     —ERIC HOFFER, *The True Believer*, 1951

If you build it, he will come.
                     —W. P. KINSELLA, *Shoeless Joe*, 1982
[The book was adapted by Phil Alden Robinson for the 1989 movie *Field of Dreams*. The line is often quoted as, "If you build it, they will come." In the movie, the line was ". . . people will come." For "Say it ain't so, Joe" see SPORTS.]

The constant assertion of belief is an indication of fear.
                     —KRISHNAMURTI, d. 1986, *The Second Penguin
                                      Krishnamurti Reader*, 1991

Faith may be defined briefly as an illogical belief in the occurrence of the improbable.
> —H. L. MENCKEN, *Prejudices: Third Series,* 1922

Faith has need of the whole truth.
> —PIERRE TEILHARD DE CHARDIN,
> d. 1955, *The Appearance of Man,* 1965

[A Jesuit priest as well as a paleontologist, Teilhard de Chardin's attempts to integrate evolutionism with religion troubled his superiors in the Church so greatly that he was forbidden to publish this and his other philosophical works during his lifetime.]

Certum est quia impossibile.
It is certain because it is impossible.
> —TERTULLIAN, *De Carne Cristi,* c. A.D. 200

[Traditionally given as *Credo quia impossibile,* "I believe because it is impossible."]

To believe in God is to yearn for His existence, and furthermore, it is to act as if He did exist.
> —MIGUEL DE UNAMUNO,
> *The Tragic Sense of Life,* 1913

A faith which does not doubt is a dead faith.
> —MIGUEL DE UNAMUNO, *The
> Agony of Christianity,* 1925

[For more on faith and doubt, see the first Bible quote at SKEPTICISM.]

FALL   See NATURE: SEASONS

FAME   See SUCCESS & FAME

FAMILIARITY   See INTIMACY & FAMILIARITY

FAMILY See also CHILDREN & CHILDHOOD; HOME;
              MARRIAGE; PARENTS & PARENTHOOD

He that hath a wife and children hath given hostages to fortune; for they are impediments to great enterprises.
> —FRANCIS BACON, *Of Marriage and Single Life,* 1625

[Adapted from the Roman writer Lucan: "I have a wife, I have sons; all these hostages have I given to fortune," *On the Civil War,* c. A.D. 60. Lucan's uncles were Seneca and Gallio; all three were forced by Nero to take their own lives.]

Accidents will occur in the best regulated families.
—CHARLES DICKENS, *David Copperfield,* 1849–50

It is a melancholy truth that even great men have their poor relations.   —CHARLES DICKENS, *Bleak House,* 1852

Good families are generally worse than any others.
—ANTHONY HOPE, *The Prisoner of Zenda,* 1894

Home life ceases to be free and beautiful as soon as it is founded on borrowing and debt.
—HENRIK IBSEN, *A Doll's House,* 1879

One would be in less danger
From the wiles of the stranger
If one's own kin and kith
Were more fun to be with.
—OGDEN NASH, *Family Court* in *Hard Lines,* 1931

Crabbèd age and youth cannot live together;
Youth is full of pleasance, age is full of care.
—SHAKESPEARE, *The Passionate Pilgrim,* 1599

Happy families are all alike; every unhappy family is un-happy in its own way.
—LEO TOLSTOY, *Anna Karenina,* 1875–77
[One of the best-known opening lines to a novel. For other first lines see, Jane Austen at MARRIAGE; Boccaccio at COMPASSION & PITY; Edward Bulwer-Lytton at NATURE: WIND & WEATHER; John Bunyan at SLEEP & DREAMS; Chaucer at NATURE: SEASONS; Dante at MIDDLE AGE & MID-LIFE CRISIS; Dickens at TURBULENT TIMES; Ford Madox Ford at STORIES; L. P. Hartley at PAST, THE; Marx & Engels at HISTORY; Melville at SEAS & SHIPS, SAILING & BOATING; Norman MacLean at SPORTS; Nabokov at LOVE, EXPRESSIONS OF; Spock at PARENTS.]

Birds in their little nest agree;
And 'tis a shameful sight,
When children of one family
Fall out, and chide, and fight.
—ISAAC WATTS, *Love Between Brothers
and Sisters* in *Divine Songs,* 1715

FANATICISM   See ENTHUSIASM, ENERGY, & ZEAL

FAREWELLS

All farewells should be sudden.
—LORD BYRON, *Sardanapalus,* 1821

Parting is all we know of heaven,
And all we need of hell.
—EMILY DICKINSON, poem no. 1732 (unknown date)

Good night, good night! Parting is such sweet sorrow
That I shall say good night till it be morrow.
—SHAKESPEARE, *Romeo and Juliet,* II, ii
[Shakespeare wrote several "good nights," cheerful and griev-
ous, including: "Good night, ladies, good night. Sweet ladies,
good night, good night," *Hamlet,* IV, v; and also from *Hamlet,*
Horatio's farewell to his dying friend, "Good night, sweet
Prince," V, ii.]

Forever, and forever, farewell, Cassius!
If we do meet again, why we shall smile;
If not, why then this parting was well made.
—SHAKESPEARE, *Julius Caesar,* V, i

There is a time for departure, even when there is no certain
place to go.
—TENNESSEE WILLIAMS, *Camino Real,* 1953

FASHION & CLOTHES   See also APPEARANCES;
STYLE

A little of what you call frippery is very necessary towards
looking like the rest of the world.
—ABIGAIL ADAMS, letter to John Adams, May 1, 1780

It is not only fine feathers that make fine birds.
                —AESOP, *The Jay and the Peacock,* 6th cent. B.C.

Clothes make the man.
                              —ANONYMOUS (LATIN PROVERB)

The fashion of this world passeth away.
                              —BIBLE, *I Corinthians* 7:31

Clothes never shut up.
                —SUSAN BROWNMILLER, *Femininity,* 1984

The sense of being well-dressed gives a feeling of inward
tranquillity which religion is powerless to bestow.
                —RALPH WALDO EMERSON, *Social Aims*
                              in *Letters and Social Aims,* 1876
[He was reporting a comment by Miss C. F. Forbes.]

Good clothes open all doors.
                —THOMAS FULLER, *Gnomologia,* 1732

A sweet disorder in the dress
Kindles in clothes a wantonness.

                              —ROBERT HERRICK,
                Delight in Disorder in *Hesperides,* 1648

If thou art clean and warm, it is sufficient, for more doth
but rob the poor and please the wanton.
                —WILLIAM PENN, *Some Fruits of Solitude,* 1693

Nothing is so hideous as an obsolete fashion.
                              —STENDAHL, *On Love,* 1822

The apparel oft proclaims the man.
                              —SHAKESPEARE, *Hamlet,* I, iii

Beware of all enterprises that require new clothes.
                              —HENRY DAVID THOREAU,
                              Economy in *Walden,* 1854

All dressed up, with nowhere to go.
                —WILLIAM ALLEN WHITE, attributed, 1916
[White, influential editor of the Kansas newspaper *Emporia
Gazette,* was referring to the Progressive Party after Theodore

Roosevelt, the party's presidential candidate in 1912, endorsed Republican presidential candidate Charles Evans Hughes in 1916. According to Henry F. Woods in *American Sayings* (1945), White's actual words were: "All dressed up in their fighting clothes with nowhere to go."]

FATE   See also LUCK; RESPONSIBILITY;
                                     SELF-RELIANCE

What's bred in the bone will not out of the flesh.
              —ANONYMOUS (ENGLISH PROVERB)

I want to seize fate by the throat.
              —LUDWIG VAN BEETHOVEN, letter to
                   Dr. Franz Wegeler, Nov. 16, 1801

In my beginning is my end.
              —T. S. ELIOT, *Four Quartets, East Coker,* 1940
[This opens the poem. The closing is "In my end is my beginning," which was also the motto of Mary Queen of Scots.]

A man's character is his fate.
                        —HERACLITUS, c. 500 B.C.,
                          quoted in Diogenes Laërtius,
                   Lives of Eminent Philosophers, 3rd cent. A.D.

We are spinning our own fates, good or evil, never to be undone.   —WILLIAM JAMES,
                   The Principles of Psychology, 1890

I claim not to have controlled events, but confess plainly that events have controlled me.
              —ABRAHAM LINCOLN, letter to
                   A. G. Hodges, Apr. 4, 1864

O! I am Fortune's fool.
              —SHAKESPEARE, *Romeo and Juliet,* III, i

Destiny is an invention of the weak and the resigned.
              —IGNAZIO SILONE, *Bread and Wine,* 1937

For man is man and master of his fate.
              —ALFRED, LORD TENNYSON, *Lancelot and Elaine*
                   in *Idylls of the King,* 1859–85

[For "I am the master of my fate," see W. E. Henley at SELF-RELIANCE. Henley and Tennyson were of the same generation and culture, Victorian England.]

Man may his fate foresee, but not prevent. . . .
'Tis better to be fortunate than wise.
　　　　　—JOHN WEBSTER, *The White Devil*, 1612

FATHERS　　　　　See PARENTS & PARENTHOOD

FATNESS　　　　　See BODY, HUMAN

FAULTS　　　　　See FAILINGS; MISTAKES

FEAR　　　　　See also COURAGE

A fool without fear is sometimes wiser than an angel with fear.
　　　　　—NANCY ASTOR, *My Two Countries*, 1920

Fear has many eyes and can see things underground.
　　　　　—CERVANTES, *Don Quixote*, 1605–15

I will show you fear in a handful of dust.
　　　　　—T. S. ELIOT, *The Waste Land*, 1922
[In 1937, English novelist Evelyn Waugh used *A Handful of Dust* as the title of a grim comic novel.]

The thing I fear most is fear.
　　　　　—MONTAIGNE, *Essays: To the Reader*, 1580–88
[See also Wellington, below; for Franklin D. Roosevelt's version, see AMERICAN HISTORY: MEMORABLE MOMENTS.]

Fear is the main source of superstition, and one of the main sources of cruelty. To conquer fear is the beginning of wisdom.　　　　　—BERTRAND RUSSELL, *An Outline of Intellectual Rubbish*, 1950

If we let things terrify us, life will not be worth living.
　　　　　—SENECA, *Epistles*, 1st cent. A.D.

The only thing I am afraid of is fear.
　　　　　—DUKE OF WELLINGTON, quoted in Philip Henry, Earl of Stanhope, *Notes of Conversations with . . . Wellington*, 1888
[In addition to Montaigne, quoted above, and Franklin D. Roose-

velt, cited at AMERICAN HISTORY: MEMORABLE MO-
MENTS, Francis Bacon, Henry David Thoreau, and others
made similar comments. Thoreau put it: "Nothing is so much
to be feared as fear," *Journal,* Sept. 7, 1851.]

FEMINISM   See WOMEN; WOMEN & MEN

FIGHTING BACK   See APPEASEMENT VS.
                          RESISTANCE; STRENGTH

FITNESS   See PHYSICAL FITNESS

FLAG   See PATRIOTISM

FLATTERY

Every woman is infallibly to be gained by every sort of
flattery, and every man by one sort or other.
> —EARL OF CHESTERFIELD, letter to
> his son, Mar. 16, 1752

Imitation is the sincerest form of flattery.
> —CHARLES CALEB COLTON, *The Lacon,* 1820–22

But when I tell him he hates flatterers,
He says he does, being then most flattered.
> —SHAKESPEARE, *Julius Caesar,* II, i

None are more taken in by flattery than the proud who wish
to be first and are not.   —SPINOZA, *Ethics,* 1677

Flattery is all right—if you don't inhale.
> —ADLAI STEVENSON, speech, Feb. 1, 1961
[Also used by Sen. Hubert Humphrey in the same era.]

'Tis an old maxim in the schools,
That flattery's the food of fools;
Yet now and then your men of wit
Will condescend to take a bit.
> —JONATHAN SWIFT, *Cadenus and Vanessa,* 1713

FLESH   See BODY, HUMAN

FLOWERS   See NATURE: GARDENS,
                          FLOWERS, & TREES

FOOD, WINE, & EATING
See also ALCOHOL & DRINKING;
EPITAPHS (for a waiter, McCord)

A gentleman does not go near a kitchen.
—ANONYMOUS (JAPANESE SAYING)

A man hath no better thing under the sun than to eat, and to drink, and to be merry. —BIBLE, *Ecclesiastes* 8:15

A feast is made for laughter, and wine maketh merry.
—*Ibid.* 10:19
[The passage is cited at greater length at MONEY.]

Bring hither the fatted calf and kill it; and let us eat, and be merry. —BIBLE, *Luke* 15:23

The destiny of countries depends on the way they feed themselves. —ANTHELME BRILLAT-SAVARIN,
The Physiology of Taste, 1825

Tell me what you eat, and I will tell you what you are.
—*Ibid.*

Doubtless God could have made a better berry, but doubtless God never did.
—WILLIAM BUTLER, d. 1618, attributed in Izaak
Walton, *The Compleat Angler,* 2nd ed., 1655
[This is in praise of the strawberry. Butler also provided useful advice on oysters: "It is unseasonable and unwholesome in all months that have not an *r* in their name to eat an oyster," *Dyet's Dry Dinner,* 1599.
In the 19th century, English novelist Elizabeth Gaskell agreed with Butler on the best berry, speculating that heaven must consist largely of "eating strawberries and cream forever," cited in Jenny Uglow, *Elizabeth Gaskell: A Habit of Stories,* 1993.]

Since Eve ate apples, much depends on dinner.
—LORD BYRON, *Don Juan,* 1819–24

Hunger is the best sauce in the world.
—CERVANTES, *Don Quixote,* 1605–15

If I cannot have too many truffles, I will do without truffles.
—COLETTE, cited in *Colette: A Passion for Life*, 1986

Life is too short to stuff a mushroom.
—SHIRLEY CONRAN, epigraph, *Superwoman*, 1975

It's a very odd thing—
as odd as can be—
That whatever Miss T. eats
Turns into Miss T.
—WALTER DE LA MARE, *Miss T.* in *Peacock Pie*, 1913

Gluttony is an emotional escape, a sign something is eating us.
—PETER DE VRIES, *Comfort Me with Apples*, 1956

Most vigitaryans I ever see look enough like their food to be classed as cannybals.
—FINLEY PETER DUNNE, *Casual Observations,*
in *Mr. Dooley's Philosophy*, 1900

Der Mensch ist, was er isst.
Man is what he eats.
—LUDWIG FEUERBACH,
Blätter für Literarische Unterhaltung, Nov. 12, 1850

Eat to live, and not live to eat. —BENJAMIN FRANKLIN,
Poor Richard's Almanac, May, 1733
[The idea is old and has been attributed to Socrates.]

More die in the United States of too much food than of too little.
—JOHN KENNETH GALBRAITH,
The Affluent Society, 1958

I want there to be no peasant in my kingdom so poor that he cannot have a chicken in his pot every Sunday.
—HENRY IV, attributed
[The modern political slogan "A chicken in every pot" was the title of a Republican campaign flyer in the 1928 presidential election. In his nomination acceptance speech, the Republican candidate, Pres. Herbert Hoover, prophesied an end to poverty in America, but did not specifically call for a chicken in every pot.]

He was a bold man who first swallowed an oyster.
>—JAMES I, attributed by Thomas Fuller,
>Jonathan Swift, and others

Oats, n. A grain, which in England is generally given to horses, but in Scotland supports the people.
>—SAMUEL JOHNSON, *Dictionary,* 1755
[Lord Elibank countered, "Very true, and where will you find such horses, and such men?"]

Some people have a foolish way of not minding, or pretending not to mind, what they eat. For my part, I mind my belly very studiously, and very carefully; for I look upon it, that he who does not mind his belly will hardly mind anything else. —SAMUEL JOHNSON, Aug. 5, 1763, quoted in
>James Boswell, *Life of Johnson,* 1791

Qu'ils mangent de la brioche.
Let them eat cake. —MARIE ANTOINETTE,
>traditional but wrong attribution
[The remark, perhaps apocryphal, was attributed to others much earlier.]

Lunch kills half of Paris, supper the other half.
>—MONTESQUIEU, d. 1755, *Variétés*

A good cook is like a sorceress who dispenses happiness.
>—ELSA SCHIAPARELLI, *Shocking Life,* 1954

He hath eaten me out of house and home.
>—SHAKESPEARE, *Henry IV, Part II,* II, i

I am a great eater of beef and I believe that does harm to my wit. —SHAKESPEARE, *Twelfth Night,* I, iii

Digestion is the great secret of life. —SYDNEY SMITH,
>letter to Arthur Kinglake, Sept. 30, 1837
[Rev. Smith, an Anglican clergyman, was a leading scholar and wit of his day. As a young man, he tutored at Edinburgh University, where he co-founded the prestigious *Edinburgh Review.* While at that university, he also studied medicine, and thus developed a professional appreciation of digestion.]

In eating, a third of the stomach should be filled with food, a third with drink, and the rest left empty.   —TALMUD

It's a naïve domestic burgundy, without any breeding, but I think you'll be amused by its presumption.
                                        —JAMES THURBER, cartoon caption,
                                            The New Yorker, Mar. 27, 1937

It's broccoli dear.
I say it's spinach, and I say the hell with it.
                            —E. B. WHITE, caption for a Carl Rose cartoon,
                                            The New Yorker, Dec. 8, 1928

One cannot think well, love well, sleep well, if one has not dined well.
        —VIRGINIA WOOLF, *A Room of One's Own*, 1929

FOOLS & STUPIDITY   See also TALK

Never give a sucker an even break.   —ANONYMOUS
[Popularized by Prohibition-era nightclub owner Texas Guinan about 1925, according to H. L. Mencken. Possibly originated by Edward F. Albee, co-owner of the Keith-Albee circuit of vaudeville theaters. Others credit W. C. Fields, who ad-libbed the line in the 1923 play *Poppy* and used it as a movie title in 1941.]

There's a sucker born every minute.
                                    —P. T. BARNUM, attributed
[Robert Pelton, curator of the Barnum Museum in Bridgeport, Conn., maintains that credit for the quote actually should be given to a friend of Barnum's, a con man by the name of Joseph "Paper Collar" Bessimer.]

A fool uttereth all his mind.   —BIBLE, *Proverbs* 29:11

For ye suffer fools gladly, seeing ye yourselves are wise.
                                    —BIBLE, *II Corinthians* 11:19

Wise men profit more by fools, than fools by wise men; for wise men avoid the mistakes of fools, but fools do not imitate the good examples of wise men.
                            —CATO THE ELDER, c. 200 B.C., quoted in
                                Plutarch's *Parallel Lives*, c. A.D. 100

A fool must now and then be right by chance.
                        —WILLIAM COWPER, *Conversation*, 1782

We are the hollow men
We are the stuffed men
Leaning together
Headpiece filled with straw. Alas!
                        —T. S. ELIOT, *The Hollow Men*, 1925

Nothing is more humiliating than to see idiots succeed in enterprises we have failed in.
                        —FLAUBERT, *Sentimental Education*, 1869
[The proverbial consolation is: Fortune favors fools. Ben Jonson in *The Alchemist* (1610) referred to "Fortune, that favors fools," while John Gay, in *Fables* (1727, 1738—two books of verse) wrote: " 'Tis a gross error held in schools / That Fortune always favors fools."]

There are some who speak one moment before they think.
                        —LA BRUYÈRE, *Les Caractères*, 1688

Small things amuse small minds.   —DORIS LESSING,
        A Woman on a Roof in *A Man and Two Women*, 1965
[A popular saying.]

For fools rush in where angels fear to tread.
                        —ALEXANDER POPE, *An Essay on Criticism*, 1711

Against stupidity, the gods themselves struggle in vain.
                        —J. C. F. VON SCHILLER, *The Maid of Orleans*, 1801

Lord, what fools these mortals be!
                        —SHAKESPEARE, *A Midsummer Night's Dream*, III, ii
[Seneca said the same thing in the first century A.D., though in Latin, in his *Epistles*: "*Tanta stultitia mortalium est.*"]

Let us be thankful for the fools. But for them the rest of us could not succeed.   —MARK TWAIN, *Pudd'nhead Wilson's New Calendar* in *Following the Equator*, 1897

There is no sin except stupidity.   —OSCAR WILDE,
                        The Critic as Artist, 1891

FORCE   See VIOLENCE & FORCE

FORGIVENESS & MERCY   See also COMPASSION &
PITY; ENEMIES; TOLERANCE
& UNDERSTANDING

Blessed are the merciful: for they shall obtain mercy.
—BIBLE, *Matthew* 5:7
[For other verses from the Sermon on the Mount, see VIRTUE.]

Forgive, and ye shall be forgiven.   —BIBLE, *Luke* 6:37
[More of this verse is cited under TOLERANCE & UNDER-
STANDING.]

Rejoice with me; for I have found my sheep which was
lost. . . . joy shall be in heaven over one that repenteth,
more than over ninety and nine just persons, which need no
repentance.   —BIBLE, *Luke* 15:6,7

Father forgive them; for they know not what they do.
—*Ibid.* 23:34

Forgive but never forget.   —JOHN F. KENNEDY, d. 1963,
saying attributed by Theodore Sorenson in *Kennedy*, 1965

To err is human, to forgive, divine.
—ALEXANDER POPE,
An Essay on Criticism, 1711

The quality of mercy is not strained.
It droppeth as the gentle rain from heaven.
—SHAKESPEARE, *The Merchant of Venice*, IV, i

Sweet mercy is nobility's true badge.
—SHAKESPEARE, *Titus Andronicus*, I, i

It is by forgiving that one is forgiven.
—MOTHER TERESA, *For the Brotherhood of Man*, 1980

Love truth, but pardon error.
—VOLTAIRE, *Sept discours en vers sur l'homme*, 1738

FORM   See ARTS: AESTHETICS

FORTUNE   See FATE; HAPPINESS; LUCK; MONEY

FRANCE   See NATIONS

FREEDOM See also APPEASEMENT VS. RESISTANCE;
DEMOCRACY; FREE SPEECH; RIGHTS

Let my people go.   —BIBLE, *Exodus* 5:1

The condition upon which God has given liberty to man is
eternal vigilance.
            —JOHN PHILPOT CURRAN, speech, July 10, 1790
[Curran, an Irish orator and magistrate, inspired the American
abolitionist Wendell Phillips, who said, "Eternal vigilance is
the price of liberty" in a speech entitled *Public Opinion,* given
at the Massachusetts Anti-Slavery Society, Jan. 28, 1852.]

You can only protect your liberties in this world by protecting the other man's freedom. You can only be free if I
am free.   —CLARENCE DARROW, address to the jury,
                                        People v. Lloyd, 1920

I only ask to be free. The butterflies are free.
            —CHARLES DICKENS, *Bleak House,* 1852

Liberty lies in the hearts of men and women; when it dies
there, no constitution, no law, no court can save it.
            —LEARNED HAND, *The Spirit of Liberty,*
                                        speech, May 21, 1944

There can be no real freedom without the freedom to fail.
            —ERIC HOFFER, *The Ordeal of Change,* 1964

What stands if freedom fall?
      —RUDYARD KIPLING, *For All We Have and Are,* 1914

Those who deny freedom to others deserve it not for
themselves. —ABRAHAM LINCOLN, letter to H. L. Pierce
                                        et al., Apr. 6, 1859

Like bone to the human body, and the axle to the wheel,
and the song to a bird, and air to the wing, thus is liberty
the essence of life. Whatever is done without it is imperfect.
            —JOSÉ MARTÍ, d. 1895, quoted by William Pfaff,
                                        The New Yorker, May 27, 1985

License they mean when they cry liberty.
            —JOHN MILTON, *On the Same,* written c. 1645
["The Same" refers to his sonnet *On the Detraction which Followed Upon My Writing Certain Treatises.*]

A nation may lose its liberties in a day, and not miss them for a century. —MONTESQUIEU, *The Spirit of Laws,* 1748

Liberty is the right to do everything which the laws allow.
—*Ibid.*

Those men and women are fortunate who are born at a time when a great struggle for human freedom is in progress.
—EMMELINE PANKHURST, *My Own Story,* 1914

Fais ce que voudras.
Do what thou wilt.
—FRANÇOIS RABELAIS, *Gargantua,* Book I, 1532
[This was the only rule at Gargantua's Abbey of Thélème; the rationale was: "because men and women that are free, well born, well instructed, and conversant in honest Companies, have naturally an instinct and spur that prompteth them ever to virtuous actions, and withdraws them from vice, the which is called honor."
For a modern update see Joseph Campbell at HAPPINESS.]

O liberty, O liberty, what crimes are committed in your name. —MADAME ROLAND, en route to the guillotine in 1793, attributed in Lamartine, *Histoire des Girondins,* 1847

We look forward to a world founded upon four essential freedoms [freedom of speech, freedom of worship, freedom from want, freedom from fear].
—FRANKLIN D. ROOSEVELT, speech, Jan. 6, 1941

Man is condemned to be free. —JEAN-PAUL SARTRE, *Existentialism Is a Humanism,* 1946

Carelessness about our security is dangerous; carelessness about our freedom is also dangerous.
—ADLAI STEVENSON, speech, Oct. 7, 1952

The secret of happiness is freedom, and the secret of freedom, courage.
—THUCYDIDES, funeral speech for Pericles, 429 B.C., in *The History of the Peloponnesian War,* c. 400 B.C.

I had reasoned this out in my mind: There was two things
I had a right to, liberty and death. If I could not have one,
I would have the other, for no man should take me alive.
>—HARRIET TUBMAN, quoted in Sarah H. Bradford,
>*Harriet, The Moses of Her People,* 1869

Caged birds accept each other but flight is what they long
for.   —TENNESSEE WILLIAMS, *Camino Real,* 1953

FREE SPEECH   See also CENSORSHIP;
FREEDOM; PRESS, THE

In a free state there must be free speech.
>—DOMITIAN, d. A.D. 96, attributed
[Domitian's rule of the Roman Empire—from A.D. 81–96—
became increasingly despotic, ending in a reign of terror.]

Let reason be opposed to reason, and argument to argument, and every good government will be safe.
>—THOMAS ERSKINE, *In Defense of
>Thomas Paine,* Dec. 20, 1792

The most stringent protection of free speech would not protect a man in falsely shouting fire in a theater and causing
a panic.   —OLIVER WENDELL HOLMES, JR.,
Schenck v. U.S., 1919

When men have realized that time has upset many fighting
faiths, they may come to believe . . . that the ultimate good
desired is reached by the free trade in ideas—that the best
test of truth is the power of the thought to get itself accepted
in the competition of the market. . . . That at any rate is
the theory of our Constitution.
>—OLIVER WENDELL HOLMES, JR.,
>dissent, *Abrams v. the U.S.,* 1919

I disapprove of what you say, but I will defend to the death
your right to say it.   —VOLTAIRE, d. 1778, attributed
[The source for the attribution is E. Beatrice Hall's *The Friends
of Voltaire.* But the author later said that the statement was
meant as a paraphrase, not an exact quote. *Bartlett's* credits
Norbert Guterman's *A Book of French Quotations* with finding
the closest verifiable quotation, in a letter from Voltaire to

M. le Riche, Feb. 6, 1770: "I detest what you write, but I would give my life to make it possible for you to continue to write."]

FREE WILL
See WILL

FRIENDS & FRIENDSHIP
See also OLD THINGS, OLD FRIENDS

Friends are born, not made.
—HENRY ADAMS,
The Education of Henry Adams, 1907

One friend in a life is much, two are many, three are hardly possible.
—*Ibid.*

Greater love hath no man than this, that a man lay down his life for his friends.
—BIBLE, *John* 15:13

Forsake not an old friend; for the new is not comparable to him; a new friend is as new wine; when it is old, thou shalt drink it with pleasure.
—BIBLE, *Ecclesiasticus* 9:10

My true friends have always given me that supreme proof of devotion, a spontaneous aversion for the man I loved.
—COLETTE, *Break of Day,* 1928

Have no friends not equal to yourself.
—CONFUCIUS, *Analects,* 6th–5th cent. B.C.

A friend may well be reckoned the masterpiece of nature.
—RALPH WALDO EMERSON,
Friendship in *Essays: First Series,* 1841

A friend is a person with whom I may be sincere. Before him, I may think aloud.
—*Ibid.*

If I had to choose between betraying my country and betraying my friend, I hope I should have the guts to betray my country.
—E. M. FORSTER, *What I Believe* in
Two Cheers for Democracy, 1951

Friendship needs no words—it is solitude delivered from the anguish of loneliness.
—DAG HAMMARSKJÖLD, *Markings,* 1964

If a man does not make new acquaintances as he advances through life, he will soon find himself left alone.
—SAMUEL JOHNSON, Apr. 1775, quoted in
James Boswell, *Life of Johnson,* 1791

A true friend is the most precious of all possessions and the one we take the least thought about acquiring.
—LA ROCHEFOUCAULD, *Maxims,* 1678

The zeal of friends it is that knocks me down, and not the hate of enemies. —J.C.F. VON SCHILLER,
The Death of Wallenstein, 1798
[See also the remark by the Duc de Villars, below.]

Those friends thou hast, and their adoption tried,
Grapple them to thy soul with hoops of steel.
—SHAKESPEARE, *Hamlet,* I, iii

To me, fair friend, you never can be old.
—SHAKESPEARE, sonnet 104

The holy passion of friendship is so sweet and steady and loyal and enduring in nature that it will last through a whole lifetime, if not asked to lend money.
—MARK TWAIN, *Pudd'nhead Wilson's Calendar*
in *Pudd'nhead Wilson,* 1894

May God defend me from my friends; I can defend myself from my enemies. —DUC DE VILLARS, c. 1700
[Sometimes attributed to Voltaire.]

It is not often that someone comes along who is a true friend and a good writer. —E. B. WHITE, *Charlotte's Web,* 1952

FUTURE, THE See also ENVIRONMENT, THE;
POPULATION; PROGRESS

The future struggles against being mastered.
—ANONYMOUS (LATIN PROVERB)

You cannot fight against the future. Time is on our side.
—WILLIAM GLADSTONE, speech on
the Reform Bill, 1866

I hold that man is in the right who is most closely in league with the future.
　　—HENRIK IBSEN, letter to Georg Brandes, Jan. 3, 1882

I like the dreams of the future better than the history of the past.　　　　　　　　　—THOMAS JEFFERSON, letter to
John Adams, Aug. 1, 1816

You ain't heard nothin' yet, folks.
　　　　　　　—AL JOLSON, *The Jazz Singer,* 1927

But this *long run* is a misleading guide to current affairs. *In the long run* we are all dead.
　　　　　　—JOHN MAYNARD KEYNES,
The Tract on Monetary Reform, 1923

I'll think of it all tomorrow at Tara. . . . After all, tomorrow is another day.
　　—MARGARET MITCHELL, *Gone With the Wind,* 1936

If you want a picture of the future, imagine a boot stamping on a human face—forever.
　　　　　　—GEORGE ORWELL, *1984,* 1948

There's a gude time coming.
　　　　　—SIR WALTER SCOTT, *Rob Roy,* 1817

I have seen the future and it works.
—LINCOLN STEFFENS, letter to Marie Howe, Apr. 3, 1919
[Steffens made this remark after visiting post-Revolutionary Russia, and it became a favorite saying of his. In his *Autobiography* (1931), Steffens wrote that after returning from Russia he told financier Bernard Baruch, "I have been over into the future and it works."]

Time and space—time to be alone, space to move about—these may well be the greatest scarcities of tomorrow.
　　—EDWIN WAY TEALE, *Autumn Across America,* 1956

G

GAMBLING See GAMES

GAMES See also SPORTS; WINNING & LOSING, VICTORY & DEFEAT

To play billiards well is a sign of misspe.t youth.
—ANONYMOUS
[Often attributed to the Herbert Spencer, the 19th-century philosopher and advocate of Darwin's theory of evolution. In a letter to a Mr. Charles Roupell, he wrote, "It was remarked to me . . . that to play billiards was the sign of an ill-spent youth."]

There are two great pleasures in gambling: winning and losing. —ANONYMOUS (FRENCH PROVERB)

Life's too short for chess.
—HENRY J. BYRON, d. 1839, *Our Boys*

Poets do not go mad, but chess players do.
—G. K. CHESTERTON, *Orthodoxy*, 1908

When in doubt, win the trick. —EDMOND HOYLE,
rule 12 for whist, *Hoyle's Games*, 1746

I am sorry I have not learnt to play at cards. It is very useful in life: it generates kindness and consolidates society.
—SAMUEL JOHNSON, Nov. 21, 1773,
quoted by James Boswell,
Journal of a Tour to the Hebrides, 1785

Cards are war in disguise of a sport. —CHARLES LAMB,
Mrs. Battle's Opinions on Whist in *Essays of Elia*, 1825

The roulette table pays nobody except him who keeps it. Nevertheless, a passion for gaming is common, though a passion for keeping roulette wheels is unknown.
—GEORGE BERNARD SHAW,
Maxims for Revolutionists in *Man and Superman,* 1903

GARDENS   See NATURE: GARDENS, FLOWERS, & TREES

GENERATIONS   See also AGE & AGING; FAMILY; LIFE; YOUTH

One generation passeth away, and another generation cometh: but the earth abideth forever.
The sun also ariseth.   —BIBLE, *Ecclesiastes* 1:4-5

Let us now praise famous men, and our fathers that begat us.   —*Ibid.* 44:1

The gods
Visit the sins of the fathers upon the children.
—EURIPIDES, *Phrixus,* fragment, 5th cent. B.C.
[Similar lines are found in *Exodus, The Merchant of Venice,* and elsewhere.]

As is the generations of leaves, so is that of humanity.
The wind scatters the leaves on the ground, but the live timber
Burgeons with leaves again in the season of spring returning.
So one generation of men will grow while another
Dies.   —HOMER, *Iliad,* 8th cent. B.C.

The generations of living things pass in a short time, and like runners hand on the torch of life.   —LUCRETIUS,
On the Nature of Things, c. 57 B.C.

Each generation wastes a little more of the future with greed and lust for riches.   —DON MARQUIS,
archy and mehitabel, 1927

Every generation revolts against its fathers and makes friends with its grandfathers.
—LEWIS MUMFORD, *The Brown Decades,* 1931

The oldest hath borne most: we that are young,
Shall never see so much, nor live so long.
                              —SHAKESPEARE, *King Lear*, V, iii

You are all a lost generation.   —GERTRUDE STEIN,
                              letter to Ernest Hemingway, 1926
[Hemingway used this as the epigraph of *The Sun Also Rises*,
1926. Stein herself picked up this observation from a French
garage owner who called his young mechanics, *"une généra-
tion perdue."*]

Every moment dies a man,
Every moment one is born.
  —ALFRED, LORD TENNYSON, *The Vision of Sin*, 1842
[Charles Babbage, inventor of the analytical engine, forerunner
of the modern computer, put matters this way in a letter to
Tennyson: "Every moment dies a man. Every moment one and
one sixteenth is born."]

GENEROSITY   See CHARITY: PHILANTHROPY;
                                      HOSPITALITY

GENIUS   See also GREATNESS; MADNESS (Dryden);
                      MIND, THOUGHT, & UNDERSTANDING;
                             VISION & VISIONARIES

A genius is a man who has two great ideas.
              —JACOB BRONOWSKI, *The Ascent of Man*, 1973

Genius . . . means transcendent capacity of taking trouble.
                              —THOMAS CARLYLE,
                      Life of Frederick the Great, 1858–65

Genius is one percent inspiration and ninety-nine percent
perspiration.   —THOMAS ALVA EDISON, said c. 1903,
                      reported in *Harper's* magazine, Sept. 1932

Towering genius disdains a beaten path. It seeks regions
hitherto unexplored.   —ABRAHAM LINCOLN,
                              speech, Jan. 27, 1838

Genius is an African who dreams up snow.
                      —VLADIMIR NABOKOV, *The Gift*, 1937–38

There is no great genius without some touch of madness.
—SENECA, *On Tranquillity of the Mind,* 1st cent. A.D.
[Based on Aristotle; see MADNESS.]

Everybody is born with genius, but most people only keep
it a few minutes.
—EDGARD VARÈSE quoted by Martha Graham,
interview, *The New York Times,* Mar. 31, 1985

GERMANY   See NATIONS

GETTING AWAY FROM IT ALL   See ESCAPE;
                                          TRAVEL

GIVING   See CHARITY: PHILANTHROPY

GLORY   See SUCCESS & FAME; WAR

GOD   See also CREATION, DIVINE; FAITH;
                    JESUS; NATURE; PRAYERS;
                    PROVIDENCE, DIVINE; RELIGION

God is not dead but alive and well and working on a much
less ambitious project.   —ANONYMOUS
[This reported graffito has been widely quoted, but it may be
apocryphal. Some sources trace it to London; *The Penguin Dictionary of Modern Quotations* says that it was noted in the
Guardian newspaper, Nov. 27, 1975.]

I am all that has been, and that is, and that shall remain,
and no one unworthy has ever unraveled, loosened, or even
touched the surface of my woven veil.   —ANONYMOUS,
carving on an ancient statue of Pallas Athena,
cited in Plutarch's *Parallel Lives,* c. A.D. 100

God is that, the greater than which cannot be conceived.
—ST. ANSELM, *Proslogion*

We know what God is not, but we cannot know what he is.
—ST. AUGUSTINE, *On the Trinity,* A.D. 400–16

And God said unto Moses, I AM THAT I AM.
—BIBLE, *Exodus* 3:14

The Lord is my shepherd; I shall not want.

—BIBLE, *Psalms* 23:1

[The entire psalm is given at PROVIDENCE, DIVINE.]

God is our refuge and strength, a very present help in trouble. —*Ibid.* 46:1

Thy word is a lamp unto my feet, and a light unto my path.

—*Ibid.* 119:25

His mercy endureth forever. —*Ibid.* 136:1

With God all things are possible. —BIBLE, *Matthew* 19:26

Thou shalt love the Lord thy God with all thy heart, and with all thy soul, and with all thy mind. —*Ibid.* 22:37

I am the resurrection, and the life. —BIBLE, *John* 11:25

In my Father's house are many mansions. —*Ibid.* 14:2

I am the way, the truth, and the life: no man cometh unto the Father, but by me. —*Ibid.* 14:6

God is no respecter of persons. —BIBLE, *Acts* 10:34

All things work together for good to them that love God.

—BIBLE, *Romans* 8:28

If God be for us, who can be against us? —*Ibid.* 8:31

He that loveth not knoweth not God, for God is love.

—BIBLE, *I John* 4:8

I am the Alpha and the Omega, the beginning and the end, the first and the last. —BIBLE, *Revelation* 22:13

A God who would let us prove his existence would be an idol. —DIETRICH BONHOEFFER, *No Rusty Swords,* translated posthumously, 1965

God is under repair. —CÉLINE, epigraph, *The School for Corpses,* 1938

Do not take liberties with the gods, or weary them.
—CONFUCIUS, *The Book of Rites,* 6th–5th cent. B.C.

Oh! for a closer walk with God.   —WILLIAM COWPER,
Walking with God in *Olney Hymns,* 1779

God moves in a mysterious way
His wonders to perform;
He plants his footsteps in the sea
And rides upon the storm.

—WILLIAM COWPER,
Light Shining out of Darkness in *Ibid.*

It is the final proof of God's omnipotence that he need not
exist in order to save us.
—PETER DE VRIES, *The Mackerel Plaza,* 1958

Raffiniert ist der Herr Gott, aber boshaft ist er nicht.
God is subtle, but he is not malicious.

—ALBERT EINSTEIN,
d. 1955, inscription in Fine Hall, Princeton University
[Alan L. Mackay, in *The Harvest of a Quiet Eye,* gives Ein-
stein's own translation as "God is slick, but he ain't mean." For
Einstein's dictum on God playing dice, see under SCIENCE:
PHYSICS & COSMOLOGY.]

God is a circle whose center is everywhere and whose circumference is nowhere.
—EMPEDOCLES, fragment, 5th cent. B.C.

At bottom God is nothing more than an exalted father.
—SIGMUND FREUD, *Totem and Taboo,* 1913

God, to me, it seems is a verb.
—R. BUCKMINSTER FULLER,
No More Secondhand God, 1963

Toward what should we aim if not toward God?
—ANDRÉ GIDE, *Thésée,* 1946

God lies ahead. . . . He depends on us. It is through us that
God is achieved.   —ANDRÉ GIDE, *Journals,* tr. 1948–51

God will forgive me, it is his business.
                                —HEINRICH HEINE,
        last words, Feb. 17, 1856, attributed in many sources,
            including the contemporaneous *Goncourt Journals*
[Heine spent the last eight years of his life suffering from a spinal disease on what he called his "mattress grave."]

The world is charged with the grandeur of God.
                                —GERARD MANLEY HOPKINS,
                                d. 1889, *God's Grandeur*
[Hopkins, a Jesuit priest and professor at Dublin University, sent his poems with letters to a longtime friend and fellow poet, Robert Bridges. None were published until Bridges assembled them in a single volume in 1918, nearly thirty years after Hopkins' death.]

An honest God's the noblest work of man.
                                —ROBERT G. INGERSOLL,
                        The Gods, and Other Lectures, 1876
[Also in *Further Extracts from the Notebooks* of Samuel Butler, published in 1934, more than three decades after the English writer's death. Both are a play on Alexander Pope's "An honest man's the noblest work of God." —see HONESTY & SINCERITY.]

My dear child, you must believe in God despite what the clergy tell you.   —BENJAMIN JOWETT, d. 1893,
                quoted by Margot Asquith, *Autobiography*, 1922
[For more on Jowett, see H. C. Beeching at EDUCATION.]

He is to us all-thing that is good and comfortable for our help. He is our clothing, for love; He enwraps us and envelops us, embraces and encloses us for tender love, that He may never leave us.   —JULIANA OF NORWICH,
                        Revelations of Divine Love, c. 1373–93

Nam homo proponit, sed Deus disponit.
For man proposes, but God disposes.
                                —THOMAS à KEMPIS,
                        Of the Imitation of Christ, c. 1420

A man with God is always in the majority.
                                —JOHN KNOX, d. 1572,
        inscription on the Reformation Monument in Geneva
[See also Andrew Jackson under COURAGE.]

He is the first and the last, the manifest and the hidden: and He knoweth all things. —KORAN, c. 610–32

Though the mills of God grind slowly, yet they grind exceedingly small. —FRIEDRICH VON LOGAU, *Retribution* in *Poetic Aphorisms*, 1654, translated by Henry Wadsworth Longfellow

[Cf. Zenobius, below.]

A mighty fortress is our God.
A bulwark never failing.
—MARTIN LUTHER, *A Mighty Fortress*, 1529

A safe stronghold our God is still,
A trusty shield and weapon. —*Ibid.*

It takes a long while for a naturally trustful person to reconcile himself to the idea that after all God will not help him.
—H. L. MENCKEN, *Minority Report: H. L. Mencken's Notebooks*, 1956

There is a very good saying that if triangles invented a god, they would make him three-sided.
—MONTESQUIEU, *Persian Letters*, 1721

Coincidence is God's way of remaining anonymous.
—BILL MOYERS, in *The New York Times*, Mar. 20, 1998

God is dead: but considering the state the species Man is in, there will perhaps be caves, for ages yet, in, which his shadow will be shown. —FRIEDRICH NIETZSCHE, *Die fröhliche Wissenschaft*, 1882

It is convenient that there be gods, and, as it is convenient, let us believe there are.
—OVID, *The Art of Love*, c. 2 B.C.

Be comforted. You would not be seeking Me if you had not found Me. —PASCAL, *Pensées*, 1670

He was a wise man who invented God.
—PLATO, *Sisyphus*, 4th cent. B.C.

[See also Voltaire, below.]

Lo, the poor Indian! whose untutored mind
Sees God in clouds, or hears him in the wind;
His soul proud science never taught to stray
Far as the solar walk, or milky way.
>—ALEXANDER POPE, *Essay on Man*, 1733–34

As flies to wanton boys are we to the gods.
They kill us for their sport.
>—SHAKESPEARE, *King Lear*, IV, i

Closer is He than breathing, and nearer than hands and feet.
>—ALFRED LORD TENNYSON,
>*The Higher Pantheism*, 1869

Let us do something beautiful for God.
>—MOTHER TERESA, motto,
>quoted in her *New York Times* obituary, 1997

A god does not change his ways.
>—TERTULLIAN, *The Christian's Defense*, c. A.D. 200

I fled Him, down the nights and down the days;
I fled Him, down the arches of the years;
I fled Him, down the labyrinthine ways
Of my own mind. >—FRANCIS J. THOMPSON,
>*The Hound of Heaven*, 1893

If God did not exist, it would be necessary to invent him.
>—VOLTAIRE, *A l'auteur du livre des trois imposteurs*,
>Nov. 10, 1770

If God made us in His image, we have certainly returned
the compliment. >—VOLTAIRE, *Le Sottisier*

Jupiter is slow looking into his notebook, but he always
looks. >—ZENOBIUS, *Sententiae*, c. 2nd cent. B.C.

GOOD-BYES See FAREWELLS

GOODNESS See VIRTUE

GOSSIP See CONVERSATION; RUMOR

GOVERNMENT
See also DIPLOMACY;
HIGH POSITION: RULERS & LEADERS;
LAW; POLITICS; SECURITY; TAXES;
TYRANNY & TOTALITARIANISM

A government of laws, and not of men.
—JOHN ADAMS, *Novanglus,* 1775
[For more see Adams at LAW.]

Divide et impera.
Divide and rule. —ANONYMOUS (LATIN PROVERB)
[Also appears as *Divide ut regnes*—"Divide in order to rule."]

A public office is a public trust.
—ANONYMOUS (AMERICAN POLITICAL SAYING)
[This was the motto of Pres. Grover Cleveland's administrations (1885–89 and 1893–97). A similar concept was voiced earlier by Thomas Jefferson; see under POLITICS. In 1829, Henry Clay said: "Government is a trust, and the officers of the government are trustees; and both the trust and the trustees are created for the benefit of the people." Others reiterated the concept, and the phrase "public office is a public trust" became a political byword.]

Government is a contrivance of human wisdom to provide for human wants. Men have a right that these wants should be provided for by this wisdom. —EDMUND BURKE,
Reflections on the Revolution in France, 1790
[For Burke on government and compromise, see under Bismarck at POLITICS, the second quote.]

The less government we have, the better.
—RALPH WALDO EMERSON,
Politics in *Essays: First Series,* 1841

In every society some men are born to rule, and some to advise. —RALPH WALDO EMERSON,
The Young American in *Addresses and Lectures,* 1849

A government that is big enough to give you all you want is big enough to take it all away.
—BARRY GOLDWATER, speech, Oct. 21, 1964

A civil servant doesn't make jokes.
                    —EUGENE IONESCO, *The Killer,* 1958

The natural progress of things is for liberty to yield and government to gain ground.   —THOMAS JEFFERSON, letter to Colonel Edward Carrington, May 27, 1788

The whole art of government consists in being honest.
                    —THOMAS JEFFERSON, *Works,* VI, 1786

The great task remaining before us . . . that government of the people, by the people, for the people, shall not perish from the earth.   —ABRAHAM LINCOLN, Address at Gettysburg, Nov. 19, 1863
[Lincoln may have been familiar with Daniel Webster's reference to "the people's government, made for the people, made by the people, and answerable to the people," speech, Jan. 26, 1830. In 1850, the social reformer and theologian Theodore Parker, in a speech in Boston, declaimed, "This is what I call the American idea—a government of all the people, by all the people, for all the people." A possible early source is said to be the prologue to John Wycliffe's translation of the Bible in 1382: "This Bible is for the government of the people, by the people, and for the people." However, this attribution remains unverified.]

It is perfectly true that the government is best which governs least. It is equally true that the government is best which provides most.
        —WALTER LIPPMANN, *A Preface to Politics,* 1913
[Political columnist Lippmann was referring to John O'Sullivan's maxim, see below.]

Every nation has the government that it deserves.
        —JOSEPH DE MAISTRE, letter to X, Aug. 15, 1811

The worst government is the most moral. One composed of cynics is often very tolerant and humane. But when fanatics are on top there is no limit to oppression.
                    —H. L. MENCKEN, *Minority Report: H. L. Mencken's Notebooks,* 1956

To govern is to choose.
                    —PIERRE MENDÈS-FRANCE, maxim
[Mendès-France, one of France's most influential post-war politicians, served as Prime Minister in 1954–55.]

All government is evil. . . . The best government is that which governs least.   —JOHN L. O'SULLIVAN,
                    *Introduction, The United States Magazine
                    and Democratic Review,* 1837
[For a response, see Walter Lippmann, above.]

Society in every state is a blessing, but government even in its best state, is but a necessary evil; in its worst state, an intolerable one.   —THOMAS PAINE, *Common Sense,* 1776

For forms of government let fools contest,
Whate'er is best administered is best.
                    —ALEXANDER POPE, *Essay on Man,* 1733–34

Government is not the solution to our problem. Government is the problem.   —RONALD REAGAN,
                    Presidential Inaugural Address, 1981
[Another antigovernment Reagan saying, dating back to his 1966 campaign for governor of California, was: "Government is like a big baby—an alimentary canal with a big appetite at one end and no responsibility at the other."]

GRACE   See also BEAUTY; CHARM; STYLE; VIRTUE

A soft answer turneth away wrath. —BIBLE, *Proverbs* 15:1

There be three things which are too wonderful for me, yea, four which I know not.
   The way of an eagle in the air; the way of a serpent upon a rock; the way of a ship in the midst of the sea; and the way of a man with a maid.   —*Ibid.* 30:18, 19

Whatever is worth doing at all, is worth doing well.
                    —EARL OF CHESTERFIELD,
                    letter to his son, Mar. 10, 1746

To learn to dance by practicing dancing or to live by practicing living, the principles are the same. . . . One becomes, in some area, an athlete of God.
                              —MARTHA GRAHAM, May 15, 1945

Grace is the absence of everything that indicates pain or difficulty, hesitation or incongruity.
                              —WILLIAM HAZLITT,
                    On Beauty in *The Round Table*, 1817

Grace under pressure.   —ERNEST HEMINGWAY,
                              definition of guts, 1926, quoted in
                    John F. Kennedy, *Profiles in Courage*, 1956
[According to Dorothy Parker, in *The Artist's Reward* in *The New Yorker*, Nov. 20, 1929, Hemingway used the phrase originally to describe Gerald Murphy's first efforts at downhill skiing. Later, describing the bullfighter Antonio Ordoñez, Hemingway wrote: "He had the three great requisites of a matador: courage, skill in his profession, and grace in the presence of the danger of death," *The Dangerous Summer*.]

Do every act of your life as if it were your last.
                    —MARCUS AURELIUS, *Meditations*, 2nd cent. A.D.

To know how to live is my trade and my art.
                              —MONTAIGNE, *Essays*, 1580–88

GRACE, DIVINE   See FAITH; PROVIDENCE, DIVINE

GREATNESS   See also AMBITION; GENIUS; HEROES;
                    HIGH POSITION: RULERS & LEADERS;
                              SUCCESS & FAME

A great man is always willing to be little.
                              —RALPH WALDO EMERSON,
                    Compensation in *Essays: First Series*, 1841

To be great is to be misunderstood.
                    —RALPH WALDO EMERSON, *Self-Reliance* in *Ibid.*

Great deeds are usually wrought at great risks.
                              —HERODOTUS, *Histories*, 5th cent. B.C.

Four things greater than all things are,—Women and Horses and Power and War. —RUDYARD KIPLING,
 The Ballad of the King's Jest in *Barrack-Room Ballads*, 1892

The great man is he who does not lose his child's heart.
 —MENCIUS, *Works*, 3rd cent. B.C.

Great men can't be ruled.
 —AYN RAND, *The Fountainhead*, 1943

Be not afraid of greatness. Some are born great, some achieve greatness, and some have greatness thrust upon them. —SHAKESPEARE, *Twelfth Night,* II, v

In order to carry out great enterprises, one must live as if one will never have to die.
 —MARQUIS DE VAUVENARGUES,
 Réflexions et maximes, c. 1747

Le mieux est l'ennemi du bien.
The best is the enemy of the good. —VOLTAIRE,
 Art dramatique in *Dictionnaire philosophique,* 1764

GREECE   See NATIONS (Ancient World and Greece)

GREED   See SELF-INTEREST

GUILT   See also CRIME; EVIDENCE; EVIL;
 INNOCENCE

The wicked flee when no man pursueth.
 —BIBLE, *Proverbs* 28:1
[Often misquoted as "The guilty flee . . ." for example by Robert Bork in his Supreme Court nomination confirmation hearings, 1987.]

The guilty think all talk is of themselves.
—GEOFFREY CHAUCER, *The Canterbury Tales,* 1387–1400

Where guilt is, rage and courage doth abound.
 —BEN JONSON, *Sejanus,* 1603

Alas! how difficult it is not to betray guilt by our countenance.
 —OVID, *Metamorphoses,* c. A.D. 5

Nobody becomes guilty by fate.
—SENECA, *Oedipus,* 1st cent. A.D.

The lady doth protest too much, methinks.
—SHAKESPEARE, *Hamlet,* III, ii

Here's the smell of the blood still. All the perfumes of Arabia will not sweeten this little hand.
—SHAKESPEARE, *Macbeth,* V, i

H

HABIT

See also CUSTOM

The nature of men is always the same; it is their habits that separate them. —CONFUCIUS, *Analects*, 6th–5th cent. B.C.

Nothing is more powerful than habit.
—OVID, *The Art of Love*, c. 2 B.C.

Habit is a second nature that prevents us from knowing the first, of which it has neither the cruelties nor the enchantments. —MARCEL PROUST, *Remembrance of Things Past: The Guermantes Way*, 1913–27

To fall into a habit is to begin to cease to be.
—MIGUEL DE UNAMUNO,
The Tragic Sense of Life, 1913

Rigid, the skeleton of habit alone upholds the human frame.
—VIRGINIA WOOLF, *Mrs. Dalloway*, 1925

HAPPINESS

See also ETHICS & MORALITY;
HAPPINESS, EXPRESSIONS OF;
HEDONISM; LOVE, EXPRESSIONS OF

A joy that's shared is a joy made double.
—ANONYMOUS (ENGLISH PROVERB),
recorded by John Ray, *English Proverbs*, 1670

One half of the world cannot understand the pleasures of the other. —JANE AUSTEN, *Mansfield Park*, 1819

Weeping may endure for a night, but joy cometh in the morning. —BIBLE, *Psalms* 30:5

Judge none blessed before his death.
> —BIBLE, *Ecclesiasticus* 11:28

[This concept was expressed in other ancient texts; for example, see Solon, below.]

The joyfulness of a man prolongeth his days. —*Ibid.*, 30:22

The secret of happiness is to admire without desiring. And that is not happiness. —F. H. BRADLEY, *Aphorisms*, 1930

Make us happy and you make us good.
> —ROBERT BROWNING,
> *The Ring and the Book*, 1868–69

Follow your bliss. —JOSEPH CAMPBELL, motto

[See also Rabelais at FREEDOM.]

The latter end of joy is woe. —GEOFFREY CHAUCER,
> *The Canterbury Tales*, 1387–1400

All seek joy, but it is not found on earth.
> —ST. JOHN CHRYSOSTOM, *Homilies*, c. 386–98

Great joys must be controlled. —COLETTE, *The Seamstress*
> in *My Mother's House*, 1922

Sweet is pleasure after pain. —JOHN DRYDEN,
> *Alexander's Feast*, 1697

[More at ALCOHOL & DRINKING.]

It is neither wealth nor splendor, but tranquillity and occupation, which give happiness. —THOMAS JEFFERSON,
> letter to Mrs. A. S. Marks, 1788

We are never so happy or as unhappy as we imagine.
> —LA ROCHEFOUCAULD, *Maxims*, 1678

To live happily is an inward power of the soul.
> —MARCUS AURELIUS, *Meditations*, 2nd cent. A.D.

toujours gai, archy, toujours gai.
> —DON MARQUIS, *the life of
> mehitabel the cat* in *archy's life of mehitabel*, 1933

Ask yourself whether you are happy, and you will cease to be so. —JOHN STUART MILL, *Autobiography,* 1873 [Mill ranked happiness below mind and understanding: "It is better to be a human being dissatisfied than a pig satisfied; better to be Socrates dissatisfied than a fool satisfied," *Utilitarianism,* 1863.]

The secret of happiness is to face the fact that the world is horrible, horrible, horrible. —BERTRAND RUSSELL, quoted in Alan Wood, *Bertrand Russell: The Passionate Skeptic,* 1956

Happiness is the only sanction in life; where happiness fails, existence remains a mad and lamentable experiment. —GEORGE SANTAYANA, *The Life of Reason: Reason in Common Sense,* 1905–06

We have no more right to consume happiness without producing it than to consume wealth without producing it. —GEORGE BERNARD SHAW, *Candida,* 1908

A lifetime of happiness! No man alive could bear it: it would be hell on earth. —GEORGE BERNARD SHAW, *Man and Superman,* 1903

There are two things to aim at in life: first, to get what you want; and, after that, to enjoy it. Only the wisest of mankind achieve the second. —LOGAN PEARSALL SMITH, *Afterthoughts,* 1931

Call no man happy until he dies; he is at best but fortunate. —SOLON, 6th cent. B.C., quoted in Herodotus, *Histories,* 5th cent. B.C.

Our happiness depends on wisdom all the way. —SOPHOCLES, *Antigone,* 6th cent. B.C.

The world is so full of a number of things. I'm sure we should all be as happy as kings. —ROBERT LOUIS STEVENSON, *Happy Thought* in *A Child's Garden of Verses,* 1885

Happiness is an imaginary condition formerly often attributed by the living to the dead, now usually attributed by
adults to children, and by children to adults.
>   —THOMAS SZASZ, *Emotions* in *The Second Sin*, 1973

For he knew that the secret of happiness was freedom, and
the secret of freedom a brave heart; and he did not stand
idly aside from the onset of the enemy.
>   —THUCYDIDES, funeral oration of Pericles, 429 B.C.

HAPPINESS, EXPRESSIONS OF   See also HAPPINESS;
>   LOVE, EXPRESSIONS OF

The morning stars sang together, and all the sons of God
shouted for joy.   —BIBLE, *Job* 38:7

"And hast thou slain the Jabberwock?
Come to my arms, my beamish boy!
O frabjous day! Callooh! Callay!"
He chortled in his joy.
>   —LEWIS CARROLL, *Jabberwocky*
>   in *Through the Looking-Glass*, 1872

We were very tired, we were very merry—
We had gone back and forth all night on the ferry.
>   —EDNA ST. VINCENT MILLAY, *Recuerdo*
>   in *A Few Figs from Thistles*, 1920

Everyone suddenly burst out singing.
>   —SIEGFRIED SASSOON,
>   *Everyone Sang* in *War Poems*, 1910

O wonderful, wonderful, and most wonderful! and yet again
wonderful, and after that, out of all whooping!
>   —SHAKESPEARE, *As You Like It*, III, ii

HASTE

Festina lente.
Hasten slowly.   —ANONYMOUS (PROVERB)

What is done well is done quickly enough.
>   —AUGUSTUS CAESAR, favorite proverbial saying,
>   quoted in Suetonius, *Lives of the Caesars*, c. 100

No man who is in a hurry is quite civilized.
—WILL DURANT, d. 1981, *What Is Civilization?*

Nothing is more vulgar than haste.
—RALPH WALDO EMERSON,
Behavior in *The Conduct of Life,* 1860

Haste in every business brings failures.
—HERODOTUS, *Histories,* 5th cent. B.C.

We haven't the time to take our time.
—EUGENE IONESCO, *Exit the King,* 1963

Wisely and slowly; they stumble that run fast.
—SHAKESPEARE, *Romeo and Juliet,* II, iii

More haste, less speed.
—THEOGNIS, fragment, 6th cent. B.C.

Never hurry and never worry!
—E. B. WHITE, *Charlotte's Web,* 1952
[Charlotte's advice to Wilbur.]

HATE   See also ANGER; MISANTHROPY; REVENGE

Hatred watches while friendship sleeps.
—ANONYMOUS (FRENCH PROVERB)

Thou shalt not hate thy brother in thy heart.
—BIBLE, *Leviticus* 19:17

The bloodthirsty hate the upright. —BIBLE, *Proverbs* 29:10

Now hatred is by far the longest pleasure;
Men love in haste, but they detest at leisure.
—LORD BYRON, *Don Juan,* 1819–24

I tell you there is such a thing as creative hate.
—WILLA CATHER, *The Song of the Lark,* 1915

Heaven has no rage like love to hatred turned,
Nor hell a fury like a woman scorned.
—WILLIAM CONGREVE, *The Mourning Bride,* 1697

Violent antipathies are always suspicious, and betray a secret affinity.   —WILLIAM HAZLITT, *Table Talk*, 1821–22

We can scarcely hate anyone that we know.
   —WILLIAM HAZLITT, *On Criticism* in *Table Talk*, 1822

Hatred, as well as love, renders its votaries credulous.
   —JEAN-JACQUES ROUSSEAU, *Confessions*, 1781–88

Hate is the coward's revenge for being humiliated.
   —GEORGE BERNARD SHAW, *Major Barbara*, 1907

It is human to hate those whom we have injured.
   —TACITUS, *Life of Agricola*, c. A.D. 98

HAVES & HAVE-NOTS   See also COMPASSION & PITY;
   MONEY; POVERTY & HUNGER;
   POWER; RUIN; WINNING & LOSING,
   VICTORY & DEFEAT

The rich would have to eat money, but luckily the poor provide food.   —ANONYMOUS (RUSSIAN PROVERB)

The poor is hated even of his own neighbor, but the rich have many friends.   —BIBLE, *Proverbs* 14:20

For unto everyone that hath shall be given, and he shall have abundance: but from him that hath not shall be taken even that which he hath.   —BIBLE, *Matthew* 25:29

There are only two families in the world, my old grandmother used to say, the Haves and the Have-nots.
   —CERVANTES, *Don Quixote*, 1605–15

I was told . . . that an impassable gulf divided the Rich from the Poor; I was told that the Privileged and the People formed Two Nations. —BENJAMIN DISRAELI, *Sybil*, 1845

The meek shall inherit the earth but not the mineral rights.
   —J. PAUL GETTY, d. 1976, attributed

If you are poor today, you will always be poor. Only the rich acquire riches.   —MARTIAL, *Epigrams*, 1st cent. A.D.

Wealth is the parent of luxury and indolence, and poverty of meanness and viciousness, and both of discontent.
                    —PLATO, *The Republic,* 4th cent. B.C.
[More at ART & THE ARTS.]

Half the world does not know how the other half lives.
        —RABELAIS, *Gargantua and Pantagruel,* 1532–52

Each belongs here or anywhere as much as the well-off . . . just as much as you or I. Each has his or her place in the procession.   —WALT WHITMAN, *Leaves of Grass,* 1855

Really, if the lower orders don't set us a good example, what on earth is the use of them?
    —OSCAR WILDE, *The Importance of Being Earnest,* 1895

HEALTH   See also DOCTORS & THE PRACTICE OF
              MEDICINE; FOOD, WINE, & EATING;
              ILLNESS & REMEDIES; MADNESS;
              PHYSICAL FITNESS

There is a limit to the best of health: disease is always a near neighbor. —AESCHYLUS, *Agamemnon,* 5th cent. B.C.

Health and good estate of body are above all good.
                    —BIBLE, *Ecclesiasticus* 30:15

To lengthen thy life lessen thy meals.
                    —BENJAMIN FRANKLIN,
              Poor Richard's Almanac, Oct. 1733

Early to bed and early to rise, makes a man healthy, wealthy, and wise.   —*Ibid.,* 1733

Orandum est ut sit mens sana in corpore sano.
We should pray for a sound mind in a sound body.
                    —JUVENAL, *Satires,* c. A.D. 100

A sound mind in a sound body is a short but full description of a happy state in this world.   —JOHN LOCKE,
              Some Thoughts Concerning Education, 1693

Non est vivere, sed valera vita est.
Life is not merely living, but living in health.
> —MARTIAL, *Epigrams,* 1st cent. A.D.

Too much attention to health is a hindrance to learning, to invention, and to studies of any kind, for we are always feeling suspicious shootings and swimmings in our heads, and we are prone to blame our studies for them.
> —PLATO, *The Republic,* 4th cent. B.C.

People who feel well are sick people neglecting themselves.
> —JULES ROMAINS, *Dr. Knock,* 1923

Use your health, even to the point of wearing it out. That is what it is for. Spend all you have before you die; and do not outlive yourself. —GEORGE BERNARD SHAW,
> *The Doctor's Dilemma,* 1906

Keep breathing [key to longevity.] —SOPHIE TUCKER,
> newspaper reports, Jan. 13, 1964

HEART

See also AGE & AGING (Yeats);
EMOTIONS; LOVE

The heart is deceitful above all things, and desperately wicked. Who can know it? —BIBLE, *Jeremiah* 17:9

What other dungeon is so dark as one's own heart!
> —NATHANIEL HAWTHORNE,
> *The House of the Seven Gables,* 1851

[More at SELF.]

When I was one-and-twenty I heard a wise man say,
Give crowns and pounds and guineas
But not your heart away.
> —A. E. HOUSMAN, *A Shropshire Lad,* 1896

The intellect is always fooled by the heart.
> —LA ROCHEFOUCAULD, *Maxims,* 1678

In the human heart, there is a ceaseless birth of passions, so that the destruction of one is almost always the establishment of another.
> —*Ibid.*

The holiest of holidays are those
Kept by ourselves in silence and apart;
The secret anniversaries of the heart.
>—HENRY WADSWORTH LONGFELLOW,
>*From My Arm-Chair,* 1879

The human heart is like a ship on a stormy sea driven about by winds blowing from all four corners of heaven.
>—MARTIN LUTHER, preface to his
>translation of the Psalms, 1534

My heart is a lonely hunter that hunts on a lonely hill.
>—FIONA MacLEOD, *The Lonely Hunter,* c. 1900

[Popularized by Carson McCullers in the title of her 1940 novel, *The Heart Is a Lonely Hunter.*]

La coeur a ses raisons que la raison ne connaît point.
The heart has its reasons which reason does not know at all.
>—BLAISE PASCAL, *Pensées,* 1670

It is only with the heart that one can see rightly; what is essential is invisible to the eye.
>—ANTOINE DE SAINT EXUPÉRY,
>*The Little Prince,* 1943

I follow my heart for I can trust it.
>—J.C.F. VON SCHILLER,
>*The Death of Wallenstein,* 1798

The heart is forever inexperienced.
>—HENRY DAVID THOREAU,
>*A Week on the Concord and Merrimack Rivers,* 1849

Great thoughts always come from the heart.
>—MARQUIS DE VAUVENARGUES,
>*Réflexions et maximes,* c. 1747

Now that my ladder's gone,
I must lie down where all the ladders start,
In the foul rag-and-bone shop of the heart.
>—WILLIAM BUTLER YEATS,
>*The Circus Animals' Desertion* in *Last Poems,* 1936–39

[These famous lines were written in the poet's old age; the

missing "ladder" has been interpreted as the creative power of the mind.]

HEAVEN   See IMMORTALITY; LAST JUDGMENT &
                                    THE HEREAFTER

HEAVENS, THE   See NATURE: THE HEAVENS,
                                            THE SKY

HEDONISM   See also EXCESS; FREEDOM (Rabelais);
                                HAPPINESS; SEX & SENSUALITY

Who loves not wine, women, and song
Remains a fool his whole life long.   —ANONYMOUS
[Traditionally but probably wrongly attributed to Martin
Luther.]

Let us eat and drink; for tomorrow we shall die.
                                    —BIBLE, *Isaiah* 22:13
[Also at *I Corinthians* 15:32, "Let us eat and drink; for tomorrow we die."]

Pleasure after all is a safer guide than either right or duty.
        —SAMUEL BUTLER, *The Way of All Flesh*, 1903

Gather ye rosebuds while ye may,
Old Time is still a-flying;
And this same flower that smiles today,
Tomorrow will be dying.
        —ROBERT HERRICK, *To the Virgins,
                To Make Much of Time* in *Hesperides*, 1648
[For "the days of wine and roses," see Ernest Dowson at
YOUTH.]

Had we but world enough, and time,
This coyness, Lady, were no crime.
        —ANDREW MARVELL, *To His Coy Mistress*, 1650–52

But at my back I always hear
Time's wingèd chariot hurrying near;
And yonder all before us lie
Deserts of vast eternity.
                                            —*Ibid.*

The grave's a fine and private place,
But none, I think, do there embrace.　　　　　—*Ibid.*

I seek the utmost pleasure and the least pain.
　　　　　—PLAUTUS, *The Captives*, c. 200 B.C.

Pleasure is the only thing to live for. Nothing ages like
happiness.　　　—OSCAR WILDE, *An Ideal Husband*, 1895

Give me the luxuries of life and I will willingly do without
the necessities.　　　—FRANK LLOYD WRIGHT, quoted in
　　　　　The New York Times, obituary, Apr. 9, 1959
[Similarly, *The New York Times* reported that an aphorism favored by painter Elaine de Kooning was "Take care of the luxuries, the necessities will take care of themselves." Mrs. de
Kooning was a person of great grace. Once when asked what it
was like to live in the "shadow" of her husband (abstract expres-
sionist Willem de Kooning), she replied, "I live in his light."]

HELL　　　See also DEVIL; EVIL; LAST JUDGMENT &
　　　　　　　　　　THE HEREAFTER

Hell, madame, is to love no more.
　　　　　—GEORGES BERNANOS,
　　　　　The Diary of a Country Priest, 1936

All hope abandon, ye who enter here!
　　　　　—DANTE, *Inferno* in *The Divine Comedy*, c. 1310–20

Hell is oneself.　　　—T. S. ELIOT, *The Cocktail Party*, 1950
[See also Robert Lowell and John Milton, below.]

I myself am hell.　　—ROBERT LOWELL, *Skunk Hour*, 1959
[More at MADNESS.]

When all the world dissolves,
And every creature shall be purified,
All place shall be hell that is not heaven.
　　　　　—CHRISTOPHER MARLOWE, *Dr. Faustus*, 1604

The road to Hell is paved with good intentions.
　　　　　—KARL MARX, *Capital*, 1867–83
[Essentially proverbial. Also attributed to St. Bernard—"Hell
is full of good intentions and desires"—and others.]

Long is the way
And hard, that out of hell leads up to light.
> —JOHN MILTON, *Paradise Lost*, 1667

Which way I fly is hell; myself am hell;
And in the lowest deep a lower deep
Still threatening to devour me opens wide,
To which the hell I suffer seems a heaven.
> —*Ibid.*

Hell has no terrors for pagans.   —ARTHUR RIMBAUD,
> *Mauvais Sang* in *A Season in Hell,* 1873

To work hard, to live hard, to die hard, and then to go to
hell after all would be too damned hard.
> —CARL SANDBURG, *The People, Yes,* 1936

Hell is other people.
> —JEAN-PAUL SARTRE, *No Exit,* 1944

Hell is a city much like London—
A populous and smoky city.
> —PERCY BYSSHE SHELLEY, *Peter Bell the Third,* 1819

The way down to hell [Hades] is easy.
The gates of black Dis stand open night and day.
But to retrace one's steps and escape to the upper air
That is toil, that is labor.   —VIRGIL, *Aeneid,* c. 19 B.C.

HEROES
See also COURAGE; GREATNESS; HIGH POSITION: RULERS & LEADERS

No hero is mortal till he dies.
> —W. H. AUDEN, *A Short Ode to a Philologist,* 1962

Unhappy the land that needs heroes.
> —BERTOLT BRECHT, *Galileo,* 1938–39

[See also Plato under TYRANNY & TOTALITARIANISM.]

Down these mean streets a man must go who is not himself
mean; who is neither tarnished nor afraid.
> —RAYMOND CHANDLER,
> *The Simple Art of Murder,* 1950

[Chandler also wrote of his detective-hero, "He must be, to
use a rather weathered phrase, a man of honor, by instinct and

inevitability, and certainly without saying it. He must be the best man in his world, and a good enough man for any world."]

Every hero becomes a bore at last.
—RALPH WALDO EMERSON,
Representative Men, 1850

Show me a hero and I will write you a tragedy.
—F. SCOTT FITZGERALD, *Notebooks*, 1978

The boy stood on the burning deck
Whence all but he had fled.
—FELICIA HEMANS, *Casabianca*, c. 1798
[The boy was Giacomo Casabianca, who died on watch during the Battle of the Nile on the French flagship *L'Orient*. Giacomo remained at his post as the ship burned and eventually exploded. His father, Louis, the ship's captain, also died during the all-night battle, which began on August 1, 1798. [The victorious commander was Adm. Sir Horatio Nelson.]

Listen, my children, and you shall hear,
Of the midnight ride of Paul Revere,
On the eighteenth of April, in Seventy-five;
Hardly a man is now alive
Who remembers that famous day and year.
—HENRY WADSWORTH LONGFELLOW,
The Landlord's Tale: Paul Revere's Ride in
Tales of a Wayside Inn, 1863–74

One if by land, and two if by sea;
And I on the opposite shore will be,
Ready to ride and spread the alarm
Through every Middlesex village and farm.   —*Ibid.*

Then out spake brave Horatius,
The Captain of the Gate:
"To every man upon this earth
Death cometh soon or late.
And how can man die better
Than facing fearful odds,
For the ashes of his fathers,
And the temples of his Gods?"
—THOMAS BABINGTON MACAULAY,
Horatius in *Lays of Ancient Rome*, 1842
[In the 6th century B.C., Horatius Cocles defended a bridge over the Tiber into Rome. Details of the legend vary, but es-

sentially Horatio and two companions held off the entire Etruscan army while the Romans destroyed the bridge behind them.]

See, the conquering hero comes!
Sound the trumpets, beat the drums!
                    —THOMAS MORELL, *Joshua,* 1798

They seek him here, they seek him there,
Those Frenchies seek him everywhere.
Is he in heaven?
Is he in hell?
That demmed, elusive Pimpernel.
        —BARONESS ORCZY, *The Scarlet Pimpernel,* 1905
[The fictional Pimpernel was an apparently feckless English dandy, who, disguised as the mysterious, dashing Pimpernel, rescued French aristocrats from the bloodthirsty leaders of the French Revolution. This verse was adapted to refer to a real-life fugitive, English suffragist Christabel Pankhurst (1880–1958), while she was in hiding to avoid arrest: "Is she in heaven? / Is she in hell? / That damned elusive Christabel!"]

The hero is strangely akin to those who die young.
            —RAINER MARIA RILKE, *Duino Elegies,* 1923

He was born with the gift of laughter and a sense that the world was mad. —RAFAEL SABATINI, *Scaramouche,* 1921

Hail to the chief who in triumph advances!
        —SIR WALTER SCOTT, *The Lady of the Lake,* 1810

O, young Lochinvar is come out of the west.
            —SIR WALTER SCOTT, *Marmion,* 1808

He was a man, take him for all in all. I shall not look upon his like again.   —SHAKESPEARE, *Hamlet,* I, ii
[Hamlet is speaking of his father.]

This was the noblest Roman of them all. . . .
His life was gentle, and the elements
So mixed in him that Nature might stand up
And say to all the world, "This was a man."
>—SHAKESPEARE, *Julius Caesar*, V, v

[The reference is to Brutus.]

Arms and the man I sing, the first who came,
Compelled by fate, an exile out of Troy,
To Italy and the Lavinian coast.
>—VIRGIL, *The Aeneid*, c. 19 B.C.

HIGHLANDS OF SCOTLAND   See NATIONS

HIGH POSITION: See also GOVERNMENT; HEROES;
RULERS & LEADERS   MILITARY, THE;
                   POLITICS; POWER; SUCCESS & FAME

He who is to be a good ruler must first have been ruled.
>—ARISTOTLE, *Politics*, 4th cent. B.C.

Princes are like to heavenly bodies, which cause good or
evil times, and which have much veneration but no rest.
>—FRANCIS BACON, *Of Empire*, 1625

It is a miserable state of mind to have few things to desire,
and many things to fear; and yet that commonly is the case
of kings. >—*Ibid.*

The people's leaders have taken the wrong turning, and
those who are led are lost. >—BIBLE, *Isaiah* 9:16

Put not your trust in princes. >—BIBLE, *Psalms* 146:3

I had rather be right than be President.
>—HENRY CLAY, speech, U. S. Senate, 1850

I have to be seen to be believed.
>—ELIZABETH II, saying, quoted in
The Wall Street Journal, Apr. 21, 1986

To be a leader of men one must turn one's back on men.
>—HAVELOCK ELLIS, Introduction to
A Rebours, by J. K. Huysmans, 1884

The art of leadership . . . consists in consolidating the attention of the people against a single adversary and taking care that nothing will split up that attention.
—ADOLF HITLER, *Mein Kampf,* 1933

A president's hardest task is not to do what is right but to know what is right.   —LYNDON B. JOHNSON,
State of the Union speech, 1965

Caesar's wife must be above suspicion.
—JULIUS CAESAR, 62 B.C.,
based on Plutarch's biography of Caesar in
Parallel Lives, c. A.D. 100

A leader is best
When people hardly know that he exists.
Not so good when people obey and acclaim him.
Worst when they despise him.
—LAO-TZU, *Tao Te Ching,* 6th cent. B.C.

I am their [the people's] chief; I must follow them.
—ALEXANDRE AUGUSTE LEDRU-ROLLIN,
attributed in E. de Mirecourt, *Les Contemporains,*
Vol. 14, 1857
[Ledru-Rollin was a leader in the French Revolution of 1848, the February Revolution. His biographer Alvin R. Calman concluded that Ledru-Rollin probably did not utter this phrase, but the remark lives on in various forms. Thus, Leon Howell, in a 1966 article on Gandhi, reports him as saying, "I must follow the people, for I am their leader."]

Noblesse oblige.
Nobility [or, rank] has its obligations.
—DUC DE LÉVIS, *Maxims and Reflections,* 1808

L'état c'est moi.
I am the state.   —LOUIS XIV, speech, Apr. 13, 1665
[This is the traditional citation, but the remark may be apocryphal—see also Napoleon Bonaparte at TYRANNY & TOTALITARIANISM.]

A prince who desires to maintain his position must learn to be not always good, but to be so or not, as needs require.
—MACHIAVELLI, *The Prince*, 1532

A prince who is a man of courage and is able to command, who knows how to preserve order in his state, need never regret having founded his security on the affection of the people. —*Ibid.*

On the highest throne in the world, we still sit only on our own rumps. —MONTAIGNE, *Essays*, Book III, 1595

A leader is a dealer in hope.
—NAPOLEON BONAPARTE, *Maxims*, 1804–15

It is impossible to reign innocently.
—LOUIS DE SAINT-JUST, speech, 1793
[Saint-Just, a zealot leader in the French Revolution, was speaking of the doomed king Louis XVI. A year later, Saint-Just himself was guillotined.]

Uneasy lies the head that wears a crown.
—SHAKESPEARE, *Henry IV, Part II,* III, i

And what have kings that privates have not too,
Save ceremony, save general ceremony.
—SHAKESPEARE, *Henry V,* IV, i

Nice customs curtsey to great kings. —*Ibid.,* V, ii

I would not be a queen
For all the world. —SHAKESPEARE, *Henry VIII,* II, iii

For God's sake, let us sit upon the ground
And tell sad stories of the death of kings.
—SHAKESPEARE, *Richard II,* III, ii

Now is the winter of our discontent
Made glorious summer by this sun of York.
—SHAKESPEARE, *Richard III,* I, i

I met a traveler from an antique land
Who said: "Two vast and trunkless legs of stone
Stand in the desert. . . . Near them, on the sand,
Half sunk, a shattered visage lies, whose frown,
And wrinkled lip, and sneer of cold command,
Tell that its sculptor well those passions read.
            —PERCY BYSSHE SHELLEY, *Ozymandias*, 1817

"My name is Ozymandias, king of kings:
Look on my works, ye Mighty, and despair!"
Nothing beside remains. Round the decay
Of that colossal wreck, boundless and bare,
The lone and level sands stretch far away.   —*Ibid.*

To know nor faith, nor love nor law; to be
Omnipotent but friendless is to reign.
            —PERCY BYSSHE SHELLEY,
                Prometheus Unbound, 1819

Princes are the lamps that light this world.
            —MURASAKI SHIKIBU,
                The Tale of Genji, 1001–15

The only emperor is the emperor of ice-cream.
            —WALLACE STEVENS,
                The Emperor of Ice-Cream, 1923

All kings is mostly rapscallions.
            —MARK TWAIN, *The Adventures of
                Huckleberry Finn*, 1885

O Captain! my Captain! our fearful trip is done,
The ship has weathered every rack, the prize we sought is
    won.
    —WALT WHITMAN, *O Captain! My Captain!*, 1865–66
[Whitman was writing of the Civil War and Lincoln's death.
The poem ends, ". . . on the deck my Captain lies, / Fallen
cold and dead."]

HISTORY   See also PAST, THE

History repeats itself.
            —ANONYMOUS (ENGLISH PROVERB)
[H. L. Mencken wrote that this proverb, which appears in many

languages, may derive from Thucydides' *The History of the Peloponnesian War* (400 B.C.), in which the author refers to "those inquirers who desire an exact knowledge of the past as an aid to the interpretation of the future." Mark Twain is said to have commented, "History may not repeat itself, but it does rhyme." See also Karl Marx below.]

Man is a history-making creature who can neither repeat his past nor leave it behind.
—W. H. AUDEN, *The Dyer's Hand*, 1962

Happy is the nation without a history.
—CESARE BECCARIA,
Essay on Crimes and Punishments, 1764
[See also Thomas Carlyle below.]

History, n. an account mostly false, of events mostly unimportant, which are brought about by rulers, mostly knaves, and soldiers, mostly fools.
—AMBROSE BIERCE, *The Devil's Dictionary*, 1906

That great dust-heap called "history."
—AUGUSTINE BIRRELL,
Carlyle in *Obiter Dicta*, 1884–87
[The phrase is often given as "the ash-heap of history."]

Happy the people whose annals are blank in history books!
—THOMAS CARLYLE, *Frederick the Great*, 1858–65

The history of the world is but the biography of great men.
—THOMAS CARLYLE, *Heroes and Hero-Worship*,
The Hero as Divinity, 1840

History has many cunning passages, contrived corridors
And issues. —T. S. ELIOT, *Gerontion*, 1920

History is more or less bunk. —HENRY FORD, quoted in
Chicago Tribune, May 25, 1916
[Ford continued: "It's tradition. We don't want tradition. We want to live in the present, and the only history that is worth a tinker's damn is the history we make today."]

The End of History.
—FRANCIS FUKUYAMA, essay title, 1989

History . . . is indeed little more than the register of the crimes, follies, and misfortunes of mankind.
—EDWARD GIBBON, *The Decline and Fall of the Roman Empire,* 1776–88
[See also Voltaire below.]

What experience and history teach is this—that people and governments never have learned anything from history or acted on principles deduced from it.
—G. W. F. HEGEL, *Philosophy of History,* Introduction, 1832

History is the autobiography of a madman.
—ALEXANDER HERZEN, d. 1870, *Dr. Krupov*

It is not the neutrals or the lukewarms who make history.
—ADOLF HITLER, speech, Apr. 23, 1933

History, Stephen said, is a nightmare from which I am trying to awake.   —JAMES JOYCE, *Ulysses,* 1922

The history of all hitherto existing society is the history of class struggles.   —KARL MARX & FRIEDRICH ENGELS, *The Communist Manifesto,* 1848

Hegel remarks somewhere that all great historical facts and personages occur, as it were, twice. He has forgotten to add: the first time as tragedy, the second time as farce.
—KARL MARX, *The Eighteenth Brumaire of Louis Bonaparte,* opening sentences, 1852
[For more first lines, see the note under Tolstoy at FAMILY.]

Men make their own history, but they do not make it just as they please.   —*Ibid.*

World history is the world's verdict.
—J.C.F. VON SCHILLER, *Resignation,* 1786

A historian is a prophet in reverse.
—FRIEDRICH VON SCHLEGEL, *Athenaeum,* 1798

History is no more than the portrayal of crimes and misfortunes.   —VOLTAIRE, *L'Ingénu,* 1767

History can be well written only in a free country.
  —VOLTAIRE, letter to Frederick the Great, May 27, 1773

Human history becomes more and more a race between education and catastrophe.
              —H. G. WELLS, *The Outline of History,* 1920

Nothing has really happened until it has been recorded.
              —VIRGINIA WOOLF, d. 1941, quoted in
              Harold Nicolson, *Diaries and Letters,* 1968

HOLIDAYS   See CHRISTMAS; HEART (Longfellow);
                THANKSGIVING; NEW YEAR

HOME   See also ARTS: ARCHITECTURE; FAMILY;
            MARRIAGE; PRIVACY; TRAVEL

To make a happy fireside clime
To wean and wife,
That's the true pathos and sublime
Of human life. —ROBERT BURNS, *To Dr. Blacklock,* 1789

For a man's house is his castle, *et domus sua cuique tutissimum refugium* [and one's home is the safest refuge to everyone].   —EDWARD COKE, *Third Institute,* 1644
[This great English jurist was an ardent supporter of common law against royal perogatives. The Latin portion of this passage comes from *The Pandects,* or *Digest of Justinian,* a codification of Roman law in the sixth century A.D. See also James Otis at PRIVACY.]

Home is where one starts from.
        —T. S. ELIOT, *Four Quartets: East Coker,* 1940

[Husband:] "Home is the place where when you have to go
    there
They have to take you in."
[Wife:] "I should have called it
Something you somehow haven't to deserve."
    —ROBERT FROST, *The Death of the Hired Man,* 1914

It takes a heap o' livin' in a house t' make it home.
              —EDGAR A. GUEST, *Home* in
              The Collected Works of Edgar Guest, 1934

[Ogden Nash added that to make a house a home also "takes a heap o' payin'," *A Heap o' Livin'*.]

I remember, I remember,
The house where I was born,
The little window where the sun
Came peeping in at morn.
        —THOMAS HOOD, *I Remember, I Remember*, 1827

A man travels the world over in search of what he needs and returns home to find it.
        —GEORGE MOORE, *The Brook Kerith*, 1916

'Mid pleasures and palaces though we may roam,
Be it ever so humble, there's no place like home.
        —JOHN HOWARD PAYNE, *Home, Sweet Home*,
          song for the opera *Clari, or The Maid of Milan*, 1823

Happy the man whose wish and care
A few paternal acres bound,
Content to breathe his native air
In his own ground.
        —ALEXANDER POPE, *Ode on Solitude*, 1717

Home is the girl's prison and the woman's workhouse.
        —GEORGE BERNARD SHAW, *Maxims for
          Revolutionists* in *Man and Superman*, 1903

Home is the sailor, home from the sea,
And the hunter home from the hill.
        —ROBERT LOUIS STEVENSON,
          Requiem in *Underwoods*, 1887
[More at EPITAPHS.]

You Can't Go Home Again.
        —THOMAS WOLFE, book title, 1940

HONESTY & SINCERITY   See also TRUTH

An honest man's word is as good as his bond.
        —CERVANTES, *Don Quixote*, 1605–15

A few honest men are better than numbers.
—OLIVER CROMWELL,
letter to Sir W. Spring, Sept. 1643

Being entirely honest with oneself is a good exercise.
—SIGMUND FREUD,
letter to Wilhelm Fliess, Oct. 15, 1897

He that resolves to deal with none but honest men must leave off dealing. —THOMAS FULLER, *Gnomologia,* 1732

The secret of success is sincerity. Once you can fake that, you've got it made.
—JEAN GIRAUDOUX, d. 1944, quoted by
A. Bloch, *Murphy's Law Book Two,* 1980
[Also attributed to Samuel Goldwyn and others.]

Honesty is praised and starves.
—JUVENAL, *Satires,* c. A.D. 100

We only confess our little faults to persuade people that we have no large ones.
—LA ROCHEFOUCAULD, *Maxims,* 1678

Children and fools speak true.
—JOHN LYLY, *Endymion,* 1591

Some persons are likeable in spite of their unswerving integrity. —DON MARQUIS, d. 1937, quoted by
Edward Anthony, *O Rare Don Marquis,* 1962

It's annoying to be honest for nothing.
—OVID, *Letter from Pontus,* c. A.D. 10

Honesty is for the most part less profitable than dishonesty.
—PLATO, *The Republic,* 4th cent. B.C.
[See also Gandhi at MONEY.]

An honest man's the noblest work of God.
—ALEXANDER POPE, *An Essay on Man,* 1733–34
[Cf. Robert Ingersoll at GOD.]

God looks at the clean hands, not the full ones.
—PUBLILIUS SYRUS, *Moral Sayings,* 1st cent. B.C.

To be honest, as this world goes,
Is to be one man picked out of ten thousand.
—SHAKESPEARE, *Hamlet,* II, ii

The weight of this sad time we must obey.
Speak what we feel, not what we ought to say.
—SHAKESPEARE, *King Lear,* V, iii

Men should be what they seem.
—SHAKESPEARE, *Othello,* III, iii

Take note, take note, O world!
To be direct and honest is not safe.   —*Ibid.*

Every man has his fault, and honesty is his.
—SHAKESPEARE, *Timon of Athens,* III, i

Though I am not naturally honest,
I am so sometimes by chance.
—SHAKESPEARE, *The Winter's Tale,* IV, iii

I hold the maxim no less applicable to public than to private
affairs, that honesty is the best policy.
—GEORGE WASHINGTON,
Farewell Address, Sept. 17, 1796
[The maxim was already time-honored; for example, Cervantes
used it in *Don Quixote:* "Honesty's the best policy." According
to Herbert Stein, Richard Nixon used to say, "Honesty may
not be the best policy, but it is worth trying once in a while."
Stein was chairman of the President's Council of Economic
Advisers under presidents Nixon and Gerald Ford; he quoted
Nixon in *The New York Times,* Op-Ed page, July 31, 1996.]

A little sincerity is a dangerous thing, and a great deal of it
is absolutely fatal.
—OSCAR WILDE, *The Picture of Dorian Gray,* 1891

If you do not tell the truth about yourself you cannot tell it
about other people.   —VIRGINIA WOOLF,
The Moment and Other Essays, 1952

HONOR   See REPUTATION; VIRTUE

HOPE   See also OPTIMISM & PESSIMISM

Hope is a waking dream.   —ARISTOTLE, 4th cent. B.C.,
                    quoted in Diogenes Laërtius, *Lives of
                        Eminent Philosophers,* 3rd cent. A.D.
[Cf. Matthew Prior, below.]

Hope is a good breakfast, but it is a bad supper.
                    —FRANCIS BACON, *Apothegms,* 1624

Hope deferred maketh the heart sick.
                    —BIBLE, *Proverbs* 13:12

Hope is the thing with feathers
That perches in the soul
And sings the tune without the words
And never stops—at all.
                    —EMILY DICKINSON, poem no. 254, c. 1861

He that lives upon hope will die fasting.
                    —BENJAMIN FRANKLIN,
                Poor Richard's Almanac, Preface, 1758
(Or, in the adult version: "He that lives upon hope, dies fart-
ing," *Poor Richard's Almanac,* 1736.]

If it were not for hopes, the heart would break.
                    —THOMAS FULLER, *Gnomologia,* 1732

Hope, like the gleaming taper's light,
Adorns and cheers our way;
And still, as darker grows the night,
Emits a lighter ray.   —OLIVER GOLDSMITH,
                    The Captivity, An Oratorio, 1764

Hope springs eternal in the human breast:
Man never is, but always to be blest.
                    —ALEXANDER POPE, *An Essay on Man,* 1733–34

For hope is but the dream of those that wake.
                    —MATTHEW PRIOR, *Solomon,* 1718
[Cf. Aristotle, above.]

Extreme hopes are born of extreme misery.
　　　　　　　　　　—BERTRAND RUSSELL,
　　　　The Future of Mankind in *Unpopular Essays,* 1950

The miserable hath no other medicine
But only hope.
　　　　　　—SHAKESPEARE, *Measure for Measure,* III, i

True hope is swift and flies with swallow's wings;
Kings it makes Gods, and meaner creatures kings.
　　　　　　　　—SHAKESPEARE, *Richard III,* V, ii

Hope deceives more men than cunning can.
　　　　　　　—MARQUIS DE VAUVENARGUES,
　　　　　　　　　Réflexions et maximes, c. 1747

HORSES　　　　　　　　　See NATURE: ANIMALS

HOSPITALITY

What is there more kindly than the feelings between host
and guest?　　　　—AESCHYLUS, *The Libation Bearers,*
　　　　　　　　　　　　　5th–6th cent. B.C.

One cannot have too large a party.
　　　　　　　　　—JANE AUSTEN, *Emma,* 1815

Go out into the highways and hedges, and compel them to
come in, that my house may be filled. —BIBLE, *Luke* 14:23

Be not forgetful to entertain strangers: for thereby some
have entertained angels unawares.　—BIBLE, *Hebrews* 13:1

Use hospitality one to another without grudging.
　　　　　　　　　　　—BIBLE, *I Peter 4:9*

You can never have less than the graces nor more than the
muses.　　　　　　—HENRY STEELE COMMAGER, on the
　　　　　　　　appropriate size of a dinner party, quoted at
　　　　　　　　　　his memorial service, May 9, 1998
[The company should number between three and nine.]

Hospitality consists in a little fire, a little food, and an im-
mense quiet. —RALPH WALDO EMERSON, *Journal,* 1856

Why don't you come up sometime, 'n see me?
— MAE WEST, *She Done Him Wrong*, 1933
[Essentially the same line is in her play *Diamond Lil*, 1928.]

HUMANS & HUMAN NATURE   See also BODY, HUMAN; LIFE; MEN; MIND, THOUGHT, & UNDERSTANDING (Pascal); MISANTHROPY; WOMEN

And the Lord God formed man of the dust of the ground, and breathed into his nostrils the breath of life; and man became a living soul.   — BIBLE, *Genesis* 2:7

What is man, that thou art mindful of him?
— BIBLE, *Psalms*, 8:4
[King David to the Lord.]

Thou hast made him a little lower than the angels.
— *Ibid.*, 8:5

For Mercy has a human heart,
Pity a human face,
And Love, the human form divine,
And Secrecy, the human dress.
— WILLIAM BLAKE, *The Divine Image*
in *Songs of Innocence*, 1789–90

Cruelty has a human heart,
And Jealousy a human face;
Terror, the human form divine,
And Secrecy, the human dress.
— WILLIAM BLAKE, *A Divine Image*
in *Songs of Experience*, 1794

Man's inhumanity to man makes countless thousands mourn.
— ROBERT BURNS, *Man Was Made to Mourn*, 1786

Man is a tool-using animal. . . . Without tools he is nothing, with tools, he is all.
— THOMAS CARLYLE, *Sartor Resartus*, 1833–34
[Earlier, James Boswell ascribed the definition of man as "a tool-making animal" to Benjamin Franklin (*The Life of Samuel Johnson*, April 7, 1778). Johnson retorted: "But many a man never made a tool; and suppose a man without arms, he could not make a tool."]

Human nature is the same all over the world.
—EARL OF CHESTERFIELD,
letter to his son, Oct. 2, 1747

No man is an island entire of itself; every man is a part of
the continent, a part of the main.   —JOHN DONNE,
Devotions Upon Emergent Occasions, XVII, 1624

Any man's death diminishes me, because I am involved in
mankind. And therefore never send to know for whom the
bell tolls. It tolls for thee.   —*Ibid.*

Man is slightly nearer to the atom than the star. . . . From
his central position man can survey the grandest works of
nature with the astronomer, or the minutest works with the
physicist.   —SIR ARTHUR EDDINGTON,
Stars and Atoms, 1928

In spite of everything I still believe that people are really
good at heart.   —ANNE FRANK,
The Diary of a Young Girl,
July 15, 1944 (published 1952)

Men and melons are hard to know.
—BENJAMIN FRANKLIN, *Poor Richard's Almanac*, 1733

Wild animals never kill for sport. Man is the only one to
whom the torture and death of his fellow creatures is amusing in itself.   —JAMES A. FROUDE, *Oceana*, 1886

When God at first made man,
Having a glass of blessings standing by,
Let us, said he, pour on him all we can.
Let the world's riches, which dispersèd lie
Contract into a span.

—GEORGE HERBERT,
The Pulley in *The Temple*, 1633
[But God withholds one gift—rest—for the reason below.]

At last,
If goodness lead him not, yet weariness
May toss him to My breast.   —*Ibid.*

Out of the crooked timber of humanity no straight thing ever can be made.   —IMMANUEL KANT, *Idee zu Einer Allgemeinen Geschichte in Weltgebürglicher Absicht,* 1784

We has met the enemy, and it is us.
                    —WALT KELLY, *Pogo,* 1970
[For Oliver Hazard Perry's version, see under AMERICAN HISTORY: MEMORABLE MOMENTS.]

I teach you the superman. Man is something to be surpassed.
                    —FRIEDRICH NIETZSCHE,
                    Thus Spake Zarathustra, 1883–91

If the universe were to crush him, man would still be more noble than that which killed him, because he knows that he dies and the advantage which the universe has over him; the universe knows nothing of this.   —PASCAL, *Pensées,* 1670
[This follows the philosopher's famous observation that man is a "thinking reed"; see MIND, THOUGHT, & UNDERSTANDING.]

Homo homini lupus.
Man is a wolf to man.
          —PLAUTUS, *The Comedy of Asses,* c. 200 B.C.
[This is the common rendering of a longer sentence, which reads, "Man is a wolf—not a man—to another man, when he has not yet gotten to know him." The image was used by Bartolomeo Vanzetti in a written statement to Judge Webster Thayer, Apr. 9, 1927. "Your name . . . your laws, institutions, and your false god are but a deem rememoring (sic) of a cursed past in which man was wolf to the man." Professed anarchists Vanzetti and Nicola Sacco were convicted of robbery and murder in Massachusetts in 1921, in highly controversial proceedings. They were executed in 1927.]

Man is the only animal that knows nothing, and can learn nothing without being taught. —PLINY, *Natural History,* A.D. 77

Nothing is more wretched or more proud than man.
                    —*Ibid.*

The glory, jest, and riddle of the world.
>   —ALEXANDER POPE, *An Essay on Man*, 1733–34
[The full sentence runs: "Great lord of all things, yet a prey to all: / Sole judge of truth, in endless error hurled: / The glory, jest, and riddle of the world."]

Man is the measure of all things, of things that are, that they are, of things that are not, that they are not.
>   —PROTAGORAS, 5th cent. B.C., quoted in
>   Diogenes Laërtius, *Lives of Eminent Philosophers*,
>   3rd cent. A.D.

Everything is good when it leaves the Creator's hands; everything degenerates in the hands of man.
>   —JEAN JACQUES ROUSSEAU, *Émile*, 1762

Brief and powerless is man's life; on him and all his race the slow, sure doom falls pitiless and dark.
>   —BERTRAND RUSSELL, *The Free Man's*
>   *Worship* in *Philosophical Essays*, 1903

We are such stuff
As dreams are made on, and our little life
Is rounded with a sleep.
>   —SHAKESPEARE, *The Tempest*, IV, i

How beauteous mankind is! O brave new world,
That has such people in it.   *Ibid.*, V, i

Wonders are many, and none is more wonderful than man.
>   —SOPHOCLES, *Antigone*, 5th cent. B.C.

Man is a social animal.   —SPINOZA, *Ethics*, 1677

We feel and know that we are eternal.   —*Ibid*

I am a man; nothing human is alien to me.
>   —TERENCE, *The Self-Tormentor*, 163 B.C.

Man is the only animal that blushes. Or needs to.
>   —MARK TWAIN, *Pudd'nhead Wilson's*
>   *New Calendar* in *Following the Equator*, 1897

If you pick up a starving dog and make him prosperous, he will not bite you. This is the principal difference between a dog and a man. —MARK TWAIN, *Pudd'nhead Wilson's Calendar* in *Pudd'nhead Wilson*, 1894

The still, sad music of humanity.
—WILLIAM WORDSWORTH, *Lines Composed a Few Miles Above Tintern Abbey*, 1798

HUMOR See also LAUGHTER

A man who could make so vile a pun would not scruple to pick a pocket. —JOHN DENNIS, *The Gentleman's Magazine*, Vol. LI, 1781

There is no better role to play among the great than that of jester. —DENIS DIDEROT, *Rameau's Nephew*, 1762

A difference of taste in jokes is a great strain on the affections. —GEORGE ELIOT, *Daniel Deronda*, 1874–76

Wit makes its own welcome and levels all distinctions.
—RALPH WALDO EMERSON, *The Comic* in *Letters and Social Aims*, 1876

Humor is an affirmation of dignity, a declaration of man's superiority to all that befalls him.
—ROMAIN GARY, *Promise at Dawn*, 1961

You can pretend to be serious; but you can't pretend to be witty. —SACHA GUITRY, quoted in *Workshop on World Humor*, Nov. 1984, cited by Donal Henahan in *The New York Times*, Mar. 17, 1985

Leave jesting while it pleaseth, lest it turn to earnest.
—GEORGE HERBERT, *Jacula prudentum*, 1651

Impropriety is the soul of wit.
—SOMERSET MAUGHAM, *The Moon and Sixpence*, 1919

Everybody likes a kidder, but nobody lends him money.
—ARTHUR MILLER, *Death of a Salesman*, 1949

Wit is the epitaph of an emotion.
—FRIEDRICH NIETZSCHE,
Miscellaneous Maxims and Opinions, 1879

Even the gods love their jokes.
—PLATO, *Cratylus,* 4th cent. B.C.

Everything is funny as long as it happens to somebody else.
—WILL ROGERS, *Warning to Jokers:*
Lay Off the Prince in *The Illiterate Digest,* 1924

The quality of wit inspires more admiration than confidence.
—GEORGE SANTAYANA,
Wit in *The Sense of Beauty,* 1896

Comedy is the last refuge of the noncontormist mind.
—GILBERT SELDES, *The New Republic,* Dec. 20, 1954

My way of joking is to tell the truth.
—GEORGE BERNARD SHAW,
John Bull's Other Island, 1907

The wit makes fun of other persons; the satirist makes fun
of the world; the humorist makes fun of himself.
—JAMES THURBER, d. 1961, in Edward R. Murrow
television interview

Humor . . . is emotional chaos remembered in tranquillity.
—JAMES THURBER, *New York Post,* Feb. 29, 1960
[Thurber was referring here to Wordsworth's immortal defini-
tion of poetry; see under ARTS: POETRY & POETS.]

The secret source of humor itself is not joy but sorrow.
There is no humor in heaven.
—MARK TWAIN, *Pudd'nhead Wilson's*
New Calendar in *Following the Equator,* 1897
[Samuel Beckett, in *Endgame,* 1957, expressed a similar thought:
"Nothing is funnier than unhappiness."]

We are not amused. —QUEEN VICTORIA, after seeing an
imitation of herself by a groom-in-waiting,
quoted in *Notebooks of a Spinster,* Jan. 2, 1900

It's hard to be funny when you have to be clean.
—MAE WEST, quoted in Joseph Weintraub, ed.,
The Wit and Wisdom of Mae West, 1967

HUNGER See FOOD, WINE, & EATING;
POVERTY & HUNGER

HURRYING See HASTE

HYPOCRISY See also CRAFTINESS;
DISHONESTY & LIES

It is the wisdom of the crocodiles, that shed tears when they
would devour. —FRANCIS BACON, *Of Wisdom
for a Man's Self* in *Essays,* 1625

And when thou prayest, thou shalt not be as the hypocrites
are: for they love to pray standing in the synagogues and in
the corners of the streets, that they may be seen of men.
—BIBLE, *Matthew* 6:6

Beware of false prophets, which come to you in sheep's
clothing, but inwardly they are ravening wolves.—*Ibid.* 7:15
[For other prophets to avoid, see VISION & VISIONARIES.]

Woe unto you, scribes and Pharisees, hypocrites! for ye are
like unto whitened sepulchres, which indeed appear beautiful outward, but are within full of dead men's bones, and of
all uncleanness. —*Ibid.* 23:27

Be a hypocrite if you like; but don't talk like one!
—DENIS DIDEROT, *Rameau's Nephew,* 1762

I detest that man who hides one thing in the depth of his
heart and speaks forth another.
—HOMER, *Iliad,* 8th cent. B.C.

No man is a hypocrite in his pleasures.
—SAMUEL JOHNSON, quoted in
James Boswell, *Life of Johnson,* June 19, 1784

Hypocrisy is the homage which vice pays to virtue.
—LA ROCHEFOUCAULD, *Maxims,* 1678

A hypocrite is a person who . . . but who isn't?
—DON MARQUIS, d. 1937, quoted by Frederick B. Wilcox,
A Little Book of Aphorisms, 1947

For neither man nor angel can discern
Hypocrisy, the only evil that walks
Invisible, except to God alone.
—JOHN MILTON, *Paradise Lost,* 1667

Being a hypocrite has marvelous advantages!
—MOLIÈRE, *Don Juan or The Stone Guest,* 1665

With devotion's usage
And pious action we do sugar o'er
The devil himself.   —SHAKESPEARE, *Hamlet,* III, i

A nice man is a man of nasty ideas.
—JONATHAN SWIFT, *A Critical Essay
upon the Faculties of the Mind,* 1709

As for conforming outwardly, and living your own life inwardly, I don't think much of that.
—HENRY DAVID THOREAU, *Excursions*
(letter to Harrison Blake, Aug. 9, 1850)

I

IDEAS & IDEALS See also ETHICS & MORALITY;
MIND, THOUGHT, & UNDERSTANDING;
VISION & VISIONARIES

If you believe in an ideal, you don't own you, it owns you.
—RAYMOND CHANDLER, d. 1959; quoted by
Frank MacShane, *The Life of Raymond Chandler,* 1978

There is no force so democratic as the force of an ideal.
—CALVIN COOLIDGE, speech, Nov. 27, 1920

You can't shoot an idea.
—THOMAS E. DEWEY, debate with Harold Stassen
on whether to outlaw the Communist party, 1948

An invasion of armies can be resisted, but not an idea whose
time has come.
—VICTOR HUGO, *Histoire d'un crime,* 1852 (published 1877)
[The famous line is a free translation of the original, which
reads "One can resist the invasion of armies; one cannot resist
an invasion of ideas." The *crime* in this instance was Prince-
President Louis Napoleon Bonaparte's coup d'état of Dec. 2,
1851, which converted the Second Republic into the Second
Empire and himself into Napoleon III. Hugo fled to Brussels,
where he wrote *Histoire d'un crime,* and remained in exile, on
Guernsey, until the Empire dissolved in 1870.]

In a war of ideas, it is people who get killed.
—STANISLAW LEC, *Unkempt Thoughts,* 1962

An idea isn't responsible for the people who believe in it.
—DON MARQUIS, *The Sun Dial,*
column, New York *Sun,* 1913–22

To die for an idea: it is unquestionably noble. But how much nobler would it be if men died for ideas that were true.
　　　　　　—H. L. MENCKEN, *Prejudices: Fifth Series,* 1926

As there are misanthropists, or haters of mankind, so there are misologists, or haters of ideas.
　　　　　　—PLATO, *Phaedo,* 4th cent. B.C.

Loyalty to petrified opinion never yet broke a chain or freed a human soul.
　　　　　　—MARK TWAIN, d. 1910, attributed, inscribed beneath
　　　　　　his bust in the Hall of Fame

Serious people have few ideas. People with ideas are never serious.
　　　　　　—PAUL VALÉRY, *Mauvaises pensées et autres,* 1941

The true God, the mighty God, is the God of ideas.
　　　　　　—ALFRED DE VIGNY, *La Bouteille à la mer,*
　　　　　　in *Les Destinées,* 1864

All great ideas are dangerous.
　　　　　　—OSCAR WILDE, *De Profundis,* 1905

IDLENESS　　　　　　　See LAZINESS; LEISURE;
　　　　　　　　　　　　　　PROCRASTINATION

ILLNESS & REMEDIES　　See also DEATH; DOCTORS
　　　　　　　　　　& THE PRACTICE OF MEDICINE;
　　　　　　　　　HEALTH; MADNESS; REVOLUTION
(Guy Fawkes & Shakespeare); SELF (Shakespeare)

Illness tells us what we are.
　　　　　　—ANONYMOUS (ITALIAN PROVERB)

The greatest evil is physical pain.
　　　　　　—ST. AUGUSTINE, *Soliloquies,* c. A.D. 410

I reckon being ill as one of the great pleasures of life, provided one is not too ill and is not obliged to work till one is better. —SAMUEL BUTLER, *The Way of All Flesh,* 1903

Look into the depths of your own soul and learn first to know yourself, then you will understand why this illness was bound to come upon you and perhaps you will thenceforth avoid falling ill.
>—SIGMUND FREUD, *One of the Difficulties of Psychoanalysis* in *Collected Papers,* 1924–50

Natural forces within us are the true healers of disease.
>—HIPPOCRATES, *Aphorisms,* c. 400 B.C.

The patient must combat the disease along with the physician. —*Ibid.*

To live by medicine is to live horribly.
>—LINNAEUS, d. 1778, Introduction, *Diaeta naturalis*

Illness is not something a person has. It's another way of being.
>—JONATHAN MILLER, *The Body in Question,* 1978

Nearly all men die of their medicines, and not of their illnesses. —MOLIÈRE, *The Imaginary Invalid,* 1673

Brightness falls from the air;
Queens have died young and fair;
Dust hath closed Helen's eye.
I am sick, I must die.
Lord have mercy on us.
>—THOMAS NASHE, *Litany in Time of Plague,* 1600
["Brightness falls" was used by James Joyce in *A Portrait of the Artist as a Young Man,* 1916, and by Jay McInerney as the title of his 1992 novel. In that story, one of the characters refers to scholarly speculation that the opening line originally read, "Brightness falls from the hair."]

Everything great that we know has come to us from neurotics. They alone have founded our religions and created our masterpieces. Never will the world be aware of how much it owes to them, nor above all what they have suffered in order to bestow their gifts on it.
>—MARCEL PROUST, *Remembrance of Things Past: The Guermantes Way,* 1913–27

There are some maladies we must not seek to cure because they alone protect us from others that are more serious.
—*Ibid.*

There never was yet philosopher
That could endure the toothache patiently.
—SHAKESPEARE, *Much Ado About Nothing*, V, i

Everyone who is born holds dual citizenship, in the kingdom of the well and the kingdom of the sick.
—SUSAN SONTAG, *Illness as Metaphor*, 1978

There are some remedies worse than the disease.
—PUBLILIUS SYRUS, *Moral Sayings*, 1st cent. B.C.
[Francis Bacon resurrected a variant in *Of Seditions and Troubles* (1625): "The remedy is worse than the disease." Also in the early 17th century, the playwrights Francis Beaumont and John Fletcher wrote in *Love's Cure*: "I find the medicine worse than the malady."]

ILLUSIONS   See REALITY & ILLUSIONS

IMAGINATION   See MIND, THOUGHT & UNDERSTANDING; VISION & VISIONARIES

IMMORTALITY   See also DEATH; LAST JUDGMENT & THE HEREAFTER; LIFE

I don't want to achieve immortality through my work. . . . I want to achieve it through not dying.
—WOODY ALLEN, quoted in
E. Lax, *Woody Allen and His Comedy*

A man should have a child, plant a tree, and write a book.
—ANONYMOUS (CHINESE PROVERB)

God created man to be immortal, and made him to be an image of his own eternity.
—BIBLE, *The Wisdom of Solomon* 2:23

When all the desires that enter one's heart are abandoned, then does the mortal become immortal.
—BRIHADARANYAKA UPANISHAD, c. 800–500 B.C.

If I err in my belief that the souls of men are immortal, I err gladly, and do not wish to lose so delightful an error.
—CICERO, *De senectute*, 44 B.C.

I shall see the Son of God, the Sun of glory, and shine myself, as that sun shines. —JOHN DONNE, *Sermons*, 1640

He had decided to live forever or die in the attempt.
—JOSEPH HELLER, *Catch-22*, 1961

I long to believe in immortality.
—JOHN KEATS, letter to Fanny Brawne, July 1820

INACTION   See INDECISION; LAZINESS; PROCRASTINATION

INDECISION   See also PROCRASTINATION

Adamant for drift.
—WINSTON CHURCHILL, *While England Slept*, 1936
[This is the most repeated phrase from Churchill's acid characterization of Stanley Baldwin's politics: "Decided only to be undecided, resolved to be irresolute, adamant for drift, solid for fluidity, all-powerful to be impotent."]

There is no more miserable human being than one in whom nothing is habitual but indecision.
—WILLIAM JAMES, *The Principles of Psychology*, 1890

It is human nature to stand in the middle of a thing.
—MARIANNE MOORE,
A Grave in *Collected Poems*, 1951

Not to decide is to decide.   —LAURENCE J. PETER,
On Leaving It to the Snake, 1967
[A condensation of a comment by Harvey G. Cox. See also PROBLEMS.]

I've made up my mind both ways.
—"CASEY" STENGEL, d. 1975, quoted in
the Ken Burns television series *Baseball*, Part IV, 1994

He who hesitates is sometimes saved.
—JAMES THURBER, *The Glass in the
Field* in *Fables for Our Time,* 1940

INDIANS   See RACES & PEOPLES

INDIVIDUALITY   See also AMERICA &
AMERICANS (Hoover);
SELF-RELIANCE; SOLITUDE; VARIETY

Individuality is the aim of political liberty.
—JAMES FENIMORE COOPER,
The American Democrat, 1838

He may well win the race that runs by himself.
—BENJAMIN FRANKLIN,
Poor Richard's Almanac, 1747

Whatever crushes individuality is despotism, by whatever
name it may be called.
—JOHN STUART MILL, *On Liberty,* 1859
[Mill ranked individuality and eccentricity high among human
and social virtues. He wrote, "That so few now dare to be
eccentric marks the chief danger of the time," *Ibid.*]

If a man does not keep pace with his companions, perhaps
it is because he hears a different drummer. Let him step to
the music which he hears, however measured or far away.
—HENRY DAVID THOREAU,
Conclusion in *Walden,* 1854

INFORMATION   See also EDUCATION & LEARNING;
FACTS

Information wants to be free.   —STEWART BRAND,
Whole Earth Review, May 1985
[The quote comes from the transcript of the first Hackers' Conference in the fall of 1984. In a book, *The Media Lab* (1987),
Mr. Brand set the idea in context in a section that begins:
"Information Wants To Be Free. Information also wants to be
expensive. Information wants to be free because it has become
so cheap to distribute, copy, and recombine—too cheap to
meter. It wants to be expensive because it can be immeasurably
valuable to the recipient. The tension will not go away. It leads

to endless wrenching debate about price, copyright, 'intellectual property,' the moral rightness of casual distribution, because each round of new devices makes the tension worse, not better."]

INITIATIVE   See BOLDNESS & INITIATIVE;
                          SELF-RELIANCE

INNOCENCE   See also CHILDREN & CHILDHOOD;
                        SILENCE (Shakespeare); VIRTUE

Where, my God, where, Oh Lord, where or when was I, Your servant, innocent?
                    —ST. AUGUSTINE, *Confessions,* 397–401

God will not cast away an innocent man.
                                    —BIBLE, *Job* 8:20

Blessed are the pure in heart: for they shall see God.
                                —BIBLE, *Matthew* 5:8

Except ye be converted and become as little children, ye shall not enter into the kingdom of heaven.   —*Ibid.* 18:3
[For other verses from the Sermon on the Mount see VIRTUE.]

Innocence dwells with wisdom, but never with ignorance.
      —WILLIAM BLAKE, *The Four Zoas,* c. 1794–1804

The innocent are God's elect. —ST. CLEMENT, fl. A.D. 96,
                          First Epistle to the Corinthians

Teach us delight in simple things,
And mirth that has no bitter springs.
                  —RUDYARD KIPLING, *The Children's
                    Song* in *Puck of Pook's Hill,* 1906

Innocence is ashamed of nothing.
              —JEAN JACQUES ROUSSEAU, *Émile,* 1762

I used to be Snow White—but I drifted.
      —MAE WEST, d. 1980, quoted in Joseph Weintraub, ed.,
              The Wit and Wisdom of Mae West, 1967

INNOVATION   See NEW THINGS; SCIENCE:
                        DISCOVERY & EXPLORATION

INSANITY   See MADNESS

INSIGHT See MIND, THOUGHT, & UNDERSTANDING;
            SCIENCE: DISCOVERY & EXPLORATION;
            VISION & VISIONARIES

INSULTS & PUT-DOWNS   See also MANNERS;
                                NATIONS

There is less in this than meets the eye.
                        —TALLULAH BANKHEAD
[Remark to critic Alexander Woollcott at a performance of
Maurice Maeterlinck's *Aglavaine and Selysette,* Jan. 3, 1922.]

A sphinx without a riddle.
                        —OTTO VON BISMARCK, d. 1898,
                        comment on Napoleon III, attributed

The souls of women are so small,
That some believe they've none at all.
    —SAMUEL BUTLER, d. 1680, *Miscellaneous Thoughts*
[Butler specialized in satire.]

ASTOR: If I were your wife, I would put poison in your
coffee!
CHURCHILL: And if I were your husband, I would drink it.
        —WINSTON CHURCHILL to Nancy Astor, c. 1912
[Cited in Consuelo Vanderbilt Balsan, *Glitter and Gold,* 1952.]

BRADDOCK: Mr. Churchill, you are drunk.
CHURCHILL: And you, madam, are ugly. But I shall be sober
tomorrow.   —WINSTON CHURCHILL to Elizabeth
                    Margaret ("Bessie") Braddock,
                    attributed, possibly apocryphal

What a dump!
    —LENORE COFFEE, screenplay, *Beyond the Forest,* 1949
[Line uttered by Bette Davis.]

There goes the famous good time that was had by all.
>—BETTE DAVIS, d. 1989, speaking of a starlet,
>quoted in Leslie Halliwell,
>*The Filmgoer's Book of Quotes,* 1990

Another damned, thick square book! Always scribble, scribble, scribble! Eh! Mr. Gibbon?
>—WILLIAM HENRY, DUKE OF GLOUCESTER,
>upon receiving from Edward Gibbon in 1781 Vol. II
>of his *Decline and Fall of the Roman Empire,* as quoted
>in note to James Boswell's *Life of Johnson,* 1791

They teach the morals of a whore, and the manners of a dancing master.
>—SAMUEL JOHNSON, 1754, speaking of the
>Earl of Chesterfield's letters, in James Boswell,
>*Life of Johnson,* 1791

Sir, a woman's preaching is like a dog's walking on his hinder legs. It is not done well; but you are surprised to find it done at all.
>—*Ibid.,* July 31, 1763

She looked as though butter wouldn't melt in her mouth—or anywhere else.
>—ELSA LANCHESTER, d. 1986, cited in
>Leslie Halliwell, *The Filmgoer's Book of Quotes,* 1973

My dear, I don't give a damn.
>—MARGARET MITCHELL, *Gone With the Wind,* 1936
[In the movie, the line is "Frankly, my dear, I don't give a damn." Producer David O. Selznick had to fight for the "damn," and pay a $5,000 fine for breaking the Motion Picture Production Code.]

She ran the whole gamut of emotions from A to B.
>—DOROTHY PARKER, attributed,
>re Katharine Hepburn in *The Lake,* 1933

It is not a novel to be thrown aside lightly. It should be thrown aside with great force.
>—DOROTHY PARKER, d. 1967, book review,
>quoted by A. Johnston, *Legend of a
>Sport* in *The New Yorker*

House Beautiful is the play lousy.

—DOROTHY PARKER,
theater review, *The New Yorker,* 1933

[He] never said a foolish thing
Nor ever did a wise one. —EARL OF ROCHESTER,
impromptu on Charles II, c. 1676?
[Reported to have been posted on White Hall Gate after the King said he would give everyone the liberty of speaking freely in his presence or, another version, to have been an impromptu comment on the King's praise of a new translation of the Psalms. The King's rejoinder, so it is said, was, "My words are my own, my actions are those of my ministers."]

No more backbone than a chocolate éclair.

—THEODORE ROOSEVELT, characterization of
Pres. William McKinley, c. 1897, cited in V. C. Jones,
Last of the Rough Riders, American Heritage, July 1969.
[Roosevelt, then Assistant Secretary of the Navy, may have borrowed the éclair metaphor from Speaker of the House Thomas B. Reed. Variants from this era include Ulysses S. Grant's complaint that James A. Garfield was "not possessed of the backbone of an angleworm," and a comment by Oliver Wendell Holmes, Jr., on a colleague: "I could carve out of a banana a judge with more backbone than that."]

You blocks, you stones, you worse than senseless things!
—SHAKESPEARE, *Julius Caesar,* I, i

Dear Sir, Your profession has, as usual, destroyed your brain. —GEORGE BERNARD SHAW, d. 1950, letter to
a journalist, Dan H. Laurence, ed., *Collected Letters,* 1972

No matter how thin you slice it, it's still baloney.
—ALFRED E. SMITH, campaign speeches, 1936
[He had broken from the Democratic Party to support the Republican candidate for president, Alf Landon.]

I am just going to pray for you at St. Paul's, but with no very lively hope of success.
—REV. SYDNEY SMITH, d. 1845, quoted by
H. Pearson, *The Smith of Smiths,* 1934

I regard you with an indifference closely bordering on aversion. —ROBERT LOUIS STEVENSON,
Story of the Bandbox in *New Arabian Nights,* 1882

INTEGRITY   See HONESTY & SINCERITY;
SELF; VIRTUE

INTELLIGENCE   See GENIUS; MIND, THOUGHT, &
UNDERSTANDING

INTIMACY & FAMILIARITY

Familiarity breeds contempt.
—AESOP, *The Fox and the Lion,* 6th cent. B.C.
[See Mark Twain's amendment, below.]

No man is a hero to his valet.
—ANNE BIGOT DU CORNUEL,
quoted in *Lettres de Mme. Aissé,* Aug. 13, 1728

Many a man has been a wonder to the world, whose wife and valet have seen nothing in him that was even remarkable. Few men have been admired by their servants.
—MONTAIGNE, *Essays,* 1580–88

Familiarity breeds contempt—and children.
—MARK TWAIN, d. 1910,
Albert B. Paine, ed., *Mark Twain's Notebook,* 1935

INVENTION See NEW THINGS; SCIENCE: DISCOVERY;
SCIENCE: TECHNOLOGY & EXPLORATION

IRELAND   See NATIONS

ITALY   See NATIONS

J

JEALOUSY

Jealousy is nothing but the foolish child of pride.
        —PIERRE-AUGUSTIN DE BEAUMARCHAIS,
                The Marriage of Figaro, 1784

Love is as strong as death; jealousy is as cruel as the grave.
                —BIBLE, *Song of Solomon* 8:6

The ear of jealousy heareth all things.
                —BIBLE, *Wisdom of Solomon*, 1:10

It is not love that is blind, but jealousy.
                —LAWRENCE DURRELL, *Justine*, 1957

Jealousy is always born with love, but does not always die
with it.   —LA ROCHEFOUCAULD, *Maxims*, 1678

O! beware, my lord, of jealousy.
It is the green-eyed monster which doth mock the meat it
    feeds on.   —SHAKESPEARE, *Othello*, III, iii

There is no greater glory than love, nor any greater punishment than jealousy.
        —LOPE DE VEGA, d. 1635, *Cantorcillo de la Virgen*

JERUSALEM   See CITIES

JESUS   See also CHRISTMAS; GOD; PROVIDENCE, DIVINE; RELIGION

And the angel came in unto her, and said, Hail, thou that art highly favored, the Lord is with thee; blessed art thou among women. . . .

Thou shalt conceive in thy womb, and bring forth a son, and shalt call his name Jesus.   —BIBLE, *Luke* 1:28 & 31

In the beginning was the Word, and the Word was with God, and the Word was God.   —BIBLE, *John* 1:1

In him was life; and the life was the light of men.
And the light shineth in darkness; and the darkness comprehended it not.   —*Ibid.* 1:4 & 5

And the Word was made flesh, and dwelt among us (and we beheld his glory, the glory as of the only begotten of the Father), full of grace and truth.   —*Ibid.* 1:14

For God so loveth the world, that he gave his only begotten son, that whosoever believeth in him should not perish, but have everlasting life.   —*Ibid.* 3:16

I am the good shepherd. The good shepherd giveth his life for the sheep.   —*Ibid.* 10:11

Jesus Christ the same yesterday, and today, and forever.
—BIBLE, *Hebrews* 13:8

Christ is all, and in all.   —BIBLE, *Colossians* 3:11

If Jesus Christ were to come today, people would not even crucify him. They would ask him to dinner, and hear what he had to say, and make fun of it.
—THOMAS CARLYLE, comment, in D. A. Wilson, *Carlyle at His Zenith: 1848–53, Life of Carlyle,* 1923–34

Stand Up, Stand Up for Jesus.
—GEORGE DUFFIELD, hymn title, 1818

Christ of his gentleness,
Thirsting and hungering
Walked in the wilderness;
Soft words of grace he spoke
Unto lost desert-folk
That listened wondering.
—ROBERT GRAVES, *In the Wilderness*, c. 1914

Have you been to Jesus for the cleansing power?
Are you washed in the blood of the Lamb?
—ELISHA B. HOFFMAN, hymn

Thou hast conquered, Galilean!
—JULIAN THE APOSTATE,
attributed deathbed words, A.D. 363

Jesus died too soon. He would have repudiated his doctrine
if he had lived to my age. —FRIEDRICH NIETZSCHE,
Thus Spake Zarathustra, 1883–91

Whether you think Jesus was God or not, you must admit
he was a first-rate political economist.
—GEORGE BERNARD SHAW, *Jesus as Economist*
Preface to *Androcles and the Lion*, 1912

Thou hast conquered, O pale Galilean; the world has grown
gray from thy breath;
We have drunken of things Lethean, and fed on the fullness
of death. —ALGERNON C. SWINBURNE,
Hymn to Proserpine, 1866

Jesus, lover of my soul,
Let me to thy bosom fly,
While the nearer waters roll,
While the tempest still is high.
—CHARLES WESLEY, *In Temptation*, 1740

Christ is God clothed with human nature.
—BENJAMIN WHICHCOTE,
Moral and Religious Aphorisms, 1753

JEWS   See RACES & PEOPLES

JOY   See HAPPINESS; HAPPINESS, EXPRESSIONS OF

JUDGES See also JUSTICE; LAW

Tell God the truth, but give the judge money.
——ANONYMOUS (RUSSIAN PROVERB)

Oh that I were made judge. ——BIBLE, *II Samuel* 15:4
[A heartfelt prayer as common today as in ancient times. The speaker here is Absalom, whose wish is granted and who uses the position to win allies in his ill-fated rebellion against his father, King David.]

Judges are the weakest link in our system of justice, and they are also the most protected.
——ALAN DERSHOWITZ, *Newsweek*, Feb. 20, 1978
[For Oliver Wendell Holmes, Jr., on a weak judge, see under INSULTS & PUT-DOWNS.]

The Law is the true embodiment
Of everything that's excellent.
It has no kind of fault or flaw,
And I, my lords, embody the Law.
——W. S. GILBERT, *Iolanthe*, 1882
[Sung by the Lord Chancellor.]

Even judges sometimes progress.
——EMMA GOLDMAN, *The Social Aspects of Birth Control* in *Mother Earth* magazine, Apr. 1916

The acme of judicial distinction means the ability to look a lawyer straight in the eyes for two hours and not to hear a damned word he says.
——JOHN MARSHALL, quoted in Albert J. Beveridge, *The Life of John Marshall*, 1916–19

We must never forget that the only real source of power that we as judges can tap is the respect of the people.
——THURGOOD MARSHALL, *Chicago Tribune*, Aug. 15, 1981

A judge is not supposed to know anything about the facts of life until they have been presented into evidence and explained to him at least three times.
——HUBERT LISTER PARKER, quoted in the *Observer*, Mar. 12, 1961
[Parker was Lord Chief Justice.]

When a judge sits in judgment over a fellow man, he should feel as if a sword is pointed at his own heart.
—TALMUD, compiled c. 6th cent. A.D., *Sanhedrin*

Disaster comes because of the kind of judges we have.
—TALMUD, compiled c. 6th cent. A.D., *Shabbat*

JUDGING OTHERS See EVIDENCE; FORGIVENESS &
MERCY; JUDGES; JUSTICE;
TOLERANCE & UNDERSTANDING

JUNE See NATURE: SEASONS

JUSTICE See also EVIDENCE; FORGIVENESS
& MERCY; JUDGES; LAW; LAWYERS;
PUNISHMENT; REVENGE

All virtue is summed up in dealing justly.
—ARISTOTLE, *Nicomachean Ethics,* 4th cent. B.C.

Let judgment run down as waters, and righteousness as a mighty stream.   —BIBLE, *Amos* 5:24
[See also Martin Luther King, Jr., at RACES & PEOPLES.]

With what measure ye mete, it shall be meted to you.
—BIBLE, *Mark* 4:24

God is not mocked: for whatsoever a man soweth, that shall he also reap.   —BIBLE, *Galatians* 6:7

For justice, though she's painted blind,
Is to the weaker side inclined.
—SAMUEL BUTLER, *Hudibras,* 1663

Justice is not to be taken by storm. She is to be wooed by slow advances.   —BENJAMIN N. CARDOZO,
The Growth of the Law, 1924

Justice is the crowning glory of the virtues.
—CICERO, *De officiis,* 44 B.C.

There is no such thing as justice—in or out of court.
—CLARENCE DARROW, interview,
The New York Times, Apr. 19, 1936

Justice is truth in action.
>—BENJAMIN DISRAELI, speech, Feb. 11, 1851

Justice . . . is a kind of compact not to harm or be harmed.
>—EPICURUS, *Principal Doctrines,* 4th–3rd cent. B.C.,
>quoted in Diogenes Laërtius, *Lives of Eminent*
>*Philosophers,* 3rd cent. A.D.

Only the just man enjoys peace of mind.
>—EPICURUS, fragment, c. 300 B.C.

Justice is the means by which established injustices are sanctioned. —ANATOLE FRANCE, *Crainquebille,* 1907

Thou shalt not ration justice.
>—LEARNED HAND, speech to the
>Legal Aid Society of New York, Feb. 16, 1951

It is of fundamental importance that justice should not only be done, but should manifestly and undoubtedly be seen to be done. —GORDON HEWART, *Rex v. Sussex Justices,*
>Nov. 9, 1923
[The comment came in Lord Chief Justice Hewart's judicial opinion in this case.]

Justice consists in taking from no man what is his.
>—THOMAS HOBBES, *Leviathan,* 1651

Injustice anywhere is a threat to justice everywhere.
>—MARTIN LUTHER KING, JR.,
>letter from the Birmingham, Ala., jail, Apr. 16, 1963

Love of justice in most men is no more than the fear of suffering injustice.
>—LA ROCHEFOUCAULD, *Maxims,* 1678

Your justice would freeze beer!
>—ARTHUR MILLER, *The Crucible,* 1953

I shalt temper . . . justice with mercy.
>—JOHN MILTON, *Paradise Lost,* 1667

Justice without force is impotent; force without justice is tyranny. —PASCAL, *Pensées,* 1670

Everywhere there is one principle of justice, which is the interest of the stronger.
>   —PLATO, *The Republic*, 4th cent. B.C.

All justice comes from God—he alone is its source.
>   —JEAN JACQUES ROUSSEAU,
>   *The Social Contract*, 1762

There are times when even justice brings harm with it.
>   —SOPHOCLES, *Electra*, 5th cent. B.C.

If they are just, they are better than clever.
>   —SOPHOCLES, *Philoctetes*, 5th cent. B.C.

There is one universal law. . . . That law is justice. Justice forms the cornerstone of each nation's law.
>   —ALEXIS DE TOCQUEVILLE,
>   *Democracy in America*, 1835–39

The laws of changeless justice bind
Oppressor and oppressed;
And close as sin and suffering joined,
We march to fate abreast.
>   —JOHN GREENLEAF WHITTIER, *At Port Royal*, 1862

The good ended happily, and the bad unhappily. That is what Fiction means.
>   —OSCAR WILDE,
>   *The Importance of Being Earnest*, 1895

K

KINDNESS   See CHARITY: PHILANTHROPY;
COMPASSION & PITY; FORGIVENESS &
MERCY; VIRTUE

KINGS   See HIGH POSITION: RULERS & LEADERS

KNOWLEDGE   See EDUCATION & LEARNING;
PHILOSOPHY; QUESTIONS & ANSWERS;
SCIENCE; WISDOM

L

LABOR   See WORK & WORKERS

LAISSEZ-FAIRE   See CAPITALISM

LANGUAGE & WORDS   See also ARTS: STYLE IN
                         WRITING & EXPRESSION; ARTS:
WRITING; CONVERSATION; EVIDENCE (Butler);
                         NAMES; SILENCE; TALK

Words are slippery.   —HENRY ADAMS,
                    The Education of Henry Adams, 1907
[The full sentence runs, "No one means all he says, yet very
few say all they mean, for words are slippery and thought is
viscous."]

A word said is a shot fired.
                    —ANONYMOUS (UZBEK PROVERB)
[Uzbekistan is north of Afghanistan.]

By thy words thou shalt be justified, and by thy words thou
shalt be condemned.   —BIBLE, *Matthew* 12:37
[More at TALK.]

What so wild as words are?
    —ROBERT BROWNING, *A Woman's Last Word,* 1855

A blow with a word strikes deeper than a blow with a sword.
                    —ROBERT BURTON,
                    The Anatomy of Melancholy, 1621–51

"When I use a word," Humpty Dumpty said, in a rather scornful tone, "it means just what I choose it to mean—neither more nor less."

"The question is," said Alice, "whether you can make words mean so many different things."

"The question is," said Humpty Dumpty, "which is to be master—that's all."
—LEWIS CARROLL, *Through the Looking-Glass,* 1872

I speak Spanish to God, Italian to women, French to men, and German to my horse.
—EMPEROR CHARLES V, attributed

It depends what the meaning of *is* is.
—WILLIAM JEFFERSON CLINTON,
grand jury testimony, Aug. 17, 1998
[The issue was whether the president should have corrected his lawyer during a deposition on Jan. 17, 1998, when the lawyer said regarding an affidavit by White House intern Monica Lewinsky, "There is absolutely no sex of any kind in any manner, shape or form." The president contended that he was not obligated to speak up because the lawyer had used the present tense and he himself had not engaged in "improper contact" with Ms. Lewinsky for some time previously.]

Fine words and an insinuating appearance are seldom associated with true virtue. —CONFUCIUS, *Analects,* 6–5 B.C.

A word is dead
When it is said,
Some say.
I say it just
Begins to live
That day. —EMILY DICKINSON, poem no. 1212, c. 1872

Language is the archives of history.
—RALPH WALDO EMERSON,
The Poet in *Essays: Second Series,* 1844
[And from the same essay, "Language is fossil poetry."]

You can stroke people with words.
—F. SCOTT FITZGERALD,
The Note-Books in *The Crack-Up,* 1945

The chief merit of language is clarity, and we know that nothing detracts so much from this as do unfamiliar terms.
—GALEN, *On the Natural Faculties*, 2nd cent. A.D.

Fair words cost nothing. —JOHN GAY, *The Mohocks*, 1712

Words are mere sound and smoke, dimming the heavenly light.
—GOETHE, *Faust*, 1808

In two words: im-possible.
—SAMUEL GOLDWYN, d. 1974, attributed

Language is the house of Being. In its home man dwells.
—MARTIN HEIDEGGER, c. 1959
[Cited in *The New York Times Book Review*, May 3, 1998.]

The tongue of man is a twisty thing.
—HOMER, *Iliad*, 8th cent. B.C.

Once a word has been allowed to escape, it can never be recalled.
—HORACE, *Epistles*, Book I, 20 B.C.

Language is the dress of thought. —SAMUEL JOHNSON,
Lives of the English Poets, 1779–81
[For a similar thought, see Wesley at ARTS: STYLE IN WRITING & EXPRESSION. Lord Chesterfield, in a letter from 1749, wrote "Style is the dress of thoughts."]

My heavens! I've been talking prose for the last forty years without knowing it. —MOLIÈRE, *Le Bourgeois Gentilhomme*, 1670

Grammar, which can govern even kings.
—MOLIÈRE, *Les Femmes savantes*, 1672

Every word is a preconceived judgment.
—FRIEDRICH NIETZSCHE,
Human All-Too-Human, 1878

The use of language is all we have to pit against death and silence. —JOYCE CAROL OATES, speech,
National Book Awards, Mar. 12, 1969

The great enemy of clear language is insincerity.
—GEORGE ORWELL, *Politics and
the English Language,* 1946

What we have here is a failure to communicate.
—FRANK R. PIERSON, screenplay,
Cool Hand Luke, 1967

One of our defects as a nation is a tendency to use what
have been called "weasel words."
—THEODORE ROOSEVELT, speech, May 31, 1916
[Elsewhere Roosevelt explained that such words "weasel the
meaning out of the words in front of them, just like a weasel
when he sucks the meat out of an egg." "Weasel words" was
Roosevelt's label for Woodrow Wilson's call for "universal vol-
untary" military training.]

Slang is a language that rolls up its sleeves, spits on its
hands, and goes to work.   —CARL SANDBURG,
The New York Times, Feb. 13, 1959

Words are weapons, and it is dangerous . . . to borrow them
from the arsenal of the enemy.
—GEORGE SANTAYANA,
Obiter Scripta, 1936

These are but wild and whirling words.
—SHAKESPEARE, *Hamlet,* I, v

They have been at a great feast of languages, and stolen the
scraps.   —SHAKESPEARE, *Love's Labour's Lost,* V, i

Taffeta phrases, silken terms precise,
Three-piled hyperboles, spruce affectation,
Figures pedantical.   —*Ibid.,* V, ii

Words pay no debts.
—SHAKESPEARE, *Troilus and Cressida,* III, ii
[Also, "Words are no deeds," *Henry VIII,* III, ii.]

Silence hides nothing. Words conceal.
—AUGUST STRINDBERG, *The Ghost Sonata,* 1907

An idea does not pass from one language to another without
change.   —MIGUEL DE UNAMUNO,
                                                The Tragic Sense of Life, 1913

The limits of my language mean the limits of my world.
                                                —LUDWIG WITTGENSTEIN,
                                                Tractatus logico-philosophicus, 1922

LAST JUDGMENT   See also HELL;
& THE HEREAFTER   IMMORTALITY;
                                                WORLD, END OF

But many that are first shall be last; and the last shall be
first.   —BIBLE, *Matthew* 19:30

And whosoever shall exalt himself shall be abased; and he
that shall humble himself shall be exalted.   —*Ibid.* 23:12

He shall separate them one from another, as a shepherd
divideth his sheep from his goats.   —*Ibid.* 25:32

Don't wait for the Last Judgment. It takes place every day.
                                                —ALBERT CAMUS, *The Fall*, 1956

Abou Ben Adhem (may his tribe increase!)
Awoke one night from a deep dream of peace,
And saw, within the moonlight of the room,
Making it rich, and like a lily in bloom,
An angel writing in a book of gold.
     —LEIGH HUNT, *Abou Ben Adhem and the Angel*, 1838

Write me as one that loves his fellow men.   —*Ibid.*
[Ben Adhem's words to the angel.]

The angel wrote, and vanished. The next night
It came again with a great wakening light,
And showed the names whom love of God had blessed
And lo! Ben Adhem's name led all the rest.   —*Ibid.*

The bottom line is in heaven.
                                                —EDWIN HERBERT LAND,
                                                shareholders' meeting, Polaroid Corp.,
                                                Apr. 26, 1977

Now hast thou but one bare hour to live
And then thou must be damned perpetually!
Stand still you ever-moving spheres of heaven,
That time may cease and midnight never come.
    —CHRISTOPHER MARLOWE, *Dr. Faustus*, 1604

The way to heaven out of all places is of like length and
distance.   —THOMAS MORE, *Utopia*, 1516

LAUGHTER   See also HUMOR

Meaningless laughter is a sign of ill-breeding.
    —ANONYMOUS (ARAB PROVERB)

A maid that laughs is half taken.
    —ANONYMOUS (ENGLISH PROVERB),
    quoted in John Ray, *English Proverbs*, 1670
[St. John Chrysostom may have had this in mind when he related laughter to sin; see below.]

He laughs best who laughs last.
    —ANONYMOUS (ENGLISH PROVERB)
[H. L. Mencken noted that this appears to be proverbial in all
European languages.]

Man thinks. God laughs.
    —ANONYMOUS (JEWISH PROVERB)

I force myself to laugh at everything for fear of being
obliged to weep.
    —PIERRE-AUGUSTIN DE BEAUMARCHAIS,
    The Barber of Seville, 1775

Laughter has no greater enemy than emotion.
    —HENRI BERGSON, *Laughter: An Essay
    on the Meaning of the Comic*, 1910
[Bergson went on to say that laughter requires "a momentary
anesthesia of the heart."]

No man who has once heartily and wholly laughed can be
altogether irreclaimably bad.
    —THOMAS CARLYLE, *Sartor Resartus*, 1833–34

Nothing is sillier than silly laughter.
—CATULLUS, *Carmina,* c. 60 B.C.

The most wasted of all days is that in which we have not
laughed. —SÉBASTIEN R. N. CHAMFORT,
Maximes et pensées, 1805

In my mind, there is nothing so illiberal and so illbred as
audible laughter.
—EARL OF CHESTERFIELD, letter to his son, Mar. 9, 1748

Laughter does not seem to be a sin, but it leads to sin.
—ST. JOHN CHRYSOSTOM, *Homilies,* c. 386–98

One must laugh before one is happy or one may die without
ever having laughed at all.
—LA BRUYÈRE, *Les Caractères,* 1688
To laugh is proper to man.
—FRANÇOIS RABELAIS, *Gargantua,* Book I, 1532

Laugh, and the world laughs with you;
Weep, and you weep alone.
—ELLA WHEELER WILCOX,
Solitude in *Collected Poems,* 1917

LAW See also EVIDENCE; GOVERNMENT;
JUDGES; JUSTICE; LAWYERS

A government of laws, and not of men.
—JOHN ADAMS, *Novanglus* papers,
No. 7, *Boston Gazette,* 1774
[Adams, who used the pseudonym "Novanglus," credited the
above phrase to James Harrington. In his utopian work, *The
Commonwealth of Oceana* (1656), Harrington wrote of government as "the empire of laws and not of men." Adams used his
own rephrased version in the Massachusetts Constitution Bill
of Rights (1780).]

Go to law for a sheep and lose your cow.
—ANONYMOUS (GERMAN PROVERB)

Law is a Bottomless Pit.
—JOHN ARBUTHNOT, pamphlet title, 1712

Law means good order.
>—ARISTOTLE, *Politics,* 4th cent. B.C.

All law has for its object to confirm and exalt into a system the exploitation of the workers by a ruling class.
>—MIKHAIL A. BAKUNIN, *God and the State,* 1882

If you like laws and sausage, you should never watch either being made. —OTTO VON BISMARCK, attributed
[In *Respectfully Quoted,* published by the Library of Congress, the widely accepted Bismarck attribution is described as unverified.]

It is better that ten guilty persons escape than one innocent suffer. —WILLIAM BLACKSTONE, *Commentaries on the Laws of England,* 1765–79
[See also Voltaire, below.]

One law for the lion and ox is oppression.
>—WILLIAM BLAKE, *The Marriage of Heaven and Hell,* 1790–93

If we would guide by the light of reason, we must let our minds be bold. —LOUIS D. BRANDEIS, *N.Y. State Ice Co. v. Liebmann,* 1932

There is but one law for all, namely, that law which governs all law, the law of our Creator, the law of humanity, justice, equity—the law of nature, and of nations.
>—EDMUND BURKE, speech, May 28, 1794
[And similarly, "There is a higher law than the Constitution," William Henry Seward, speech, U.S. Senate, Mar. 11, 1850. Seward was protesting the Compromise of 1850, a set of bills that permitted slavery in some parts of the U.S.]

The people's good is the highest law.
>—CICERO, *De legibus,* c. 52 B.C.

How long soever it hath continued, if it be against reason, it is of no force in law.
>—EDWARD COKE, *Commentary on Littleton* in *First Institute,* 1628

Conscience and law never go together.
>—WILLIAM CONGREVE, *The Double Dealer,* 1694

One with the law is a majority.
>—CALVIN COOLIDGE, speech, July 27, 1920

Law [is] a horrible business.
>—CLARENCE DARROW, interview,
>*The New York Times,* Apr. 19, 1936

"If the law supposes that," said Mr. Bumble . . . "the law is a ass—a idiot."
>—CHARLES DICKENS, *Oliver Twist,* 1837–38

Good men must not obey the laws too well.
>—RALPH WALDO EMERSON,
>*Politics* in *Essays: Second Series,* 1844

A fox should not be of the jury at a goose's trial.
>—THOMAS FULLER, *Gnomologia,* 1732

Public opinion is always in advance of the law.
>—JOHN GALSWORTHY, *Windows,* 1922

There is no better way of exercising the imagination than the study of law. No poet ever interpreted nature as freely as a lawyer interprets the truth.
>—JEAN GIRAUDOUX, *Tiger at the Gates,* 1935

Law is mighty, mightier necessity.
>—GOETHE, *Faust,* Part II, 1832

[For more on necessity and law, see NECESSITY.]

Laws grind the poor, and rich men rule the law.
>—OLIVER GOLDSMITH, *The Traveller,* 1764

A verbal contract isn't worth the paper it's printed on.
>—SAMUEL GOLDWYN, d. 1974, attributed

The law is not the same at morning and at night.
>—GEORGE HERBERT, *Jacula prudentum,* 1651

The life of the law has not been logic; it has been experience. —OLIVER WENDELL HOLMES, JR.,
The Common Law, 1881

Great cases like hard cases make bad law.
  —OLIVER WENDELL HOLMES, JR.,
Northern Securities Co. v. U.S., 1904
[Holmes was alluding to the legal byword: "Hard cases make bad law."]

The execution of the laws is more important than the making of them. —THOMAS JEFFERSON, letter to the
Abbé Arnoux, July 19, 1789

It is a fortunate thing for society that the courts do not get the same chance at the Ten Commandments as they do at the Constitution of the United States.
  —PHILANDER C. JOHNSON,
Senator Sorghum's Primer of Politics, 1906

Morality cannot be legislated but behavior can be regulated. Judicial decrees may not change the heart, but they can restrain the heartless. —MARTIN LUTHER KING, JR.,
Strength to Love, 1963

Wherever law ends, tyranny begins.
  —JOHN LOCKE, *Two Treatises on Government*, 1690
[The almost identical observation was made, or borrowed, by William Pitt, see below.]

Useless laws weaken the necessary laws.
  —MONTESQUIEU, *The Spirit of Laws*, 1748

Laws were made to be broken.
  —CHRISTOPHER NORTH, *Noctes Ambrosianae*
in *Blackwood's Magazine*, May 1830

Where laws end, tyranny begins.
  —WILLIAM PITT, EARL OF CHATHAM,
speech on the Wilkes case, Jan. 9, 1770
[Note similarity to John Locke's comment, above. John Wilkes, a notorious libertine and opponent of George III, was constantly in trouble with the government and the law—and was elected four times to Parliament while in prison. "Wilkes and

Liberty" became a rallying cry in Britain and the American colonies, where he and a fellow radical, Isaac Barré, are commemorated in the name of Wilkes-Barre, Pa. Pitt was one of Wilkes' supporters.]

The law must be stable, but it must not stand still.
> —ROSCOE POUND, *Introduction to the*
> *Philosophy of Law,* 1922

The law does not generate justice. The law is nothing but a declaration and application of what is just.
> —PIERRE-JOSEPH PROUDHON, *Of Justice*
> *in the Revolution and the Church,* 1858

Give me six lines written by the most honorable of men, and I will find an excuse in them to hang him.
> —CARDINAL RICHELIEU, *Mirame,* attributed, 1641

[The busy Cardinal hired various writers, Corneille included, to help realize his ideas for plays, and it is not known exactly who wrote what in the dramas that were produced under his name.]

No man is above the law and no man is below it; nor do we ask any man's permission when we require him to obey it. —THEODORE ROOSEVELT, speech, Jan. 1904

Laws are always useful to persons of property and hurtful to those who have none.
> —JEAN JACQUES ROUSSEAU,
> *The Social Contract,* 1762

[A century later, Anatole France referred ironically to "the majestic equality of the law, which forbids the rich as well as the poor to sleep under bridges, to beg in the streets, and to steal bread," *The Red Lily,* 1894.]

Ignorance of the law excuses no man: not that all men know the law, but because 'tis an excuse every man will plead, and no man can tell how to refute him.
> —JOHN SELDEN, *Law* in *Table Talk,* 1689

[Assembled and published thirty-five years after Selden's death.]

The law hath not been dead, though it hath slept.
> —SHAKESPEARE, *Measure for Measure,* II, ii

Pity is the virtue of the law.
> —SHAKESPEARE, *Timon of Athens,* III, v

[The meaning is that pity, or mercy, is the best characteristic of law.]

Laws are like spiders' webs: If some poor weak creature come up against them, it is caught; but a big one can break through and get away. —SOLON, 6th cent. B.C., quoted in
> Diogenes Laërtius, *Lives of Eminent Philosophers,* 3rd cent. A.D.

The law at its most rigorous is often injustice at its worst.
> —TERENCE, *The Self-Tormentor,* 163 B.C.

It is better to risk saving a guilty man than to condemn an innocent one. —VOLTAIRE, *Zadig,* 1747

[The idea is probably better known in Blackstone's formulation, see above.]

LAWYERS   See also LAW

The Pharisees and lawyers rejected the counsel of God.
> —BIBLE, *Luke* 7:30

Lawyer, n. One skilled in circumvention of the law.
> —AMBROSE BIERCE, *The Devil's Dictionary,* 1906

Our wrangling lawyers . . . are so litigious and busy here on earth, that I think they will plead their clients' causes hereafter, some of them in hell. —ROBERT BURTON,
> *The Anatomy of Melancholy,* 1621–51

Resolve to be honest at all events: and if in your judgment you cannot be an honest lawyer, resolve to be honest without being a lawyer. Choose some other occupation.
> —ABRAHAM LINCOLN, notes for a lecture, 1850

They have no lawyers among them [in Utopia] for they consider them as the sort of people whose profession it is to disguise matters. —THOMAS MORE, *Utopia,* 1516

The first thing we do, let's kill all the lawyers.
> —SHAKESPEARE, *Henry VI, Part II,* IV, ii

[One of the most popular Shakespearian quotes, even though

the speaker—Dick the Butcher—is not a likable character, and lawyers in this context represent order and justice.]

LAZINESS   See also LEISURE; PHYSICAL FITNESS; PROCRASTINATION; PRUDENCE & PRACTICAL WISDOM

Laziness is often mistaken for patience.
                              —ANONYMOUS (FRENCH PROVERB)

Go to the ant, thou sluggard; consider her ways, and be wise.   —BIBLE, *Proverbs* 6:6
[More at WORK & WORKERS.]

Laziness travels so slowly that poverty soon overtakes him.
                              —BENJAMIN FRANKLIN,
                              The Way to Wealth, July 7, 1757

Idle men are dead all their life long.
                              —THOMAS FULLER, *Gnomologia,* 1732

I have all my life long been lying [in bed] till noon; yet I tell all young men, and tell them with great sincerity, that nobody who does not rise early will ever do any good.
                              —SAMUEL JOHNSON, quoted by
                              James Boswell, *Journal of a Tour to
                              the Hebrides,* Sept. 14, 1773

If you are idle, be not solitary; if you are solitary, be not idle.   —SAMUEL JOHNSON, letter to James Boswell, 1779
[A variation of Robert Burton's advice for curing melancholy; see WORK & WORKERS.]

Lazy people are always looking for something to do.
                              —MARQUIS DE VAUVENARGUES,
                              Maximes et pensées, c. 1747

Iron rusts from disuse, stagnant water loses its purity and in cold weather becomes frozen; even so does inaction sap the vigors of the mind.   —LEONARDO DA VINCI,
                              Notebooks, 1508–18
[See also "rust" quote from Sir Walter Scott at LEISURE.]

LEADERS See HIGH POSITION: RULERS & LEADERS

LEARNING   See EDUCATION & LEARNING

LEISURE   See also LAZINESS; WORK & WORKERS

Better to idle well than to work badly.
          —ANONYMOUS (SPANISH PROVERB)

Rest is for the dead.
          —THOMAS CARLYLE, *Journal,* June 22, 1830

What is this life, if full of care,
We have no time to stand and stare.
          —W. H. DAVIES, *Leisure* in *Songs of Joy,* 1911
[Davies was a well-traveled vagrant; see his classic *Autobiography of a Super-Tramp,* 1908. Bernard Shaw, in 1905, had recognized his talent and set him on the road to fame.]

The occupation most becoming a civilized man is to do nothing.   —THÉOPHILE GAUTIER,
          Caprices and Zigzags, 1845

Too much rest itself becomes a pain.
          —HOMER, *Odyssey,* 8th cent. B.C.

Too much rest is rust.
          —SIR WALTER SCOTT, *The Betrothed,* 1825
[A saying that has been widely used. Wilhelm II of Germany as a youth adopted the motto, "If I rest, I rust." See also the Leonardo da Vinci passage at LAZINESS.]

It is a great art to saunter.
          —HENRY DAVID THOREAU,
          Journal, Apr. 26, 1841

The man who does not betake himself at once and desperately to sawing is called a loafer, though he may be knocking at the doors of heaven all the while.
          —HENRY DAVID THOREAU,
          The Pond in Winter in *Walden,* 1854

For Satan finds some mischief still
For idle hands to do.
          —ISAAC WATTS, *Against Idleness and
          Mischief* in *Divine Songs,* 1715

LIBERTY   See FREEDOM

LIES   See DISHONESTY & LIES

LIFE   See also EXPERIENCE; GENERATIONS;
               HEDONISM; HUMANS & HUMAN NATURE

And we are here as on a darkling plain
Swept with confused alarms of struggle and flight,
Where ignorant armies clash by night.
                    —MATTHEW ARNOLD, *Dover Beach,* 1867

All creatures live bewildered.
                    —BHAGAVAD GITA, c. 250 B.C.–A.D. 250
[The Lord Krishna is speaking.]

Life is a long lesson in humility.
                    —JAMES M. BARRIE, *The Little Minister,* 1891

To every thing there is a season, and a time to every purpose
    under the heaven:
A time to be born and a time to die; a time to plant, and
    a time to pluck up that which is planted;
A time to kill, and a time to heal; a time to break down,
    and a time to build up;
A time to weep, and a time to laugh; a time to mourn, and
    a time to dance;
A time to cast away stones, and a time to gather stones
    together; a time to embrace, and a time to refrain from
    embracing;
A time to get, and a time to lose; a time to keep, and a
    time to cast away;
A time to rend, and a time to sew; a time to keep silence,
    and a time to speak;
A time to love, and a time to hate; a time of war, and a
    time of peace.   —BIBLE, *Ecclesiastes* 3:1–8

Oh, the wild joys of living!
                    —ROBERT BROWNING, *Saul,* 1855

How good is man's life, the mere living! how fit to employ
All the heart and the soul and the sense for ever in joy!
                    —*Ibid.*

We are involved in a life that passes understanding and our highest business is our daily life.
> —JOHN CAGE, *Where Are We Going and What Are We Doing?* in *Silence,* 1961

There are only two or three human stories, and they go on repeating themselves as fiercely as if they had never happened before. —WILLA CATHER, *O Pioneers,* 1913

If life had a second edition, how I would correct the proofs.
> —JOHN CLARE, letter to a friend, quoted in J. W. Tibble and Anne Tibble, *John Clare: A Life,* 1932

Life always has the last word.
> —LE CORBUSIER, d. 1963, quoted in Witold Rybczynski, *A Journey Through Architecture,* 1992

What is life? It is a flash of a firefly in the night. It is the breath of a buffalo in the wintertime. It is the little shadow which runs across the grass and loses itself in the sunset.
> —CROWFOOT, last words, 1890

That it will never come again
Is what makes life so sweet.
> —EMILY DICKINSON, d. 1886; poem no. 1741, date unknown

What we anticipate seldom occurs; what we least expected generally happens. —BENJAMIN DISRAELI, *Henrietta Temple,* 1837

I have measured out my life with coffee spoons.
> —T. S. ELIOT, *The Love Song of J. Alfred Prufrock,* 1917

Birth, copulation, and death.
That's all the facts when you come to brass tacks.
> —T. S. ELIOT, *Sweeney Agonistes,* 1932

We are always getting ready to live but never living.
> —RALPH WALDO EMERSON, *Journal,* Apr. 13, 1834

Life consists in what a man is thinking of all day.
> —*Ibid.,* July–Aug. 1847

Only connect . . .
        —E. M. FORSTER, *Howards End,* epigraph, 1910
[What Forster had in mind is conveyed in this passage in the book: "Only connect! That was the whole of her sermon. Only connect the prose and the passion, and both will be exalted, and human love will be seen at its height. Live in fragments no longer. Only connect, and the beast and the monk, robbed of the isolation that is life to either, will die."]

Life is a jest; and all things show it.
I thought so once; but now I know it.
        —JOHN GAY, *My Own Epitaph,* 1720

A useless life is an early death.
        —GOETHE, *Iphigenia in Tauris,* 1787

Life is made up of marble and mud.
        —NATHANIEL HAWTHORNE,
        The House of the Seven Gables, 1851

Life is short, art long, opportunity fleeting, experience treacherous, judgment difficult.
        —HIPPOCRATES, *Aphorisms,* c. 400 B.C.
[For the proverbial version, see under ART & THE ARTS, the first quote. See also Hippocrates at WORK & WORKERS.]

The condition of man . . . is a condition of war of everyone against everyone.   —THOMAS HOBBES, *Leviathan,* 1651

. . . the life of man, solitary, poor, nasty, brutish, and short.
        —*Ibid.*

Life is just one damn thing after another.
        —ELBERT HUBBARD, *The Roycroft
        Dictionary and Book of Epigrams,* 1923
[For Edna St. Vincent Millay's response, see below.]

How small it's all. —JAMES JOYCE, *Finnegans Wake,* 1939

There is always inequity in life. Some men are killed in a war and some men are wounded, and some men never leave the country. . . . Life is unfair.
        —JOHN F. KENNEDY, press conference, Mar. 23, 1962

Life can only be understood backwards, but it must be lived
forwards. —SØREN KIERKEGAARD, *Either/Or:*
A Fragment of Life, 1843

For men must work and women must weep,
And the sooner it's over, the sooner to sleep.
  —CHARLES KINGSLEY, *The Three Fishers,* 1851

Life is real! Life is earnest!
And the grave is not its goal;
Dust thou art, to dust returnest,
Was not spoken of the soul.
  —HENRY WADSWORTH LONGFELLOW,
A Psalm of Life, 1839

Ships that pass in the night, and speak each other in passing;
Only a signal shown and a distant voice in the darkness;
So on the ocean of life we pass and speak one another,
Only a look and a voice; then darkness again and a silence.
  —HENRY WADSWORTH LONGFELLOW,
The Theologian's Tale: Elizabeth in
Tales of a Wayside Inn, 1863–74

Life is one long struggle in the dark.
  —LUCRETIUS, *On the Nature of Things,* c. 57 B.C.

The world has always been the same; and there has always
been as much good fortune as bad in it.
  —MACHIAVELLI, Introduction, *Discourse upon the*
First Ten Books of Livy, 1531

It is not true that life is one damn thing after another—it is
one damn thing over and over.
  —EDNA ST. VINCENT MILLAY, letter to
Arthur Davison Ficke, Oct. 24, 1930

The value of life lies not in the length of days, but in the
use we make of them; a man may live long yet live very
little. —MONTAIGNE, *Essays,* 1580–88

Those who have compared life to a dream were right. . . .
We sleep when we are awake, and awake when sleeping.
  —*Ibid.*

La vie est vaine:
Un peu d'amour,
Un peu de haine,
Et puis—bonjour!
La vie est brève:
Un peu d'espoir,
Un peu de rêve,
Et puis—bon soir!

Life is aimless: a little love, a little hate, and then good day!
Life is short: a little hope, a little dreaming, and then—
    goodnight!
    —LÉON MONTENAEKEN, *Peu de chose,* c. 1900

Our existence is but a brief crack of light between two eter-
nities of darkness.
    —VLADIMIR NABOKOV, *Speak, Memory,* 1951

Our existence is but a series of footnotes to a vast obscure
unfinished masterpiece.
    —VLADIMIR NABOKOV, *Pale Fire,* 1962
[The sentence begins, "The cradle rocks above an abyss, and
common sense tells us that our existence is . . ."]

To burn always with this hard gem-like flame, to maintain
this ecstasy, is success in life.
    —WALTER PATER, *Studies in the
        History of the Renaissance, Conclusion,* 1873

The world itself is but a large prison out of which some
daily are led to execution.
    —SIR WALTER RALEIGH, remark, 1603
[Sir Walter made this comment while being led back to prison
after his trial for treason. He spent most of the next fifteen
years in confinement, not being executed until 1618.]

There is no wealth but life.
    —JOHN RUSKIN, *Unto This Last,* 1862

There must be more to life than having everything!
    —MAURICE SENDAK, *Higglety Pigglety Pop!,* 1967

All the world's a stage,
And all the men and women merely players.
    —SHAKESPEARE, *As You Like It,* II, vii

Life is as tedious as a twice-told tale
Vexing the dull ear of a drowsy man.
                    —SHAKESPEARE, *King John*, III, iv

When we are born, we cry that we are come
To this great stage of fools.
                    —SHAKESPEARE, *King Lear*, IV, vi

Life's but a walking shadow, a poor player
That struts and frets his hour upon the stage
And then is heard no more. It is a tale
Told by an idiot, full of sound and fury,
Signifying nothing.   —SHAKESPEARE, *Macbeth*, V, v

Dying is no big deal. The least of us will manage that. Living
is the trick.   —WALTER ("RED") SMITH, funeral eulogy
                    for golf impresario Fred Corcoran, 1977

Old and young, we are all on our last cruise.
                    —ROBERT LOUIS STEVENSON,
          Crabbèd Age and Youth in *Virginibus Puerisque*, 1881
[For the origin of Stevenson's title, see Shakespeare at
FAMILY.]

If a person saves one life it is as if he had saved the whole
world.   —TALMUD, compiled 6th cent. A.D.

While there's life, there's hope.
                    —TERENCE, *The Self-Tormentor*, 163 B.C.

The mass of men lead lives of quiet desperation.
                    —HENRY DAVID THOREAU,
                    Economy in *Walden*, 1854

Life is so unlike theory.
          —ANTHONY TROLLOPE, *Phineas Finn*, 1869

The world is a comedy to those that think, a tragedy to
those that feel.   —HORACE WALPOLE, letter to the
                    Countess of Upper Ossory, Aug. 16, 1776

Life is an offensive, directed against the repetitious mechanism of the universe.
—ALFRED NORTH WHITEHEAD,
Adventures of Ideas, 1933

Life imitates art far more than art imitates life.
—OSCAR WILDE, *The Decay of Lying*
in *Intentions,* 1891
[Cf. Seneca under ART & THE ARTS.]

The world is too much with us; late and soon,
Getting and spending, we lay waste our powers:
Little we see in Nature that is ours;
We have given our hearts away.
—WILLIAM WORDSWORTH,
The World Is Too Much with Us, 1807

Cast a cold eye
On life, on death.
Horseman, pass by!   —WILLIAM BUTLER YEATS,
Under Ben Bulben in *Last Poems,* 1936–39

LIMITS   See also FAILINGS

A man cannot jump over his own shadow.
—ANONYMOUS (YIDDISH PROVERB)
[Sometimes used in the sense: one cannot escape the consequences of one's acts.]

Beyond his strength no man can fight, though he be eager.
—HOMER, *The Iliad,* 8th cent. B.C.

He who stands on his tiptoes does not stand firm.
—LAO-TZU, *Tao Te Ching,* c. 6th cent. B.C.

Tempt us not to bear above our power!
—SHAKESPEARE, *King John,* V, vi

LITERATURE   See ARTS entries; BOOKS & READING

LITTLE THINGS   See DETAILS & OTHER SMALL
THINGS; THINGS & POSSESSIONS

LIVING WELL   See GRACE; HEDONISM; LIFE

LOGIC See MIND; PHILOSOPHY;
REASON & REASONS; REASONABLE &
UNREASONABLE PEOPLE

LONDON See CITIES

LONELINESS See SOLITUDE

LOS ANGELES See CITIES

LOSERS See HAVES AND HAVE-NOTS; RUIN;
WINNING & LOSING, VICTORY & DEFEAT

LOVE See also HEART; JEALOUSY; LOVE,
EXPRESSIONS OF; LOVE & CHARITY:
BIBLICAL REFERENCES; MARRIAGE;
SEX & SENSUALITY; WOMEN & MEN

Love teaches even asses to dance.
—ANONYMOUS (FRENCH PROVERB)

The heart that loves is always young.
—ANONYMOUS (GREEK PROVERB)

It is impossible to love and be wise.
—FRANCIS BACON, *Of Love,* 1625

Absence makes the heart grow fonder.
—T. H. BAYLY, d. 1839, *Isle of Beauty*
[The expression is proverbial, dating at least to the Roman
poet Sextus Propertius in the first century A.D.]

Where love is concerned, too much is not even enough.
—PIERRE-AUGUSTIN DE BEAUMARCHAIS,
The Marriage of Figaro, 1784

Who can give law to lovers? Love is a greater law to itself.
—BOETHIUS, *De consolatione philosophiae,* c. 524
[See also John Lyly, below.]

Man's love is of man's life a thing apart,
'Tis woman's whole existence.
—LORD BYRON, *Don Juan,* 1819–24

In her first passion woman loves her lover,
In all the others, all she loves is love.   —*Ibid.*
[Byron might have credited La Rochefoucauld, see below.]

Love, such as it is in society, is only the exchange of two
fantasies, and the contact of two bodies.
                              —SÉBASTIEN R. N. CHAMFORT,
                                        Maximes et pensées, 1805

Love is blind.   —GEOFFREY CHAUCER, *The Merchant's
                         Tale* in *The Canterbury Tales,* 1387–1400
[Essentially proverbial; see variations by Menander and Shakespeare, below.]

Can there be a love which does not make demands on its
object?   —CONFUCIUS, *Analects,* 6th–5th cent. B.C.

Love and murder will out.
        —WILLIAM CONGREVE, *The Double Dealer,* 1694
[For more on revelations of murder, see under CRIME.]

Love, all alike, no season knows, nor clime,
Nor hours, days, months, which are the rags of time.
              —JOHN DONNE, *The Sun Rising,* c. 1591–1601

For heaven be thanked, we live in such an age,
When no man dies for love, but on the stage.
            —JOHN DRYDEN, Epilogue, *Mithridates,* 1678

All mankind love a lover.
                          —RALPH WALDO EMERSON,
                            Love in *Essays: First Series,* 1841

Love is all we have, the only way that each can help the
other.   —EURIPIDES, *Orestes,* 408 B.C.

Earth's the right place for love;
I don't know where it's likely to go better.
                          —ROBERT FROST, *Birches,* 1916

The only regret I will have in dying is if it is not for love.
                          —GABRIEL GARCÍA MÁRQUEZ,
                            Love in the Time of Cholera, 1988
[In a *New York Times* interview, Aug. 21, 1991, García Már-

quez remarked that the Latin view of love was well put by
Brazilian songwriter Vinicius de Moralis: "Love is eternal as
long as it lasts."]

She who has never loved has never lived.
—JOHN GAY, *Captives*, 1724

It's love that makes the world go round!
—W. S. GILBERT, *Iolanthe*, 1882
[Probably proverbial. The French say, "*L'amour fait tourner
le monde.*"]

Love knows nothing of order.
—ST. JEROME, letter 7, c. 400

Love is swift, sincere, pious, pleasant, generous, strong, patient, faithful, prudent, long-suffering, manly, and never
seeking her own; for wheresoever a man seeketh his own,
there he falleth from love.   —THOMAS à KEMPIS,
Imitation of Christ, c. 420

A fool there was and he made his prayer
(Even as you and I!)
To a rag and a bone and a hank of hair
(We called her the woman who did not care)
But the fool he called her his lady fair—
Even as you and I.   —RUDYARD KIPLING,
The Vampire, 1897

If one judges love by the majority of its effects, it is more
like hatred than friendship.
—LA ROCHEFOUCAULD, *Maxims*, 1678

There is no disguise which can hide love for long where it
exists, or simulate it where it does not.   —*Ibid.*

In their first passion, women love their lovers; in all the
others, they love love.   —*Ibid.*
[See also Byron, above.]

It requires far more genius to make love than to command
armies.   —NINON DE LENCLOS, d. 1705, attributed

Two souls with but a single thought,
Two hearts that beat as one.
　　　　　　—MARIA LOVELL, *Ingomar the Barbarian*, 1896

Love is a product of habit.　　　　　　—LUCRETIUS,
　　　　　　　　　　On the Nature of Things, c. 57 B.C.
[A similar thought occurred to Jane Austen: "I am pleased
that you have learned to love a hyacinth, the mere habit of
learning to love is the thing."]

Love knoweth no laws.　　　—JOHN LYLY, *Euphues: The
　　　　　　　　　　　　Anatomy of Wit, 1579
[See also Boethius, above.]

Delicacy is to love what grace is to beauty.
　　　　　　—MADAME DE MAINTENON,
　　　　　　Maximes de Mme. de Maintenon, 1686

It is love, not reason, that is stronger than death.
　　　　　　—THOMAS MANN, *The Magic Mountain*, 1924

Who ever loved that loved not at first sight?
　　　　　　—CHRISTOPHER MARLOWE,
　　　　　　　　　　Hero and Leander, 1598
[Picked up by Shakespeare in *As You Like It*, III, v.]

When you have loved as she has loved, you grow old
beautifully.
　　　　　　—W. SOMERSET MAUGHAM, *The Circle*, 1921

Love blinds all men alike, both the reasonable and the
foolish.　　　　　　—MENANDER, *Andria*, 4th cent. B.C.

We are easily duped by those we love.
　　　　　　—MOLIÈRE, *Tartuffe*, 1664

No, there's nothing half so sweet in life
As love's young dream.
　　　　　　—THOMAS MOORE, *Love's Young Dream*
　　　　　　　　　　in *Irish Melodies*, 1807–34

This is the hardest of all: to close the open hand out of love, and to keep modest as a giver.
—FRIEDRICH NIETZSCHE,
Thus Spake Zarathustra, 1883–91

Love is a kind of warfare.
—OVID, *The Art of Love*, c. 2 B.C.

Oh, life is a glorious cycle of song,
A medley of extemporanea;
And love is a thing that can never go wrong,
And I am Marie of Roumania.   —DOROTHY PARKER,
Comment in *Enough Rope*, 1927

By the time you swear you're his
Shivering and sighing,
And he vows his passion is
Infinite, undying—
Lady make a note of this:
One of you is lying.   —DOROTHY PARKER,
Unfortunate Coincidence in *Ibid.*

[Love is] the joy of the good, the wonder of the wise, the amazement of the gods.   —PLATO, *The Symposium*,
4th cent. B.C.

There can be no peace of mind in love since the advantage one has secured is never anything but a fresh starting point for further desire.   —MARCEL PROUST, *Remembrance of Things Past: Within a Budding Grove*, 1913–27

Love consists in this, that two solitudes protect and border and salute each other.   —RAINER MARIA RILKE,
Letters to a Young Poet, May 14, 1904

What is life without the radiance of love?
—J.C.F. VON SCHILLER,
The Death of Wallenstein, 1798

Love means not ever having to say you're sorry.
—ERICH SEGAL, *Love Story*, 1970

Love is little;
Love is low;
Love will make our spirit grow;
Grow in peace,
Grow in light,
Love will do the thing that's right.—SHAKER song, c. 1800

Men have died from time to time and worms have eaten them, but not for love.
                    —SHAKESPEARE, *As You Like It,* IV, i

Love is a familiar. Love is a devil. There is no evil angel but Love.   —SHAKESPEARE, *Love's Labour's Lost,* I, ii

But love is blind, and lovers cannot see
The pretty follies that themselves commit.
                    —SHAKESPEARE, *The Merchant of Venice,* II, vi

The course of true love never did run smooth.
                    —SHAKESPEARE, *A Midsummer Night's Dream,* I, i

Speak low, if you speak love.
                    —SHAKESPEARE, *Much Ado About Nothing,* II, i

Speak of me as I am . . . Of one that loved not wisely but too well.   —SHAKESPEARE, *Othello,* V, ii

They do not love that do not show their love.
                    —SHAKESPEARE, *The Two
                    Gentlemen of Verona,* I, ii

Let me not to the marriage of true minds
Admit impediments. Love is not love
Which alters when it alteration finds,
Or bends with the remover to remove.
Oh no! It is an ever-fixèd mark
That looks on tempests and is never shaken.
It is the star to every wandering bark,
Whose worth's unknown, although his height be taken.
                    —SHAKESPEARE, sonnet 116

Love comforteth like sunshine after rain.
                    —SHAKESPEARE, *Venus and Adonis*

Familiar acts are beautiful through love.
—PERCY BYSSHE SHELLEY,
Prometheus Unbound, 1819

All love is sweet,
Given or returned. Common as light is love,
And its familiar voice wearies not ever. —*Ibid.*

All's fair in love and war.
—FRANCIS EDWARD SMEDLEY,
Frank Fairlegh, 1850

One word frees us of all the weight and pain of life: That
word is love. —SOPHOCLES, *Oedipus at Colonus,*
5th cent. B.C.

'Tis better to have loved and lost
Than never to have loved at all.
—ALFRED, LORD TENNYSON, *In Memoriam,* 1850

O, tell her, brief is life but love is long.
—ALFRED, LORD TENNYSON, *The Princess,* 1847

All, everything that I understand, I understand only because
I love. —LEO TOLSTOY, *War and Peace,* 1865–69

Love is the child of illusion, and the parent of disillusion.
—MIGUEL DE UNAMUNO,
The Tragic Sense of Life, 1913

Omnia vincit Amor: et nos cedamus Amori.
Love conquers all: and let us too surrender to love.
—VIRGIL, *Eclogues,* c. 37 B.C.

Love those who love you. —VOLTAIRE, letter to
d'Alembert, Nov. 28, 1762
[This is the last, often overlooked phrase in the noted *écrasez
l'infâme* exhortation, cited in full at RELIGION.]

'Tis said that some have died for love.
—WILLIAM WORDSWORTH, poem title, 1800

A pity beyond all telling
is hid in the heart of love.

—WILLIAM BUTLER YEATS,
The Pity of Love in *The Rose,* 1893

LOVE & CHARITY: See also LOVE
BIBLICAL REFERENCES

Thou shalt love thy neighbor as thyself.

—BIBLE, *Leviticus* 19:18
[Also found in several other places in the Bible, including most
notably *Matthew* 22:39, where in the next verse it is described
as one of the two essential commandments, along with the
commandment to love God—see under GOD.]

A new commandment I give unto you, that you love one
another.   —BIBLE, *John* 13:34

Though I speak with the tongues of men and of angels, and
have not charity, I am become as sounding brass, or a tin-
kling cymbal.   —BIBLE, *I Corinthians* 13:1

Charity suffereth long and is kind; charity envieth not; charity vaunteth not itself, is not puffed up.   —*Ibid.* 13:4

And now abideth faith, hope, and charity, these three; but
the greatest of these is charity.   —*Ibid.* 13:13

There is no fear in love; but perfect love casteth out fear.

—BIBLE, *I John* 4:18

He that loveth not his brother whom he hath seen, how can
he love God whom he hath not seen?   —*Ibid.* 4:20

LOVE, EXPRESSIONS OF   See also HAPPINESS,
EXPRESSIONS OF (Millay);
HEDONISM; LOVE; MARRIAGE;
WOMEN, BEAUTIFUL & HOMELY

Western Wind, when wilt thou blow,
That the small rain down can rain?
Christ if my love were in my arms
And I in my bed again.   —ANONYMOUS

He was my North, my South, my East and West.
My working week and my Sunday rest,
My noon, my midnight, my talk, my song;
I thought that love would last forever; I was wrong.
                    —W. H. AUDEN, *Twelve Songs*, 1936

Arise, my love, my fair one, and come away.
                    —BIBLE, *The Song of Solomon* 2:10–13
[The quote is given in full at NATURE: SEASONS.]

If ever two were one, then surely we.
If ever man were loved by wife, then thee.
                    —ANNE BRADSTREET,
                    To My Dear and Loving Husband, 1698

These I have loved:
White plates and cups, clean-gleaming,
Ringed with blue lines.
                    —RUPERT BROOKE, *The Great Lover*, 1914

Then, the cool kindliness of sheets, that soon
Smooth away trouble; and the rough male kiss
Of blankets; grainy wood; live hair that is
Shining and free; blue massing clouds; the keen
Unpassioned beauty of a great machine.   —*Ibid.*

How do I love thee? Let me count the ways.
I love thee to the depth and breadth and height
My soul can reach, when feeling out of sight
For the ends of being and ideal grace.
                    —ELIZABETH BARRETT BROWNING,
                    Sonnets from the Portuguese, 43, 1850

I love thee with the breath,
Smiles, tears, of all my life!—and, if God choose,
I shall but love thee better after death.   —*Ibid.*

But to see her was to love her,
Love but her, and love for ever.
                    —ROBERT BURNS, *Ae Fond Kiss*
                    in *Johnson's Musical Museum*, 1787–96
[In another poem, *Saw Ye Bonnie Lesley*, Burns wrote almost
identical lines: "To see her is to love her, / And love but her

for ever: / For Nature made her what she is, and never made sic anither!"]

O, my luve's like a red red rose
That's newly sprung in June:
O my luve's like the melodie
That's sweetly played in tune.
> —ROBERT BURNS, *A Red Red Rose* in
> *Scots Musical Museum*, 1796

O whistle an' I'll come to ye, my lad,
O whistle an' I'll come to ye, my lad,
Tho' father an' mother an' a' should gae mad,
O whistle an' I'll come to ye, my lad.
> —ROBERT BURNS, *O Whistle an' I'll Come to Ye,
> My Lad,* in George Thomson's *A Select
> Collection of Original Scottish Airs,* 1792–96

Come live with me, and be my love,
And we will some new pleasures prove
Of golden sands, and crystal brooks,
With silken lines, and silver hooks.
> —JOHN DONNE, *The Baite,* c. 1591–1601

[See below the similar but more famous verse by Christopher Marlowe, probably written a few years before Donne's version.]

I have found it impossible to carry the heavy burden of responsibility and to discharge my duties as king as I would wish without the help and support of the woman I love.
> —EDWARD VIII, abdication speech, Dec. 11, 1936

A book of verses underneath the bough
A jug of wine, a loaf of bread—and thou
Beside me singing in the wilderness.
> —EDWARD FITZGERALD,
> *The Rubáiyát of Omar Khayyám,* 1879

Why don't you speak for yourself, John?
> —HENRY WADSWORTH LONGFELLOW,
> *The Courtship of Miles Standish,* 1858

[Priscilla Mullens to John Alden, who had been speaking for his friend Miles Standish. Longfellow was descended from John and Priscilla.]

Come live with me and be my love,
And we will all the pleasures prove
That valleys, groves, hills, and fields,
Woods or steepy mountain yields.
　　　　　—CHRISTOPHER MARLOWE,
　　　　　　The Passionate Shepherd to His Love, c. 1589
[Cf. John Donne, above]

Lolita, light of my life, fire of my loins. My sin. My soul.
　　　　　　—VLADIMIR NABOKOV, *Lolita*, 1955
[The first line of the novel. For other first lines, see the list at
FAMILY, the Tolstoy quote.]

I was a child and she was a child,
In this kingdom by the sea;
But we loved with a love that was more than love
I and my Annabel Lee.
　　　　　—EDGAR ALLAN POE, *Annabel Lee*, 1849

What's mine is yours, and what is yours is mine.
　　　　　　—SHAKESPEARE, *Measure for Measure*, V, i
[Plautus used the same line.]

But, soft! What light through yonder window breaks?
It is the east, and Juliet is the sun.
　　　　　—SHAKESPEARE, *Romeo and Juliet*, II, ii

See how she leans her cheek upon her hand!
Oh, that I were a glove upon that hand,
That I might touch that cheek!　　　　　　　　　　*—Ibid.*

O Romeo, Romeo, wherefore art thou Romeo?
Deny thy father and refuse thy name,
Or, if thou wilt not, be but sworn my love
And I'll no longer be a Capulet.　　　　　　　　　*—Ibid.*

Parting is such sweet sorrow
That I shall say goodnight till it be morrow.　　　*—Ibid.*

When he shall die,
Take him and cut him out in little stars,
And he will make the face of heaven so fine
That all the world will be in love with night.　　　*—Ibid.*

Kiss me, Kate!
—SHAKESPEARE, *The Taming of the Shrew,* II, i

Shall I compare thee to a summer's day?
Thou art more lovely and more temperate.
—SHAKESPEARE, sonnet 18

•

Nothing in the world is single;
All things by a law divine
In one spirit meet and mingle.
Why not I with thine?   —PERCY BYSSHE SHELLEY,
Love's Philosophy, 1819

One can't live on love alone; and I am so stupid that I can
do nothing but think of him.
—SOPHIE TOLSTOY, Nov. 13, 1862,
in *A Diary of Tolstoy's Wife, 1860–91*

When you are old and gray and full of sleep
And nodding by the fire, take down this book,
And slowly read. . . .

How many loved your moments of glad grace,
And loved your beauty with love false or true;
But one man loved the pilgrim soul in you,
And loved the sorrows of your changing face.
—WILLIAM BUTLER YEATS,
When You Are Old in *The Rose,* 1893

LOYALTY   See UNITY AND LOYALTY

LUCK   See also FATE; WINNING & LOSING,
VICTORY & DEFEAT (Amundsen)

Throw a lucky man in the sea, and he will come up with a
fish in his mouth.   —ANONYMOUS (ARAB PROVERB)

The race is not to the swift, nor the battle to the strong,
neither yet bread to the wise, nor yet riches to men of understanding, nor yet favor to men of skill; but time and chance
happeneth to them all.   —BIBLE, *Ecclesiastes* 9:11

Who has good luck is good. Who has bad luck is bad.
—BERTOLT BRECHT,
The Exception and the Rule, 1937

Heaven's help is better than early rising.
—CERVANTES, *Don Quixote,* 1605–15
[Probably proverbial—Mencken cites as an Irish proverb,
"Good luck beats early rising."]

Luck is not chance—
It's toil—
Fortune's expensive smile
Is earned.   —EMILY DICKINSON, poem no. 1350, c. 1876

The lucky person passes for a genius.
—EURIPIDES, *Herakleidai,* c. 428 B.C.

Have but luck, and you will have the rest; be fortunate, and
you will be thought great.
—VICTOR HUGO, *Les Misérables,* 1862

A lucky man is rarer than a white cow.
—JUVENAL, *Satires,* c. A.D. 100

If it wasn't for bad luck, I wouldn't have no luck at all.
—ALBERT KING, *Born Under a Bad Sign,* 1993
[A folk saying that appears in many forms, including King's
blues classic, cited here.]

Now and then
there is a person born
who is so unlucky
that he runs into accidents
which started out to happen to somebody else.
—DON MARQUIS, *archy says*
in *archy's life of mehitabel,* 1933

Chance favors the prepared mind.
—LOUIS PASTEUR, speech, Dec. 7, 1854

Luck is the Residue of Design.
—BRANCH RICKEY, lecture title, 1950
[At the time, Rickey was running the Brooklyn Dodgers.]

Luck never made a man wise.
> —SENECA, *Letters to Lucilius,* 1st cent. A.D.

Fortune favors the brave.   —TERENCE, *Phormio,* 161 B.C.

'Tis better to be fortunate than wise.
> —JOHN WEBSTER, *The White Devil,* 1612

[More at FATE.]

Luck is not something you can mention in the presence of self-made men.
> —E. B. WHITE, *Control* in *One Man's Meat,* 1944

LUXURY   See EXCESS; HEDONISM

LYING   See DISHONESTY & LIES

M

MACHINES	See SCIENCE: TECHNOLOGY
MADNESS	See also ALIENATION; DESPAIR, DEPRESSION & MISERY; ILLNESS & REMEDIES (Freud and Proust); SCIENCE: PSYCHOLOGY

No excellent soul is exempt from a mixture of madness.
      —ARISTOTLE, d. 322 B.C., *Problemata* 30, 1.
[The citation is from Seneca, whose adaption is usually given a different translation; see GENIUS.]

We are all born mad. Some remain so.
      —SAMUEL BECKETT, *Waiting for Godot,* 1952

My name is Legion: for we are many.   —BIBLE, *Mark* 5:9
[The speaker is a devil inhabiting a madman of the Gadarenes. Jesus sent the devils to enter a herd of two thousand swine.]

Great wits are sure to madness near allied;
And thin partitions do their bonds divide.
      —JOHN DRYDEN, *Absalom and Achitophel,* 1680
[Popularized: There's a thin line between genius and madness.]

There is a pleasure sure
In being mad, which none but madmen know.
      —JOHN DRYDEN, *The Spanish Friar,* 1681

Sanity is very rare.
      —RALPH WALDO EMERSON, *Journal,* 1836

Those whom God wishes to destroy, he first makes mad.
      —EURIPIDES, fragment, 455–405 B.C.
[A proverbial comment, found in numerous other sources. In

a modern revision, Cyril Connolly wrote, "Whom the gods wish to destroy they first call promising," *Enemies of Promise.*]

I saw the best minds of my generation destroyed by madness. —ALLEN GINSBERG, *Howl,* 1956

The only people for me are the mad ones, the ones who are mad to live, mad to talk, mad to be saved, desirous of everything at the same time, the ones who never yawn or say a commonplace thing, but burn, burn like fabulous yellow roman candles exploding like spiders across the stars and in the middle you see the blue centerlight pop and everybody goes "Aww!" —JACK KEROUAC, *On the Road,* 1957

Everyone is more or less mad on one point.
> —RUDYARD KIPLING, *On the Strength of a Likeness* in *Plain Tales from the Hills,* 1888

My mind's not right.
. . .
I myself am hell;
nobody's here. —ROBERT LOWELL, *Skunk Hour,* 1959

Men . . . go mad in herds, while they only recover their senses slowly, and one by one.
> —CHARLES MacKAY, *Extraordinary Popular Delusions, and the Madness of Crowds,* 1852

As I was going up the stair,
I met a man who wasn't there.
He wasn't there again today.
I wish, I wish he'd stay away.
> —HUGHES MEARNS, *The Psycho-ed,* 1910

From childhood's hour I have not been
As others were—I have not seen
As others saw. —EDGAR ALLAN POE, *Alone,* 1829

Our occasional madness is less wonderful than our occasional sanity.
> —GEORGE SANTAYANA, *The Life of Reason: Reason in Common Sense,* 1905–06

There is no great genius without some touch of madness.
> —SENECA, *On Tranquillity of the Mind,* 1st cent. A.D.

Madness in great ones must not unwatched go.
—SHAKESPEARE, *Hamlet*, III, i
[See also *Hamlet* under METHOD.]

Is this a dagger which I see before me,
The handle toward my hand? Come let me clutch thee.
—SHAKESPEARE, *Macbeth*, II, i

Art thou but
A dagger of the mind, a false creation
Proceeding from the heat-oppressèd brain?   —*Ibid.*

It is an accustomed action with her to seem thus washing
her hands. I have known her continue in this a quarter of
an hour.   —*Ibid.*, V, i

Out, damned spot! Out, I say! One, two, why, then 'tis time
to do't. Hell is murky!   —*Ibid.*
[Lady Macbeth is speaking. See also GUILT.]

When we remember that we are all mad, the mysteries dis-
appear and life stands explained.
—MARK TWAIN, d. 1910, Albert B. Paine, ed.,
Mark Twain's Notebook, 1935

My apprehensions come in crowds;
I dread the rustling of the grass;
The very shadows of the clouds
Have power to shake me as they pass:
I question things and do not find
One that will answer to my mind;
And all the world appears unkind.
—WILLIAM WORDSWORTH,
The Affliction of Margaret, 1807

MAGIC   See OCCULT, THE

MAJORITY   See PEOPLE, THE

MALAYA   See NATIONS

MANDALAY   See CITIES

MANKIND   See HUMANS & HUMAN NATURE;
                    MEN; WOMEN & MEN

MANNERS   See also CUSTOM; GRACE;
                    HOSPITALITY; INSULTS & PUT-DOWNS

Whatsoever ye would that men should do to you, do ye
even so to them.   —BIBLE, *Matthew* 7:12
[Often paraphrased; known as the Golden Rule. See also related quotes from Confucius and Shaw, below.]

An injury is much sooner forgotten than an insult.
                            —EARL OF CHESTERFIELD,
                            letter to his son, Oct. 9, 1746

Take the tone of the company you are in.
                            —*Ibid.,* Oct. 9, 1747
[See also St. Ambrose at TRAVEL.]

O tempora! O mores!
O the times! O the manners!
                            —CICERO, *In catilinam,* 63 B.C.

To be audacious with tact, you have to know to what point
you can go too far.
                    —JEAN COCTEAU, *Le Coq et l'arlequin,*
                            1918, in *Le Rappel à l'ordre,* 1926
[The phrase "to know to what point you can go too far"—
savoir jusqu'ou on peut aller trop loin—has become a common
expression among French speakers.]

It is good manners which make the excellence of a neighborhood. No wise man will settle where they are lacking.
                    —CONFUCIUS, *Analects,* 6th–5th cent. B.C.

Behave to everyone as if you were receiving a great guest; . . .
[do not] do to others what you would not wish done to
yourself.   —*Ibid.*

The trouble with treating people as equals is that the first
thing you know they may be doing the same thing to you.
                    —PETER DE VRIES, *The Prick of Noon,* 1985

The art of pleasing consists in being pleased
> —WILLIAM HAZLITT, *On Manners*
> in *The Round Table*, 1817

[See also Samuel Johnson, below.]

You never want to give a man a present when he's feeling good. You want to do it when he's down.
> —LYNDON B. JOHNSON, quoted in Doris Kearns,
> *Lyndon Johnson and the American Dream*, 1976

He who endeavors to please must appear to be pleased.
> —SAMUEL JOHNSON, *The Rambler*, Aug. 31, 1751

Punctuality is the politeness of kings.
> —LOUIS XVIII, attributed

My father used to say
"Superior people never make long visits."
> —MARIANNE MOORE, *Silence*
> in *Collected Poems*, 1935

It is almost a definition of a gentleman to say that he is one who never inflicts pain.
> —CARDINAL NEWMAN,
> *The Idea of a University*, 1873

Manners go on deteriorating.
> —PLAUTUS, *The Merchant*, c. 200 B.C.

Etiquette can be at the same time a means of approaching people and of staying clear of them.
> —DAVID RIESMAN, *The Lonely Crowd*, 1950

Rudeness is better than any argument; it totally eclipses intellect.
> —ARTHUR SCHOPENHAUER,
> *Position* in *Essays*, 1851

Is there no respect of place, persons, nor time, in you?
> —SHAKESPEARE, *Twelfth Night*, II, iii

Do not do unto others as you would they should do unto you. Their tastes may not be the same.
> —GEORGE BERNARD SHAW, *Maxims for*
> *Revolutionists* in *Man and Superman*, 1903

Good breeding consists in concealing how much we think of ourselves and how little we think of the other person.
　　　　　　—MARK TWAIN, died 1910, Albert B. Paine, ed.,
　　　　　　　　　　　　　　　Mark Twain's Notebook, 1935

MARRIAGE　　　　　See also FAMILY; HOME; LOVE;
　　　LOVE, EXPRESSIONS OF; WOMEN & MEN

Those marriages generally abound most with love and constancy that are preceded by a long courtship.
　　　　　　—JOSEPH ADDISON, *The Spectator,* Dec. 29, 1711

When a match has equal partners, then I fear not.
　　　　　　—AESCHYLUS, *Prometheus Bound,* 5th cent. B.C.

First marriage to please one's parents; second marriage to please oneself.　　　—ANONYMOUS (CHINESE ADAGE)
[*The New York Times* reported on June 4, 1998, that this ancient adage is enjoying a new popularity in China as married people chafe under the regimented morality imposed by Communist rulers.]

Autant de mariages, autant ménages.
As many as there are marriages, so many living arrangements.　　　　　—ANONYMOUS (FRENCH PROVERB)

Se marie, c'est apprendre être seul.
To marry is to learn to be alone.
　　　　　　—ANONYMOUS (FRENCH PROVERB)

Marriage, to women as to men, must be a luxury, not a necessity; an incident of life, not all of it.
　　　　　　—SUSAN B. ANTHONY, speech, 1875

I married beneath me—all women do.
　　　　　　—NANCY ASTOR, speech, Oldham, England, 1951

It is a truth universally acknowledged, that a single man in possession of a good fortune must be in want of a wife.
　　　　　　—JANE AUSTEN, *Pride and Prejudice,* 1813
[The first line of the novel. For other first lines, see the list under Tolstoy at FAMILY. For more of Austen on marriage, see WOMEN & MEN.]

It is better to marry than to burn.
> —BIBLE, *I Corinthians* 7:9

One was never married, and that's his hell; another is, and that's his plague.
> —ROBERT BURTON, *The Anatomy of Melancholy*, 1621–51

Polygamy may well be held in dread,
Not only as a sin but as a bore.
> —LORD BYRON, *Don Juan*, 1819–24

Marriage is a result of the longing for the deep, deep peace of the double bed after the hurly-burly of the chaise-longue.
> —MRS. PATRICK CAMPBELL, 1914, quoted in Ralph G. Martin, *Jenny*, 1971

The divorce will be gayer than the wedding.
> —COLETTE, *Cheri*, 1920

I am not against hasty marriages, where a mutual flame is fanned by an adequate income.
> —WILKIE COLLINS, *No Name*, 1862

Married in haste, we may repent at leisure.
> —WILLIAM CONGREVE, *The Old Bachelor*, 1693
[The proverb "Marry in haste, repent at leisure" predates Congreve.]

A single man . . . is an incomplete animal. He resembles the odd half of a pair of scissors.
> —BENJAMIN FRANKLIN, letter to a young man, June 25, 1745

Where there's marriage without love, there will be love without marriage.
> —BENJAMIN FRANKLIN, *Poor Richard's Almanac*, May 1734

I think it can be stated without denial that no man ever saw a man he would be willing to marry if he were a woman.
> —GEORGE GIBBS, *How to Stay Married*, 1925

Let there be spaces in your togetherness.
> —KAHLIL GIBRAN, *The Prophet*, 1923

A wife loves out of duty, and duty leads to constraint, and constraint kills desire.
—JEAN GIRAUDOUX, *Amphitryon 38*, 1929

Faithful women are all alike. They think only of their fidelity and not of their husbands. —*Ibid.*

When a woman gets married, it's like jumping into a hole in the ice in the middle of winter: you do it once and you remember it the rest of your days.
—MAXIM GORKY, *The Lower Depths*, 1903

[A gentleman who had been very unhappy in marriage, married immediately after his wife died: Johnson said] it was the triumph of hope over experience.
—SAMUEL JOHNSON, quoted in
James Boswell, *Life of Johnson*, 1791

Marriage has many pains, but celibacy has no pleasures.
—SAMUEL JOHNSON, *Rasselas*, 1759

There are few women so perfect that their husbands do not regret having married them at least once a day.
—LA BRUYÈRE, *Les Caractères*, 1688

Two can live cheaper than one.
—RING LARDNER, *Big Town*, 1921

There are some good marriages, but no delightful ones.
—LA ROCHEFOUCAULD, *Maxims*, 1678

There is no more lovely, friendly, and charming relationship, communion, or company than a good marriage.
—MARTIN LUTHER, *Table Talk*, 1569

Marriages are made in heaven.
—JOHN LYLY, *Euphues and His England*, 1580

"That's bigamy."
"Yes and it's big of me, too. It's big of all of us. I'm sick of these conventional marriages. One woman and one man was good enough for your grandmother. But who wants to marry your grandmother?"
—GROUCHO MARX, in *Animal Crackers*, 1930

Marriage, to tell the truth, is an evil, but it is a necessary evil. —MENANDER, fragment, 4th cent. B.C.

It [marriage] is like a cage; one sees the birds outside desperate to get in, and those inside desperate to get out.
—MONTAIGNE, *Essays,* 1580–88

Not louder shrieks to pitying heaven are cast,
When husbands or when lapdogs breathe their last.
—ALEXANDER POPE, *The Rape of the Lock,* 1714

More marriages have been ruined by boredom than by sexual betrayal. —MORDECAI RICHLER, *New York Times Book Review,* Apr. 11, 1999

A good marriage is that in which each appoints the other the guardian of his solitude.
—RAINER MARIA RILKE, *Letters,* 1892–1926

It doesn't much signify whom one marries, for one is sure to find out the next morning that it was someone else.
—SAMUEL ROGERS, *Table Talk,* 1860

Love, the quest; marriage, the conquest; divorce, the inquest.
—HELEN ROWLAND, *A Guide to Men,* 1922

Marriage is for woman the commonest mode of livelihood, and the total amount of undesired sex endured by women is probably greater in marriage than in prostitution.
—BERTRAND RUSSELL, *Marriage and Morals,* 1929

It takes patience to appreciate domestic bliss; volatile spirits prefer unhappiness. —GEORGE SANTAYANA, *The Life of Reason,* 1905–06

To marry is to halve your rights and double your duties.
—ARTHUR SCHOPENHAUER, *The World as Will and Idea,* 1819

Marriage is a desperate thing.
—JOHN SELDEN, *Marriage* in *Table Talk,* 1689

The ancient saying is no heresy,
Hanging and wiving goes by destiny.
    —SHAKESPEARE, *The Merchant of Venice,* II, ix
[Another form of this proverb was cited by John Heywood in the mid-sixteenth century: "Wedding is destiny, / And hanging likewise."]

A light wife doth make a heavy husband.   *—Ibid.,* V, i

Item: I give unto my wife my second best bed.
    —SHAKESPEARE, his will, Mar. 25, 1616
[This may have been the bed they slept in as opposed to the bed for guests, which was the better for being less often slept in. He died the following month, April 23, also thought to be his birthday.]

When two people are under the influence of the most violent, most insane, most delusive and most transient of passions, they are required to swear that they will remain in that excited, abnormal and exhausting condition continuously until death do them part.
    —GEORGE BERNARD SHAW,
    Preface, *Getting Married,* 1908

It is a woman's business to get married as soon as possible, and a man's to keep unmarried as long as he can.
    —GEORGE BERNARD SHAW,
    Man and Superman, 1903

Marriage is popular because it combines the maximum of temptation with the maximum of opportunity.
    —Maxims for Revolutionists in *Ibid.*

The married state is the completest image of heaven and hell we are capable of receiving in this life.
    —RICHARD STEELE, *The Spectator,* Sept. 9, 1712

In marriage, a man becomes slack and selfish, and undergoes a fatty degeneration of his moral being.
    —ROBERT LOUIS STEVENSON,
    Virginibus Puerisque, 1881

Oh husbands, oh, my married friends, what comfort is there to be derived from a wife well obeyed!
—ANTHONY TROLLOPE, *Barchester Towers*, 1857

In married life, three is company and two is none.
—OSCAR WILDE, *The Importance of Being Earnest*, 1895

The world has grown suspicious of anything that looks like a happy married life.
—OSCAR WILDE, *Lady Windermere's Fan*, 1892

Men marry because they are tired; women because they are curious. Both are disappointed.
—OSCAR WILDE, *A Woman of No Importance*, 1893

MARXISM   See COMMUNISM

MASSES   See PEOPLE, THE

MATHEMATICS   See SCIENCE: MATHEMATICS & STATISTICS

MAXIMS   See QUOTATIONS, MAXIMS, & PROVERBS

MAY   See NATURE: SEASONS

MEANS   See ENDS & MEANS

MEDIA   See also ADVERTISING; PRESS, THE; SCIENCE: TECHNOLOGY

One picture is worth a thousand words.
—FRED R. BARNARD, in *Printers' Ink*, Mar. 10, 1927
[Barnard called this a Chinese proverb, but actually it is a rewrite of an earlier Barnard maxim, "One look is worth a thousand words," *Printers' Ink*, Dec. 8, 1921.]

The printing press is either the greatest blessing or the greatest curse of modern times, one sometimes forgets which.
—J. M. BARRIE, *Sentimental Tommy*, 1896

Publicity is justly recommended as a remedy for social and industrial diseases. Sunlight is said to be the best of disinfectants; electric light the most efficient policeman.
—LOUIS D. BRANDEIS, *What Publicity Can Do*
in *Harper's Weekly,* Dec. 20, 1913

Some television programs are so much chewing gum for the eyes. —JOHN MASON BROWN, interview, July 28, 1955
[This also has been attributed to Frank Lloyd Wright and Fred Allen.]

Now Barabbas was a publisher.
—LORD BYRON, d. 1824; traditional attribution
[Some feel that a more likely source is Thomas Campbell.]

Television is a form of soliloquy.
—SIR KENNETH CLARK, in the *Guardian,* Nov. 26, 1977

Because television can make so much money doing its worst, it often cannot afford to do its best.
—FRED W. FRIENDLY, *Due to
Circumstances Beyond Our Control,* 1967

The hand that rules the press, the radio, the screen, and the far-spread magazine rules the country.
—LEARNED HAND, speech, Dec. 21, 1942

Television kills telephony in brothers' broil.
—JAMES JOYCE, *Finnegans Wake,* 1939
[Robert Sullivan in *The New York Times Book Review,* June 16, 1996, identified this as the first significant mention of television in a work of fiction.]

It is characteristic of the present time always to be conscious of the medium. It is almost bound to end in madness, like a man who whenever he looked at the sun and the stars was conscious of the world going round.
—SØREN KIERKEGAARD, 1839

[Television:] a medium, so called because it is neither rare nor well done. —ERNIE KOVACS, d. 1962, quoted in
Leslie Halliwell, *The Filmgoer's Book of Quotes,* 1973

The new electronic interdependence re-creates the world in the image of a global village.
—MARSHALL McLUHAN, *The Gutenberg Galaxy*, 1962

The medium is the message.
—MARSHALL McLUHAN, *Understanding Media*, 1964

[If you watch television from morning to night] I can assure you that you will observe a vast wasteland.
—NEWTON MINOW, speech to the
National Association of Broadcasters, May 9, 1961

It is not enough to cater to the nation's whims—you must also serve the nation's needs. —*Ibid.*

The more we elaborate our means of communication, the less we communicate. —J. B. PRIESTLEY, *Televiewing*, in
Thoughts in the Wilderness, 1957

The New Yorker will be the magazine that is not edited for the old lady in Dubuque.
—HAROLD R. ROSS, prospectus
for *The New Yorker*, 1924

I believe television is going to be the test of the modern world, and that in this new opportunity to see beyond the range of our vision we shall discover either a new and unbearable disturbance of the general peace or a saving radiance in the sky. We shall stand or fall by television.
—E. B. WHITE, *Removal* in *Harper's Magazine*, 1938

MEDICINE   See DOCTORS & THE PRACTICE OF
MEDICINE; ILLNESS & REMEDIES;
MADNESS; SCIENCE: PSYCHOLOGY

MEDIOCRITY

Be not righteous over much; neither make thyself over wise.
—BIBLE, *Ecclesiastes* 7:16

The world is a republic of mediocrities, and always was.
—THOMAS CARLYLE, letter to Emerson, May 13, 1853

The only sin is mediocrity.
>—MARTHA GRAHAM, quoted in
>*The New York Times,* Mar. 31, 1985

The way to get on in the world is to be neither more nor less wise, neither better nor worse than your neighbors.
>—WILLIAM HAZLITT, *On Knowledge of the World* in *Sketches and Essays,* 1839

Some men are born mediocre, some men achieve mediocrity, and some men have mediocrity thrust upon them. With Major Major it had been all three.
>—JOSEPH HELLER, *Catch-22,* 1961

[See also Shakespeare at GREATNESS.]

Even if he is mediocre, there are lots of mediocre judges, and people, and lawyers. They are entitled to a little representation, too, aren't they?
>—ROMAN L. HRUSKA, Senate hearings on the nomination of G. Harrold Carswell to the Supreme Court, in *The New York Times,* Mar. 17, 1970

[Hruska, a Republican senator from Nebraska, was attempting to defend Pres. Richard Nixon's nominee. The comment, however, was not helpful. The Senate rejected Judge Carswell. See also Bryce at POLITICS.]

There are certain things in which mediocrity is insupportable—poetry, music, painting, public speaking.
>—LA BRUYÈRE, *Les Caractères,* 1688

MELANCHOLY   See DESPAIR, DEPRESSION, & MISERY; SORROW, SADNESS, & SUFFERING

MEMORY   See also PAST, THE

Memory is the mother of all wisdom.
>—AESCHYLUS, *Prometheus Bound,* 5th cent. B.C.

Memories are hunting horns
Whose sound dies on the wind.
>—GUILLAUME APOLLINAIRE,
>*Cors de chasse* in *Alcools,* 1913

I have more memories than if I were a thousand years old.
—CHARLES BAUDELAIRE, *Spleen et idéal*, 1861

Some memories are realities, and are better than anything
that can ever happen to one again.
—WILLA CATHER, *My Antonia*, 1918

Memory is the treasury and guardian of all things.
—CICERO, *De Oratore*, 55 B.C.

It is an art to recollect. —SØREN KIERKEGAARD,
Stages on Life's Way, 1845

The richness in life lies in the memories we have forgotten.
—CESARE PAVESE, *This Business of Living:
A Diary, 1935–1950*, Feb. 13, 1944

Good memories are lost jewels.
—PAUL VALÉRY, *Mauvaises Pensées et autres*, 1941

In memory everything seems to happen to music.
—TENNESSEE WILLIAMS,
The Glass Menagerie, 1945

MEN   See also HUMANS & HUMAN NATURE;
WOMEN & MEN

If there is anything disagreeable going on, men are sure to
get out of it. —JANE AUSTEN, *Northanger Abbey*, 1818

As long as you know that most men are like children, you
know everything. —COCO CHANEL, d. 1971, attributed

A man is a god in ruins.
—RALPH WALDO EMERSON, *Nature*, 1836

Every man has a wild animal in him.
—FREDERICK THE GREAT, letter to Voltaire, 1759

There's nothing so stubborn as a man when you want him
to do something. —JEAN GIRAUDOUX, *The Madwoman
of Chaillot*, 1945

What a piece of work is a man! How noble in reason! How infinite in faculty! In form, in moving, how express and admirable! In action how like an angel! In apprehension how like a god! The beauty of the world! The paragon of animals!
—SHAKESPEARE, *Hamlet*, II, ii

Sigh no more, ladies, sigh no more,
Men were deceivers ever;
One foot in sea, and one on shore,
To one thing constant never.
—SHAKESPEARE, *Much Ado About Nothing*, II, iii

Every man over forty is a scoundrel.
—GEORGE BERNARD SHAW, *Maxims for Revolutionists* in *Man and Superman,* 1903

A man in the house is worth two in the street.
—MAE WEST, *Belle of the Nineties,* 1934

MERCY   See FORGIVENESS & MERCY; JUSTICE

METAPHYSICS   See ETHICS & MORALITY; PHILOSOPHY

METHOD   See also ENDS & MEANS; WORK & WORKERS

Chaos often breeds life, when order breeds habit.
—HENRY ADAMS, *The Education of Henry Adams,* 1907
[In our time, Bob Dylan, explaining his music, said, "Chaos is a friend of mine," *Newsweek,* Dec. 9, 1985. See also Melville below.]

If there are obstacles, the shortest line between two points may be the crooked line.
—BERTOLT BRECHT, *Galileo,* 1938–39

There's a way to do it better—Find it.
—THOMAS ALVA EDISON, directive to a research assistant, c. 1919, attributed

There are some enterprises in which a careful disorderliness is the true method.
—HERMAN MELVILLE, *Moby-Dick*, 1851

Though this be madness, yet there is method in it.
—SHAKESPEARE, *Hamlet*, II, ii

MEXICO See NATIONS

MIDDLE AGE & MID-LIFE CRISIS

Midway in our life's journey, I went astray from the straight road and woke to find myself alone in a dark wood.
—DANTE, *Inferno* in *The Divine Comedy*, c. 1310–20
[Opening lines. See the list of first lines at FAMILY in the note to the Tolstoy quote.]

After thirty, a man wakes up sad every morning, excepting perhaps five or six, until the day of his death.
—RALPH WALDO EMERSON, *Journal*, 1834

By the time a person has achieved years adequate for choosing a direction, the die is cast and the moment has long since passed which determined the future.
—ZELDA FITZGERALD, *Save Me the Waltz*, 1932

Whoever, in middle age, attempts to realize the wishes and hopes of his early youth invariably deceives himself. Each ten years of a man's life has its own fortunes, its own hopes, its own desires.   —GOETHE, *Elective Affinities*, 1808

Men, like peaches and pears, grow sweet a little while before they begin to decay.
—OLIVER WENDELL HOLMES, SR.,
The Autocrat of the Breakfast Table, 1858

[Middle age is] the time when a man is always thinking that in a week or two he'll feel just as good as ever.
—DON MARQUIS, d. 1937, quoted in
B. Wilcox, *A Little Book of Aphorisms*, 1947

Maturity hath her defects, as well as greenness, or worse.
—MONTAIGNE, *Essays*, 1580–88

From forty to fifty, a man is at heart either a stoic or a satyr.   —A. W. PINERO, *The Second Mrs. Tanqueray,* 1893

Life Begins at Forty. —WALTER PITKIN, book title, 1932

What is the prime of life? May it not be defined as a period of about twenty years in a woman's life, and thirty in a man's?   —PLATO, *The Republic,* 4th cent. B.C.

One's prime is elusive.
   —MURIEL SPARK, *The Prime of Miss Jean Brodie,* 1962

MIGHT   See STRENGTH; VIOLENCE & FORCE

MILITARY, THE   See also ELITE, THE
                              (U.S. Army Service Forces);
                              MILITARY BATTLES; WAR

If it moves, salute it. If it doesn't move, pick it up. If you can't pick it up, paint it.   —ANONYMOUS

If the trumpet give an uncertain sound, who shall prepare himself to the battle?   —BIBLE, *I Corinthians* 14:8

Don't talk to me about naval tradition. It's nothing but rum, sodomy, and the lash.
               —WINSTON CHURCHILL, d. 1965, quoted by
               Sir Peter Gretton, *Former Naval Person,* 1968

The services in wartime are fit only for desperadoes, but in peace are fit only for fools.
               —BENJAMIN DISRAELI, *Vivian Grey,* 1826

There are all sorts of things to be done in this country. I see no reason why the sums which are now going into these sterile, negative mechanisms that we call war munitions shouldn't go into something positive.
               —DWIGHT D. EISENHOWER, d. 1969, quoted in
               Stephen E. Ambrose, *Eisenhower: The President,* 1983
[For the renowned "military-industrial establishment" speech, see AMERICAN HISTORY: MEMORABLE MOMENTS.]

A large army is always disorderly.
> —EURIPIDES, *Hecuba*, c. 425 B.C.

Stick close to your desks and never go to sea,
And you all may be Rulers of the Queen's Navee!
> —W. S. GILBERT, *H.M.S. Pinafore*, 1878

I am the very model of a modern Major-General;
I've information vegetable, animal and mineral;
I know the kings of England, and I quote the fights historical,
From Marathon to Waterloo in order categorical.
> —W. S. GILBERT, *The Pirates of Penzance*, 1879

Ask any soldier. To kill a man is to merit a woman.
> —JEAN GIRAUDOUX, *Tiger at the Gates*, 1935

There was only one catch and that was Catch-22.
> —JOSEPH HELLER, *Catch-22*, 1961

["Orr would be crazy to fly more missions and sane if he didn't, but if he was sane he had to fly them. If he flew them he was crazy and didn't have to; but if he didn't want to he was sane and had to."]

For a people who are free, and who mean to remain so, a well-organized and armed militia is their best security.
> —THOMAS JEFFERSON,
> message to Congress, Nov. 8, 1808

Every citizen [should] be a soldier. This was the case with the Greeks and the Romans, and must be that of every free state.
> —THOMAS JEFFERSON, letter to James Monroe, 1813

For it's Tommy this, an' Tommy that, an' "Chuck him out, the brute!"
But it's "Savior of 'is country" when the guns begin to shoot.
> —RUDYARD KIPLING, *Tommy* in
> *Ballads and Barrack Room Ballads*, 1892, 1893

[A Tommy is a British soldier.]

The people are like water and the army is like fish.
> —MAO ZEDUNG, *Aspects of China's
> Anti-Japanese Struggle*, 1948

The greatest general is he who makes the fewest mistakes.
—NAPOLEON BONAPARTE, *Maxims,* 1804–15

Soldiers generally win battles; generals generally get credit for them.   —NAPOLEON BONAPARTE, to Gaspard Gourgaud at St. Helena, 1815–18

An army marches on its stomach.
—NAPOLEON BONAPARTE, d. 1821, attributed

Russia has two generals whom she can trust—Generals Janvier and Février [Generals January and February].
—NICHOLAS I, quoted in *Punch,* Mar. 10, 1853

I never expect a soldier to think.
—GEORGE BERNARD SHAW, *The Devil's Disciple,* 1897

The British soldier can stand up to anything except the British War Office.   —*Ibid.*

To fight and conquer in all your battles is not supreme excellence; supreme excellence consists in breaking the enemy's resistance without fighting.
—SUN TZU, *The Art of War,* 4th cent. B.C.

Theirs not to reason why.
Theirs but to do and die.
—ALFRED LORD TENNYSON, *The Charge of the Light Brigade,* 1854
[For more, see under MILITARY BATTLES, below.]

The strength of an army lies in strict discipline and undeviating obedience to its officers.
—THUCYDIDES, *The History of the Peloponnesian War,* c. 400 B.C.

The chief attraction of military service has consisted and will consist in this compulsory and irreproachable idleness.
—LEO TOLSTOY, *War and Peace,* 1865–69

God is always on the side of the big battalions.
—MARSHAL TURENNNE, attributed, c. 1650
[Sometimes also attributed to Voltaire, Frederick the Great,

and others, but it was already established by then. *Bartlett's* suggests that it may date from Tacitus; see under STRENGTH.]

The army is a nation within the nation: it is a vice of our time.   —ALFRED DE VIGNY, *Servitude et grandeur militaires*, 1835

Military intelligence—a contradiction in terms.
            —OSWALD GARRISON VILLARD, lecture, c. 1920, personal report by a member of the audience

In this country we find it pays to shoot an admiral from time to time to encourage the others.
                              —VOLTAIRE, *Candide*, 1759

Discipline is the soul of an army. It makes small numbers formidable; procures success to the weak and esteem to all.
                  —GEORGE WASHINGTON, letter to the Captains of the Virginia Regiments, July 1759

Who is this happy warrior? Who is he
That every man in arms should wish to be?
                        —WILLIAM WORDSWORTH, *Character of the Happy Warrior*, 1807
[The "happy warrior" in U.S. politics was New York governor Al Smith, nominated for president by Franklin D. Roosevelt at the Democratic National Convention in 1928. Smith lost to Herbert Hoover.]

MILITARY BATTLES   See also AMERICAN HISTORY: MEMORABLE MOMENTS; MILITARY, THE; NATIONS (England); WAR

Gentlemen, we are being killed on the beaches. Let's go inland and be killed.
                  —GEN. NORMAN COTA, attributed, Omaha Beach, Normandy, June 6, 1944

My center is giving way, my right is in retreat; situation excellent. I am attacking.
                  —MARSHAL FERDINAND FOCH, attributed
[Usually dated Sept. 1914, the Battle of the Marne.]

Get there first with the most men.
> —NATHAN BEDFORD FORREST,
> saying during the Civil War, 1861–65

[Sometimes rendered as "Git thar firstest with the mostest." But Gen. Forrest, a Confederate cavalry commander, evidently spoke standard English.]

Die hard, men, die hard!   —WILLIAM INGLIS, battle of
> Albuera, Spain, May 16, 1811

[Because of this order by Col. Inglis, the 57th Foot Regiment of Middlesex came to be known as "the Diehards." In the battle, a combined force of British, Portuguese, and Spanish defeated the French.]

Veni, vidi, vici.
I came, I saw, I conquered.
> —JULIUS CAESAR, quoted in Suetonius,
> *Lives of the Caesars,* c. A.D. 121

Sighted sub, sank same.
> —DONALD F. MASON, radio dispatch, Jan. 28, 1942

Soldiers, consider that from the summit of these pyramids, forty centuries look down upon you.
> —NAPOLEON BONAPARTE, address to the troops
> before the Battle of the Pyramids, July 21, 1798

England expects every man will do his duty.
> —HORATIO, LORD NELSON, signal to the British
> fleet, prior to the battle of Trafalgar, Oct. 21, 1805

Ils ne passeront pas.
They shall not pass.
> —ROBERT-GEORGES NIVELLE, Verdun, Feb. 1916

[In this form, the order became a slogan, however, the actual wording was, *"Vous ne laisserez pas passer"* ("You shall not let them pass.") In the Spanish Civil War, the Republicans used *No pasarán*; see under Ibarruri at APPEASEMENT VS. RESISTANCE.]

Don't cheer, men, those poor devils are dying.
> —JOHN WOODWARD PHILIP,
> the Battle of Santiago, July 3, 1898

[Capt. Philip, later Rear Admiral Philip, commanded the U.S.S.

Texas in the blockade of Santiago during the brief Spanish-American War. The dying men were from the the Spanish flagship *Viscaya*, which exploded under U.S. fire.]

One more such victory, and we are undone.
>   —KING PYRRHUS OF EPIRUS,
>   after fighting the Romans at Asculum, 279 B.C.

[One of two pyrrhic victories. His victory at Heraclea in 280 B.C. also cost many lives.]

Go, tell the Spartans, thou who passeth by:
Carrying out their orders, here we lie.
>   —SIMONIDES, epitaph for the Spartan dead at
>   Thermopylae, 480 B.C., quoted in Herodotus, *Histories*

It is the beginning of the end.
>   —TALLEYRAND, after the Battle of
>   Borodino, Sept. 7, 1812

Half a league, half a league,
Half a league onward,
All in the valley of Death
Rode the six hundred.   —ALFRED, LORD TENNYSON,
>   *The Charge of the Light Brigade*, 1854

Cannon to right of them
Cannon to left of them,
Cannon behind them
Volleyed and thundered.   *—Ibid.*

Into the jaws of death,
Into the mouth of hell
Rode the six hundred.   *—Ibid.*

[This was the "death charge of the 600" in the Battle of Balaclava in the Crimea, Sept. 20, 1854. Under orders, the British cavalry brigade charged the Russian line, despite recognizing that they would likely be destroyed. But "Theirs not to make reply, / Theirs not to reason why, / Theirs but to do and die. / Into the valley of Death / Rode the six hundred."]

Nothing except a battle lost can be half so melancholy as a battle won.   —DUKE OF WELLINGTON, dispatch after
>   the Battle of Waterloo, June 18, 1815

The battle of Waterloo was won on the playing fields of Eton.   —DUKE OF WELLINGTON, d. 1852, attributed, but apparently invented several years after Wellington's death

MIND, THOUGHT, & UNDERSTANDING
See also GENIUS; IDEAS & IDEALS;
MADNESS; PROGRESS; REASON & REASONS;
REASONABLE & UNREASONABLE PEOPLE;
SOUL; VISION & VISIONARIES

The march of the human mind is slow.
—EDMUND BURKE, speech on conciliation
with the American colonies, Mar. 22, 1775

The empires of the future are the empires of the mind.
—WINSTON CHURCHILL, address at
Harvard University, Sept. 6, 1943

The mind of man is capable of anything—because everything is in it, all the past as well as all the future.
—JOSEPH CONRAD, *Heart of Darkness*, 1902

Cogito ergo sum.
I think therefore I am.
—RENÉ DESCARTES, *Discourse on Method*, 1637
[Probably the most famous maxim in the history of philosophy. Folklorist Roger Welsch, in the September 1992 issue of *Natural History*, reported seeing on a newlywed's car: *Coito ergo sum.* See also Bishop Berkeley at PHILOSOPHY.]

Being and thought are one.
—JEAN DUBUFFET, quoted in his obituary,
The New York Times, May 15, 1985

What once was thought can never be undone.
—FRIEDRICH DÜRRENMATT, *The Physicists*, 1962

Imagination is more important than knowledge.
—ALBERT EINSTEIN, d. 1955, *On Science*

On earth there is nothing great but man; in man there is nothing great but mind.   —SIR WILLIAM HAMILTON,
Lectures on Metaphysics, 1859–60

What we call a mind is nothing but a heap or collection of different perceptions, united together by certain relations and supposed, though falsely, to be endowed with a perfect simplicity and identity.   —DAVID HUME, *A Treatise of Human Nature,* 1739

Sooner or later, false thinking brings wrong conduct.
        —JULIAN HUXLEY, *Essays of a Biologist,* 1923

Meditation is not a means to an end. It is both the means and the end.   —KRISHNAMURTI, d. 1986, *The Second Penguin Krishnamurti Reader,* 1991

Intelligence forbids tears.
        —DORIS LESSING, *To Room 19* in *A Man and Two Women,* 1965

Stone walls do not a prison make
Nor iron bars a cage.
        —RICHARD LOVELACE, *To Althea, From Prison* in *Lucasta,* 1649

Our life is what our thoughts make it.
        —MARCUS AURELIUS, *Meditations,* 2nd cent. A.D.

It is not the consciousness of men that determines their existence, but on the contrary, their social existence determines their consciousness.
        —KARL MARX, *Critique of Political Economy,* 1859

The mind is its own place, and in itself
Can make a heaven of Hell, a hell of Heaven.
        —JOHN MILTON, *Paradise Lost,* 1667

Man is no more than a reed, the weakest in nature. But he is a thinking reed.   —PASCAL, *Pensées,* 1670
[For more from this passage, see HUMANS & HUMAN NATURE.]

The Power of Positive Thinking.
        —NORMAN VINCENT PEALE, book title, 1952
[The enormously successful Rev. Peale was an all-American cleric, who urged: "Pray big! Believe big! Act big!" For an

example of positive thinking, see Coué at OPTIMISM & PESSIMISM.]

[There is no] Ghost in the Machine.
>—GILBERT RYLE, *The Concept of Mind,* 1949

Our dignity is not in what we do but what we understand. The whole world is doing things.
>—GEORGE SANTAYANA, *Winds of Doctrine,* 1913

A good mind is a lord of a kingdom.
>—SENECA, *Thyestes,* 1st cent. A.D.

There is nothing either good or bad but thinking makes it so.   —SHAKESPEARE, *Hamlet,* II, ii

Thy wish was father, Harry, to that thought.
>—SHAKESPEARE, *Henry IV, Part II,* IV, v
[Prince Henry has just said to his aged father, the king, who appeared to have died in his sleep, "I never thought to hear you speak again."]

He gave man speech, and speech created thought,
Which is the measure of the universe.
>—PERCY BYSSHE SHELLEY,
>*Prometheus Unbound,* 1819

It is the mind that maketh good or ill,
That maketh wretch or happy, rich or poor.
>—EDMUND SPENSER, *The Faerie Queene,* 1596

Intellect does not attain its full force until it attacks power.
>—MADAME DE STAËL, *De la littérature considerée*
>*dans ses rapports avec les institutions sociales,* 1800

Consciousness is a disease.   —MIGUEL DE UNAMUNO,
>*The Tragic Sense of Life,* 1913

A mind is a terrible thing to waste.
>—UNITED NEGRO COLLEGE FUND,
>advertising slogan, adopted 1983

Intellectual passion drives out sensuality.
—LEONARDO DA VINCI,
Notebooks, 1508–18

MINORITIES   See RACES & PEOPLE

MIRACLES

Behold, the bush burned with fire, and the bush was not consumed.   —BIBLE, *Exodus* 3:2

Rise, take up thy bed, and walk.   —BIBLE, *John* 5:8

The distance is nothing. It's only the first step that's important.   —MARQUISE DU DEFFAND, comment on the legend that St. Denis walked six miles with his head in his hand, letter to d'Alembert, July 7, 1763

No testimony is sufficient to establish a miracle, unless the testimony be of such a kind that its falsehood would be more miraculous than the fact which it endeavors to establish.
—DAVID HUME, *Enquiry Concerning Human Understanding,* 1748

Everything is miraculous. It is miraculous that one does not melt in one's bath.   —PICASSO, d. 1973, attributed
[The *Penguin Dictionary of Modern Quotations* indicates that Jean Cocteau reported this delightful observation.]

There have been rains of milk, blood, flesh, iron, sponges, wool, and baked bricks. —PLINY, *Natural History,* A.D. 77
[As Pliny notes, quite a variety of miraculous heavenly omens were reported in ancient times.]

Miracles are propitious accidents, the natural causes of which are too complicated to be readily understood.
—GEORGE SANTAYANA, *The Ethics of Spinoza,* 1910

They say miracles are past.
—SHAKESPEARE, *All's Well That Ends Well,* II, iii
[For the modern "age of miracles," see Carlyle at MODERN TIMES.]

Macbeth shall never vanquished be until
Great Birnam Wood to high Dunsinane Hill
Shall come against him.

> —SHAKESPEARE, *Macbeth*, IV, i

[Macbeth, bolstered by this prophecy, later boasts, "I will not
be afraid of death and bane / Till Birnam Forest come to Dunsinane." He expects neither a miracle nor a trick. For more on
Macbeth's wonders and witches, see OCCULT, THE.]

MISANTHROPY   See also HATE

I do not want people to be very agreeable, as it saves me
the trouble of liking them a great deal.

> —JANE AUSTEN, letter to her
> sister Cassandra, Dec. 24, 1798

[The date suggests the author may have been suffering a holiday depression.]

I do not love thee, Doctor Fell.
The reason why I cannot tell.
But this alone I know full well.
I do not love thee, Doctor Fell.

> —THOMAS ("TOM") BROWN, c. 1680

[Brown is said to have staved off expulsion from Oxford University with this variation on epigram 33 by Martial when Dr.
John Fell, dean of Christ Church, offered to let him remain as
a student if he could produce an impromptu translation of it.
Martial's epigram begins, *Non te amo, Sabidi*.]

I wish I loved the human race;
I wish I loved its silly face;
I wish I loved the way it walks;
I wish I loved the way it talks;
And when I'm introduced to one,
I wish I thought *What jolly fun*.

> —SIR WALTER A. RALEIGH, *Wishes of an
> Elderly Man* in *Laughter from a Cloud*, 1923

Any man who hates dogs and babies can't be all bad.

> —LEO C. ROSTEN, speaking of
> W. C. Fields, Masquers' Club, 1939

[Often attributed to Fields in the form: "Anyone who hates children and dogs can't be all bad." William Safire, thanks to a corre-
spondent, unearthed an earlier version, from *Harper's* magazine,

1937, penned by Cedric Worth: "No man who hates dogs and children can be all bad." Worth, in turn, was recalling comments by a *New York Times* reporter, Byron Darton, after a party in 1930, at which conversation was dominated by a man who detested dogs.]

Plus je connais les hommes, plus j'aime mon chien.
The more I know men, the more I like my dog.
　　　　　—MADAME DE SÉVIGNÉ, d. 1696, attributed

Man delights not me; no, nor woman either.
　　　　　—SHAKESPEARE, *Hamlet,* II, ii

MISERY　　　See DESPAIR, DEPRESSION, & MISERY;
　　　SORROW, SADNESS, & SUFFERING; TROUBLE

MISFORTUNE　　　　　See LUCK; RUIN; TROUBLE

MISTAKES　　　　　　　　See also FAILINGS

He is always right who suspects that he makes mistakes.
　　　　　—ANONYMOUS (SPANISH PROVERB)

C'est pire qu'un crime, c'est une faute.
It's worse than a crime, it's a blunder.
　　　　　—ANTOINE BOULAY DE LA MEURTHE,
　　　　　　　on the execution of the Duc d'Enghien, 1804
[Attributed also to Talleyrand and Joseph Fouché.]

Mistakes have been made.　　　　　—ULYSSES S. GRANT,
　　　　　　　report to Congress, Dec. 5, 1876
[This admission appears in an unprecedented apology that Grant appended to his final annual report to Congress. But Grant shed personal responsibility for the scandals that plagued his two presidential terms by casting the apology in passive-evasive terms that later political leaders have found equally useful. For example, President Bill Clinton glossed over improper Democratic party fundraising activities by saying "Mistakes were made" (press conference, Jan. 20, 1998); Israeli Prime Minister Benjamin Netanyahu reacted to the news that he had escaped indictment in a scandal with the same "Mistakes were made" (*New York Times,* Apr. 21, 1998); and Pol Pot, former leader of Cambodia, alluded to the killing of some two million of his fellow citizens, with the similarly bland "Our movement (the Khmer Rouge) made mistakes" (*New York Times,* Oct. 23, 1998).]

It is the true nature of mankind to learn from mistakes, not from example.   —FRED HOYLE, *Into Deepest Space*, 1974

When I make a mistake, it's a beaut!
          —FIORELLO LA GUARDIA, d. 1947;
     attributed remark referring to a bad job appointment

The only one who makes no mistakes is one who never does anything!   —THEODORE ROOSEVELT, d. 1919; saying
              inscribed on the Theodore Roosevelt Birthplace
              National Historic Site, New York City

A life spent in making mistakes is not only more honorable but more useful than a life spent doing nothing.
                    —GEORGE BERNARD SHAW,
              Preface, *The Doctor's Dilemma*, 1906

Mistakes live in the neighborhood of truth and therefore delude us.   —RABINDRANATH TAGORE, *Fireflies*, 1928

MODERATION   See PRUDENCE
                          & PRACTICAL WISDOM

MODERN TIMES   See also CIVILIZATION;
            ENVIRONMENT; MEDIA; PROGRESS;
      SCIENCE: TECHNOLOGY; TURBULENT TIMES

In the nightmare of the dark
All the dogs of Europe bark,
And the living nations wait,
Each sequestered in its hate.
          —W. H. AUDEN, *In Memory of W. B. Yeats*, 1940

This society is going smash;
They cannot fool us with how fast they go,
How much they cost each other and the gods!
A culture is no better than its woods.
     —W. H. AUDEN, *Bucolics* in *The Shield of Achilles*, 1955

We have grasped the mystery of the atom and rejected the Sermon on the Mount.
     —GEN. OMAR BRADLEY, speech, Armistice Day, 1948

The age of chivalry is gone. That of sophisters, economists, and calculators has succeeded, and the glory of Europe is extinguished forever.   —EDMUND BURKE, *Reflections on the Revolution in France,* 1790

The age of miracles is forever here!
            —THOMAS CARLYLE, *The Hero as Priest* in *On Heros and Hero Worship,* 1840
[But see Shakespeare at MIRACLES.]

Perfection of means and confusion of goals seem, in my opinion, to characterize our age.
            —ALBERT EINSTEIN, *Out of My Later Years,* 1950

The lamps are going out all over Europe; we shall not see them lit again in our lifetime.
            —VISCOUNT GREY OF FALLODEN, Aug. 3, 1914
[The remark was made while Grey was standing at a window in the Foreign Office, London, watching lamp-lighters at work. War was declared the next day.]

One of the crying needs of the time is for a suitable burial service for the admittedly damned.
            —H. L. MENCKEN, *Prejudices,* 1919–27

There are evidently limits to the achievements of science; and there are irresolvable contradictions both between prosperity and virtue, and between happiness and "the good life," which had not been anticipated in our philosophy. The discovery of these contradictions threatens our culture with despair.   —REINHOLD NIEBUHR, *The Irony of American History,* 1952

Morality in Europe today is herd morality.
            —FRIEDRICH NIETZSCHE, *Beyond Good and Evil,* 1885–86

Today violence is the rhetoric of the period.
            —ORTEGA Y GASSET, *The Revolt of the Masses,* 1930

We are suffering today from a greed for knowledge of evil.
            —CHRISTABEL PANKHURST, speech, 1930, quoted in David Mitchell, *The Fighting Pankhursts,* 1967

All the modern inconveniences.
>—MARK TWAIN, *Life on the Mississippi*, 1883

The century on which we are entering can be and must be the century of the common man.
>—HENRY A. WALLACE, speech, May 8, 1942

Plain living and high thinking are no more.
>—WILLIAM WORDSWORTH,
>*Written in London, September 1802*, 1807

Things fall apart; the center cannot hold;
Mere anarchy is loosed upon the world.
>—WILLIAM BUTLER YEATS, *The Second Coming*
>in *Michael Robartes and the Dancer*, 1921

The best lack all conviction, while the worst
Are full of passionate intensity.
>—*Ibid.*

MONEY   See also BUSINESS; CAPITALISM;
ECONOMICS; HAVES & HAVE-NOTS;
POVERTY & HUNGER; SELF-INTEREST

Money disappears like magic.
>—ANONYMOUS (ARAB PROVERB)

Every man thinks God is on his side. The rich and powerful know he is.   —JEAN ANOUILH, *The Lark*, 1953

It is very difficult for the prosperous to be humble.
>—JANE AUSTEN, *Emma*, 1815
[Cf. Epictetus, below.]

A large income is the best recipe for happiness I ever heard of.   —JANE AUSTEN, *Northanger Abbey*, 1818

Money is like muck, not good except it be spread.
>—FRANCIS BACON, *Of Seditions and Troubles*, 1625

If you want to know what the Lord God thinks of money, you have only to look at those to whom he gives it.
>—MAURICE BARING, d. 1945, quoted by
>Dorothy Parker, *Writers at Work: First Series*, 1958

Wealth maketh many friends.   —BIBLE, *Proverbs* 19:4

He that maketh haste to be rich shall not be innocent.
   —*Ibid.* 28:20

A feast is made for laughter, and wine maketh merry: but money answereth all things.   —BIBLE, *Ecclesiastes* 19:10

It is easier for a camel to go through the eye of a needle, than for a rich man to enter into the kingdom of God.
   —BIBLE, *Matthew* 19:24
[Also *Mark* 10:25, and *Luke* 18:25. The "needle" was actually a narrow city gate—too narrow for a camel loaded with baggage.]

The love of money is the root of all evil.
   —BIBLE, *I Timothy* 6:10

Money, n. A blessing that is of no advantage to us excepting when we part with it.
   —AMBROSE BIERCE, *The Devil's Dictionary,* 1906

A rich man's joke is always funny.
   —THOMAS E. BROWNE, *The Doctor* in
   Poems of T. E. Brown, 1900

It has been said that the love of money is the root of all evil. The want of money is so quite as truly.
   —SAMUEL BUTLER, *Erewhon,* 1872
[Cf. George Bernard Shaw, below.]

Ready money is Aladdin's lamp.
   —LORD BYRON, *Don Juan,* 1819–24

Money you know will hide many faults.
   —CERVANTES, *Don Quixote,* 1605–15

I knew once a very covetous, sordid fellow, who used to say, "Take care of the pence, for the pounds will take care of themselves."   —EARL OF CHESTERFIELD,
   letter to his son, Nov. 6, 1747

To be clever enough to get all the money, one must be stupid enough to want it.   —G. K. CHESTERTON,
   The Innocence of Father Brown, 1911

Show me the money! —CAMERON CROWE, screenplay,
Jerry McGuire, 1996

Annual income twenty pounds, annual expenditure nineteen
pounds six, result happiness. Annual income twenty pounds,
annual expenditure twenty pounds ought and six, result
misery.
—CHARLES DICKENS, *David Copperfield,* 1849–50

A billion here and a billion there and pretty soon you're
talking big money.
—EVERETT DIRKSEN, d. 1969, attributed
[*The Wall Street Journal* reported on Jan. 1, 1985, that the curator
of the Dirksen Congressional Center could not track down the
quote, but had noted, "That doesn't mean he didn't say it." Sen.
Dirksen of Illinois was a Republican.]

All heiresses are beautiful.
—JOHN DRYDEN, *King Arthur,* 1681

Money, which represents the prose of life . . . is, in its effects
and laws, as beautiful as roses.
—RALPH WALDO EMERSON, *Nominalist
and Realist* in *Essays: Second Series,* 1844

It is difficult for a rich person to be modest, or a modest
person rich. —EPICTETUS, *Encheiridion,* c. A.D. 100

Money's the wise man's religion.
—EURIPIDES, *The Cyclops,* 423 B.C.

Money is far more persuasive than logical arguments.
—EURIPIDES, *Medea,* 431 B.C.

Ah, take the Cash, and let the Credit go,
Nor heed the rumble of a distant Drum!
—EDWARD FITZGERALD,
The Rubáiyát of Omar Khayyám, 1879

Let me tell you about the very rich. They are different from
you and me. —F. SCOTT FITZGERALD,
The Rich Boy, 1926
[Ernest Hemingway, in *The Snows of Kilimanjaro* (1936), reported a humorous quip made by "someone" on the subject

of this quote. The quip was, "Yes, they have more money." Hemingway himself accepted credit for being the witty some-one, but evidently the correct attribution is to critic Mary Colum. At a lunch in 1936 with Colum and famed editor Max-well Perkins, Hemingway is said to have boasted, "I am getting to know the rich," and Colum replied, "The only difference between the rich and other people is that the rich have more money," Matthew J. Bruccoli, *Scott and Ernest,* 1978.

In *The Snows of Kilimanjaro* Hemingway himself came up with a quotable description of the wealthy: "The rich were dull and they drank too much."]

Money is like an arm or leg: use it or lose it.
      —HENRY FORD, *The New York Times,* Nov. 8, 1931

If you would know the value of money, go and try to borrow some.   —BENJAMIN FRANKLIN,
                                  Poor Richard's Almanac, 1758

Money is a singular thing. It ranks with love as man's great-est source of joy. And with his death as his greatest source of anxiety.   —JOHN KENNETH GALBRAITH,
                                  The Age of Uncertainty, 1977

Honesty is incompatible with amassing a large fortune.
                                  —MOHANDAS GANDHI,
                                  Non-Violence in Peace and War, 1942

I am indeed rich since my income is superior to expenses, and my expense is equal to my wishes.
                                  —EDWARD GIBBON, *Memoirs,* 1796

Follow the money.   —WILLIAM GOLDMAN, screenplay,
                                  All the President's Men, 1976
[This instruction from "Deep Throat," the mystery source in the Watergate case, is so memorable that people tend to forget that the line appeared first in the movie, not in the 1974 book by investigative reporters Bob Woodward and Carl Bernstein.]

Money is life to us wretched mortals.
                                  —HESIOD, *Works and Days,* c. 700 B.C.

He is almost always a slave who cannot live on little.
                                  —HORACE, *Satires,* 35–30 B.C.

The almighty dollar, that great object of universal devotion throughout our land.
> —WASHINGTON IRVING, *The Creole Village*
> in *The New Yorker*, Nov. 12, 1836

There are few ways in which a man can be more innocently employed than in getting money.
> —SAMUEL JOHNSON, letter to
> William Strahan, Mar. 27, 1775

The human species, according to the best theory I can form of it, is composed of two distinct races, the men who borrow and the men who lend.
> —CHARLES LAMB, *The Two Races of Men*
> in *Essays of Elia*, 1823

Nothing hurts worse than the loss of money.
> —LIVY, *History of Rome*, c. A.D. 14

All wealth is the product of labor.
> —JOHN LOCKE, *Two Treatises of Government*, 1692

When a man tells you that he got rich through hard work, ask him: "Whose?"   —DON MARQUIS, c. 1930, quoted in
> Edward Anthony, *O Rare Don Marquis*, 1962

What's a thousand dollars? Mere chicken feed. A poultry matter.   —GROUCHO MARX, *The Cocoanuts*, film, 1929

Money is like a sixth sense without which you cannot make a complete use of the other five.
> —W. SOMERSET MAUGHAM,
> *Of Human Bondage*, 1915

He must have killed a lot of people to have gotten so rich.
> —MOLIÈRE, *The Imaginary Invalid*, 1673
[Similar to Balzac: "Behind every great fortune there is a crime."]

You can never be too skinny or too rich.
> —BARBARA "BABE" PALEY, attributed
[Also attributed to the Duchess of Windsor and Gloria Vanderbilt.]

The rich have many consolations.
> —PLATO, *The Republic*, 4th cent. B.C.

The tears of an heir are masked laughter.
  —PUBLILIUS SYRUS, *Moral Sayings,* 1st cent. B.C.

I believe the power to make money is a gift of God.
  —JOHN D. ROCKEFELLER, interview, 1905,
  quoted in Matthew Josephson, *The Robber Barons,* 1934

A full pocketbook often groans more loudly than an empty stomach.
  —FRANKLIN D. ROOSEVELT, speech, Nov. 1, 1940

Never invest in anything that eats or needs repainting.
  —BILLY ROSE, in the *New York Post,* Oct. 26, 1957

Neither a borrower nor a lender be.
  —SHAKESPEARE, *Hamlet,* I, iii

Lack of money is the root of all evil.
  —GEORGE BERNARD SHAW, *Maxims for
  Revolutionists* in *Man and Superman,* 1903
[Cf. Samuel Butler, above.]

The universal regard for money is the one hopeful fact in our civilization.   —GEORGE BERNARD SHAW,
  Preface, *Major Barbara,* 1907

There are few sorrows, however poignant, in which a good income is of no avail.   —LOGAN PEARSALL SMITH,
  Afterthoughts, 1931

For money you would sell your soul.
  —SOPHOCLES, *Antigone,* 5th cent. B.C.

There is nothing in the world so demoralizing as money.
  —*Ibid.*

That man is the richest whose pleasures are the cheapest.
  —HENRY DAVID THOREAU, *Journal,* Mar. 3, 1856

In order to stand well in the eyes of the community, it is necessary to come up to a certain, somewhat indefinite, conventional standard of wealth.
  —THORSTEIN VEBLEN, *The Theory
  of the Leisure Class,* 1899

[For Veblen's phrase "conspicuous consumption," see CAPITALISM.]

All those men have their price.
>   —SIR ROBERT WALPOLE, d. 1745, referring to
>   certain members of Parliament, in William Coxe,
>   *Memoirs of Walpole,* 1798

[The popular version is: "Every man has his price."]

Money should circulate like rainwater.
>   —THORNTON WILDER, *The Matchmaker,* 1954

MOON, THE See NATURE: THE HEAVENS, THE SKY

MORNING See NATURE: TIMES OF DAY

MORALITY See ETHICS & MORALITY

MORTALITY See DEATH; GENERATIONS; HEDONISM; ILLNESS & REMEDIES; IMMORTALITY; LIFE

MOTHERS See PARENTS & PARENTHOOD

MURDER See CRIME

MUSIC See ARTS: MUSIC & DANCE

MYSTICISM See also PRAYER; RELIGION

The most beautiful thing we can experience is the mysterious. It is the source of all true art and science.
>   —ALBERT EINSTEIN, *What I Believe*

Without mysticism man can achieve nothing great.
>   —ANDRÉ GIDE, *The Counterfeiters,* 1926

The dark night of the soul through which the soul passes on its way to the Divine Light.
>   —ST. JOHN OF THE CROSS,
>   *The Ascent of Mount Carmel,* 1578

[He also used the phrase "The Dark Night of the Soul" as the title of a treatise in 1583. The metaphor is the most famous expression of the despair that often precedes intense mystical experience. See also F. Scott Fitzgerald at DESPAIR, DE-PRESSION, & MISERY.]

The Way [Tao] that can be told is not the eternal way.
—LAO-TZU, *Tao Te Ching*, 6th cent. B.C.

The Way is like an empty vessel that yet may be drawn from.　　　　　　　　　　　　　　　　　　—*Ibid.*

Mysticism is, in essence, little more than a certain intensity and depth of feeling in regard to what is believed about the universe.　　　　　　　　　　　　—BERTRAND RUSSELL,
Mysticism and Logic, title essay, 1918

The more mysterious, the more imperfect: that which is mystically spoken is but half spoken.
—BENJAMIN WHICHCOTE,
Moral and Religious Aphorisms, 1753

N

NAMES

Nomen est omen.
In name is destiny.   —ANONYMOUS (ROMAN SAYING)

What's in a name? That which we call a rose
By any other name would smell as sweet.
                    —SHAKESPEARE, *Romeo and Juliet,* II, ii

NAPLES   See CITIES

NATIONS   See also AMERICA & AMERICANS; CITIES;
                    RACES & PEOPLES; TRAVEL

A nation does not have friends, it has interests.
                    —ANONYMOUS, quoted by Thomas Polgar,
                         The New York Times, Nov. 11, 1993
[Polgar, an intelligence expert, identified this as an old saying.]

Behold, the nations are as a drop of a bucket, and are
counted as the small dust of the balance.
                              —BIBLE, *Isaiah* 40:151

Africa

It is still yesterday in Africa. It will take millions of tomor-
rows to rectify what has been done here.
                    —LORRAINE HANSBERRY, *Les Blancs,* 1972

Let freedom reign. God bless Africa.
                    —NELSON MANDELA, presidential inaugural speech,
                         Pretoria, South Africa, May 10, 1994

The wind of change is blowing through this Continent, and whether we like it or not, this growth of national conscious-ness is a political fact.   —HAROLD MACMILLAN,
speech in Cape Town, Feb. 3, 1960
[Macmillan drew on a traditional image here. In his *Political Dictionary*, William Safire cites, among several precedents, In-dian Prime Minister Jawaharlal Nehru, "Strong winds are blow-ing all over Asia," 1947; and British Prime Minister Stanley Baldwin, "There is a wind of nationalism and freedom blowing around the world," 1934.]

There is always something new out of Africa.
—PLINY, *Natural History*, A.D. 77

Ancient World

The Naiad airs have brought me home
To the glory that was Greece,
And the grandeur that was Rome.
—EDGAR ALLAN POE, *To Helen*, 1831
[See also **Greece** below and **Rome** at CITIES.)

Brazil

Brazil is not a serious country.
—CHARLES DE GAULLE, d. 1970, attributed
[De Gaulle evidently never said this, nevertheless it is a fa-mous quote.]

Canada

I am rather inclined to believe that this is the land God gave to Cain.   —JACQUES CARTIER, *Relation Originale du voyage de Jacques Cartier au Canada en 1534*

China

In Xanadu did Kubla Khan
A stately pleasure dome decree:
Where Alph, the sacred river ran
Through caverns measureless to man
Down to a sunless sea.
—SAMUEL TAYLOR COLERIDGE, *Kubla Khan*, 1797

Very big, China.   —NOEL COWARD, *Private Lives*, 1930

There does not appear the slightest probability that Hong Kong will ever become a place of trade.
                          —ROBERT MONTGOMERY MARTIN,
                                report from Hong Kong, 1844
[Mr. Martin was the British colonial treasurer.]

East, The

The power that rules the Pacific . . . is the power that rules the world.
      —ALBERT J. BEVERIDGE, speech, U.S. Senate, 1900

The mysterious East, perfumed like a flower, silent like death, dark like a grave.
                      —JOSEPH CONRAD, *Youth*, 1902

Oh, East is East, and West is West, and never the twain shall meet, / Till Earth and Sky stand presently at God's great Judgment Seat.   —RUDYARD KIPLING,
                        The Ballad of East and West, 1889

England

Great Britain has lost an empire and has not yet found a role.   —DEAN ACHESON, speech,
                  U.S. Military Academy, Dec. 5, 1962

If I should die, think only this of me:
That there's some corner of a foreign field
That is forever England.
                    —RUPERT BROOKE, *The Soldier*, 1914

Oh, to be in England now that April's there.
                              —ROBERT BROWNING,
                        Home Thoughts from Abroad, 1845

I have nothing to offer but blood, toil, tears, and sweat,
            —WINSTON CHURCHILL, speech, May 13, 1940

We shall go on to the end . . . we shall defend our island, whatever the cost may be, we shall fight on the beaches, we shall fight on the landing grounds, we shall fight in the fields and in the streets, we shall fight in the hills; we shall never surrender. —WINSTON CHURCHILL, speech, June 4, 1940
[Churchill may have remembered French Premier Georges Clemenceau's defiance of the German army in 1918: "I shall fight in front of Paris, within Paris, behind Paris." See also Churchill on victory at WINNING & LOSING, VICTORY & DEFEAT.]

This was their finest hour.   —WINSTON CHURCHILL,
                                              speech, June 18, 1940
[Conclusion of an urgent appeal: "Let us . . . brace ourselves to our duties, and so bear ourselves that if the British Empire and its Commonwealth last for a thousand years, men will still say: 'This was their finest hour.' "]

Never in the field of human conflict was so much owed by so many to so few.   —WINSTON CHURCHILL,
                                              speech, Aug. 20, 1940
[He was speaking of the Royal Air Force.]

England is the paradise of women, the purgatory of men, and the hell of horses.
                              —JOHN FLORIO, *Second Frutes*, 1591
[See also **Italy,** the Burton quote.]

The stately homes of England!
How beautiful they stand.   —FELICIA HEMANS,
                                              The Homes of England, 1827
[For a different perspective, see Virginia Woolf below.]

Continental people have a sex life; the English have hot-water bottles.   —GEORGE MIKES, *How to Be an Alien,* 1946

England is a nation of shopkeepers.
                              —NAPOLEON BONAPARTE, d. 1821,
                       attributed, B. E. O'Meara, *Napoleon in Exile,* 1922
[This is the usual attribution, but the adage was going around. *Bartlett's* cites the description "a shop-keeping nation" in a tract by Josiah Tucker dated 1763. Samuel Adams is said to have called England a nation of shopkeepers in 1776. And Adam Smith in *The Wealth of Nations* (1776) wrote: "To found

a great empire for the sole purpose of raising up a people of customers, may at first sight appear a project fit only for a nation of shopkeepers. It is, however, a project altogether unfit for a nation of shopkeepers; but extremely fit for a nation whose government is influenced by shopkeepers."]

There'll Always Be an England.
 —ROSS PARKER & HUGH CHARLES, song title, 1939

England is the paradise of individuality, eccentricity, heresy, anomalies, hobbies, and humors.
     —GEORGE SANTAYANA,
      Soliloquies in England, 1922

Once more unto the breach, dear friends, once more,
Or close the wall up with our English dead!
    —SHAKESPEARE, *Henry V,* III, i

The game's afoot.
Follow your spirit, and upon this charge
Cry "God for Harry, England, and Saint George!" —*Ibid.*

This England never did, nor never shall,
Lie at the proud foot of a conqueror.
     —SHAKESPEARE, *King John,* V, vii

This royal throne of kings, this sceptered isle.
     —SHAKESPEARE, *Richard II,* II, i

This happy breed of men, this little world
This precious stone set in the silver sea.   —*Ibid.*

This blessed plot, this earth, this realm, this England.
         —*Ibid.*

An Englishman thinks he is moral when he is only uncomfortable. —GEORGE BERNARD SHAW,
       Man and Superman, 1903

The English take their pleasures sadly after the fashion of their country. —DUC DE SULLY, *Memoirs,* c. 1630

Those comfortably padded lunatic asylums which are known, euphemistically, as the stately homes of England.
> —VIRGINIA WOOLF, *Lady Dorothy Nevill*
> in *The Common Reader,* 1925

Europe

I want to travel in Europe . . . I know that I am only going to a graveyard, but it's a most precious graveyard.
> —FEODOR DOSTOEVSKI,
> *The Brothers Karamazov,* 1879–80

Je regrette l'Europe aux anciens parapets!
I long for Europe of the ancient parapets.
> —ARTHUR RIMBAUD, *Le bateau ivre,* 1871

This agglomeration which was called, and still calls itself, the Holy Roman Empire was neither holy, nor Roman, nor any empire in any way. —VOLTAIRE, *Essai sur les moeurs*
> *et l'esprit des nations,* 1756

France

Fifty million Frenchmen can't be wrong.
> —ANONYMOUS, saying of American
> troops in World War I, 1917–18

France was a long despotism tempered by epigrams.
> —THOMAS CARLYLE, *History of the*
> *French Revolution,* 1837

How can you be expected to govern a country that has two hundred and forty-six kinds of cheese?
> —CHARLES DE GAULLE, *Newsweek,* Oct. 1, 1962

Gallia est omnis divisa in partes tres.
All Gaul is divided in three parts.
> —JULIUS CAESAR, *Commentarii de*
> *bello Gallico,* c. 58–52 B.C.

Germany

Everything ponderous, viscous, and solemnly clumsy, all long-winded and boring types of style are developed in profuse variety among Germans. —FRIEDRICH NIETZSCHE,
Beyond Good and Evil, 1855–56

Whenever the literary German dives into a sentence, that is the last you are going to see of him till he emerges on the other side of the Atlantic with his verb in his mouth.
—MARK TWAIN, *A Connecticut Yankee
in King Arthur's Court,* 1889

Greece

They [the Greeks] were the first Westerners; the spirit of the West, the modern spirit, is a Greek discovery.
—EDITH HAMILTON, *The Greek Way,* 1930
[See also **Ancient World** above.]

Greece is the home of the gods.
—HENRY MILLER, *The Colossus of Maroussi,* 1941

We are all Greeks. Our laws, our literature, our religion, our arts have their roots in Greece.
—PERCY BYSSHE SHELLEY, Preface, *Hellas,* 1821

We [Greeks] are lovers of the beautiful, yet simple in our tastes, and we cultivate the mind without loss of manliness.
—THUCYDIDES, *The History of the
Peloponnesian War,* c. 400 B.C.

I fear the Greeks even when they bring gifts.
—VIRGIL, *Aeneid,* c. 19 B.C.

Ireland

If you begin in Ireland, Ireland remains the norm; like it or not.
—ELIZABETH BOWEN,
Pictures and Conversations, 1975

For the great Gaels of Ireland
Are the men that God made mad,
For all their wars are merry,
And all their songs are sad.   —G. K. CHESTERTON,
                                The Ballad of the White Horse, 1911

The Irish are a fair people;—they never speak well of one
another.   —SAMUEL JOHNSON, Mar. 20, 1775,
                        quoted in James Boswell, *Life of Johnson,* 1791

Ireland is the old sow that eats her farrow.
                            —JAMES JOYCE, *A Portrait of the
                                Artist As a Young Man,* 1916

I'm troubled, I'm dissatisfied. I'm Irish.
                        —MARIANNE MOORE, *Spenser's Ireland,* 1941

Romantic Ireland's dead and gone,
It's with O'Leary in the grave.
                            —WILLIAM BUTLER YEATS,
                        September 1913 in *Responsibilities,* 1914

Italy

England is a paradise for women, and hell for horses; Italy
is a paradise for horses, hell for woman, as the diverb [prov-
erb] goes.   —ROBERT BURTON, *The Anatomy
                                of Melancholy,* 1621–51
[See also **England**, the Florio quote.]

A man who has not been in Italy is always conscious of an
inferiority.   —SAMUEL JOHNSON, April 1776,
                        quoted in James Boswell, *Life of Johnson,* 1791

A race corrupted by a bad government and a bad religion,
long renowned for skill in the arts of voluptuousness, and
tolerant of all the caprices of sensuality.
                        —THOMAS BABINGTON MACAULAY,
                Moore's Life of Lord Byron in *Edinburgh Review,*
                                        June 1831
[An attack on Italians that makes them sound quite appealing.
For an appreciation of Italians' accomplishments, see the Orson
Welles quote under **Switzerland**.]

Japan

The real man in Japan is the one who keeps his feelings to himself, so as not to disturb the harmony of others.
—SADUHARU OH, quoted by Robert Whiting,
The New York Times, Op-Ed, Oct. 7, 1992
[Sadaharu Oh, a famed baseball player, hit 868 career home runs.]

While we spend energy and imagination on new ways of cleaning the floors of our houses, the Japanese solve the problem by not dirtying them in the first place.
—BERNARD RUDOFSKY, *The Kimono Mind,* 1965

The Japanese have perfected good manners and made them indistinguishable from rudeness.
—PAUL THEROUX, *The Great Railway Bazaar,* 1975

Malaya

This is Malaya. Everything takes a long, a very long time in Malaya. Things get done, occasionally, but more often they don't, and the more in a hurry you are, the quicker you break down.   —HAN SUYIN, *And the Rain My Drink,* 1956

Mexico

Poor Mexico! So far from God and so close to the United States.
—PORFIRIO DÍAZ, attributed, in John S. D. Eisenhower,
The U.S. War with Mexico, 1846–48, 1989
[Gen. Díaz was president of Mexico from 1877–1911.]

Russia

Russia is omnipotence . . . who can ever penetrate that polar mystery?
—HENRY ADAMS, letter to Brooks Adams, June 5, 1895
[On January and February in Russia, see Nicholas I at MILITARY, THE.]

It [Russia] is a riddle wrapped in a mystery inside an enigma.
—WINSTON CHURCHILL, radio speech, Oct. 1, 1939

Our fatal troika dashes on in her headlong flight, perhaps to destruction.　　　　　—FEODOR DOSTOEVSKI,
The Brothers Karamazov, 1879–80

An evil empire.
　　　　　—RONALD REAGAN, speech, Mar. 9, 1983
[Pres. Reagan here borrowed a designation made famous in the 1977 film *Star Wars* by George W. Lucas.]

And grasping tight her pot of vodka, our Holy Russia lies in interminable sleep.
　　　　　—IVAN TURGENEV, *Virgin Soil,* 1868

Scotland

My heart's in the Highlands, my heart is not here,
My heart's in the Highlands a-chasing the deer.
　　　　　—ROBERT BURNS, *My Heart's in the Highlands*
in *Johnson's Musical Museum,* 1787–96

The noblest prospect that a Scotchman ever sees is the high road that leads to London.
　　　　　—SAMUEL JOHNSON, Nov. 10, 1773, quoted by
James Boswell, *Journal of a Tour to the Hebrides,* 1785

Sri Lanka

What though the spicy breezes
Blow soft o'er Ceylon's isle;
Though every prospect pleases,
And only man is vile.　　　　　—REGINALD HEBER, *From*
Greenland's Icy Mountains, 1819

Switzerland

The Swiss are not a people so much as a neat clean quite solvent business.
　　　　　—WILLIAM FAULKNER, *Intruder in the Dust,* 1948

In Italy for thirty years under the Borgias, they had warfare, terror, murder, bloodshed. They produced Michelangelo, Leonardo da Vinci, and the Renaissance. In Switzerland, they had brotherly love, five hundred years of democracy and peace, and what did they produce? The cuckoo clock.
　　　　　—ORSON WELLES, screenplay, *The Third Man,* 1949

[The script writer was Graham Greene, but Welles reportedly added this passage himself.]

Turkey

A humorless soldierly people whose arts are courage, honor and bloodletting.
—NELSON ALGREN, *Who Lost an American,* 1963

We have a sick man—a seriously sick man on our hands.
—NICHOLAS I of Russia, quoted by
Sir G. H. Seymour, letter, Jan. 11, 1853
[In *The Real World,* 1980, Richard M. Nixon wrote: "Before World War I, Turkey was known as the 'Sick Man of Europe'; now it is almost a terminal case."]

NATURE   See also COUNTRY, THE; CREATION, DIVINE; ENVIRONMENT; SEAS & SHIPS, SAILING & BOATING; UNIVERSE; and NATURE subcategories, below

Natura genetrix.
Nature is our mother.
—ANONYMOUS (LATIN PROVERB)

Nature, to be commanded, must be obeyed.
—FRANCIS BACON, *Novum Organum,* 1620

La nature est un temple où de vivants piliers
Laissent parfois sortir de confuses paroles;
L'homme y passe à travers des forêts de symboles
Qui l'observent avec des regards familiers.
Nature is a temple where living pillars
Sometimes emit confused words;
There man passes through forests of symbols
Which observe him with familiar looks.
—CHARLES BAUDELAIRE, *Correspondences,* 1861

What I know of the divine science and Holy Scripture I learnt in woods and fields.
—ST. BERNARD, *Epistle 106,* 12th cent.

Listen to a man of experience: thou wilt learn more in the woods than in books.   —*Ibid.*

Speak to the earth, and it shall teach thee.
—BIBLE, *Job* 12:8

For the earth is the Lord's, and the fulness thereof.
—BIBLE, *I Corinthians* 10:26

To see a world in a grain of sand
And a heaven in a wild flower,
Hold infinity in the palm of your hand
And eternity in an hour.
—WILLIAM BLAKE, *Auguries of Innocence*
in *Poems from the Pickering Manuscript,* c. 1805

All things are artificial, for nature is the art of God.
—THOMAS BROWNE, *Religio medici,* 1643

There is a pleasure in the pathless woods,
There is a rapture on the lonely shore,
There is a society where none intrudes,
By the deep sea, and music in its roar:
I love not man the less, but nature more.
—LORD BYRON, *Childe Harold's Pilgrimage,* 1812–18

The works of nature must all be accounted good.
—CICERO, *De senectute,* 44 B.C.

Earth, with her thousand voices, praises God.
—SAMUEL TAYLOR COLERIDGE,
Hymn Before Sun-Rise in the Vale of Chamount, 1802

Whatever nature has in store for mankind, unpleasant, as it
may be, men must accept, for ignorance is never better than
knowledge. —ENRICO FERMI, d. 1954, quoted in
Laura Fermi, *Atoms in the Family,* 1955

Nature goes her own way, and all that to us seems an exception is really according to order.
—GOETHE, quoted in Johann Peter Eckermann,
Conversations with Goethe, 1836

Glory be to God for dappled things.
—GERARD MANLEY HOPKINS, d. 1889,
Pied Beauty in *Poems,* 1918

The world is charged with the grandeur of God.
> —GERARD MANLEY HOPKINS,
> *God's Grandeur* in *Ibid.*

Though you drive away nature with a pitchfork, she always returns.   —HORACE, *Epistles,* Book I, 20 B.C.

Never does nature say one thing and wisdom another.
> —JUVENAL, *Satires,* c. A.D. 100

The poetry of earth is never dead.
> —JOHN KEATS, *On the Grasshopper
> and the Cricket* in *Poems,* 1817

The roaring of the wind is my wife and the stars through the window pane are my children.
> —JOHN KEATS, letter to George and
> Georgina Keats, Oct. 14, 1818

Nature is not human-hearted.
> —LAO-TZU, *Tao Te Ching,* 6th cent. B.C.

The clearest way into the universe is through a forest wilderness.   —JOHN MUIR, *John of the Mountains,* 1938
[See also Muir at ENVIRONMENT.]

Nature is an infinite sphere of which the center is everywhere and the circumference nowhere.
> —PASCAL, *Pensées,* 1670

It were happy if we studied nature more in natural things, and acted according to nature, whose rules are few, plain, and most reasonable.
> —WILLIAM PENN, *Some Fruits of Solitude,* 1693

All nature is but art, unknown to thee;
All chance, direction, which thou canst not see;
All discord, harmony not understood;
All partial evil, universal good.
> —ALEXANDER POPE, *An Essay on Man,* 1733–34

Perhaps nature is our best assurance of immortality.
> —ELEANOR ROOSEVELT,
> *My Day* newspaper column, Apr. 24, 1945

What else is nature but God?
>—SENECA, *De beneficiis,* 1st cent. A.D.

One touch of nature makes the whole world kin.
>—SHAKESPEARE, *Troilus and Cressida,* III, iii

The earth and ocean seem
To sleep in one another's arms, and dream
Of waves, flowers, clouds, woods, rocks, and all that we
Read in their smiles, and call reality.
>—PERCY BYSSHE SHELLEY, *Epipsychidion,* 1821

In nature, there is less death and destruction than death and transmutation.
>—EDWIN WAY TEALE, *Circle of the Seasons,* 1953

Nature, red in tooth and claw.
>—ALFRED, LORD TENNYSON, *In Memoriam,* 1850

For men may come and men may go,
But I go on forever.
>—ALFRED, LORD TENNYSON, *The Brook,* 1855

I have learned
To look on nature, not as in the hour
Of thoughtless youth; but hearing oftentimes
The still, sad music of humanity.
>—WILLIAM WORDSWORTH, *Lines Composed
a Few Miles Above Tintern Abbey,* 1798

Nature never did betray the heart that loved her.   *—Ibid.*

NATURE: ANIMALS

The dog was created especially for children. He is the god of frolic.
>—HENRY WARD BEECHER,
Proverbs from Plymouth Pulpit, 1887

Hast thou given the horse strength? hast thou clothed his
neck with thunder?. . . .
   He paweth in the valley, and rejoiceth in his strength; he
goeth on to meet the armed men. . . .
   He saith among the trumpets, Ha, ha; and he smelleth the
battle afar off, the thunder of the captains, and the shouting.
                                        —BIBLE, *Job* 39:19, 21, 25

A robin red breast in a cage
Puts all heaven in a rage.
                     —WILLIAM BLAKE, *Auguries of Innocence*
                     in *Poems from the Pickering Manuscript,* c. 1805

Tiger! Tiger! burning bright
In the forests of the night,
What immortal hand or eye
Could frame thy fearful symmetry?
In what distant deeps or skies
Burnt the fire of thine eyes?
On what wings dare he aspire?
What the hand dare seize the fire?   —WILLIAM BLAKE,
                     The Tiger in *Songs of Experience,* 1794

When the stars threw down their spears,
And watered heaven with their tears,
Did he smile his work to see?
Did he who made the Lamb make thee?   —*Ibid.*

That's the wise thrush; he sings each song twice over,
Lest you think he never could recapture
The first fine careless rapture!   —ROBERT BROWNING,
                     Home Thoughts from Abroad, 1845

An animal's eyes have the power to speak a great language.
                     —MARTIN BUBER, *I and Thou,* 1923

Wee, sleekit, cow'ring, tim'rous beastie,
O what a panic's in thy breastie!
                     —ROBERT BURNS, *To a Mouse,* 1786

A hen is only an egg's way of making another egg.
                     —SAMUEL BUTLER, *Life and Habit,* 1877

The greatest pleasure of a dog is that you may make a fool of yourself with him and not only will he not scold you, but he will make a fool of himself too. —SAMUEL BUTLER,
Higgledy-Piggledy in *Notebooks,* 1912

Near this spot are deposited the remains of one who possessed beauty without vanity, strength without insolence, courage without ferocity, and all the virtues of Man without his vices. —LORD BYRON, epitaph for
his Newfoundland, Boatswain, 1808
[A similar sentiment is expressed in an anonymous American epitaph: "MAJOR / Born a Dog / Died a Gentleman." *American Heritage,* Feb. 1973, identified this as from an old Maryland gravestone.]

A cat looks down upon a man, and a dog looks up to a man, but a pig will look a man in the eye and see his equal.
—WINSTON CHURCHILL, remark to his grandson,
c. 1950, cited in *Scientific American,* May 1966

A canter is the cure for every evil.
—BENJAMIN DISRAELI, *The Young Duke,* 1831

Everything belonging to the spider is admirable.
—JONATHAN EDWARDS, *The Spider,* c. 1714
[American theologian Edwards was a promising scientist in his youth; he was about 12 when he wrote about spiders.]

Animals are such agreeable friends—they ask no questions, they pass no criticisms.
—GEORGE ELIOT, *Mr. Gilfil's Love Story*
in *Scenes of Clerical Life,* 1857

The Creator, if He exists, has a special preference for beetles. —J.B.S. HALDANE, Apr. 7, 1951
[Sometimes the line is given as "God has an inordinate fondness for beetles." Haldane reportedly based this conclusion on the grounds that there are 400,000 species of beetles, versus 8,000 species of mammals. The quote, and beetles, are discussed in Stephen J. Gould's column in *Natural History* magazine, Jan. 1993.]

The Cat. He walked by himself, and all places were alike to him.   —RUDYARD KIPLING, *The Cat That Walked by Himself* in *Just-So Stories,* 1902

Only animals were not expelled from Paradise.
                    —MILAN KUNDERA, *The Unbearable Lightness of Being,* 1984

I never saw a wild thing
Sorry for itself.
A small bird will drop frozen dead
From a bough
Without ever having felt sorry for itself.
                    —D. H. LAWRENCE, *Self-Pity,* 1923

O, a wondrous bird is the pelican,
His beak will hold more than his belican.
He takes in his beak
Enough food for a week,
But I'm darned if I know how the helican.
                    —DIXON MERRITT, *The Pelican* in the *Nashville Banner,* Apr. 22, 1913

When I play with my cat, who knows whether she is not amusing herself with me more than I with her.
                    —MONTAIGNE, *Essays,* 1580–88

The turtle lives 'twixt plated decks
Which practically conceal its sex.
I think it's clever of the turtle
In such a fix to be so fertile.
                    —OGDEN NASH, *Autres Bêtes, Autres Moeurs* in *Hard Lines,* 1931

The song of canaries
Never varies,
And when they're moulting
They're pretty revolting.
                    —OGDEN NASH, *The Canary* in *The Face Is Familiar,* 1941

Dogs display reluctance and wrath
If you try to give them a bath.
They bury bones in hideaways
And half the time they trot sideaways.
                    —OGDEN NASH, *An Introduction to Dogs* in *Ibid.*

The trouble with a kitten is
That
Eventually it becomes a
Cat.   —OGDEN NASH, *The Kitten* in *Ibid.*

There is something about the unselfish and self-sacrificing
love of a brute, which goes directly to the heart of him who
has had frequent occasion to test the paltry friendship and
gossamer fidelity of mere man.
           —EDGAR ALLAN POE, *The Black Cat*, 1843

I am his Highness' dog at Kew;
Pray tell me, sir, whose dog are you?
                    —ALEXANDER POPE, d. 1744,
                         couplet for a dog's collar

A horse! A horse! my kingdom for a horse!
                —SHAKESPEARE, *Richard III*, V, iv

Hail to thee, blithe Spirit!
Bird thou never wert,
That from Heaven, or near it,
Pourest thy full heart
In profuse strains of unpremeditated art.
           —PERCY BYSSHE SHELLEY, *To a Skylark*, 1819

So, naturalists observe, a flea
Hath smaller fleas that on him prey;
And these have smaller fleas to bite 'em
And so proceed ad infinitum.
                —JONATHAN SWIFT, *On Poetry*, 1733
[Swift's conclusion, less well-known, is: "Thus every poet, in
his kind, / Is bit by him that comes behind."]

He clasps the crag with crooked hands;
Close to the sun in lonely lands,
Ringed with the azure world, he stands.
The wrinkled sea beneath him crawls;
He watches from his mountain walls,
And like a thunderbolt he falls.
           —ALFRED, LORD TENNYSON, *The Eagle*, 1842

The bluebird carries the sky on its back.
           —HENRY DAVID THOREAU, *Journal*, Apr. 3, 1852

Cheerfulness is proper to the cock, which rejoices over every little thing, and crows with varied and lively movements.
—LEONARDO DA VINCI, *Notebooks*, 1508–18

If a dog jumps in your lap, it is because he is fond of you; but if a cat does the same thing, it is because your lap is warmer.
—ALFRED NORTH WHITEHEAD, *Dialogues*, 1955

I think I could turn and live with animals, they are so placid and self-contained,
I stand and look at them long and long.
—WALT WHITMAN,
Song of Myself in *Leaves of Grass*, 1855

The best thing about animals is that they don't talk much.
—THORNTON WILDER, *The Skin of Our Teeth*, 1942

NATURE: GARDENS,   See also ENVIRONMENT
FLOWERS, & TREES   (Voltaire)

Flowers are my music. —DR. THOMAS ARNOLD, d. 1842,
quoted by Arthur Stanley, *Life of Dr. Arnold*, 1844

God almighty first planted a garden.
—FRANCIS BACON, *Of Gardens*, 1625

Flowers are the sweetest things that God ever made, and forgot to put a soul into.
—HENRY WARD BEECHER, *Life Thoughts*, 1887

The Lord God planted a garden eastward in Eden.
—BIBLE, *Genesis* 2:8

Consider the lilies of the field, how they grow; they toil not, neither do they spin:
    And yet I say unto you, That even Solomon in all his glory was not arrayed like one of these.
—BIBLE, *Matthew* 6:28, 29

A garden is a lovesome thing, God wot!
—THOMAS E. BROWN, *My Garden of Cyrus*, 1658

The groves were God's first temples.
—WILLIAM CULLEN BRYANT, *A Forest Hymn*, 1852

The dandelion's pallid tube
Astonishes the grass,
And winter instantly becomes
An infinite alas.
—EMILY DICKINSON, poem no. 1519, c. 1881

Earth laughs in flowers. —RALPH WALDO EMERSON,
Hamatreya in *Poems*, 1847

There are fairies at the bottom of our garden!
—ROSE FYLEMAN,
The Fairies in *Fairies and Chimneys*, 1920

Verde que te quiero verde
Verde viento. Verde ramas.
Green I love you green.
Green wind. Green branches.
—FEDERICO GARCÍA LORCA,
Romance sonámbulo, 1928

The kiss of the sun for pardon,
The song of the birds for mirth.
One is nearer God's heart in a garden
Than anywhere else on earth.
—DOROTHY GURNEY, *God's Garden*, 1913

But though I am an old man, I am but a young gardener.
—THOMAS JEFFERSON, letter to
Charles Wilson Peale, Aug. 20, 1811

I think that I shall never see
A poem lovely as a tree. —JOYCE KILMER, *Trees*, 1913

Poems are made by fools like me,
But only God can make a tree. —*Ibid.*

I want death to find me planting my cabbages.
—MONTAIGNE, *To the Reader* in *Essays*, Book I, 1880
[Another great writer fond of cabbages was Rabelais; see
below.]

The last rose of summer.
> —THOMAS MOORE, *'Tis the Last
> Rose* in *Irish Melodies*, 1807–34

[More at NATURE: SEASONS below.]

Woodman, spare that tree!
Touch not a single bough!
In youth it sheltered me,
And I'll protect it now.   —GEORGE POPE MORRIS,
Woodman, Spare That Tree, 1830

Each flower is a soul opening out to nature.
> —GÉRARD DE NERVAL, d. 1855, *Vers dorés,*

Where'er you walk, cool gales shall fan the glade,
Trees where you sit shall crowd into a shade:
Where'er you tread, the blushing flowers shall rise,
And all things flourish where you turn your eyes.
> —ALEXANDER POPE, *Summer* in *Pastorals*, 1709

Oh thrice and four times happy those who plant cabbages!
> —FRANÇOIS RABELAIS, *Gargantua
> and Pantagruel*, Book IV, 1548

There is material enough in a single flower for the ornament
of a score of cathedrals.
> —JOHN RUSKIN, *The Stones of Venice*, 1851–53

There's rosemary, that's for remembrance—pray you love,
remember. And there is pansies, that's for thoughts.
> —SHAKESPEARE, *Hamlet*, IV, v

I know a bank where the wild thyme blows,
Where oxlips and the nodding violet grows
Quite overcanopied with lucious woodbine,
With sweet musk-roses and with eglantine.
> —SHAKESPEARE, *A Midsummer-Night's Dream*, II, i

For you there's rosemary and rue, these keep
Seeming and savor all the winter long.
> —SHAKESPEARE, *The Winter's Tale*, IV, iii

The summer's flower is to the summer sweet,
Though to itself it only live and die.
—SHAKESPEARE, sonnet 94

There's a tree that grows in Brooklyn. Some people call it
the Tree of Heaven. No matter where its seed falls, it makes
a tree which struggles to reach the sky.
—BETTY SMITH, *A Tree Grows in Brooklyn,* 1943
[The tree is the ailanthus.]

Rose is a rose is a rose.
—GERTRUDE STEIN, *Sacred Emily,* 1913

One morning, very early, before the sun was up,
I rose and found the shining dew on every buttercup.
—ROBERT LOUIS STEVENSON,
A Shadow in *A Child's Garden of Verses,* 1885

Flower in the crannied wall,
I pluck you out of the crannies,
I hold you here, root and all, in my hand,
Little flower—but *if* I could understand
What you are, root and all, and all in all,
I should know what God and man is.
—ALFRED, LORD TENNYSON,
Flower in the Crannied Wall, 1869

I was determined to know beans.
—HENRY DAVID THOREAU, *Walden,* 1854

To own a bit of ground, to scratch it with a hoe, to plant
seeds and watch their renewal of life—this is the commonest
delight of the race, the most satisfactory thing a man can
do. —CHARLES DUDLEY WARNER,
My Summer in a Garden, 1870

I wandered lonely as a cloud
That floats on high o'er vales and hills,
When all at once I saw a crowd,
A host of golden daffodils. —WILLIAM WORDSWORTH,
I Wandered Lonely as a Cloud, 1807

A primrose by a river's brim
A yellow primrose was to him,
And it was nothing more.
—WILLIAM WORDSWORTH, *Peter Bell,* 1819

NATURE: See also SCIENCE: PHYSICS
THE HEAVENS, THE SKY   & COSMOLOGY

I do set my bow in the cloud, and it shall be for a token of
a covenant between me and the earth.
—BIBLE, *Genesis* 9:13

The heavens declare the glory of God; and the firmament
showeth his handiwork.   —BIBLE, *Psalms* 19:1

The moon like a flower
In heaven's high bower,
With silent delight,
Sits and smiles on the night.
—WILLIAM BLAKE, *Night* in *Poetical Sketches,* 1783

The moon is a different thing to each one of us.
—FRANK BORMAN, from Apollo 8, Dec. 24, 1968

The heavens call to you, and circle around you, displaying
to you their eternal splendours, and your eye gazes only to
earth.   —DANTE, *Purgatorio* in
The Divine Comedy, c. 1310–20

A man is a small thing, and the night is very large and full
of wonders.
—LORD DUNSANY, *The Laughter of the Gods,* 1916

Space is the stature of God.
—JOSEPH JOUBERT, *Pensées,* 1842

Now the bright morning star, day's harbinger,
Comes dancing from the east.
—JOHN MILTON, *On May Morning,* 1645

The evening star,
Love's harbinger, appeared.
—JOHN MILTON, *Paradise Lost,* 1667

The moon was a ghostly galleon tossed upon cloudy skies.
> —ALFRED NOYES, *The Highwayman* in
> *Forty Singing Seamen and Other Poems,* 1907

The eternal silence of these infinite spaces frightens me.
> —PASCAL, *Pensées,* 1670

I have a horror of sunsets, they're so romantic, so operatic.
> —MARCEL PROUST, *Remembrance of Things Past:*
> *The Guermantes Way,* 1913–27

My heart leaps up when I behold
A rainbow in the sky.
> —WILLIAM WORDSWORTH, *My Heart Leaps Up,* 1807

And pluck till time and times are done
The silver apples of the moon,
The golden apples of the sun.
> —WILLIAM BUTLER YEATS, *The Song of the*
> *Wandering Aengus* in *The Wind Among the Reeds,* 1899

NATURE: THE OCEAN   See also SEAS & SHIPS,
SAILING & BOATING

Roll on, thou deep and dark blue ocean—roll!
Ten thousand fleets sweep over thee in vain;
Man marks the earth with ruin—his control
Stops with the shore.
> —LORD BYRON, *Childe Harold's Pilgrimage,* 1812–18

For all at last returns to the sea—to Oceanus, the ocean
river, like the everflowing stream of time, the beginning and
the end.   —RACHEL CARSON, *The Sea Around Us,* 1951

The sea never changes and its works, for all the talk of men,
are wrapped in mystery.
> —JOSEPH CONRAD, *Typhoon,* 1902

Never trust her at any time, when the calm sea shows her
false alluring smile.
> —LUCRETIUS, *On the Nature of Things,* c. 57 B.C.

NATURE: SEASONS   See also LIFE (Bible)

November is the most disagreeable month in the entire year.
—LOUISA MAY ALCOTT, *Little Women*, 1868

Sumer is icumen in,
Lhude sing cuccu!
Groweth sed, and bloweth med,
And springth the wude nu
Sing cuccu!   —ANONYMOUS
[Cf. Ezra Pound, below.]

Rise up, my love, my fair one, and come away.
    For lo, the winter is past, the rain is over and gone;
    The flowers appear on the earth; the time of the singing
of birds is come, and the voice of the turtle is heard in
our land;
    The fig tree putteth forth her green figs, and the vines
with the tender grape give a good smell. Arise, my love, my
fair one, and come away.
—BIBLE, *The Song of Solomon* 2:10–13

Autumn arrives in the early morning, but spring at the close
of a winter day.
—ELIZABETH BOWEN, *The Death of the Heart*, 1938

The year's at the spring
And day's at the morn;
Morning's at seven;
The hillside's dew-pearled;
The lark's on the wing;
The snail's on his thorn:
God's in his heaven—
All's right with the world.
—ROBERT BROWNING, *Pippa Passes*, 1841

Hard is his herte that loveth nought
In May.   —GEOFFREY CHAUCER,
                            The Romaunt of the Rose, c. 1370
[A translation of the French *Romance of the Rose*.]

Whan that Aprill with his shoures soote
The droghte of March hath perced to the roote.
　　　　　—GEOFFREY CHAUCER, Prologue, lines 1–2,
　　　　　　　　The Canterbury Tales, c. 1387
[For other first lines, see Tolstoy at FAMILY.]

There's a certain slant of light,
Winter afternoons
That oppresses like the heft
Of cathedral tunes.
　　　　　—EMILY DICKINSON, poem no. 258, c. 1861

A little madness in the Spring
Is wholesome even for the king.
　　　　　—EMILY DICKINSON, poem no. 1333, c. 1875

April is the cruellest month, breeding
Lilacs out of the dead land, mixing
Memory and desire, stirring
Dull roots with spring rain.
　　　　　—T. S. ELIOT, *The Waste Land,* 1922

Snowy, Flowy, Blowy,
Showery, Flowery, Bowery,
Hoppy, Croppy, Droppy,
Breezy, Sneezy, Freezy.
　　　　　—GEORGE ELLIS, d. 1815, *The Twelve Months*

Alas, that Spring should vanish with the Rose!
　　　　　—EDWARD FITZGERALD,
　　　　　The Rubáiyát of Omar Khayyám, 1879
[More at YOUTH.]

I saw old autumn in the misty morn
Stand shadowless like silence, listening
To silence.　　　　—THOMAS HOOD, *Ode: Autumn,* 1827

Summer afternoon—summer afternoon; to me those have
always been the two most beautiful words in the English
language.　　　　　—HENRY JAMES, d. 1916, quoted in
　　　　　Edith Wharton, *A Backward Glance,* 1934

His soul swooned slowly as he heard the snow falling faintly through the universe and faintly falling, like the descent of their last end, upon all the living and the dead.
> —JAMES JOYCE, *The Dead* in *Dubliners*, 1914

Season of mists and mellow fruitfulness.
> —JOHN KEATS, *To Autumn* in *Poems*, 1820

In a summer season when soft was the sun.
> —WILLIAM LANGLAND, *The Vision of Piers the Plowman*, 1362–90

What is so rare as a day in June?
Then, if ever, come perfect days.
> —JAMES RUSSELL LOWELL, Prelude, *The Vision of Sir Launfal*, 1846

'Tis the last rose of summer
Left blooming alone;
All her lovely companions
Are faded and gone.
> —THOMAS MOORE, *'Tis the Last Rose* in *Irish Melodies*, 1807–34

It snowed and snowed, the whole world over,
Snow swept the world from end to end.
A candle burned on the table;
A candle burned.
> —BORIS PASTERNAK, *Doctor Zhivago*, 1958

Winter is icumen in,
Lhude sing Goddamm,
Raineth drop and staineth slop,
And how the wind doth ramm!
Sing: Goddamm.
> —EZRA POUND, *Ancient Music*, c. 1917

[For the original ancient verse, see the first entry in this section.]

O, it sets my heart a-clickin' like the tickin' of a clock
When the frost is on the punkin and the fodder's in the shock.
> —JAMES WHITCOMB RILEY, *When the Frost Is on the Punkin*, 1883

The seasons . . . are authentic; there is no mistake about them, they are what a symphony ought to be: four perfect movements in intimate harmony with one another.
　　　　　—ARTHUR RUBINSTEIN, *My Young Years,* 1973

Summer makes a silence after spring.
　　　　　—VITA SACKVILLE-WEST, *The Land,* 1926

November's sky is chill and drear,
November's leaf is red and sear.
　　　　　—SIR WALTER SCOTT, Introduction, *Marmion,* 1808

Why, this is very midsummer madness.
　　　　　—SHAKESPEARE, *Twelfth Night,* III, iv

Rough winds do shake the darling buds of May,
And summer's lease hath all too short a date.
　　　　　—SHAKESPEARE, sonnet 18

If winter comes, can spring be far behind?
　　　　　—PERCY BYSSHE SHELLEY,
　　　　　　Ode to the West Wind, 1819

In winter I get up by night
And dress by yellow candlelight.
In summer quite the other way,
I have to go to bed by day.
　　　　　—ROBERT LOUIS STEVENSON, *Bed in Summer*
　　　　　　in *A Child's Garden of Verses,* 1885

In the spring a young man's fancy lightly turns to thoughts of love.
　　　　　—ALFRED, LORD TENNYSON, *Locksley Hall,* 1842

Years and years and years ago, when I was a boy, when there were wolves in Wales . . . when we rode the daft and happy hills bareback, it snowed and it snowed.
　　　　　—DYLAN THOMAS, *A Child's Christmas in Wales,* 1954

NATURE: TIMES OF DAY

The morning is wiser than the evening.
　　　　　—ANONYMOUS (RUSSIAN PROVERB)

The night
Hath been to me a more familiar face
Than that of man; and in her starry shade
Of dim and solitary loveliness
I learned the languages of another world.
—LORD BYRON, *Manfred*, 1817

Night is the mother of thoughts.
—JOHN FLORIO, *First Frutes*, 1578

Awake! for Morning in the Bowl of Night
Has flung the Stone that puts the Stars to Flight.
—EDWARD FITZGERALD, *The Rubáiyát
of Omar Khayyám*, 1859

I have been one acquainted with the night.
I have walked out in rain—and back in rain.
I have outwalked the furthest city light.
—ROBERT FROST, *Acquainted with the Night*, 1928

Night is the other half of life, and the better half.
—GOETHE, *Wilhelm Meister's Apprenticeship*, 1795–96

The curfew tolls the knell of parting day,
The lowing herd wind slowly o'er the lea,
The plowman homeward plods his weary way,
And leaves the world to darkness and to me.
—THOMAS GRAY, *Elegy Written in
a Country Churchyard*, 1750

The day is done, and the darkness
Falls from the wings of night,
As a feather is wafted downward
From an eagle in his flight.
—HENRY WADSWORTH LONGFELLOW,
The Day Is Done, 1845
[More at ARTS: MUSIC & DANCE.]

Night hath a thousand eyes.
—JOHN LYLY, *Maides Metamorphose*, 1600

Is not the night mournful, sad, and melancholy?
—RABELAIS, *Gargantua and Pantagruel*, 1532–52

Night, when words fade and things come alive.
—ANTOINE DE SAINT-EXUPÉRY,
Flight to Arras, 1942

Each day is a little life; every waking and rising a little birth; every fresh morning a little youth; every going to rest and sleep a little death.   —ARTHUR SCHOPENHAUER,
Our Relation to Ourselves in *Essays*, 1851

'Tis now the very witching time of night,
When churchyards yawn and hell itself breathes out
Contagion to this world. —SHAKESPEARE, *Hamlet*, III, ii

I arise from dreams of thee
In the first sweet sleep of night
When the winds are breathing low,
And the stars are shining bright.
—PERCY BYSSHE SHELLEY,
The Indian Serenade, 1819

Never greet a stranger in the night, for he may be a demon.
—TALMUD, compiled c. 6th cent. A.D.

Outside the open window
The morning air is all awash with angels.
—RICHARD WILBUR, *Love Calls Us
to the Things of This World*, 1956

NATURE: WIND & WEATHER   See also NATURE:
TIMES OF DAY

A cloudy day or a little sunshine have as great an influence on many constitutions as the most real blessings or misfortunes.
—JOSEPH ADDISON, *The Spectator*, Sept. 5, 1711

It was a dark and stormy night.
—EDWARD BULWER-LYTTON, *Paul Clifford*, 1840
[Opening words. See the list of first lines at FAMILY, under Tolstoy.]

It ain't a fit night out for man or beast.
—W. C. FIELDS, *The Fatal Glass of Beer*, 1933

Not snow, no, nor rain, nor heat, nor night keeps them from accomplishing their appointed courses with all speed.

—HERODOTUS, *Histories*, 5th cent. B.C.
[The version inscribed on the main Post Office in Manhattan is: "Neither snow, nor rain, nor gloom of night stays these couriers from the swift completion of their appointed rounds."]

Who has seen the wind? Neither you nor I:
But when the trees bow down their heads
The wind is passing by.

—CHRISTINA ROSSETTI, *Who Has
Seen the Wind?*, 1872

There is really no such thing as bad weather, only different kinds of good weather.

—JOHN RUSKIN, d. 1900, attributed

The fog comes in on little cat feet.

—CARL SANDBURG, *Fog*, 1916

O Wild West Wind, thou breath of Autumn's being,
Thou from whose unseen presence the leaves dead
Are driven like ghosts from an enchanter fleeing,
Yellow and black, and pale, and hectic red,
Pestilence-stricken multitude.

—PERCY BYSSHE SHELLEY,
Ode to the West Wind, 1819

Thank heaven, the sun has gone in, and I don't have to go out and enjoy it.

—LOGAN PEARSALL SMITH, *Afterthoughts*, 1931

Sweet and low, sweet and low,
Wind of the western sea.

—ALFRED, LORD TENNYSON, *The Princess*, 1847

Everybody talks about the weather, but nobody does anything about it.   —MARK TWAIN, editorial, Hartford
Courant, Aug. 24, 1897
[The editorial was unsigned. Twain is a likely author, and in Robert Wood Johnson's memoirs is quoted as saying, "We all grumble about the weather, but nothing is *done* about it." On the other hand, the author may have been Charles Dudley Warner, associate editor of the *Courant*.]

NAVY See MILITARY, THE

NECESSITY See also EXPEDIENCY

Necessity, the tyrant's plea.
—JOHN MILTON, *Paradise Lost*, 1667

Necessity is the plea for every infringement of human freedom. It is the argument of tyrants; it is the creed of slaves.
—WILLIAM PITT, speech, Nov. 18, 1783

The true creator is necessity, which is the mother of our invention. —PLATO, *The Republic*, 4th cent. B.C.
[Jonathan Swift used the modern variant "Necessity is the mother of invention" in *Gulliver's Travels*, 1726.]

Necessity knows no law.
—PUBLILIUS SYRUS, *Moral Sayings*, 1st cent. B.C.
[The adage was used by St. Augustine and Oliver Cromwell, among others. In *Piers the Plowman* (1362–90), William Langland put it: "Need has no law." See also the Goethe quote under LAW.]

Teach thy necessity to reason thus;
There is no virtue like necessity.
—SHAKESPEARE, *Richard II*, I, iii

I know this—a man got to do what he got to do.
—JOHN STEINBECK, *The Grapes of Wrath*, 1939

NEGOTIATION See also DIPLOMACY

Make sure you leave some fat for the other side.
—ANONYMOUS (CHINESE SAYING)

"Let us agree not to step on each other's feet," said the cock to the horse.
—ANONYMOUS (ENGLISH PROVERB)

Never hold discussions with the monkey when the organ grinder is in the room.
—WINSTON CHURCHILL, attributed
[William Safire, in his *Political Dictionary*, writes that Churchill is supposed to have said this in answer to a query from his foreign minister on whether to raise a certain point with Musso-

lini or Count Ciano, the Italian foreign minister. In another context, in 1957, British Labour leader Aneurin Bevan advised: "If we complain about the tune, there is no reason to attack the monkey while the organ grinder is present."]

Let us never negotiate out of fear, but let us never fear to negotiate.   —JOHN F. KENNEDY,
                                    Inaugural Address, Jan. 20, 1961

This offer proceeds from policy, not love.
                    —SHAKESPEARE, *Henry IV, Part II,* IV, i
[Lord Mowbray assessing an offer from the king.]

NEUROSIS   See ILLNESS & REMEDIES

NEWS   See also MEDIA; PRESS, THE; RUMOR

How beautiful upon the mountain are the feet of him that bringeth good tidings.   —BIBLE, *Isaiah* 52:7

Though it be honest, it is never good to bring bad news.
                —SHAKESPEARE, *Antony and Cleopatra,* II, v
[And especially not in time of crisis; see Hiram Johnson at WAR.]

What news on the Rialto?
                —SHAKESPEARE, *The Merchant of Venice,* I, iii
[The Rialto is a bridge in Venice, formerly a commercial center. The phrase also appears at III, i.]

Nobody likes the bringer of bad news.
                    —SOPHOCLES, *Antigone,* 5th cent. B.C.

NEW THINGS   See also CHANGE; SCIENCE:
                    DISCOVERY & EXPLORATION; SCIENCE:
                        TECHNOLOGY; VARIETY

He that will not apply new remedies must expect new evils; for time is the greatest innovator.
                    —FRANCIS BACON, *Of Innovations,* 1625

There is nothing new except that which has been forgotten.
                    —MLLE. BERTIN, *fl.* 1770–90, ascribed
[She was the dressmaker of Marie Antoinette.]

There is no new thing under the sun.
—BIBLE, *Ecclesiastes* 1:9

Neither do men put new wine into old bottles.
—BIBLE, *Matthew* 9:17

Men love . . . newfangledness.
—GEOFFREY CHAUCER, *The Squire's Tale* in
The Canterbury Tales, 1387–1400

Nothing quite new is perfect.   —CICERO, *Brutus,* 46 B.C.

Mr. and Mrs. Veneering were bran-new people in a bran-new house in a bran-new quarter of London. Everything about the Veneerings was spick-and-span new. All their furniture was new, all their friends were new, all their servants were new, their plate was new, their carriage was new, their harness was new, their horses were new, their pictures were new, they themselves were new, they were as newly married as was lawfully compatible with having a bran-new baby, and if they had set up a great-grandfather, he would have come in matting from the Pantechnicon, without a scratch upon him, French polished to the crown of his head.
—CHARLES DICKENS, *Our Mutual Friend,* 1864–65

If a man write a better book, preach a better sermon, or make a better mousetrap than his neighbor, tho' he build his house in the woods, the world will make a beaten path to his door.   —RALPH WALDO EMERSON, lecture,
attributed in Sarah B. Yule & Mary S. Keene,
Borrowings, 1889
[A somewhat similar passage can be found in Emerson's *Journal,* Feb. 1855. The version here was written down by Yule during a lecture by Emerson in 1871 in California, either in San Francisco or Oakland.]

It is always the latest song that an audience applauds the most.   —HOMER, *Odyssey,* 8th cent. B.C.

New opinions are always suspected, and usually opposed, without any other reason but because they are not already common.   —JOHN LOCKE, *Essay Concerning
Human Understanding,* 1690

All good things which exist are the fruit of originality.
                              —JOHN STUART MILL, *On Liberty,* 1859

Nothing can be said nowadays which has not already been
said.   —TERENCE, *The Eunuch,* 161 B.C.

NEW YEAR

Now the New Year reviving old Desires,
The thoughtful Soul to Solitude retires.
                              —EDWARD FITZGERALD,
                    The Rubáiyát of Omar Khayyám, 1879

Ring out, wild bells, to the wild sky,
The flying cloud, the frosty light:
The year is dying in the night;
Ring out wild bells and let him die.

Ring out the old, ring in the new,
Ring, happy bells, across the snow:
The year is going, let him go;
Ring out the false, ring in the true.
      —ALFRED, LORD TENNYSON, *In Memoriam,* 1850

NEW YORK   See CITIES

NIGHT   See NATURE: TIMES OF DAY

NONVIOLENCE   See PACIFISM

NOSTALGIA   See also OLD THINGS, OLD FRIENDS;
                                        PAST, THE

Nostalgia Isn't What It Used To Be.   —ANONYMOUS
[A graffito used by the French actress and writer Simone Signo-
ret as the title of her 1978 autobiography.]

Play it, Sam. Play "As Time Goes By."
                    —JULIUS EPSTEIN, PHILIP EPSTEIN,
            HOWARD KOCH, screenplay, *Casablanca,* 1942

NOVELTY   See NEW THINGS

NOVEMBER   See NATURE: SEASONS

O

OBEDIENCE   See also APPEASEMENT VS.
RESISTANCE; RESIGNATION

Obedience is the mother of success, and the wife of security.
—AESCHYLUS, *The Seven Against Thebes,*
5th cent. B.C.

Obedience is in a way the mother of all virtues.
—ST. AUGUSTINE, *On the Good of Marriage,* A.D. 401

Nevertheless, not my will, but thine, be done.
—BIBLE, *Luke* 22:42

Obedience is a hard profession.
—PIERRE CORNEILLE, *Nicomède,* 1651

It is much safer to obey than to rule.
—THOMAS à KEMPIS, *Imitation of Christ,* c. 1420

It is right that what is just should be obeyed; it is necessary
that what is strongest should be obeyed.
—PASCAL, *Pensées,* 1670

He who yields a prudent obedience exercises a partial
control.
—PUBLILIUS SYRUS, *Moral Sayings,* 1st cent. B.C.

Let them obey that know not how to rule.
—SHAKESPEARE, *Henry VI, Part II,* V, i

Obedience,
Bane of all genius, virtue, freedom, truth
Makes slaves of men, and, of the human frame,
A mechanized automaton.
    —PERCY BYSSHE SHELLEY, *Queen Mab,* 1813

Learn to obey before you command.
        —SOLON, 6th cent. B.C., quoted in Diogenes Laërtius,
            Lives of Eminent Philosophers, 3rd cent. A.D.

OBJECTS   See THINGS & POSSESSIONS

OCCULT, THE   See also MIRACLES

Do you believe in fairies? . . . If you believe, clap your
hands!   —J. M. BARRIE, *Peter Pan,* 1904
[For fairies in a garden, see Rose Fyleman at NATURE: GAR-
DENS, FLOWERS, & TREES.]

To deny the possibility, nay, the actual existence of witchcraft and sorcery is flatly to contradict the revealed word
of God.
        —WILLIAM BLACKSTONE, *Commentaries on
            the Laws of England,* 1765–79

The constellations were consulted for advice, but no one
understood them.
        —ELIAS CANETTI, *The Agony of Flies,* 1994

Go and catch a falling star,
Get with child a mandrake root.
                    —JOHN DONNE, *Song: Go and
                    Catch a Falling Star,* c. 1591–1601

Nature has given us astrology as an adjunct and ally to
astronomy.   —JOHANNES KEPLER,
            De fundamentis astrologie certioribus, 1602

May the Force be with you.
    —GEORGE W. LUCAS, JR., screenplay, *Star Wars,* 1977

Astrology is framed by the devil.
                    —MARTIN LUTHER, *Table Talk,* 1569

Millions of spiritual creatures walk the earth
Unseen, both when we wake, and when we sleep.
—JOHN MILTON, *Paradise Lost,* 1667

Magic is detestable, vain and idle . . . though it has what I
might call shadows of truth.
—PLINY, *Natural History,* A.D. 77

Once upon a midnight dreary, while I pondered, weak and
    weary,
Over many a quaint and curious volume of forgotten lore—
While I nodded, nearly napping, suddenly there came a
    tapping,
As of someone gently rapping, rapping at my chamber door.
—EDGAR ALLAN POE, *The Raven,* 1845

Quoth the Raven, "Nevermore."   —*Ibid.*

GLENDOWER: I can call spirits from the vasty deep.
HOTSPUR: Why so can I, or so can any man;
But will they come when you do call for them?
—SHAKESPEARE, *Henry IV, Part I,* III, i

Double, double toil and trouble,
Fire burn and caldron bubble.
—SHAKESPEARE, *Macbeth,* IV, i

Eye of newt and toe of frog,
Wool of bat and tongue of dog,
Adder's fork and blindworm's sting,
Lizard's leg and owlet's wing,
For a charm of powerful trouble,
Like a hell broth boil and bubble.   —*Ibid.*

I'll break my staff,
Bury it certain fathoms in the earth,
And deeper than did ever plummet sound
I'll drown my book.   —SHAKESPEARE, *The Tempest,* V, i

OCEAN   See NATURE: THE OCEAN; SEAS & SHIPS,
                            SAILING & BOATING

OLD AGE   See AGE & AGING; OLD THINGS,
                            OLD FRIENDS

OLD THINGS, OLD FRIENDS   See also AGE;
NOSTALGIA; PAST, THE

I love everything that's old: old friends, old times, old manners, old books, old wines.
—OLIVER GOLDSMITH, *She Stoops to Conquer,* 1773

Is not old wine wholesomest, old pippins toothsomest, old
wood burns brightest, old linen wash whitest? Old soldiers,
sweetheart, are surest, and old lovers are soundest.
—JOHN WEBSTER, with THOMAS DEKKER,
Westward Hoe, 1607

OPPORTUNITY   See also BOLDNESS & INITIATIVE

He who sees the last blossom on the plum tree must pick
it.   —ANONYMOUS (CHINESE PROVERB)

A wise man will make more opportunities than he finds.
—FRANCIS BACON, *Of Ceremonies and
Reports* in *Essays,* 1625

Observe the opportunity.   —BIBLE, *Ecclesiasticus* 4:20

Seize the day.   —HORACE, *Odes,* 1st cent. B.C.
[More at PRESENT, THE.]

While we stop to think, we often miss our opportunity.
—PUBLILIUS SYRUS, *Moral Sayings,* 1st cent. B.C.

There is a tide in the affairs of men
Which, taken at the flood, leads on to fortune;
Omitted, all the voyage of their life
Is bound in shallows and in miseries.
—SHAKESPEARE, *Julius Caesar,* IV, iii

OPTIMISM & PESSIMISM   See also DESPAIR,
DEPRESSION, & MISERY; HOPE

The optimist proclaims that we live in the best of all possible
worlds; and the pessimist fears this is true.
—JAMES BRANCH CABELL,
The Silver Stallion, 1926

Pessimists have good appetites.   —COLETTE, *Gigi*, 1944

Every day, in every way, I'm getting better and better.
                              —EMILE COUÉ, self-improvement
                                      mantra, devised in 1920

Cheer up, the worst is yet to come.
                              —PHILANDER C. JOHNSON,
            Shooting Stars in *Everybody's Magazine*, May 1920

A pessimist is a person who has had to listen to too many
optimists.
                  —DON MARQUIS, quoted in Frederick B. Wilcox,
                              A Little Book of Aphorisms, 1947

An optimist is a guy that never has had much experience.
                  —DON MARQUIS, d. 1937, *certain maxims of archy*
                              in *archy and mehitabel*, 1927

To fear the worst oft cures the worse.
                  —SHAKESPEARE, *Troilus and Cressida*, III, ii

In this best of all possible worlds . . . all is for the best.
                  —VOLTAIRE, *Candide*, 1759

ORIENT, THE   See NATIONS; TRAVEL

P

PACIFISM   See also APPEASEMENT VS. RESISTANCE;
PEACE; RESIGNATION;
VIOLENCE & FORCE; WAR

Resist not evil: but whosoever shall smite thee on thy right
cheek, turn to him the other also.   —BIBLE, *Matthew* 5:39

Be ye therefore wise as serpents, and harmless as doves.
—*Ibid.* 10:16

Non-violence is the first article of my faith. It is also the last
article of my creed. —MOHANDAS K. GANDHI, speech in
defense against a charge of sedition, Mar. 23, 1922

Man lives freely only by his readiness to die, if need be, at
the hands of his brother, never by killing him.
—MOHANDAS K. GANDHI, d. 1948, quoted in
S. Hobhouse, ed., *True Patriotism:
Some Sayings of Mahatma Gandhi*

Pacifism is simply undisguised cowardice.
—ADOLF HITLER, speech, Aug. 21, 1926

PAINTING   See ARTS: PAINTING

PARENTS &   See also CHILDREN & CHILDHOOD;
PARENTHOOD   FAMILY; GENERATIONS

The joys of parents are secret, and so are their griefs and
fears: they cannot utter the one, nor will they utter the other.
—FRANCIS BACON, *Of Parents
and Children* in *Essays*, 1625

There is no slave out of heaven like a loving woman; and, of all loving women, there is no such slave as a mother.
> —HENRY WARD BEECHER,
> *Proverbs from Plymouth Pulpit,* 1887

What the mother sings to the cradle goes all the way down to the coffin.　　　　　　　　　　　　　　—*Ibid.*

Honor thy father and thy mother.
> —BIBLE, *Exodus* 20:12 and elsewhere

He that spareth his rod hateth his son.
> —BIBLE, *Proverbs* 13:24

Train up a child in the way he should go: and when he is old, he will not depart from it.　　　　　—*Ibid.* 22:6

Who doesn't desire his father's death?
> —FEODOR DOSTOEVSKI,
> *The Brothers Karamazov,* 1879–80

Happy that man whose children make his happiness in life and not his grief.　　　—EURIPIDES, *Orestes,* 408 B.C.

If a man has been his mother's undisputed darling, he retains throughout life the triumphant feeling, the confidence in success, which not seldom brings actual success with it.
> —SIGMUND FREUD, *A Childhood
> Memory of Goethe's,* 1917

[For the opposite view, see the first Maugham entry below.]

You are the bows from which your children are as living arrows sent forth.　—KAHLIL GIBRAN, *The Prophet,* 1923

There are some extraordinary fathers who seem, during the whole course of their lives, to be giving their children reasons for being consoled at their death.
> —LA BRUYÈRE, *Les Caractères,* 1688

He that will have his son have respect for him and his orders, must himself have a great reverence for his son.
> —JOHN LOCKE, *Some Thoughts
> Concerning Education,* 1693

wot in hell
have I done to deserve
all these kittens.　　　　—DON MARQUIS, *mehitabel and her
kittens* in *archy and mehitabel,* 1927

Few misfortunes can befall a boy which bring worse conse-
quence than to have a really affectionate mother.
　　　　　　　　　　　　—W. SOMERSET MAUGHAM,
　　　　　　　　　　　　　　A Writer's Notebook, 1949

People are always rather bored with their parents. That's
human nature.　　　　　　　—W. SOMERSET MAUGHAM,
　　　　　　　　　　　　　　The Bread-Winner, 1930

How sharper than a serpent's tooth it is
To have a thankless child.
　　　　　　　　　　—SHAKESPEARE, *King Lear,* I, iv

It is a wise father that knows his own child.
　　　　　　—SHAKESPEARE, *The Merchant of Venice,* II, ii

If parents would only realize how they bore their own
children! —GEORGE BERNARD SHAW, *Misalliance,* 1914

Trust yourself. You know more than you think you do.
　　—DR. BENJAMIN SPOCK, *Baby and Child Care,* 1946
[The opening words, addressed to new parents. For other first
lines, see the list at the Tolstoy entry at FAMILY.]

Most American children suffer too much mother and too
little father.　　　　　　　　　　—GLORIA STEINEM,
　　　　　　　　　　　　The New York Times, Aug. 26, 1971

Happy he
With such a mother! faith in womankind
Beats with his blood.
　　　　　—ALFRED, LORD TENNYSON, *The Princess,* 1847

I have found the best way to give advice to your children
is to find out what they want and then advise them to do
it.　　　　　　　—HARRY S. TRUMAN, television interview,
　　　　　　　　　　　　　　　　　　　May 27, 1955

Children begin by loving their parents. After a time they judge them. Rarely, if ever, do they forgive them.
—OSCAR WILDE, *A Woman of No Importance*, 1893
[In *The Picture of Dorian Gray,* Wilde concludes more optimistically: "*Sometimes* they forgive them" (italics added).]

All women become like their mothers. That is their tragedy. No man does. That's his.
—OSCAR WILDE, *The Importance of Being Earnest*, 1895

There are no illegitimate children—only illegitimate parents.
—JUDGE LEON R. YANKWICH,
decision in *Zipkin v. Mozon,* June 1928
[J. M. and M. J. Cohen, in *The Penguin Dictionary of Modern Quotations,* say that Yankwich was quoting the columnist O. O. McIntyre.]

PARIS See CITIES

PARTIES See CONVERSATION; HOSPITALITY; POLITICS

PARTING See FAREWELLS

PASSION See ENTHUSIASM, ENERGY, & ZEAL; LOVE; SEX

PAST, THE See also HISTORY; MEMORY; NOSTALGIA; REGRET; TIME

Of one power even God is deprived, and that is the power of making what is past never to have been.
—AGATHON, 5th cent. B.C., quoted in Aristotle,
The Nicomachean Ethics, c. 333–23 B.C.
[Often quoted as "Even God cannot change the past."]

Which of us can overcome his past?
—JAMES BALDWIN, *Alas, Poor Richard*, 1961

In the carriages of the past you can't go anywhere.
—MAXIM GORKY, *The Lower Depths*, 1903

The past is a foreign country: they do things differently
there.   —L. P. HARTLEY, *The Go-Between*, 1953
[The opening sentence. For other first lines see under Tolstoy
at FAMILY.]

Yesterday
A night-gone thing
A sun-down name.
          —LANGSTON HUGHES, *Youth* in *From My People*

The past lies like a nightmare upon the present.
          —KARL MARX, *The 18th Brumaire
                    of Louis Bonaparte*, 1852
[A somewhat free translation. A more literal version is: "The
tradition of all the dead generations weighs like a nightmare"
(or "incubus") "upon the brain of the living."]

The past is the present, isn't it? It's the future too.
          —EUGENE O'NEILL, *Long Day's
                    Journey into Night*, 1956

Only the past when you were happy is real.   —*Ibid.*

Who controls the past controls the future.
          —GEORGE ORWELL, *1984*, 1948
[More at TYRANNY & TOTALITARIANISM.]

Don't look back. Something may be gaining on you.
          —LEROY "SATCHEL" PAIGE,
                    How to Keep Young, 1953
[Possibly at least partly the invention of writer Richard Donovan, who did a profile on Paige for *Collier's* magazine, which
included a section of "typical" Paige quotes. William and Leo-
nard Safire say in their book *Good Advice* (1982) that Donovan
came up with quotes that Paige later legitimized by using in
his own autobiography. But presumably, Donovan's "typical"
quotes reflected at least to some extent comments by Paige,
himself, who was famous for his aphorisms. Paige, incidentally,
was one of the greatest baseball pitchers, a legend in the Negro
leagues, finally accepted in the majors in 1948, at age 42. He
made his last major league appearance in 1965.]

I tell you the past is a bucket of ashes.
          —CARL SANDBURG, *Prairie*, 1918

Those who cannot remember the past are condemned to
repeat it. —GEORGE SANTAYANA,
The Life of Reason, 1905–06

What's past is prologue.
—SHAKESPEARE, *The Tempest,* II, i

The world is weary of the past,
Oh, might it die or rest at last.
—PERCY BYSSHE SHELLEY, *Hellas,* 1822

They don't sell tickets to the past.
—ALEXANDER SOLZHENITSYN,
The First Circle, 1964

All things are taken from us, and become
Portions and parcels of the dreadful past.
—ALFRED, LORD TENNYSON,
The Lotos-Eaters, 1833

Mais où sont les neiges d'antan?
Where are the snows of yesteryear?
—FRANÇOIS VILLON, *Ballade des dames
du temps jadis* in *Le Grand Testament,* 1461

We live in reference to past experience and not to future
events, however inevitable.
—H. G. WELLS, *Mind at the End of Its Tether,* 1946
[See also Auden, at HISTORY.]

PATIENCE See also PERSEVERANCE & ENDURANCE

Patience is bitter but its fruit is sweet.
—ANONYMOUS (FRENCH PROVERB)
[Used by Jean-Jacques Rousseau in *Émile.*]

Sit on the bank of a river and wait: your enemy's corpse
will soon float by. —ANONYMOUS (INDIAN PROVERB)

Patience is the companion of wisdom.
—ST. AUGUSTINE, d. A.D. 430, *On Patience*

The end is not yet. —BIBLE, *Matthew* 24:6

Patience, n. A minor form of despair disguised as a virtue.
   —AMBROSE BIERCE, *The Devil's Dictionary,* 1906

Everything comes if a man will only wait.
     —BENJAMIN DISRAELI, *Tancred,* 1847
[Essentially proverbial. Rabelais wrote "Everything comes in
time to those who can wait," *Gargantua and Pantagruel,*
1532–52; and Longfellow offered, "All things come round to
him who will but wait," *The Student's Tale* in *Tales of a Wayside Inn,* 1863.]

Beware the fury of a patient man.
   —JOHN DRYDEN, *Absalom and Achitophel,* 1680

Patience and delay achieve more than force and rage.
     —LA FONTAINE, *Fables,* 1668

They also serve who only stand and wait.
     —JOHN MILTON, *On His Blindness,* 1652

How poor are they that have not patience!
What wound did ever heal but by degrees?
     —SHAKESPEARE, *Othello,* II, iii

The strongest of all warriors are these two—Time and
Patience.   —LEO TOLSTOY, *War and Peace,* 1865–69

PATRIOTISM See also AMERICA & AMERICANS;
  AMERICAN HISTORY: MEMORABLE MOMENTS
  (Nathan Hale); MILITARY BATTLES; HEROES

Patriotism is in political life what faith is in religion.
     —LORD ACTON, *Nationality* in *The Home
     and Foreign Review,* July 1862

Plus je vis d'étrangers, plus j'aimai ma patrie.
The more I saw of foreigners, the more I loved my country.
     —P. L. DE BELLOY, *The Siege of Calais,* 1764
[Madame de Staël slightly rephrased the thought in *Corinne*
(1807): "The more I see of other countries, more I love my
own."]

"My country, right or wrong," is a thing no patriot would think of saying except in a desperate case. It is like saying, "My mother, drunk or sober."
—G. K. CHESTERTON, *Defense of Patriotism*
in *The Defendant,* 1901
[He is referring to Decatur; see below.]

Our country! In her intercourse with foreign nations may she always be in the right; but our country, right or wrong.
—STEPHEN DECATUR, toast, at
Norfolk, Va., April 1816
[Cf. Chesterton above. Carl Schurz also offered a correction, in a speech on Oct. 17, 1899: "Our country, right or wrong. When right, to be kept right; when wrong, to be put right."]

When a whole nation is roaring Patriotism at the top of its voice, I am fain to explore the cleanness of its hands and purity of its heart.
—RALPH WALDO EMERSON, *Journal,* 1824

Dulce et decorum est pro patria mori.
It is a sweet and seemly thing to die for one's country.
—HORACE, *Odes,* 33–15 B.C.

Patriotism is the last refuge of a scoundrel.
—SAMUEL JOHNSON, Apr. 7, 1775, quoted in
James Boswell, *Life of Johnson,* 1791

Ask not what your country can do for you, ask what you can do for your country.
—JOHN F. KENNEDY, Inaugural Address, Jan. 20, 1961
[The *Oxford Dictionary of Quotations* notes that a similar exhortation was used in the funeral oration for John Greenleaf Whittier (d. 1892). And *Bartlett's* cites several predecessors, not including Whittier but going back to an even earlier address by Oliver Wendell Holmes, Jr., on May 30, 1884: "We pause . . . to recall what our country has done for each of us, and to ask ourselves what we can do for our country in return."]

You're not supposed to be so blind with patriotism that you can't face reality. Wrong is wrong no matter who does it or who says it.   —MALCOLM X, *Malcolm X Speaks,* 1965

Patriotism is a kind of religion; it is the egg from which wars are hatched.

> —GUY DE MAUPASSANT, *My Uncle Sosthenes*

Yes, we'll rally round the flag, boys, we'll rally once again.

> —GEORGE FREDERICK ROOT,
> *The Battle Cry of Freedom,* 1863

Breathes there the man, with soul so dead,
Who never to himself has said,
This is my own, my native land! —SIR WALTER SCOTT,
The Lay of the Last Minstrel, 1805

No one loves his country for its size or eminence, but because it is his own.

> —SENECA, *Letter to Lucilius,* 1st cent. A.D.

"Shoot, if you must, this old gray head,
But spare your country's flag," she said.

> —JOHN GREENLEAF WHITTIER,
> *Barbara Frietchie* in *The Atlantic,* Oct. 1863

PATTERNS

Perfumes, colors, and sounds echo one another.

> —CHARLES BAUDELAIRE, *Correspondances,* 1861

We all of us live too much in circles.

> —BENJAMIN DISRAELI, *Sybil,* 1845

The life of man is a self-evolving circle.

> —RALPH WALDO EMERSON,
> *Circle* in *Essays: First Series,* 1841

Network, n. Any thing reticulated or decussated at equal distances, with interstices between the intersections.

> —SAMUEL JOHNSON, *Dictionary,* 1755

Christ! What are patterns for?

> —AMY LOWELL, *Patterns* in *Men,
> Women, and Ghosts,* 1916

The wheel is come full circle.

> —SHAKESPEARE, *King Lear,* V, iii

PEACE   See also PACIFISM; WAR

They shall beat their swords into plowshares, and their spears into pruning hooks: nation shall not lift up sword against nation, neither shall they learn war any more.
> —BIBLE, *Isaiah* 2:4, also *Micah* 4:3

The wolf also shall dwell with the lamb, and the leopard shall lie down with the kid; and the calf and the young lion and the fatling together; and a little child shall lead them.
> —*Ibid.* 11:16

Saying, Peace, peace; when there is no peace.
> —BIBLE, *Jeremiah* 6:14 and 8: 11

Blessed are the peacemakers: for they shall be called the children of God.   —BIBLE, *Matthew* 5:9
[For other verses from the Sermon on the Mount, see VIRTUE.]

Give peace in our time, O Lord.
> —BOOK OF COMMON PRAYER, *Morning Prayer*
[See under APPEASEMENT VS. RESISTANCE for Neville Chamberlain's "peace for our time."]

Peace is liberty in tranquillity.
> —CICERO, *Philippics,* 44–43 B.C.

Peace I hope with honor.
> —BENJAMIN DISRAELI, speech, July 16, 1878
[Disraeli referred to the agreements at the Congress of Berlin, which ended the Russo-Turkish War, 1877–78. For another "peace with honor," see APPEASEMENT VS. RESIS-TANCE, Neville Chamberlain.]

Peace cannot be kept by force. It can only be achieved by understanding.
> —ALBERT EINSTEIN, d. 1955, *Notes on Pacifism*

The most disadvantageous peace is better than the most just war.   —ERASMUS, *Adagia,* 1500

You and me, we've made a separate peace.
> —ERNEST HEMINGWAY, *In Our Time,* 1924

Better to live in peace than to begin a war and lie dead.
—JOSEPH THE YOUNGER, c. 1870s,
quoted in Time-Life Books, *The Indians*, 1973
[Chief Joseph's Indian name was Hinmaton-Yalakktit, or Thunder Rolling the Mountains. He surrendered in Montana in 1877, thus ending the Nez Percé War. See also RESIGNATION.]

First keep peace within yourself, then you can also bring peace to others.
—THOMAS à KEMPIS, *Imitation of Christ*, c. 1420

Arms alone are not enough to keep the peace. It must be kept by men.   —JOHN F. KENNEDY, State of the Union
message, Jan. 14, 1963

Certain peace is better than anticipated victory.
—LIVY, *History of Rome*, c. A.D. 14

The inglorious arts of peace.
—ANDREW MARVELL, *Upon Cromwell's
Return from Ireland*, 1650

Peace hath her victories
No less renowned than war.   —JOHN MILTON,
To the Lord General Cromwell, 1652

The only alternative to co-existence is co-destruction.
—JAWAHARLAL NEHRU, quoted in
the *Observer*, Aug. 29, 1954

Peace is not made with friends. Peace is made with enemies.
—YITZHAK RABIN, quoted in
The New York Times, Sept. 5, 1993
[The occasion of the remark was an accord between Israel and the Palestine Liberation Organization, the first step toward signing a formal peace treaty between the two parties a year later.]

It isn't enough to talk about peace. One must believe in it. And it isn't enough to believe in it. One must work at it.
—ELEANOR ROOSEVELT,
Voice of America broadcast, Nov. 11, 1951

Peace, like charity, begins at home.
    —FRANKLIN D. ROOSEVELT, speech, Aug. 14, 1936

A peace is of the nature of a conquest;
For then both parties nobly are subdued,
And neither party loser.
    —SHAKESPEARE, *Henry IV, Part II*, IV, ii

They make a desert and call it peace.
    —TACITUS, *Agricola*, c. A.D. 98

Ring out the thousand wars of old,
Ring in the thousand years of peace.
    —ALFRED, LORD TENNYSON,
        In Memoriam, 1850

Peace hath higher tests of manhood
Than battle ever knew.
    —JOHN GREENLEAF WHITTIER,
        The Hero, 1853

Only a peace between equals can last.
    —WOODROW WILSON, speech to U.S. Senate, 1917

PEOPLE   See DANGEROUS PEOPLE;
    HUMANS & HUMAN NATURE; PEOPLE, THE;
    RACES & PEOPLES; REASONABLE &
        UNREASONABLE PEOPLE

PEOPLE, NOT LIKING   See MISANTHROPY

PEOPLE, THE   See also DEMOCRACY

Vox populi, vox Dei.
The voice of the people is the voice of God.
    —ALCUIN, letter to Charlemagne, A.D. 800
[Alexander Pope was not quite sure of this—he wrote: "The
people's voice is odd; / It is, and it is not, the voice of God,"
Epistle I, Imitations of Horace, 1733–38. William Tecumseh
Sherman simply disagreed: "Vox populi, vox humbug," letter
to his wife, June 2, 1863.]

The people want to be deceived.
    —ANONYMOUS (ROMAN EPIGRAPH)

Who builds upon the people, builds upon sand.
> —ANONYMOUS (ITALIAN PROVERB)

In the common people there is no wisdom, no penetration, no power of judgment.   —CICERO, *Pro planchio,* 54 B.C.

If it has to choose who is to be crucified, the crowd will always save Barabbas.
> —JEAN COCTEAU, *Le rappel à l'ordre,* 1926

Nor is the people's judgment always true;
The most may err as grossly as the few.
> —JOHN DRYDEN, *Absalom and Achitophel,* 1680

All the world over, I will back the masses against the classes.
> —WILLIAM GLADSTONE, speech, June 6, 1886

There is not a more mean, stupid, dastardly, pitiful, selfish, spiteful, envious, ungrateful animal than the public. It is the greatest of cowards, for it is afraid of itself.
> —WILLIAM HAZLITT, *On Living to
> One's Self* in *Table Talk,* 1820–21

The wealth of a country is its working people.
> —THEODOR HERZL, *Altneuland,* 1902

The great masses of the people will more easily fall victims to a big lie than to a small one.
> —ADOLF HITLER, *Mein Kampf,* 1935

You [the people] are a many-headed beast.
> —HORACE, *Epistles,* Book I, 20 B.C.

[In the 16th century, Machiavelli wrote, "The people resemble a wild beast," *Discourse Upon the First Ten Books of Livy.* And Alexander Hamilton protested to Thomas Jefferson, "Your *People,* Sir, is nothing but a great beast."]

The people are the only sure reliance for the preservation of our liberty.   —THOMAS JEFFERSON, letter
> to James Madison, 1787

About things on which the public thinks long it commonly thinks right.   —SAMUEL JOHNSON, *Addison*
> in *Lives of the Poets,* 1779–81

Two things only it [the public] desires: bread and circus games.   —JUVENAL, *Satires*, c. A.D. 100

Why should there not be a patient confidence in the ultimate justice of the people? Is there any better or equal hope in the world?   —ABRAHAM LINCOLN,
First Inaugural Address, Mar. 4, 1861
[See under GOVERNMENT for "government of the people."]

You may fool all the people some of the time; you can even fool some of the people all the time; but you can't fool all of the people all the time.   —ABRAHAM LINCOLN
(possibly apocryphal)
[*Bartlett's* cites Alexander K. McClure, who in *Lincoln's Yarns and Stories* (1904) claimed that Lincoln made this remark to a caller at the White House. There have been numerous updates, including: "You can fool too many people too much of the time," James Thurber, *The Owl Who Was God*, 1949; and "You can fool all the people if the advertising is right and the budget is big enough," movie producer Joseph Levine, quoted in *The New York Times*, obituary, Aug. 1, 1987.]

Every man a king!   —HUEY LONG, slogan in the 1928
Louisiana gubernatorial campaign
and title of Long's autobiography, 1933

The people, and the people alone, are the motive force in the making of world history.
—MAO ZEDUNG, *Quotations from
Chairman Mao Zedung*, 1966

No one . . . has ever lost money by underestimating the intelligence of the great masses of the plain people.
—H. L. MENCKEN, *Notes on Journalism,
Chicago Tribune*, Sept. 26, 1926
[Popularized as "No one ever lost money by underestimating the intelligence of the American people."]

I am the people—the mob—the crowd—the mass.
Do you know that all the great work of the world is done through me?   —CARL SANDBURG,
I Am the People, the Mob, 1916

The pitifulest thing out is a mob.
> —MARK TWAIN, *The Adventures of*
> *Huckleberry Finn,* 1885

PEOPLES   See NATIONS; RACES & PEOPLES

PERSEVERANCE   See also EFFORT; PATIENCE;
& ENDURANCE   SURVIVAL; WORK

Slow and steady wins the race.
> —AESOP, *The Hare and the Tortoise,* 6th cent. B.C.

He that can't endure the bad will not live to see the good.
> —ANONYMOUS (JEWISH PROVERB)

ESTRAGON: I can't go on like this.
VLADIMIR: That's what you think.
> —SAMUEL BECKETT, *Waiting for Godot,* 1952

He that endureth to the end shall be saved.
> —BIBLE, *Matthew* 10:22

Be there a will, and wisdom finds a way.
> —GEORGE CRABBE, *The Birth of Flattery,* 1807

To persevere, trusting in what hopes he has, is courage in a
man. The coward despairs.
> —EURIPIDES, *Heracles,* c. 422 B.C.

'Tis a lesson you should heed,
Try, try again.
If at first you don't succeed,
Try, try again.
> —WILLIAM E. HICKSON, d. 1870, *Try and Try Again*

Great works are performed not by strength, but by perseverance.   —SAMUEL JOHNSON, *Rasselas,* 1759

God helps those who persevere.   —KORAN, c. 610–32

Sorrow and silence are strong, and patient endurance is
godlike.   —HENRY WADSWORTH LONGFELLOW,
> *Evangeline,* 1847

Endurance is the crowning quality,
And patience all the passion of great hearts.
—JAMES RUSSELL LOWELL, *Columbus*, 1844

The struggle is my life.   —NELSON MANDELA, cited in
The New York Times, May 7, 1997

Perseverance is more prevailing than violence; and many
things which cannot be overcome when they are taken together, yield themselves up when taken little by little.
—PLUTARCH, *Life of Sertorius* in
Parallel Lives, c. A.D. 100

PESSIMISM   See DESPAIR, DEPRESSION, & MISERY;
OPTIMISM & PESSIMISM

PETS   See NATURE: ANIMALS

PHILADELPHIA   See CITIES

PHILANTHROPY   See CHARITY: PHILANTHROPY

PHILOSOPHY   See also ETHICS & MORALITY;
MIND, THOUGHT, &
UNDERSTANDING (Descartes);
SCIENCE; SKEPTICISM

To be is to be perceived.   —GEORGE BERKELEY,
Philosophical Commentaries, 1707–08
[Popular form of Bishop Berkeley's fundamental philosophical
statement, "Existence is to be perceived or to perceive, or to will,
that is, to be active." Cf. Descartes at MIND, THOUGHT, &
UNDERSTANDING.]

A metaphysician is a man who goes into a dark cellar at
midnight without a light, looking for a black cat that is not
there.   —LORD BOWEN, d. 1894, attributed
[Lord Bowen seems to have leaned on the metaphor more than
once. In *Pie-Powder* (1911), John Anderson Foote credited him
with "When I hear of an 'equity' in a case like this, I am
reminded of a blind man in a dark room—looking for a black
hat—which isn't there."]

There is but one truly serious philosophical problem, and that is suicide. Judging whether life is or is not worth living amounts to answering the fundamental question of philosophy. —ALBERT CAMUS, *The Myth of Sisyphus*, 1942

There is nothing so ridiculous but some philosopher has said it. —CICERO, *De divinatione*, 44 B.C.
[Matters did not improve in the next seventeen hundred years; see Descartes, below.]

There is nothing so strange and so unbelievable that it has not been said by one philosopher or another.
—RENÉ DESCARTES, *Discourse on Method*, 1637
[For Descartes' own fundamental dictum, the cogito argument, see under MIND, THOUGHT, & UNDERSTANDING.]

The test of a religion or philosophy is the number of things it can explain. —RALPH WALDO EMERSON, *Journal*, 1836

What is it to be a philosopher? Is it not to be prepared against events? —EPICTETUS, *Discourses*, c. A.D. 100

You can't do without philosophy, since everything has its hidden meaning which we must know.
—MAXIM GORKY, *The Zykovs*, 1914

Philosophy will clip an angel's wing.
—JOHN KEATS, *Lamia* in *Poems*, 1820

Do not all charms fly
At the mere touch of cold philosophy? —*Ibid.*

Logic is the art of making truth prevail.
—LA BRUYÈRE, *Les Caractères*, 1688

Metaphysics is almost always an attempt to prove the incredible by an appeal to the unintelligible.
—H. L. MENCKEN, *Minority Report*
in *H. L. Mencken's Notebooks*, 1956

Most philosophical treatises show the human cerebrum loaded far beyond its Plimsoll mark.
—H. L. MENCKEN, *Prejudices*, 1919–27

To philosophize is to doubt.
      —MONTAIGNE, *Essays,* 1580–88
[For more on this line, see SKEPTICISM.]

Wonder is the foundation of all philosophy, inquiry the process, ignorance the end.   *—Ibid.*
[See also Plato and Whitehead below.]

True philosophers are lovers of the vision of truth.
     —PLATO, *The Republic,* 4th cent. B.C.

Wonder is the feeling of a philosopher, and philosophy begins in wonder. —PLATO, *Theaetetus,* 4th cent. B.C.

To teach how to live without certainty and yet without being paralyzed by hesitation is perhaps the chief thing that philosophy, in our age, can do for those who study it.
     —BERTRAND RUSSELL, *History of*
        Western Philosophy, 1946

Philosophy arises from an unusually obstinate attempt to arrive at real knowledge.
 —BERTRAND RUSSELL, *An Outline of Philosophy,* 1970

There are more things in heaven and earth, Horatio,
Than are dreamt of in your philosophy.
     —SHAKESPEARE, *Hamlet,* I, v

Adversity's sweet milk, philosophy.
    —SHAKESPEARE, *Romeo and Juliet,* III, iii

The unexamined life is not worth living.
    —SOCRATES, 5th cent. B.C., quoted in
      Plato, *Apology,* 4th cent. B.C.

I am a citizen, not of Athens or Greece, but of the world.
      —SOCRATES, 5th cent. B.C.,
    quoted in Plutarch, *De exilio,* c. 100 A.D.

Nero's mother turned him from the study of philosophy, warning that it was contrary to the needs of one destined to rule. —SUETONIUS, *Nero* in *Lives of the Caesars,*
        c. A.D. 121

The safest general characterization of the European philosophical tradition is that it consists of a series of footnotes to Plato.   —ALFRED NORTH WHITEHEAD,
Process and Reality, 1929

Philosophy begins in wonder, and at the end, when philosophic thought has done its best, the wonder remains.
—ALFRED NORTH WHITEHEAD,
Modes of Thought, 1938

Philosophy is not a body of doctrine but an activity.
—LUDWIG WITTGENSTEIN,
Tractatus logico-philosophicus, 1922

Most propositions and questions that have been written about philosophical matters are not false but senseless.
—*Ibid.*

The world is everything that is the case.   —*Ibid.*

What can be said at all can be said clearly; and whereof one cannot speak thereof one must be silent.   —*Ibid.*

PHOTOGRAPHY   See ARTS: PHOTOGRAPHY

PHYSICAL FITNESS   See also HEALTH; SPORTS

People seem to think there is something inherently virtuous in the desire to go out for a walk.
—MAX BEERBOHM, *Going Out for a Walk*
in *And Even Now*, 1920
[The author confessed, "It is a fact that not once in my life have I gone out for a walk. I have been taken out for walks; but that is another matter."]

Strengthen the weak hands, and make firm the feeble knees.
—BIBLE, *Isaiah* 35:3 (Revised Standard Version)

Whenever the urge to exercise comes upon me, I lie down for a while and it passes.
—ROBERT MAYNARD HUTCHINS, d. 1977,
quoted in Harry S. Ashmore,
The Life of Robert Maynard Hutchins

[Hutchins, who headed the University of Chicago 1929 to 1951, enjoyed good health throughout his life; he died at age 78.]

The sovereign invigorator of the body is exercise, and of all exercises, walking is best.
—THOMAS JEFFERSON, letter to
Thomas Mann Randolph, Jr., Aug. 27, 1786

Bodily exercises are to be done discreetly; not to be taken evenly and alike by all men.
—THOMAS à KEMPIS, *The Imitation of Christ,* 1426

I wish to preach, not the doctrine of ignoble ease, but the doctrine of the strenuous life.
—THEODORE ROOSEVELT, speech, Apr. 10, 1899

I have never taken any exercise, except sleeping and resting, and I never intend to take any. Exercise is loathsome.
—MARK TWAIN, speech on his
70th birthday, Dec. 5, 1905

PHYSICIANS See DOCTORS & THE PRACTICE OF MEDICINE

PHYSICS See SCIENCE: PHYSICS & COSMOLOGY

PITY See COMPASSION & PITY; FORGIVENESS & MERCY

PLANS

You can never plan the future by the past.
—EDMUND BURKE, letter to a member
of the French National Assembly, 1791

The best-laid schemes o' mice an' men
Gang aft a-gley.   —ROBERT BURNS, *To a Mouse,* 1786

It's a bad plan that can't be changed.
—PUBLILIUS SYRUS,
Moral Sayings, 1st cent. B.C.

PLANTS See NATURE: GARDENS, FLOWERS, & TREES

PLEASURE　　　　　　See HAPPINESS; HEDONISM;
　　　　　　　　　　　　　　　SEX & SENSUALITY

POETRY & POETS　　　See ARTS: POETRY & POETS

POLITICS　　　　　　　　　See also CAPITALISM;
　　　　CITIES (Washington, D.C.); COMMUNISM;
　　　　DEMOCRACY; DIPLOMACY; FREEDOM;
　　　GOVERNMENT; HIGH POSITION: RULERS &
　　　LEADERS; POWER; REVOLUTION; SOCIALISM

Politics, as a practice, whatever its professions, has always
been the systematic organization of hatreds.

　　　　　　　　　　　　　　—HENRY ADAMS,
　　　　　　　　　　The Education of Henry Adams, 1907

Knowledge of human nature is the beginning and end of
political education.　　　　　　　　　　　　　—*Ibid.*

Modern politics is, at bottom, a struggle not of men but of
forces.　　　　　　　　　　　　　　　　　　　—*Ibid.*

My country has in its wisdom contrived for me the most
insignificant office [the vice-presidency] that ever the invention of man contrived or his imagination conceived.
　　—JOHN ADAMS, letter to Abigail Adams, Dec. 19, 1793

You have all the characteristics of a popular politician: a
horrible voice, bad breeding, and a vulgar manner.
　　　　　　　　　　—ARISTOPHANES, *Knights,* 424 B.C.

Man is by nature a political animal.
　　　　　　　　　　　—ARISTOTLE, *Politics,* 4th cent. B.C.

We know what happens to people who stay in the middle
of the road. They get run over.
　　　　　　　　　　　—ANEURIN BEVAN, *Observer,*
　　　　　　　　　　　　　Saying of the Week, Dec. 9, 1953
[Similarly, John Adams, "In politics the middle way is none at
all," letter to Horatio Gates, Mar. 23, 1776.]

Politics is a blood sport.
　　　　　　　　　　　—ANEURIN BEVAN, d. 1960, quoted
　　　　　　　　　　in Jennie Lee, *My Life with Nye,* 1980

Politics is not an exact science.
—OTTO VON BISMARCK, speech, Dec. 1863

Politics is the art of the possible, the attainable . . . the art of the next best.   —OTTO VON BISMARCK, conversation with Meyer von Waldeck, Aug. 11, 1867
[The saying "politics is the art of compromise" derives in part from a speech by Edmund Burke on conciliation with America, Mar. 22, 1775. The relevant passage is: "All government—indeed, every human benefit and enjoyment, every virtue and every prudent act—is founded on compromise and barter."]

Politics ruins the character.
—OTTO VON BISMARCK, quoted by Bernhard Brige, *Berlin Tägliche Rundschau,* 1881

Politics are not the task of a Christian.
—DIETRICH BONHOEFFER, d. 1945, *No Rusty Swords,* tr. 1965
[An opinion of venerable age; see Tertullian below.]

The ordinary voter does not object to mediocrity.
—JAMES BRYCE, *The American Commonwealth,* 1888
[This is from the chapter entitled "Why Great Men Are Not Chosen Presidents." Bryce explains that the American voter "likes his candidate to be sensible, vigorous, and, above all, what he calls 'magnetic.' " For more on mediocrity in politics, see Hruska at MEDIOCRITY.]

You scratch my back, I'll scratch yours.
—SIMON CAMERON, attributed, c. 1850
[Cameron, the Republican boss of Pennsylvania, was Lincoln's first Secretary of War, acquitting himself so scandalously that Lincoln had to ease him out of office—by naming him ambassador to Russia. Another famous Cameron saying was "An honest politician is one who when he's bought stays bought."]

Vain hope to make people happy by politics!
—THOMAS CARLYLE, *Journal,* Oct. 10, 1831

Persistence in one opinion has never been considered a merit in political leaders.
—CICERO, *Ad familiares,* c. 80–43 B.C.

In a smoke-filled room in some hotel.
> —HARRY M. DAUGHERTY, quoted in
> *The New York Times,* Feb. 21, 1920

[Daugherty, who was Warren G. Harding's campaign manager, was predicting that, come June, his candidate would be chosen by the Republican Convention, or more accurately, by some dozen influential politicians cutting a deal in a hotel room. He later denied using the words "smoke-filled room," but nevertheless the phrase became a metaphor for professional party politics.]

Since a politician never believes what he says, he is surprised when others believe him.
> —CHARLES DE GAULLE, quoted in
> *Newsweek,* Oct. 1, 1962

No government can long be secure without a formidable opposition.   —BENJAMIN DISRAELI, *Coningsby,* 1844

A conservative government is an organized hypocrisy.
> —BENJAMIN DISRAELI, speech, Mar. 1845

Finality is not the language of politics.
> —BENJAMIN DISRAELI, speech, Feb. 28, 1859

A party is perpetually corrupted by personality.
> —RALPH WALDO EMERSON,
> *Politics* in *Essays: Second Series,* 1844

Politics is not the art of the possible. It consists in choosing between the disastrous and the unpalatable.
> —JOHN KENNETH GALBRAITH, letter to
> John F. Kennedy, Mar. 2, 1962,
> in *Ambassador's Journal,* 1969

[This updates Bismarck; see above.]

I often think it's comical
How nature always does contrive
That every boy and every gal,
That's born into the world alive,
Is either a little Liberal
Or else a little Conservative!
> —W. S. GILBERT, *Iolanthe,* 1882

A liberal is a man who tells other people how to spend their money. —CARTER GLASS, quoted in Associated Press interview, Sept. 24, 1938

Treason doth never prosper: what's the reason? For if it prosper, none dare call it treason.
—SIR JOHN HARINGTON, *Of Treason* in *Epigrams,* 1618

You can't adopt politics as a profession and remain honest.
—LOUIS McHENRY HOWE, speech, Jan. 17, 1933
[Howe was Franklin D. Roosevelt's invaluable adviser.]

When a man assumes a public trust, he should consider himself as public property.
—THOMAS JEFFERSON, remark to Baron von Humboldt, quoted in Rayner, *Life of Jefferson,* 1834
[For more on the "public trust" concept, see GOVERNMENT, the entry and note under Anonymous (American Political Saying).]

Political action is the highest responsibility of a citizen.
—JOHN F. KENNEDY, speech, Oct. 20, 1960
[Plato is sometimes quoted on this subject: "The penalty that good men pay for indifference to politics is to be governed by evil men or men worse than themselves." Unfortunately, the source for this warning is hard to find. The attribution to Plato is listed as "unverified" in the authoritative *Respectfully Quoted,* published by the Library of Congress.]

Politicians are the same all over. They promise to build bridges, even where there are no rivers.
—NIKITA KHRUSHCHEV, to the press, Oct. 9, 1960, in Glen Cove, L.I.

What is conservatism? Is it not adherence to the old and tried, against the new and untried?
—ABRAHAM LINCOLN, speech, Feb. 27, 1860

A politician must often talk and act before he has thought and read. —THOMAS BABINGTON MACAULAY, *Gladstone on Church and State* in *Edinburgh Review,* Apr. 1839

In every age, the vilest specimens of human nature are to be found among demagogues.
　　　　　　　—THOMAS BABINGTON MACAULAY,
　　　　　　　　　History of England, 1849–61

All reactionaries are paper tigers.
　　　　　　　—MAO ZEDUNG, conversation with
　　　　　　　　Anna Louise Strong, Aug. 1946,
　　　　　　　　in *Peking Review,* Nov. 11, 1958

Politics is war without bloodshed, while war is politics with bloodshed.　　　—MAO ZEDUNG, *Quotations from*
　　　　　　　　Chairman Mao Zedung, 1966
[For Mao on the source of political power, see under POWER.]

[The Democrats] see nothing wrong in the rule that to the victors belong the spoils of the enemy.
　　—WILLIAM MARCY, speech, U.S. Senate, Jan. 25, 1832
[Sen. Marcy of New York was defending Pres. Andrew Jackson's policy of appointing supporters to government positions. This policy, which Jackson called "rotation in office," is practiced far more thoroughly today. About 1890, "Boss" Richard Croker of New York City attempted to justify Marcy's position: "Politics are impossible without spoils. . . . You have to deal with men as they are . . . you must bribe the masses with spoils," quoted in Richard Norton Smith, *Thomas E. Dewey,* 1982.]

Liberal institutions straightway cease from being liberal the moment they are soundly established.
　　　—FRIEDRICH NIETZSCHE, *Twilight of the Idols,* 1888

All politics is local.
　　　　　　　—THOMAS P. ("TIP") O'NEILL, saying
[In his 1993 autobiography, *Man of the House,* Tip O'Neill credited his father with this insight.]

In our time, political speech and writing are largely the defense of the indefensible.
　　　　　　　　—GEORGE ORWELL, *Politics and the*
　　　　　　　English Language in *Shooting an Elephant,* 1946

Never lose your temper with the press or the public is a major rule of political life.
> —CHRISTABEL PANKHURST, *Unshackled*, 1959

It is now known . . . that men enter local politics solely as a result of being unhappily married.
> —C. NORTHCOTE PARKINSON,
> *Parkinson's Law*, 1958

Party-spirit . . . at best is but the madness of many for the gain of a few. —ALEXANDER POPE, letter
to E. Blount, Aug. 27, 1714
[A similar quote, which some accredit to Pope and some to Jonathan Swift, is: "Party is the madness of many for the gain of a few." Published in Pope, *Thoughts on Various Subjects* in *Swift's Miscellanies*, 1727.]

Politics is knowing when to pull the trigger.
> —MARIO PUZO, screenplay, *Godfather III*, 1990

A statesman is a successful politician who is dead.
> —THOMAS BRACKETT REED, d. 1902,
> attributed remark to Rep. Henry Cabot Lodge
["Czar" Reed represented Maine from 1877 to 1899, serving six years as Speaker of the House. Numerous variants of this remark exist, including, "A statesman is a politician who's been dead ten or fifteen years," Harry S. Truman, *New World Telegram & Sun*, Apr. 12, 1958.]

All politics are based on the indifference of the majority.
> —JAMES RESTON,
> *The New York Times*, June 12, 1968

I tell you folks, all politics is applesauce.
> —WILL ROGERS, *The Illiterate Digest*, 1924

Politicians, after all, are not over a year behind public opinion. —WILL ROGERS, *The Autobiography
of Will Rogers*, 1949

A radical is a man with both feet firmly planted in the air. . . . A conservative is a man with two perfectly good legs who, however, has never learned how to walk forward. . . . A reactionary is a somnambulist walking backward.
—FRANKLIN D. ROOSEVELT,
radio speech, Oct. 26, 1939
[An anonymous update from the 1980s, "A conservative is a liberal who's been mugged." In *The Bonfire of the Vanities* (1987), Tom Wolfe gave the converse of this saying: "A liberal is a conservative who's been arrested."]

A politician . . . one that would circumvent God.
—SHAKESPEARE, *Hamlet*, V, i

He knows nothing and thinks he knows everything. That points clearly to a political career.
—GEORGE BERNARD SHAW, *Major Barbara*, 1907

Politics is perhaps the only profession for which no preparation is thought necessary.
—ROBERT LOUIS STEVENSON,
"Yoshida-Torajiro" in *Familiar Studies
of Men and Books*, 1882

Nothing is more foreign to us Christians than politics.
—TERTULLIAN, *The Christian's Defense*, c. A.D. 208

In politics, if you want anything said, ask a man; if you want anything done, ask a woman.
—MARGARET THATCHER, quoted in
Anthony Sampson, *The Changing Anatomy of Britain*, 1982

There is no distinctly native American criminal class except Congress.
—MARK TWAIN, *Pudd'nhead Wilson's New Calendar*
in *Following the Equator*, 1897

Money is the mother's milk of politics.
—JESSE UNRUH, saying, quoted in
The New York Times, obituary, Aug. 6, 1987
[Unruh was a Democratic power broker in California.]

Politics is the art of preventing people from taking part in affairs which properly concern them.
—PAUL VALÉRY, *Tel quel*, 1943

Politics makes strange bedfellows.
—CHARLES DUDLEY WARNER,
My Summer in a Garden, 1870
[For misery and bedfellows, see the Shakespeare quote from *The Tempest* under TROUBLE.]

Among politicians, the esteem of religion is profitable, the principles of it are troublesome.
—BENJAMIN WHICHCOTE,
Moral and Religious Aphorisms, 1753

Prosperity is necessarily the first theme of a political campaign. —WOODROW WILSON, speech, Sept. 4, 1912
[Updated in Democratic advisor James Carville's motto in the 1992 presidential campaign: "It's the economy, stupid."]

POOR, THE   See HAVES & HAVE-NOTS; MONEY;
POVERTY & HUNGER

POPULAR OPINION See PEOPLE, THE; REPUTATION

POPULATION   See also ENVIRONMENT

Population, when unchecked, increases in a geometric ratio. Subsistence increases only in an arithmetical ratio.
—THOMAS MALTHUS, *An Essay on the Principle of Population*, 1798

In a foreseeable future we shall be smothered by our own numbers. . . . Preoccupation with survival has set the stage for extinction. —JOHN STEINBECK, *Sweet Thursday*, 1954

POSSESSIONS   See THINGS & POSSESSIONS

POVERTY & HUNGER See also AMERICAN HISTORY:
MEMORABLE MOMENTS (Lyndon B. Johnson);
HAVES & HAVE-NOTS; MONEY

Hunger knows no friend but its feeder.
—ARISTOPHANES, *The Wasps*, 422 B.C.

Poverty is the parent of revolution and crime.
—ARISTOTLE, *Politics,* 4th cent. B.C.

The poor man's wisdom is despised, and his words are not heard.   —BIBLE, *Ecclesiastes* 9:16

For the poor always ye have with you. —BIBLE, *John* 12:8

Poverty makes you sad as well as wise.
—BERTOLT BRECHT, *The Threepenny Opera,* 1928

Eats first, morals after.   —*Ibid.*

If the misery of our poor be caused not by laws of nature, but by our institutions, great is our sin.
—CHARLES DARWIN, *Voyage of the Beagle,* 1840

Poverty demoralizes.   —RALPH WALDO EMERSON,
Wealth in *The Conduct of Life,* 1860

There is no scandal like rags, nor any crime so shameful as poverty.
—GEORGE FARQUHAR, *The Beaux' Stratagem,* 1707

The short and simple annals of the poor.
—THOMAS GRAY, *Elegy Written in a
Country Churchyard,* 1850

There is something about poverty that smells like death. Dead dreams dropping off the heart like leaves in a dry season and rotting around the feet.
—ZORA NEALE HURSTON,
Dust Tracks on a Road, 1942

This administration . . . declares unconditional war on poverty in America.   —LYNDON B. JOHNSON,
State of the Union speech, Jan. 8, 1964

A decent provision for the poor is the true test of civilization.   —SAMUEL JOHNSON, 1770, quoted in
James Boswell, *Life of Johnson,* 1791

A man who has nothing can whistle in a robber's face.
—JUVENAL, *Satires,* c. A.D. 100

Love in a hut, with water and a crust,
Is—Love, forgive us—cinders, ashes, dust.
> —JOHN KEATS, *Lamia* in *Poems*, 1820

If a free society cannot help the many who are poor, it cannot save the few who are rich.
> —JOHN F. KENNEDY, Inaugural Address, Jan. 20, 1961

Anticipate charity by preventing poverty.
> —MAIMONIDES, *Charity's Eight Degrees,* 12th cent.

The forgotten man at the bottom of the economic pyramid.
> —FRANKLIN D. ROOSEVELT,
> radio speech, Apr. 7, 1932

[Roosevelt borrowed this phrase from a famous 1855 speech by William Graham Sumner; see ECONOMICS.]

The more humanity owes him [the poor man], the more society denies him. Every door is shut against him, even when he has a right to its being opened: and if he ever obtains justice, it is with much greater difficulty than others obtain favors.
> —JEAN JACQUES ROUSSEAU,
> *A Discourse on Political Economy*, 1758

The greatest of evils and the worst of crimes is poverty.
> —GEORGE BERNARD SHAW, Preface, *Major Barbara*, 1907

I have been a common man and a poor man; and it has no romance for me.
> —*Ibid.*

PICKERING: Have you no morals, man?
DOOLITTLE: Can't afford them, Governor. Neither could you if you was as poor as me.
> —GEORGE BERNARD SHAW, *Pygmalion*, 1912

Poverty is no disgrace to a man, but it is profoundly inconvenient.
> —SYDNEY SMITH, *His Wit and Wisdom*, 1900

A hungry man is not a free man.
> —ADLAI STEVENSON, speech, Sept. 6, 1952

I was once so poor I didn't know where my next husband was coming from.
>   —MAE WEST, in the movie *She Done Him Wrong*,
>   1933, from her play *Diamond Lil*, 1928

No one can worship God or love his neighbor on an empty stomach.   —WOODROW WILSON, speech, May 23, 1912

POWER
See also HIGH POSITION: RULERS & LEADERS;
STRENGTH; TYRANNY & TOTALITARIANISM

Power tends to corrupt and absolute power corrupts absolutely. . . . Great men are almost always bad men.
>   —LORD ACTON, letter to
>   Bishop Mandell Creighton, Apr. 5, 1887

I am more and more convinced that man is a dangerous creature and that power, whether vested in many or a few, is ever grasping, and like the grave, cries, "Give, give."
>   —ABIGAIL ADAMS, letter to
>   John Adams, Nov. 27, 1775

A friend in power is a friend lost.   —HENRY ADAMS,
>   *The Education of Henry Adams,* 1907

Power always thinks it has a great soul and vast views beyond the comprehension of the weak; and that it is doing God's service, when it is violating all His laws.
>   —JOHN ADAMS, letter to
>   Thomas Jefferson, Feb. 2, 1816

Power is a disease one has no desire to be cured of.
>   —GIULIO ANDREOTTI, cited in
>   *The New Yorker,* Sept. 11, 1995

[Andreotti served seven times as prime minister of Italy.]

I have seen the wicked in great power, and spreading himself like a green bay tree.   —BIBLE, *Psalms* 37:35

There is no power but of God.   —BIBLE, *Romans* 13:1

The greater the power, the more dangerous the abuse.
—EDMUND BURKE, speech on
the Middlesex election, 1771

Power is the first good. —RALPH WALDO EMERSON,
Inspiration in *Letters and Social Aims,* 1876

You shall have joy, or you shall have power, said God; you shall not have both. —RALPH WALDO EMERSON,
Journal, Oct. 1842

Life is a search after power.
—RALPH WALDO EMERSON,
Power in *The Conduct of Life,* 1860

Power is precarious.
—HERODOTUS, *Histories,* 5th cent. B.C.

This is the bitterest pain among men, to have much knowledge but no power. —*Ibid.*

Power is the supreme law.
—ADOLF HITLER, *Mein Kampf,* 1973

An honest man can feel no pleasure in the exercise of power over his fellow citizens. —THOMAS JEFFERSON, letter to
John Melish, Jan. 13, 1813

All power, of whatever sort, is of itself desirable.
—SAMUEL JOHNSON, Apr. 14, 1775,
quoted in James Boswell, *Life of Johnson,* 1791

Power is the great aphrodisiac.
—HENRY KISSINGER, quoted in
The New York Times, Jan. 19, 1971

Power never takes a back step—only in the face of more power. —MALCOLM X, *Malcolm X Speaks,* 1965

Every Communist must grasp the truth: political power grows out of the barrel of a gun.
—MAO ZEDUNG, *Quotations from
Chairman Mao Zedung,* 1966

Political power is merely the organized power of one class to oppress another.
> —KARL MARX & FRIEDRICH ENGELS,
> *Communist Manifesto,* 1848

The object of power is power.
> —GEORGE ORWELL, *1984,* 1948

We cannot all be masters.   —SHAKESPEARE, *Othello,* I, i

Power, like a desolating pestilence,
Pollutes whate'er it touches —PERCY BYSSHE SHELLEY,
> *Queen Mab,* 1812–13

Power takes as ingratitude the writhing of its victims.
> —RABINDRANATH TAGORE, *Stray Birds,* 1916

In order to obtain and hold power, a man must love it.
> —LEO TOLSTOY, *The Kingdom of*
> *God Is Within You,* 1893

We have, I fear, confused power with greatness.
> —STEWART UDALL, Commencement speech,
> Dartmouth College, 1965

PRACTICAL WISDOM   See PRUDENCE
                              & PRACTICAL WISDOM

PRAYER   See also PRAYERS; RELIGION

Ask the gods nothing excessive.
> —AESCHYLUS, *The Suppliant Women,* 5th cent. B.C.

It is in vain to expect our prayers to be heard, if we do not strive as well as pray.
> —AESOP, *Hercules and the Waggoner,* 6th cent. B.C.

Orare est laborare, laborare est orare.
To pray is to work, to work is to pray.
> —BENEDICTINE ORDER, Motto

The wish to pray is a prayer in itself.
> —GEORGES BERNANOS,
> *The Diary of a Country Priest,* 1936

God is in heaven, and thou upon earth: therefore let thy words be few. —BIBLE, *Ecclesiastes* 5:5

When thou prayest, thou shalt not be as the hypocrites are: for they love to pray standing in the synagogues and in the corners of the streets that they may be seen of men. Verily I say unto you, they have their reward.

—BIBLE, *Matthew* 6:6

Watch and pray. —BIBLE, *Mark* 13:33

Pray, v. To ask that the rules of the universe be annulled in behalf of a single petitioner, confessedly unworthy.

—AMBROSE BIERCE, *The Devil's Dictionary*, 1906

Worship is transcendent wonder.

—THOMAS CARLYLE, *The Hero as Divinity*
in *On Heroes and Hero-Worship*, 1841

Prayer is conversation with God.

—CLEMENT OF ALEXANDRIA,
Stromateis, c. A.D. 193–211

He prayeth well, who loveth well
Both man and bird and beast.

—SAMUEL TAYLOR COLERIDGE,
The Rime of the Ancient Mariner, 1798

He prayeth best, who loveth best
All things both great and small;
For the dear God who loveth us,
He made and loveth all. —*Ibid.*

Prayer is the little implement
Through which men reach
Where presence—is denied them.

—EMILY DICKINSON, poem no. 437, c. 1862

Prayer is the contemplation of the facts of life from the highest point of view. —RALPH WALDO EMERSON,
Self-Reliance in *Essays: First Series*, 1841

You pray in your distress and in your need: would that you might pray also in the fullness of your joy and in your days of abundance.   —KAHLIL GIBRAN, *The Prophet*, 1923

And fools, who came to scoff, remained to pray.
     —OLIVER GOLDSMITH, *The Deserted Village*, 1770

Prayer indeed is good, but while calling on the gods, a man should himself lend a hand.
     —HIPPOCRATES, *Regimen*, c. 400 B.C.

Pray, for all men need the aid of the gods.
     —HOMER, *Odyssey*, 8th cent. B.C.

Certain thoughts are prayers. There are moments when, whatever be the attitude of the body, the soul is on its knees.
     —VICTOR HUGO, *Les Misérables*, 1862

A single grateful thought raised to heaven is the most perfect prayer.   —GOTTHOLD EPHRAIM LESSING,
Minna von Barnhelm, 1767

There are few men who would dare publish to the world the prayers they make to almighty God.
     —MONTAIGNE, *Essays*, 1580–88

My words fly up; my thoughts remain below.
Words without thoughts never to heaven go.
     —SHAKESPEARE, *Hamlet*, III, iii

His worst fault is that he is given to prayer. He is something peevish that way.
     —SHAKESPEARE, *The Merry Wives of Windsor*, I, iv

Complaint is the largest tribute Heaven receives, and the sincerest part of our devotion.
     —JONATHAN SWIFT, *Thoughts
on Various Subjects*, 1711

More things are wrought by prayer
Than this world dreams of.
     —ALFRED, LORD TENNYSON,
The Passing of Arthur in *Idylls of the King*, 1859–85

Whatever a man prays for, he prays for a miracle. Every prayer reduces itself to this: "Great God, grant that twice two be not four."
—IVAN TURGENEV, *Prayer* in *Poems in Praise*, 1881

PRAYERS   See also PRAYER

Matthew, Mark, Luke, and John,
The bed be blest that I lie on.
Four angels to my bed,
Four angels round my head,
One to watch, and one to pray,
And two to bear my soul away.
—THOMAS ADY, *A Candle in the Dark*, 1655

Now I lay me down to sleep;
I pray the Lord my soul to keep.
If I should die before I wake,
I pray the Lord my soul to take.   —ANONYMOUS

From ghoulies and ghosties and long-leggety beasties
And things that go bump in the night,
Good Lord deliver us!   —ANONYMOUS

May the road rise to meet you,
May the wind be always at your back,
May the sun shine warm upon your face,
May the rain fall soft upon your fields,
And, until we meet again,
May God hold you in the palm of his hand.
—ANONYMOUS (IRISH BLESSING)

O Lord! thou knowest how busy I must be this day; if I forget thee, do not thou forget me.
—SIR JACOB ASTY, prior to the Battle of Edgehill,
Oct. 23, 1642, quoted in Sir Philip Warwick, *Memoirs*

Give me chastity and continency, but not yet.
—ST. AUGUSTINE, *Confessions*, A.D. 397–401

The Lord bless thee, and keep thee:
   The Lord make his face shine upon thee, and be gracious unto thee:
   The Lord lift up his countenance upon thee, and give thee peace.   —BIBLE, *Numbers* 6:24–26

Out of the depths have I cried unto thee, O Lord.
> —BIBLE, *Psalms* 130:1

Glory to God in the highest, and on earth peace, good will toward men.
> —BIBLE, *Luke* 2:14

As it was in the beginning, is now, and ever shall be; world without end. Amen.
> —BOOK OF COMMON PRAYER, compiled 1662

Teach me, my God and king,
In all things thee to see;
And what I do in anything,
To do it as for thee.
> —GEORGE HERBERT, *The Elixir* in *The Temple*, 1633

And help us, this and every day,
To live more nearly as we pray.
> —JOHN KEBLE, *The Christian Year*, 1827

Would to God that we might spend a single day really well.
> —THOMAS À KEMPIS, *Imitation of Christ*, c. 1420

Lord God of Hosts, be with us yet,
Lest we forget—lest we forget.
> —RUDYARD KIPLING, *Recessional*
> in *The Times*, July 17, 1897

Sabrina fair,
Listen where thou art sitting
Under the glassy, cool, translucent wave,
In twisted braids of lilies knitting
The loose train of thy amber-dropping hair;
Listen for dear honor's sake,
Goddess of the silver lake,
Listen and save.
> —JOHN MILTON, *Comus*, 1634

What in me is dark
Illumine, what is low raise and support;
That to the height of this great argument
I may assert eternal Providence,
And justify the ways of God to men.
> —JOHN MILTON, *Paradise Lost*, 1667

Lead, Kindly Light.
> —JOHN HENRY CARDINAL NEWMAN,
> poem title in *The Pillar of Cloud,* 1833

O Lord, support us all the day long, until the shadows lengthen and the evening comes, and the busy world is hushed, and the fever of life is over, and our work is done. Then in thy mercy grant us a safe lodging and a holy rest, and peace at the last.
> —JOHN HENRY CARDINAL NEWMAN,
> sermon, 1834, included in *The Book of Common Prayer*

God, give us grace to accept with serenity the things that cannot be changed, courage to change the things which should be changed, and the wisdom to distinguish the one from the other.
> —REINHOLD NIEBUHR, *The Serenity Prayer,* 1934

O Lord, if there is a Lord, save my soul, if I have a soul.
> —ERNEST RENAN, *Prière d'un sceptique*

Angels and ministers of grace defend us.
> —SHAKESPEARE, *Hamlet,* I, iv

Good night, sweet prince,
And flights of angels sing thee to thy rest.   *—Ibid.,* V, ii

Mount, mount my soul! thy seat is up on high,
Whilst my gross flesh sinks downward, here to die.
> —SHAKESPEARE, *King Richard II,* V, v

Wild Spirit, which art moving everywhere;
Destroyer and preserver;
Hear, oh, hear!   —PERCY BYSSHE SHELLEY,
Ode to the West Wind, 1819

PREJUDICE   See RACES & PEOPLES

PRESENT, THE   See also HEDONISM;
MODERN TIMES; TIME

Take therefore no thought for the morrow: for the morrow shall take thought for the things of itself. Sufficient unto the day is the evil thereof.   —BIBLE, *Matthew* 6:34

Happy the man, and happy he alone,
He, who can call today his own:
He who, secure within, can say,
Tomorrow do thy worst, for I have lived today.
> —JOHN DRYDEN, *Imitation of Horace*, 1685

We want to live in the present, and the only history that is
worth a tinker's damn is the history we make today.
> —HENRY FORD, *Chicago Tribune*, May 25, 1916

Every situation—no, every moment—is of infinite worth; for
it is the representative of a whole eternity.
> —GOETHE, quoted in Johann Peter Eckermann,
> *Conversations with Goethe*, 1836

Carpe diem, quam minimum credula a postero.
Seize the day, and put the least possible trust in tomorrow.
> —HORACE, *Odes*, 33–15 B.C.

No mind is much employed upon the present; recollection
and anticipation fill up almost all our moments.
> —SAMUEL JOHNSON, *Rasselas*, 1759

Each day the world is born anew
For him who takes it rightly.
> —JAMES RUSSELL LOWELL, *Gold Egg:*
> *A Dream-Fantasy* in *Under the Willows*
> *and Other Poems*, 1868

[In the same spirit is the anonymous "Today is the first day of
the rest of your life," often attributed to Charles Dederich.]

Tomorrow's life is too late. Live today.
> —MARTIAL, *Epigrams*, 1st cent. A.D.

Each day provides its own gifts.
> —*Ibid.*

The word *now* is like a bomb through the window and it
ticks.   —ARTHUR MILLER, *After the Fall*, 1964

The only living life is in the past and future—the present is
an interlude—strange interlude in which we call on past and
future to bear witness we are living.
> —EUGENE O'NEILL, *Strange Interlude*, 1928

Let others praise ancient times. I am glad that I was born in these. —OVID, *The Art of Love*, c. 2 B.C.

Past, and to come, seems best; things present, worst.
—SHAKESPEARE, *Henry IV, Part I*, I, iii

Do not say, "It is morning," and dismiss it with a name of yesterday. See it for the first time as a newborn child that has no name.
—RABINDRANATH TAGORE, *Stray Birds*, 1916

Life is all memory except for the one present moment that goes by so quick you can hardly catch it going.
—TENNESSEE WILLIAMS,
The Milk Train Doesn't Stop Here Anymore, 1963

He who lives in the present lives in eternity.
—LUDWIG WITTGENSTEIN,
Tractatus logico-philosophicus, 1922

PRESS, THE   See also CENSORSHIP; FREE SPEECH;
MEDIA; NEWS

The liberty of the press is essential to the security of the state.   —JOHN ADAMS, Free-Press Clause,
Massachusetts Constitution, 1780

What the proprietorship of these newspapers is aiming at is power, and power without responsibility—the prerogative of the harlot through the ages.
—STANLEY BALDWIN, referring to press barons
Beaverbrook and Rothermere, speech, Mar. 18, 1931
[J. M. and M. J. Cohen in *The Penguin Dictionary of Modern Quotations* note that Lord Birkenhead, Kipling's biographer, credits Kipling with originating the wording here. Prime Minister Baldwin was Kipling's cousin.]

Publish, and conceal not.   —BIBLE, *Jeremiah* 50:2

The pen is mightier than the sword.
—EDWARD GEORGE BULWER-LYTTON,
Richelieu, 1839

A free press can, of course, be good or bad, but, most certainly without freedom, the press will never be anything but bad.   —ALBERT CAMUS, *Resistance, Rebellion, and Death,* 1960

When a dog bites a man, that is not news. But when a man bites a dog, that is news.
                         —CHARLES A. DANA, *What Is News?,*
                              New York *Sun* newspaper, 1882
[Sometimes attributed to *Sun* editor John B. Bogart.]

Th' newspaper does ivrything f'r us. It . . . comforts th' afflicted, afflicts th' comfortable, buries th' dead an' roasts thim afterward.   —FINLEY PETER DUNNE,
                         Observations by Mr. Dooley, 1902
[The allusion is to the adage: "The duty of a newspaper is to comfort the afflicted and afflict the comfortable."]

The press must be free; it has always been so and much evil has been corrected by it. If Government finds itself annoyed by it, let it examine its own conduct and it will find the cause.   —THOMAS ERSKINE, *Rex v. Paine,* 1792
[Erskine was Lord Chancellor.]

Madame, we are the press. You know our power. We fix all values. We set all standards. Your entire future depends on us. —JEAN GIRAUDOUX, *The Madwoman of Chaillot,* 1945

[Journalism:] The first rough draft of history.
                         —PHILIP GRAHAM, Apr. 29, 1963
[The *Washington Post* publisher's full comment, given to correspondents from *Newsweek,* was: "So let us today drudge on about our inescapably impossible task of providing every week a first rough draft of history that will never be completed about a world we can never really understand."]

You furnish the pictures and I'll furnish the war.
                         —WILLIAM RANDOLPH HEARST, telegram
                         allegedly sent to artist Frederic Remington
                              in Havana, Cuba, Mar. 1898
[Hearst denied ever sending such a telegram. Nevertheless, his newspaper, the *New York Journal,* called the brief Spanish-American War "the *Journal*'s war."]

[Editor:] A person employed on a newspaper, whose business it is to separate the wheat from the chaff, and to see that the chaff is printed.
>—ELBERT HUBBARD, *Roycroft Dictionary and Book of Epigrams,* 1923

Our liberty depends on the freedom of the press, and that cannot be limited without being lost.
>—THOMAS JEFFERSON, letter to James Currie, Jan. 28, 1786

Were it left to me to decide whether we should have a government without newspapers, or newspapers without a government, I should not hesitate a moment to prefer the latter.
>—THOMAS JEFFERSON, letter to Colonel Edward Carrington, Jan. 16, 1787

Nothing can now be believed which is seen in a newspaper.
>—THOMAS JEFFERSON, letter to J. Norville, 1807

The only security of all is in a free press.
>—THOMAS JEFFERSON, letter to Marquis de la Lafayette, 1823

If the myth gets bigger than the man, print the myth.
>—DOROTHY JOHNSON, d. 1984, *The Man Who Shot Liberty Valance*

[John Ford directed the 1962 movie adapted from Johnson's story by James Warner Bellan and Willis Goldbeck.]

Why should any man be allowed to buy a printing press and disseminate pernicious opinions calculated to embarrass the government?
>—V. I. LENIN, speech, Moscow, 1920

People everywhere confuse
What they read in the newspaper with news.
>—A. J. LIEBLING, *A Talkative Something or Other* in *The New Yorker,* May 14, 1960

Freedom of the press is guaranted only to those who own one.
>—A. J. LIEBLING, *Do You Belong in Journalism?* in Ibid.

The gallery in which the reporters sit has become a fourth estate of the realm.
—THOMAS BABINGTON MACAULAY,
On Hallam's Constitutional History, 1828
[Often attributed to Edmund Burke, because Thomas Carlyle wrote in *Heroes and Hero-Worship* (1841): "Burke said that there were three estates in Parliament; but in the reporters' gallery yonder, there sat a fourth estate more important far than them all." But the phrase has not been found in Burke, and Carlyle actually may have had Macaulay in mind.]

Once a newspaper touches a story, the facts are lost forever, even to the protagonists.
—NORMAN MAILER, in *Esquire,* June 1960

The Third World never sold a newspaper.
—RUPERT MURDOCH, in the *Observer,* Jan. 1, 1978

All I know is just what I read in the papers.
—WILL ROGERS, d. 1935,
saying used as a lead-in to his routines

There aren't any embarrassing questions—just embarrassing answers. —CARL ROWAN, *The New Yorker,* Dec. 7, 1963
[See also Sydney Harris at QUESTIONS & ANSWERS.]

The difference between burlesque and the newspapers is that the former never pretended to be performing a public service by exposure.
—I. F. STONE, *I. F. Stone's Weekly,* Sept. 7, 1952

I don't care what the papers say about me as long as they spell my name right.
—"BIG TIM" SULLIVAN, saying, c. 1900
[Numerous others are credited with this remark. Sullivan was a New York City political boss around the turn of the 20th century.]

The report of my death has been grossly exaggerated.
—MARK TWAIN, quoted in cable from London,
Associated Press, June 1897

Possible? Is anything impossible? Read the newspapers.
—DUKE OF WELLINGTON, quoted in
Sir William Fraser, *Words on Wellington,* 1889

Publish and be damned.
                              —DUKE OF WELLINGTON, attributed
[Scrawled in red ink, according to legend, across a letter from
the publisher who hoped to be paid off for not printing the
complete memoirs of the courtesan Harriette Wilson, Dec.
1824.]

In old days, men had the rack. Now they have the press.
                              —OSCAR WILDE, *The Soul of
                              Man Under Socialism*, 1895
[For another negative view of journalism from approximately
the same era, see George Bernard Shaw at INSULTS & PUT-
DOWNS.]

PRIDE & VANITY   See also AMBITION;
                                      SELF-CONFIDENCE

It's a fine thing to rise above pride, but you must have pride
in order to do so.   —GEORGES BERNANOS,
                              The Diary of a Country Priest, 1936

The Lord will destroy the house of the proud.
                              —BIBLE, *Proverbs* 15:25

Pride goeth before destruction, and an haughty spirit before
a fall.   —BIBLE, *Proverbs* 16:18

Vanity of vanities, saith the Preacher, vanity of vanities; all
is vanity.   —BIBLE, *Ecclesiastes* 1:2

Half of the harm that is done in this world
Is due to people who want to feel important.
                              —T. S. ELIOT, *The Cocktail Party*, 1950

Pride ruined the angels.   —RALPH WALDO EMERSON,
                              The Sphinx in *The Dial*, Jan. 1841

Who does not detest a haughty man?
                              —EURIPIDES, *Hippolytus*, 428 B.C.

Pride is said to be the last vice the good man gets clear of.
                              —BENJAMIN FRANKLIN,
                              Poor Richard's Almanac, 1732–57

I'm the straw that stirs the drink.
> —REGGIE JACKSON, saying, spring
> training with the New York Yankees, May 1977

Vanity is the greatest of all flatterers.
> —LA ROCHEFOUCAULD, *Maxims*, 1678

The most violent passions sometimes leave us at rest, but vanity agitates us constantly.   —*Ibid.*

I never wanted to be a crumb. If I had to be a crumb, I'd rather be dead.   —SALVATORE "LUCKY" LUCIANO,
> d. 1962, quoted in Richard Norton Smith,
> *Thomas E. Dewey*, 1982

Better to reign in hell than serve in heaven.
> —MILTON, *Paradise Lost*, 1667

For he will never follow anything
That other men begin.
> —SHAKESPEARE, *Julius Caesar*, II, i

He that is proud eats up himself.
> —SHAKESPEARE, *Troilus and Cressida*, II, iii

Nobody holds a good opinion of a man who has a low opinion of himself.
> —ANTHONY TROLLOPE, *Orley Farm*, 1862

Vanity is only being sensitive to what other people probably think of us.   —PAUL VALÉRY,
> *Mauvaises pensées et autres*, 1941

I have nothing to declare except my genius.
> —OSCAR WILDE, remark at the
> New York Customs House, Jan. 1882

PRINCES   See HIGH POSITION: RULERS & LEADERS

PRINCIPLES   See ETHICS & MORALITY;
IDEAS & IDEALS

PRISONS   See PUNISHMENT

PRIVACY   See also SOLITUDE

The right to be let alone—the most comprehensive of rights and the most valued by civilized men.
                                    —LOUIS D. BRANDEIS,
                                    Olmstead v. the U.S., 1928
[See also Ayn Rand at CIVILIZATION.]

"If everybody minded their own business," said the Duchess in a hoarse growl, "the world would go round a deal faster than it does."   —LEWIS CARROLL, *Alice's Adventures
                                    in Wonderland,* 1865

I would not open windows into men's souls.
            —ELIZABETH I, d. 1603, traditional attribution
[Charles I is said to have countered, "We have no windows into men's souls."]

The saint and poet seek privacy.
                                    —RALPH WALDO EMERSON,
                        Culture in *The Conduct of Life,* 1860

One of the most essential branches of English liberty is the freedom of one's house. A man's house is his castle; and whilst he is quiet, he is as well guarded as a prince in his castle.   —JAMES OTIS, argument on the
                        Writs of Assistance, Boston, Feb. 24, 1761
[The Writs of Assistance allowed customs officers wide freedom to search for smuggled goods. Otis used an axiom of common law, famously stated by Edward Coke; see HOME.]

PROBLEMS   See also TROUBLE

You're either part of the solution or part of the problem.
            —ELDRIDGE CLEAVER, attributed, saying, c. 1968
[Other people had the same thought at about the same time. Buell Gallagher, president of City College of New York, told the graduating class of 1964 to "Be part of the answer, not part of the problem, as the American revolution proceeds."]

Problems are only opportunities in work clothes.
                                    —HENRY J. KAISER, d. 1967, saying

Our problems are man-made; therefore they may be solved by man.   —JOHN F. KENNEDY, speech, June 10, 1963

If we can really understand the problem, the answer will come out of it, because the answer is not separate from the problem.   —KRISHNAMURTI, d. 1986, *The Penguin Krishnamurti Reader,* 1991

Some problems are so complex that you have to be highly intelligent and well informed just to be undecided about them.   —LAURENCE J. PETER, *Peter's Almanac,* 1982
[See also Peter at INDECISION.]

PROCRASTINATION   See also INDECISION; TIME

Never do today what you can do as well tomorrow.
          —AARON BURR, d. 1836, quoted in
          James Parton, *Life and Times of Aaron Burr,* 1857
[See Rands, below, for a British variant.]

Delay always breeds anger, and to protract a great design is often to ruin it.   —CERVANTES, *Don Quixote,* 1605–15

No idleness, no laziness, no procrastination; never put off till tomorrow what you can do today.
          —EARL OF CHESTERFIELD, letter to
          his son, Dec. 26, 1749
[This intolerable advice is at least as old as Hesiod; see below. For the relationship between murder and procrastination, see De Quincy under CRIME.]

Don't put things off till tomorrow or the day after!
          —HESIOD, *Works and Days,* c. 700 B.C.

Delay is preferable to error.
          —THOMAS JEFFERSON, letter to
          George Washington, May 16, 1792

The time to repair the roof is when the sun is shining.
          —JOHN F. KENNEDY,
          State of the Union address, Jan. 10, 1962

procrastination is the
art of keeping
up with yesterday.   —DON MARQUIS, *certain maxims of*
archy in *archy and mehitabel,* 1927

Never do today what you can
Put off till tomorrow.   —WILLIAM BRIGHTY RANDS,
Lilliput Levee, 1867
[The thought has occurred to many. See, for example, Aaron
Burr, above.]

Delays have dangerous ends.
              —SHAKESPEARE, *Henry VI, Part I,* III, ii

Procrastination is the thief of time.
              —EDWARD YOUNG, *Night Thoughts,* 1742–45

PROGRESS   See also CHANGE; CIVILIZATION;
                   FUTURE, THE; MIND, THOUGHT, &
                   UNDERSTANDING; MODERN TIMES;
                   SCIENCE: TECHNOLOGY

Quo vadis?
Whither goest thou?
[The Latin is in the Vulgate version.]   —BIBLE, *John* 16:5

Progress is
The law of life, man is not man as yet.
              —ROBERT BROWNING, *Paracelsus,* 1835

Progress, man's distinctive mark alone,
Not God's and not the beasts'.
              —ROBERT BROWNING, *A Death in the Desert,* 1864

The march of the human mind is slow.
              —EDMUND BURKE, Second Speech on
              Conciliation with America, Mar. 22, 1775

All progress is based upon a universal innate desire of every
organism to live beyond its means.
              —SAMUEL BUTLER, *Notebooks,* 1912

Change is certain. Progress is not.
              —E. H. CARR, *From Napoleon to Stalin,*
              and Other Essays, 1980

As natural selection works solely by and for the good of each being, all corporeal and mental endowments will tend to progress toward perfection.
—CHARLES DARWIN, *The Origin of Species,* 1859

All that is human must retrograde if it does not advance.
—EDWARD GIBBON, *The Decline and Fall of the Roman Empire,* 1776–88

We still dream what Adam dreamt.
—VICTOR HUGO, d. 1885, *Horror*

All progress is precarious, and the solution of one problem brings us face to face with another problem.
—MARTIN LUTHER KING, JR., *Strength to Love,* 1963

Is it progress if a cannibal uses a fork?
—STANISLAW J. LEC, *Unkempt Thoughts,* 1962

Human progress is furthered, not by conformity, but by aberration. —H. L. MENCKEN, *Prejudices: Third Series,* 1922

The desire to understand the world and the desire to reform it are the two great engines of progress.
—BERTRAND RUSSELL, *Marriage and Morals,* 1929

All progress means war with society.
—GEORGE BERNARD SHAW, *Getting Married,* 1908

Progress, therefore, is not an accident, but a necessity. . . . It is a part of nature.
—HERBERT SPENCER, *Social Statics,* 1850

Yet I doubt not through the ages one increasing purpose runs,
And the thoughts of men are widened,
With the process of the suns.
—ALFRED, LORD TENNYSON, *Locksley Hall,* 1842

Progress imposes not only new possibilities for the future but new restrictions. —NORBERT WIENER, *The Human Use of Human Beings,* 1954

PROPERTY See CAPITALISM; THINGS & POSSESSIONS

PROPHETS See VISION & VISIONARIES

PROVERBS See QUOTATIONS, MAXIMS, & PROVERBS

PROVIDENCE, DIVINE

The Lord is my shepherd; I shall not want.

He maketh me to lie down in green pastures; he leadeth me beside the still waters.

He restoreth my soul: he leadeth me in the paths of righteousness for his name's sake,

Yea, though I walk through the valley of the shadow of death, I will fear no evil: for thou art with me; thy rod and thy staff they comfort me.

Thou preparest a table before me in the presence of mine enemies: thou anointest my head with oil; my cup runneth over.

Surely goodness and mercy shall follow me all the days of my life: and I will dwell in the house of the Lord forever.
—BIBLE, *Psalms* 23

For he shall give his angels charge over thee, to keep thee in all thy ways.

They shall bear thee up in their hands, lest thou dash thy foot against a stone. —*Ibid.* 91:11–12

The Lord shall preserve thy going out and thy coming in.
—*Ibid.* 121:8

We degrade Providence too much by attributing our ideas to it out of annoyance at being unable to understand it.
—FEODOR DOSTOEVSKI, *The Idiot,* 1868–69

Know from the bounteous heaven all riches flow.
—HOMER, *Odyssey,* 8th cent. B.C.

PRUDENCE & See also ADVICE; CRAFTINESS;
PRACTICAL WISDOM QUOTATIONS, MAXIMS,
& PROVERBS; WISDOM

Don't count your chickens before they are hatched.
—AESOP, *The Milkmaid and Her Pail,* 6th cent. B.C.

Slow and steady wins the race.
>   —AESOP, *The Hare and the Tortoise*, 6th cent. B.C.

Never eat at a place called Mom's. Never play cards with a man named Doc. And never lie down with a woman who's got more troubles than you.
>   —NELSON ALGREN, *What Every Young Man
>   Should Know* in *A Walk on the Wild Side*, 1956

[Algren later credited "a nice old Negro lady," with these words of wisdom.]

One swallow does not make a spring.
>   —ARISTOTLE, *Nicomachean Ethics*, 4th cent. B.C.

Prudence is a rich, ugly old maid courted by Incapacity.
>   —WILLIAM BLAKE, *The Marriage of
>   Heaven and Hell*, 1790–93

A wise man does not trust all his eggs to one basket.
>   —CERVANTES, *Don Quixote*, 1605–15

[But see Mark Twain, below.]

The cautious seldom err.
>   —CONFUCIUS, *Analects*, 6th–5th cent. B.C.

Thrust [trust] ivrybody—but cut th' ca-ards.
>   —FINLEY PETER DUNNE, *Casual Observations*
>   in *Mr. Dooley's Opinions*, 1900

You have the world before you. Stoop as you go through it, and you will miss many hard thumps.
>   —COTTON MATHER, advice to
>   Benjamin Franklin, 1724

[Franklin, writing to his son on May 12, 1784, revealed that Mather had given him this valuable advice shortly before he left Boston sixty years earlier.]

You will go most safely in the middle.
>   —OVID, *Metamorphoses*, c. A.D. 5

Be not the first by whom the new are tried,
Nor yet the last to lay the old aside.
>   —ALEXANDER POPE, *An Essay on Criticism*, 1711

Be wisely worldly, be not worldly wise.
——FRANCIS QUARLES, *Emblems,* 1635

If you want to get along, go along.
——SAM RAYBURN, d. 1961, saying,
quoted in Neil MacNeil, *Forge of Democracy,*
The House of Representatives, 1963
[U.S. Rep. Sam Rayburn of Texas—Mr. Democrat—was Speaker of the House for a total of seventeen years.]

The better part of valor is discretion.
——SHAKESPEARE, *Henry IV, Part I,* V, iv

Moderation in all things.
——TERENCE, *The Woman of Andros,* 166 B.C.

Put all your eggs in one basket—and watch that basket!
——MARK TWAIN, *Pudd'nhead Wilson's*
Calendar in *Pudd'nhead Wilson,* 1894
[Always ascribed to Twain, but Twain's biographer Albert Bigelow Paine said that the comment was delivered by Andrew Carnegie at a dinner with Twain on Apr. 6, 1893.]

Common sense is not so common.   ——VOLTAIRE,
Self-Love in *Dictionnaire philosophique,* 1764

PUBLIC, THE   See PEOPLE, THE

PUBLIC OFFICE   See GOVERNMENT;
HIGH POSITION:
RULERS & LEADERS; POLITICS

PUBLICITY   See also ADVERTISING
& PUBLIC RELATIONS

You must stir it and stump it,
And blow your own trumpet,
Or trust me, you haven't a chance.
——W. S. GILBERT, *Ruddigore,* 1887

The art of publicity is a black art; but has come to stay, and every year adds to its potency.
——LEARNED HAND, address at the
Elizabethan Club, May 1951
[For a more lighthearted comment on the power of publicity

and advertising, see Joseph Levine's update of Abraham Lincoln's assessment of the possibility of fooling all of the people—at PEOPLE under Lincoln.]

It is most expedient for the wise . . . to be the trumpet of his own virtues.
                    —SHAKESPEARE, *Much Ado About Nothing,* V, ii

PUBLISHING   See BOOKS & READING; MEDIA;
                            PRESS, THE

PUNISHMENT   See also JUSTICE; REVENGE

Eye for eye, tooth for tooth, hand for hand, foot for foot.
Burning for burning, wound for wound, stripe for stripe.
                    —BIBLE, *Exodus* 21:24–25

Let the punishment match the offense.
                    —CICERO, *De legibus,* c. 52 B.C.

To punish and not prevent is to labor at the pump and leave open the leak.   —THOMAS FULLER, *Gnomologia,* 1732

If a man destroy the eye of another man, they shall destroy his eye.   —CODE OF HAMMURABI, c. 2030 B.C.

Distrust all in whom the impulse to punish is powerful.
                    —FRIEDRICH NIETZSCHE,
                    Thus Spake Zarathustra, 1883–91

Punishment brings wisdom. It is the healing art of wickedness.   —PLATO, *Gorgias,* 4th cent. B.C.

Frequent punishments are always a sign of weakness or laziness on the part of the government.
                    —JEAN JACQUES ROUSSEAU,
                    The Social Contract, 1762

The reformative effect of punishment is a belief that dies hard, chiefly I think, because it is so satisfying to our sadistic impulses.   —BERTRAND RUSSELL, *Ideas That*
                    Have Harmed Mankind, 1946

While we have prisons, it matters little which of us occupy the cells. —GEORGE BERNARD SHAW, *Maxims for Revolutionists* in *Man and Superman*, 1903

I am all for bringing back the birch but only between consenting adults.
—GORE VIDAL, television interview with David Frost, quoted in *Sunday Times Magazine*, Sept. 16, 1973

The vilest deeds like poison weeds
Bloom well in prison air:
It is only what is good in man
That wastes and withers there.
—OSCAR WILDE, *The Ballad of Reading Gaol*, 1898

Q

QUESTIONS & ANSWERS

The answer to the Great Question of . . . Life, the Universe and Everything . . . Is . . . Forty-two.
> —DOUGLAS ADAMS, *The Hitch-hiker's Guide to the Galaxy,* 1979

To ask the hard question is simple.
> —W. H. AUDEN, poem no. 27 in *Poems,* 1933

A sudden, bold, and unexpected question doth many times surprise a man and lay him open.
> —FRANCIS BACON, *Of Cunning* in *Essays,* 1625

The answer, my friend, is blowin' in the wind.
> —BOB DYLAN, *Blowin' in the Wind,* 1962

More trouble is caused in this world by indiscreet answers than by indiscreet questions.
> —SYDNEY J. HARRIS, *Chicago Daily News,* Mar. 27, 1958

[A saying sometimes used by the press in defense of probing questions. See the similar Carl Rowan quote at PRESS, THE.]

All clues, no solutions. That's the way things are.
> —DENNIS POTTER, *The Singing Detective,* 1986

Be patient toward all that is unsolved in your heart. Try to love the questions themselves.
> —RAINER MARIA RILKE, letter to Franz Xaver Kappus, July 16, 1903

[The full final sentence is: "Try to love the questions themselves like locked rooms and like books in a very foreign language."]

What is the answer? [*I was silent.*] In that case, what is the question? —GERTRUDE STEIN, last words, 1946, reported in Alice B. Toklas, *What Is Remembered?*, 1963

And so I leave it to all of you:
Which came out of the opened door,—the lady, or the tiger?
—FRANK R. STOCKTON, *The Lady or the Tiger* in *Century Magazine*, Nov. 1882
[The story, originally called *The King's Arena*, is about a young man and a princess who fall in love. Her cruel father discovers the romance, and condemns the youth to enter an arena and open one of two doors. Behind one is a beautiful maiden whom he may marry; behind the other is a tiger. The princess learns which door conceals what, and signals her beloved which door to open. The fable ends with the famous query.]

Who are we? *Where* are we?
—HENRY DAVID THOREAU, *Ktaadn*, 1848, in *The Maine Woods*, 1864

It is better to ask some of the questions than to know all of the answers.
—JAMES THURBER, *The Scottie Who Knew Too Much* in *The Thurber Carnival*, 1945

QUOTATIONS, MAXIMS, & PROVERBS

See also PRUDENCE & PRACTICAL WISDOM

A proverb is the child of experience.
—ANONYMOUS (ENGLISH PROVERB)

The maxims of men disclose their hearts.
—ANONYMOUS (FRENCH PROVERB)

Despise not the discoveries of the wise, but acquaint thyself with their proverbs. —BIBLE, *Ecclesiasticus* 8:8

It is a good thing for an uneducated man to read books of quotations. —WINSTON CHURCHILL, *Roving Commission* in *My Early Life*, 1930

Confound those who have said our remarks before us.
—AELIUS DONATUS, 4th cent. A.D., cited in St. Jerome, *Commentary on Ecclesiastes*, c. A.D. 400

Proverbs are the sanctuary of the intuitions.
—RALPH WALDO EMERSON,
Compensation in *Essays: First Series,* 1841

Next to the originator of a good sentence is the first quoter of it.   —RALPH WALDO EMERSON, *Quotation and Originality* in *Letters and Social Aims,* 1876

I hate quotation. Tell me what you know.
—RALPH WALDO EMERSON, *Journal,* May 1849

A book that furnishes no quotations is, *me judice,* no book—it is a plaything.
—THOMAS LOVE PEACOCK, *Crochet Castle,* 1831

Some, for renown, on scraps of learning dote,
And think they grow immortal as they quote.
—EDWARD YOUNG, *Love of Fame,* 1725–28

R

RACES & PEOPLES See also NATIONS

The most certain test by which we judge whether a country is really free is the amount of security enjoyed by minorities.
—LORD ACTON, *The History of Freedom in Antiquity,* 1907

The Pilgrim Fathers landed on the shores of America and fell upon their knees. Then they fell upon the aborigines.
—ANONYMOUS, c. early 20th cent.
[Attributed widely, including to William Maxwell Everts, who printed a version of this joke in the *Louisville Courier-Journal,* July 4, 1913.]

Am I not a man and a brother?
—ANONYMOUS, inscription on the seal of the Antislavery Society of London, c. 1770

We shall overcome, we shall overcome,
We shall overcome some day.
Oh, deep in my heart, I do believe
We shall overcome some day.
—ANONYMOUS, civil rights song, 1960s
[The song evidently dates from the mid-19th century. About 1900, it was adapted as a Baptist hymn, *I'll Overcome Some Day,* by C. Albert Tindley.]

Black is beautiful. —ANONYMOUS, slogan, c. 1966
[Among the forerunners of this phrase is Langston Hughes's "I am a Negro—and beautiful!" *The Negro Artist and the Racial Mountain* in *The Nation,* June 23, 1926. Also *The Song of Solomon* 1:5 in the Douay version of the Bible reads, "I am black but beautiful."]

If we do not now dare everything, the fulfillment of that prophecy, recreated from the Bible in song by a slave, is upon us:

God gave Noah the rainbow sign,
No more water, the fire next time!
—JAMES BALDWIN, *The Fire Next Time*, 1963

To be a Jew is destiny.
—VICKI BAUM, *And Life Goes On*, 1932

It is not healthy when a nation lives within a nation, as colored Americans are living inside America. A nation cannot live confident of its tomorrow if its refugees are among its own citizens.
—PEARL S. BUCK, *What America Means to Me*, 1942

Yes, I am a Jew, and when the ancestors of the right honorable gentleman were brutal savages in an unknown island, mine were priests in the temple of Solomon.
—BENJAMIN DISRAELI, reply to
Daniel O'Connell, c. 1835–37

The destiny of the colored American . . . is the destiny of America. —FREDERICK DOUGLASS, speech, Feb. 12, 1862

To be a poor man is hard, but to be a poor race in a land of dollars is the very bottom of hardships.
—W.E.B. DU BOIS, *The Souls of Black Folk*, 1903

One ever feels his twoness—an American, a Negro, two souls, two thoughts, two unreconciled strivings; two warring ideals in one dark body . . . . The history of the American Negro is the history of this strife—this longing to attain self-conscious manhood, to merge his double self into a better and truer self. —*Ibid.*

The problem of the twentieth century is the problem of the color line. —W.E.B. DU BOIS, speech, London, 1900

However painful it may be for me to accept this conclusion, I am obliged to state it: for the black man there is only one destiny. And it is white.
—FRANTZ FANON, *Black Skin, White Masks*, 1952

Death is a slave's freedom.
> —NIKKI GIOVANNI, speech at the
> funeral of Martin Luther King, Jr., Apr. 9, 1968

The American economy, the American society, the American unconscious are all racist.
> —MICHAEL HARRINGTON, *The Other America,* 1962

All those who are not racially pure are mere chaff.
> —ADOLF HITLER, *Mein Kampf,* 1933

I swear to the Lord I still can't see
Why democracy means
Everybody but me.
> —LANGSTON HUGHES, *The Black Man Speaks*
> in *Jim Crow's Last Stand,* 1943

Among the thousand white persons, I am a dark rock surged upon, and overswept.
> —ZORA NEALE HURSTON, *Mules and Men,* 1935

We will not be satisfied until justice rolls down like waters and righteousness like a mighty stream.
> —MARTIN LUTHER KING, JR., speech at
> the Lincoln Memorial, Aug. 28, 1963

[Based on *Amos* 5:24. See under JUSTICE.]

I have a dream that one day on the red hills of Georgia, the sons of former slaves and the sons of former slaveowners will be able to sit down together at the table of brotherhood.
> —*Ibid.*

I have a dream that my four little children will one day live in a nation where they will not be judged by the color of their skin but by the content of their character.　　—*Ibid.*

[King's stirring address was delivered to 200,000 civil rights marchers gathered at the Lincoln Memorial in Washington, D.C.]

You're a better man than I am, Gunga Din!
> —RUDYARD KIPLING, *Gunga Din*
> in *Barrack-Room Ballads,* 1892

All I ask for the Negro is that if you do not like him, let him alone. If God gave him but little, that little let him enjoy.   —ABRAHAM LINCOLN, speech, July 17, 1858

We didn't land on Plymouth Rock. Plymouth Rock landed on us.
          —MALCOLM X, *The Autobiography of Malcolm X,* 1965

A foreigner scarcely counts as a human being for someone of another race.   —PLINY, *Natural History,* A.D. 77

No democracy can long survive which does not accept as fundamental to its very existence the recognition of the rights of minorities.   —FRANKLIN D. ROOSEVELT,
          letter to the NAACP, June 25, 1938

We don't have to be what you want us to be.
          —BILL RUSSELL, quoted by
          George Vecsey, *The New York Times,* 1985

When the last red man shall have vanished from this earth, and his memory is only a story among the whites, these shores will still swarm with the invisible dead of my people. . . . The white man will never be alone. And when your children's children think they are alone . . . they will not be alone. . . . Your lands will throng with the returning hosts that once filled them and still love this beautiful land. The white man will never be alone.
          —SEATTLE, speech, c. 1854, quoted in
          Joseph Epes Brown, *The Spiritual Legacy
          of the American Indian,* 1964
[Seattle's speech was probably in the Salish dialect and addressed to the governor of the Washington Territory. A translation by Dr. Henry Smith was published in 1887. Since then, Seattle's comments have been richly embroidered. The 1971 film *Home* transformed them into an ecological manifesto.]

Hath not a Jew eyes? Hath not a Jew hands, organs, dimensions, senses, affections, passions? Fed with the same food, hurt with the same weapons, subject to the same diseases, healed by the same means, warmed and cooled by the same winter and summer as a Christian is? If you prick us, do we not bleed? If you tickle us, do we not laugh? If you poison us, do we not die? And if you wrong us, shall we not revenge? —SHAKESPEARE, *The Merchant of Venice,* III, i

"Do you know who made you?" "Nobody, as I knows on," said the child, with a short laugh. . . . "I 'spect I grow'd. Don't think nobody never made me."
> —HARRIET BEECHER STOWE,
> *Uncle Tom's Cabin*, 1852

The danger of a conflict between the white and the black inhabitants perpetually haunts the imagination of the Americans like a bad dream. —ALEXIS DE TOCQUEVILLE,
> *Democracy in America*, 1835–39

We have ground the manhood out of them, and the shame is ours not theirs, and we should pay for it.
> —MARK TWAIN, letter to Francis Wayland,
> Dean of Yale Law School, c. 1890, offering to
> pay the tuition and board of a black student

What a happy country this will be, if the whites will listen.
> —DAVID WALKER, *Walker's Appeal*, Sept. 28, 1829

Segregation now. Segregation tomorrow. Segregation forever. —GEORGE WALLACE, inaugural speech
> on becoming governor of Alabama, Jan. 14, 1963
[The lines were apparently written by Asa Earl Carter, a right-wing extremist, who under the pseudonym Forrest Carter was responsible for the well-received, politically correct memoirs of an Indian named Little Tree.)

The slave system on our place, in large measure, took the spirit of self-reliance and self-help out of the white people.
> —BOOKER T. WASHINGTON, *Up from Slavery*, 1901

J'accuse.
I accuse you.
> —EMILE ZOLA, title of a letter to the president
> of the French Republic, accusing the government of
> wrongdoing in the Dreyfus case, published Jan. 13, 1898

RAIN   See NATURE: SEASONS;
              NATURE: WIND & WEATHER

RAINBOW   See NATURE: THE HEAVENS, THE SKY

REALITY & ILLUSIONS

I do not know whether I was then a man dreaming I was a butterfly, or whether I am now a butterfly dreaming I am a man. —CHUANG-TZU, *On Leveling All Things,* c. 300 B.C.

Every age is fed on illusions, lest men should renounce life early and the human race come to an end.
—JOSEPH CONRAD, *Victory,* 1915

Between the idea and the reality
Between the motion
And the act
Falls the Shadow.   —T. S. ELIOT, *The Hollow Men,* 1925

Humankind
Cannot bear very much reality.
—T. S. ELIOT, *Murder in the Cathedral,* 1935

Things are not what they seem.
—HENRY WADSWORTH LONGFELLOW,
A Psalm of Life, 1839

We live in a fantasy world, a world of illusion. The great task in life is to find reality.
—IRIS MURDOCH, quoted by Rachel Billington,
The Times, London, Apr. 15, 1983

Reality is a staircase going neither up nor down; we don't move, today is today, always is today.
—OCTAVIO PAZ, *The Endless Instant*
in *Modern European Poetry,* 1966

All that we see or seem
Is but a dream within a dream.   —EDGAR ALLAN POE,
A Dream Within a Dream, 1848–49

In the American metaphysic, reality is always material reality, hard, resistant, unformed, impenetrable, unpleasant.
—LIONEL TRILLING, *Reality*
in *The Liberal Imagination,* 1950

Don't part with your illusions. When they are gone, you may still exist, but you have ceased to live.
—MARK TWAIN, *Pudd'nhead Wilson's
Calendar* in *Pudd'nhead Wilson,* 1894

REASON & REASONS See also MIND, THOUGHT, &
UNDERSTANDING; PHILOSOPHY;
REASONABLE & UNREASONABLE PEOPLE

Come now, and let us reason together.
—BIBLE, *Isaiah* 1:18
[A favorite saying of President Lyndon B. Johnson.]

Let reason go before every enterprise, and counsel before
every action. —BIBLE, *Ecclesiasticus* 37:16

Reason is the ruler and queen of all things.
—CICERO, *Tusulanae disputationes,* 44 B.C.

If everything on earth were rational, nothing would happen.
—FEODOR DOSTOEVSKI,
The Brothers Karamazov, 1879–80

Reason can wrestle and overthrow terror.
—EURIPIDES, *Iphigenia in Aulis,* c. 405 B.C.

The sleep of reason begets monsters.
—GOYA, motto for the intended frontispiece
of his 1799 graphic series, the *Caprichos*

In this world there is one terrible thing, and that is that
everyone has his reasons.
—JEAN RENOIR, screenplay, *The Rules of the Game,* 1939

Tout par raison.
Everything according to reason.
—CARDINAL RICHELIEU, *Mirame,* 1641

There is occasions and causes why and wherefore in all
things. —SHAKESPEARE, *Henry V,* V, i
["Every why hath a wherefore," *Comedy of Errors,* II, ii.]

Reason is God's crowning gift to man.
—SOPHOCLES, *Antigone,* 5th cent. B.C.

Passion and prejudice govern the world; only under the
name of reason.
—JOHN WESLEY, letter to Joseph Benson, Oct. 5, 1770

REASONABLE &   See also MIND, THOUGHT,
UNREASONABLE PEOPLE   & UNDERSTANDING;
                                                 REASON & REASONS

When a man begins to reason, he ceases to feel.
                          —ANONYMOUS (FRENCH PROVERB)

Falling in love is one of the activities forbidden that tiresome person, the consistently reasonable man.
                          —SIR ARTHUR EDDINGTON,
                              News Chronicle, London, Mar. 2, 1932

Who reasons wisely is not therefore wise;
His pride in reasoning, not in acting, lies.
                          —ALEXANDER POPE, *Moral Essays,* 1731–35

Pure logic is the ruin of the spirit.
    —ANTOINE DE SAINT-EXUPÉRY, *Flight to Arras,* 1942

The reasonable man adapts himself to the world; the unreasonable one persists in trying to adapt the world to himself. Therefore all progress depends on the unreasonable man.
                          —GEORGE BERNARD SHAW, *Maxims for
                              Revolutionists* in *Man and Superman,* 1903

A mind all logic is like a knife all blade. It makes the hand bleeds that uses it.
                          —RABINDRANATH TAGORE, *Stray Birds,* 1916

REGRET   See also DECISION; PAST, THE

If you board the wrong train, it is no use running along the corridor in the other direction.
                          —DIETRICH BONHOEFFER,
                              d. 1945, *The Way to Freedom*

We have left undone those things which we ought to have done; and we have done those things which we ought not to have done; and there is no health in us.
                          —BOOK OF COMMON PRAYER, compiled 1662

Remorse is the poison of life.
                          —CHARLOTTE BRONTË, *Jane Eyre,* 1847

Of all the horrid, hideous notes of woe,
Sadder than owl songs or the midnight blast,
Is that portentous phrase, "I told you so."
      —LORD BYRON, *Don Juan*, 1819–24

Footfalls echo in the memory
Down the passage which we did not take
Towards the door we never opened
Into the rosegarden.
      —T. S. ELIOT, *Burnt Norton* in *Four Quartets*, 1940

I shall be telling this with a sigh
Somewhere ages and ages hence:
Two roads diverged in a wood, and I—
I took the one less traveled by,
And that has made all the difference.
      —ROBERT FROST, *The Road Not Taken*, 1916

We often repent the good we have done as the ill.
      —WILLIAM HAZLITT, *Characteristics*, 1823

God has little patience with remorse.
      —MALCOLM LOWRY, *Under the Volcano*, 1947

Rosebud.
      —HERMAN J. MANKIEWICZ & ORSON WELLES,
              screenplay, *Citizen Kane*, 1941
[Kane's last word. The movie turns on discovering its meaning.
The searcher comes close: "Maybe Rosebud was something he
couldn't get or something he lost."]

When I am dead and opened, you shall find "Calais" written
on my heart.   —MARY I, d. 1558, quoted in
              Raphael Holinshed's *Chronicles*, 1577
[In some versions, it is "Philip and Calais" that is written.]

I could have had class. I could've been a contender. I
could've been somebody. Instead of a bum, which is what I
am.
—BUDD SCHULBERG, screenplay, *On the Waterfront*, 1954

Why should I mourn at the untimely fate of my people?
Tribe follows tribe, and nation follows nation, and regret is
useless.　　　　　　　　—SEATTLE, speech, c. 1854, quoted in
Joseph Epes Brown, *The Spiritual Legacy
of the American Indian,* 1964
[For more from this speech, see RACES & PEOPLES.]

What's done is done.　　　—SHAKESPEARE, *Macbeth,* III, ii

Oh, call back yesterday, bid time return.
—SHAKESPEARE, *Richard II,* III, ii

What's gone and what's past help
Should be past grief.
—SHAKESPEARE, *The Winter's Tale,* III, ii

To regret deeply is to live afresh.
—HENRY DAVID THOREAU, *Journal,* Nov. 13, 1839

For of all sad words of tongue or pen,
The saddest are these: "It might have been!"
—JOHN GREENLEAF WHITTIER, *Maud Muller,* 1856

RELIGION　　　　　　See also ATHEISM; FAITH; GOD;
JESUS; MYSTICISM; PRAYER;
SELF-RIGHTEOUSNESS

Man doth not live by bread only, but by every word that
proceedeth out of the mouth of the Lord doth man live.
—BIBLE, *Deuteronomy* 8:3
[Also *Matthew* 4:4, "Man shall not live by bread alone . . ."
—and *Luke* 4:4.]

I am holier than thou.　　　　　　—BIBLE, *Isaiah* 65:5
[More, with a note, at SELF-RIGHTEOUSNESS.]

No man can serve two masters.　　—BIBLE, *Matthew* 6:24

Ye cannot serve God and mammon.　　　　　—*Ibid.*

Thou art Peter, and upon this rock I will build my church;
and the gates of hell shall not prevail against it.
—*Ibid.* 16:18

Heathen, n. A benighted creature who has the folly to worship something that he can see and feel.
> —AMBROSE BIERCE, *The Devil's Dictionary,* 1906

To die for a religion is easier than to live it absolutely.
> —JORGE LUIS BORGES,
> *Deutsches Requiem* in *Labyrinths,* tr. 1962

How very hard it is
To be a Christian!
> —ROBERT BROWNING, *Easter-Day,* 1850

Every day, people are straying away from the church and going back to God.
> —LENNY BRUCE, *The Essential Lenny Bruce,* 1967

This Ariyan Eightfold Path, that is to say: Right view, right aim, right speech, right action, right living, right effort, right mindfulness, right contemplation.
> —BUDDHA, 6th–5th cent. B.C., from
> F. L. Woodward, *Some Sayings of the Buddha*

One religion is as true as another.   —ROBERT BURTON,
> *The Anatomy of Melancholy,* 1621–51

Wonder is the basis of worship.
> —THOMAS CARLYLE, *Sartor Resartus,* 1833–34

Religion is by no means a proper subject of conversation in mixed company.   —EARL OF CHESTERFIELD, d. 1773,
> letter to his godson, No. 112, undated

The Christian ideal has not been tried and found wanting. It has been found difficult; and left untried.
> —G. K. CHESTERTON, *The Unfinished Temple*
> in *What's Wrong with the World,* 1910

The all-male religions have produced no religious imagery. . . . The great religious art of the world is deeply involved with the female principle.
> —SIR KENNETH CLARK, *Civilization,* 1970

In my religion, there would be no exclusive doctrine; all would be love, poetry, and doubt.
> —CYRIL CONNOLLY, *The Unquiet Grave,* 1945

The cosmic religious experience is the strongest force and the noblest driving force behind scientific research.
> —ALBERT EINSTEIN, *Religion and Science,* Nov. 9, 1930

Science without religion is lame; religion without science is blind.
> —ALBERT EINSTEIN, d. 1955, quoted in
> *The Reader's Digest,* Nov. 1973

I like the silent church before the service begins, better than any preaching.
> —RALPH WALDO EMERSON,
> *Self-Reliance* in *Essays: First Series,* 1841

God builds his temple in the heart on the ruins of churches and religions.
> —RALPH WALDO EMERSON,
> *Worship* in *The Conduct of Life,* 1860

Religion is an illusion and it derives its strength from the fact that it falls in with our instinctual desires.
> —SIGMUND FREUD, *A Philosophy of Life* in
> *New Introductory Lectures in Psychoanalysis,* 1933

The Bible shows the way to go to heaven, not the way the heavens go.
> —GALILEO, d. 1642, fragment

All religions are ancient monuments to superstitions, ignorance, ferocity; and modern religions are only ancient follies rejuvenated.
> —BARON D'HOLBACH, *Le bon sens . . . ,* 1772

Writing for a penny a word is ridiculous. If a man really wants to make a million dollars, the best way would be to start his own religion.
> —L. RONALD HUBBARD, founder of Scientology,
> lecture, Eastern Science Fiction Association,
> Newark, N.J., 1947

I am for religion, against religions.
> —VICTOR HUGO, *Les Misérables,* 1862

Religion is a monumental chapter in the history of human egotism.
> —WILLIAM JAMES, *The Varieties*
> *of Religious Experience,* 1902

It does me no injury for my neighbor to say there are twenty Gods, or no God. —THOMAS JEFFERSON, *Notes on the State of Virginia*, 1782

The church must be reminded that it is not the master or the servant of the state, but rather the conscience of the state.
—MARTIN LUTHER KING, JR., *Strength to Love*, 1963

Here I stand, I cannot do otherwise; God help me; Amen.
—MARTIN LUTHER, speech, Diet of Worms, Apr. 18, 1521

Religion is the sign of the oppressed creature, the sentiment of a heartless world, and the soul of soulless conditions. It is the opium of the people. —KARL MARX, *Criticism of Hegel's Philosophy of Right*, 1844
[In the same era, Friedrich Nietzsche wrote of "the two great European narcotics, alcohol and Christianity," *Twilight of the Idols*, 1888.]

What mean and cruel things men do for the love of God.
—W. SOMERSET MAUGHAM, *A Writer's Notebook*, 1949

We must respect the other fellow's religion, but only in the sense and to the extent that we respect his theory that his wife is beautiful and his children smart.
—H. L. MENCKEN, *Minority Report: H. L. Mencken's Notebooks*, 1956

Fear of death and fear of life both become piety. —*Ibid.*

A nation must have a religion, and that religion must be under the control of the government.
—NAPOLEON BONAPARTE, to Count Thibaudeau, June 6, 1801

I want nothing to do with any religion concerned with keeping the masses satisfied to live in hunger, filth, and ignorance.
—JAWAHARLAL NEHRU, quoted in Edgar Snow, *Journey to the Beginning*, 1958

Dogma has been the fundamental principle of my religion. . . .
Religion, as mere sentiment, is to me a mockery.
> —JOHN HENRY CARDINAL NEWMAN,
> *Apologia pro Vita Sua,* 1864

Any system of religion that has anything in it that shocks
the mind of a child, cannot be a true system.
> —THOMAS PAINE, *The Age of Reason,* 1793

Men despise religion; they hate it, and they fear it is true.
> —PASCAL, *Pensées,* 1670

Religion is so great a thing that it is right that those who
will not take the trouble to seek it if it be obscure, should
be deprived of it.   *—Ibid.*

To be like Christ is to be a Christian.
> —WILLIAM PENN, last words, May 30, 1718

The world would be poorer without the antics of clergymen.
> —V. S. PRITCHETT, *The Dean*
> in *In My Good Books,* 1942

Religion is something infinitely simple, ingenuous. . . . In
the infinite extent of the universe, it is a direction of the
heart.   —RAINER MARIA RILKE, letter to
> Ilse Blumenthal-Weiss, Dec. 28, 1921

The Bible is literature, not dogma.
> —GEORGE SANTAYANA, *The Ethics of Spinoza,* 1910

Religion is the love of life in the consciousness of impotence.
> —GEORGE SANTAYANA, *Winds of Doctrine,* 1913

He worships God who knows him.
> —SENECA, *Letters to Lucilius,* 1st cent. A.D.

The devil can cite Scripture for his purpose.
> —SHAKESPEARE, *The Merchant of Venice,* I, iii

There is only one religion though there are a hundred versions of it.
—GEORGE BERNARD SHAW, *Arms and the Man,* 1898

How many divisions has the Pope?
                                      —STALIN, d. 1953, attributed

We have just enough religion to make us hate, but not
enough to make us love one another.
                                      —JONATHAN SWIFT, *Thoughts
                                        on Various Subjects,* 1711

I never saw, heard, nor read that the clergy were beloved
in any nation where Christianity was the religion of the
country. Nothing can render them popular but some degree
of persecution.   —JONATHAN SWIFT,
                                        Thoughts on Religion, 1765
[Swift, it is worth remembering, was himself a clergyman. The
Thoughts were not published until twenty years after his death.]

There is perhaps no greater hardship at present inflicted on
mankind in civilized and free countries than the necessity of
listening to sermons.
        —ANTHONY TROLLOPE, *Barchester Towers,* 1857

*Quoi que vous fassiez, écrasez l'infâme, et aimez qui vous
aime.*
Whatever you do, crush this infamy, and love those who love
you.   —VOLTAIRE, letter to d'Alembert, Nov. 28, 1762
[The "infamy," or "infamous thing," is superstition or organized religion, depending on one's interpretation.]

Orthodoxy is my doxy; heterodoxy is another man's doxy.
                            —WILLIAM WARBURTON, d. 1779,
                            quoted in Joseph Priestley, *Memoirs,* 1807
[This was Bishop Warburton's answer to a question by the Earl
of Sandwich (of comestible fame), who wanted to know the
difference between orthodoxy and heterodoxy.]

Religion is love; in no case is it logic.
    —BEATRICE POTTER WEBB, *My Apprenticeship,* 1926

As society is now constituted, a literal adherence to the
moral precepts scattered throughout the Gospels would
mean sudden death.   —ALFRED NORTH WHITEHEAD,
                        Adventures in Ideas, 1933

And I could wish my days to be
Bound each to each by natural piety.
   —WILLIAM WORDSWORTH, *My Heart Leaps Up,* 1807

REMEDIES   See ILLNESS & REMEDIES; PROBLEMS;
                       QUESTIONS & ANSWERS;
              REVOLUTION (Guy Fawkes & Shakespeare)

REMORSE   See REGRET

REPENTANCE See FORGIVENESS & MERCY; REGRET

REPUTATION

A good name is rather to be chosen than great riches.
                   —BIBLE, *Proverbs* 22:1

A good name endureth forever.
             —BIBLE, *Ecclesiasticus* 41:13

One who has a reputation for rising early can sleep until
noon.   —ALPHONSE DAUDET, *Tartarin sur les Alpes,* 1885
[Probably proverbial. *Yiddish Proverbs,* edited by Hanan J. Ay-
alti, includes the same observation.]

Reputation, like a face, is the symbol of its possessor and
creator, and another can use it only as a mask.
                   —LEARNED HAND, *Yale Electric
                       Company v. Robertson,* 1928
[A key case in trademark law.]

The worst of me is known, and I can say that I am better
than my reputation.
          —J.C.F. VON SCHILLER, *Maria Stuart,* 1801

Good name in man and woman, dear my lord,
Is the immediate jewel of their souls.
               —SHAKESPEARE, *Othello,* III, iii

The purest treasure mortal times afford
Is spotless reputation.   —SHAKESPEARE, *Richard II,* I, i

If we disregard what the world says of someone, we live to
repent it.   —LOGAN PEARSALL SMITH, *All Trivia,* 1933

RESIGNATION See also OBEDIENCE

Naked came I out of my mother's womb, and naked shall I return thither: the Lord gave, and the Lord hath taken away; blessed be the name of the Lord. —BIBLE, *Job* 1:21

Teach us to care and not to care.
Teach us to sit still. —T. S. ELIOT, *Ash Wednesday*, 1930

Better to accept whatever happens.
—HORACE, *Odes*, 33 B.C.

Hear me, my chiefs, l am tired; my heart is sick and sad. From where the sun now stands, I will fight no more forever.
—JOSEPH THE YOUNGER, speech at the
conclusion of the Nez Percé War, Oct. 1877
[See also PEACE.]

A calm despair, without angry convulsion or reproaches directed to heaven, is the essence of wisdom.
—ALFRED DE VIGNY, *Journal d'un poète*, 1832

RESISTANCE See APPEASEMENT VS. RESISTANCE;
COURAGE; REVOLUTION

RESPONSIBILITY See also FATE; SELF;
SELF-RELIANCE

Everybody's business is nobody's business.
—ANONYMOUS
[Sometimes attributed to Lord Macaulay or Izaak Walton, but evidently an ancient byword; see Aristotle, for example, on everybody's property, under COMMUNISM.]

Every man is the architect of his own fortune.
—APPIUS CLAUDIUS CAECUS, c. 300 B.C.,
quoted in Sallust, *De civitate*, 1st cent. B.C.

Am I my brother's keeper? —BIBLE, *Genesis* 4:9

Unto whomsoever much is given, of him shall be much required. —BIBLE, *Luke* 12:48

Perhaps it is better to be irresponsible and right than to be responsible and wrong.

> —WINSTON CHURCHILL, radio broadcast,
> Aug. 26, 1950

Do your duty and leave the rest to the gods.

> —PIERRE CORNEILLE, *Horace,* 1639

When your neighbor's wall is on fire, it becomes your business.

> —HORACE, *Epistles, Book I,* 20 B.C.

Our privileges can be no greater than our obligations. The protection of our rights can endure no longer than the performance of our responsibilities.

> —JOHN F. KENNEDY, speech, May 18, 1963

"Once the rockets are up, who cares where they come down?
That's not my department," says Wernher von Braun.

> —TOM LEHRER, *Wernher von Braun,* song, 1965

[Von Braun developed Germany's V-2 rocket used against Britain in World War II. Later, in the U.S., he developed the Saturn booster rocket used in the Apollo flights to the moon.]

Oh duty,
Why hast thou not the visage of a sweetie or a cutie?

> —OGDEN NASH, *Kind of an Ode*
> *to Duty* in *The Face Is Familiar,* 1941

I believe that every right implies a responsibility; every opportunity, an obligation; every possession, a duty.

> —JOHN D. ROCKEFELLER, speech, July 8, 1941

To be a man is, precisely, to be responsible.

> —ANTOINE DE SAINT-EXUPÉRY,
> *Wind, Sand, and Stars,* 1939

The fault, dear Brutus, is not in our stars,
But in ourselves, that we are underlings.

> —SHAKESPEARE, *Julius Caesar,* I, ii

The buck stops here.

> —HARRY S. TRUMAN, sign on his White House desk

REST See LEISURE; SLEEP & DREAMS

REVENGE See also JUSTICE; PUNISHMENT

Revenge is a dish that should be eaten cold.
  —ANONYMOUS (ENGLISH PROVERB)

Men regard it as their right to return evil for evil—and if
they cannot, feel they have lost their liberty.
  —ARISTOTLE, *Nicomachean Ethics,* 4th cent. B.C.

In taking revenge, a man is but even with his enemy; but in
passing it over, he is superior.
  —FRANCIS BACON, *Of Revenge,* 1625

A man that studieth revenge keeps his own wounds green,
which otherwise would heal and do well. —*Ibid.*

Thou shalt not avenge. —BIBLE, *Leviticus* 19:18

Vengeance is mine; I will repay, saith the Lord.
  —BIBLE, *Romans* 12:19

Living well is the best revenge.
  —GEORGE HERBERT, *Jacula Prudentum,* 1651
[This was also the motto of Gerald and Sara Murphy, the expa-
triate friends of F. Scott Fitzgerald who were the models for
Dick and Nicole Diver in *Tender Is the Night.*]

Revenge is the poor delight of little minds.
  —JUVENAL, *Satires,* c. A.D. 100

REVOLUTION See also APPEASEMENT VS.
RESISTANCE; TURBULENT TIMES;
VIOLENCE & FORCE

I came not to send peace, but a sword.
  —BIBLE, *Matthew* 10:34

Revolutions are not made with rosewater.
  —EDWARD GEORGE BULWER-LYTTON,
The Parisians, 1873

In the groves of their academy, at the end of every walk, you see nothing but the gallows.
—EDMUND BURKE, *Reflections on the French Revolution*, 1790

Lay the proud usurpers low!
Tyrants fall in every foe!
Liberty's in every blow!
Let us do or die!
—ROBERT BURNS, *Scots Wha Hae*, 1794

What is a rebel? A man who says no.
—ALBERT CAMUS, *The Rebel*, 1951

All modern revolutions have ended in a reinforcement of the power of the state.
—*Ibid.*

The revolutionary spirit is mighty convenient in this, that it frees one from all scruples as regards ideas.
—JOSEPH CONRAD, *A Personal Record*, 1912

The blow by which kings fall causes a long bleeding.
—PIERRE CORNEILLE, *Cinna*, 1640

Plots true or false are necessary things,
To raise up commonwealths and ruin kings.
—JOHN DRYDEN, *Absalom and Achitophel*, 1680

When you strike at a king, you must kill him.
—RALPH WALDO EMERSON, d. 1882, attributed by Oliver Wendell Holmes, Jr., cited in Max Lerner, *The Mind and Faith of Justice Holmes*, 1943

Desperate diseases require desperate remedies.
—GUY FAWKES, attributed in connection with the Gunpowder Plot to blow up Parliament, Nov. 5, 1605
[Cf. Shakespeare, below.]

A great revolution is never the fault of the people, but of the government.
—GOETHE, quoted in Johann Peter Eckermann, *Conversations with Goethe*, 1836

What happens to a dream deferred?
Does it dry up
Like a raisin in the sun? . . .
Or does it explode?
>—LANGSTON HUGHES, *Harlem,* 1951

Fire in the lake: the image of revolution.
>—*I CHING,* Book I, c. 12th cent. B.C.

The tree of liberty must be refreshed from time to time with the blood of patriots and tyrants. It is its natural manure.
>—THOMAS JEFFERSON, letter to
>Col. William S. Smith, Nov. 13, 1787

If you feed the people just with revolutionary slogans, they will listen today, they will listen tomorrow, they will listen the day after tomorrow, but on the fourth day, they will say "To hell with you."   —NIKITA KHRUSHCHEV, quoted in
>*The New York Times,* Oct. 4, 1964

When smashing monuments, save the pedestals—they always come in handy.
>—STANISLAW J. LEC, *Unkempt Thoughts,* 1962

Inciting to revolution is treason, not only against man, but also against God.
>—POPE LEO XIII, *Immortale Dei,* Nov. 1, 1855

Be not deceived. Revolutions do not go backward.
>—ABRAHAM LINCOLN, speech, May 19, 1856
[Similarly, the abolitionist William Henry Seward said: "Revolutions never go backward," in a speech on Oct. 25, 1858.]

Revolution is the proper occupation of the masses.
>—MAO ZEDUNG, *Be Concerned with the Well-Being of the Masses, Pay Attention to Methods of Work,* Jan. 27, 1934

The workers have nothing to lose in this but their chains. They have a world to gain. Workers of the world, unite!
>—KARL MARX & FRIEDRICH ENGELS,
>*The Communist Manifesto,* 1848

In revolutions everything is forgotten. . . . Gratitude, friendship, parentage; every tie vanishes, and all that is sought is self-interest.   —NAPOLEON BONAPARTE, quoted in
Barry E. O'Meara, *Napoleon in Exile,* 1822

A share in two revolutions is living to some purpose.
—THOMAS PAINE, quoted in Eric Foner,
Tom Paine and Revolutionary America, 1976

I will return and be millions.
—EVA PERON, d. 1952, saying

Apres nous le déluge.
After us, the flood.
—MADAME DE POMPADOUR, Nov. 5, 1751,
quoted in Mme. de Hausset, *Mémoires,* 1802
[The prediction was precipitated by Frederick the Great's victory over the combined French and Austrian armies at the battle of Rossbach.]

I will have no laws. I will acknowledge none. I protest against every law which an authority calling itself necessary imposes upon my free will.
—PIERRE-JOSEPH PROUDHON, *General Idea
of the Revolution in the Nineteenth Century,* 1861

Diseases desperate grown
By desperate appliance are relieved,
Or not at all.   —SHAKESPEARE, *Hamlet,* IV, iii
[Cf. Guy Fawkes above and the third of Hippocrates' adages at DOCTORS & THE PRACTICE OF MEDICINE.]

Revolutions have never lightened the burden of tyranny. They have only shifted it to another shoulder.
—GEORGE BERNARD SHAW, *The Revolutionist's
Handbook* in *Man and Superman,* 1903

All men recognize the right of revolution.
—HENRY DAVID THOREAU, *Civil Disobedience,* 1849

All changed, changed utterly:
A terrible beauty is born.
—WILLIAM BUTLER YEATS, *Easter 1916*
in *Michael Robartes and the Dancer,* 1921

RICH, THE   See HAVES & HAVE-NOTS; MONEY

RIGHT   See JUSTICE; VIRTUE

RIGHTEOUSNESS See SELF-RIGHTEOUSNESS; VIRTUE

RIGHTS   See also DEMOCRACY; EQUALITY;
        FREEDOM; FREE SPEECH; LAW;
        LAWYERS; PRESS, THE; PRIVACY

A right sometimes sleeps but it never dies.
        —ANONYMOUS (LEGAL MAXIM)

Rights are lost by disuse.
        —ANONYMOUS (LEGAL MAXIM)
[These contradictory maxims cover both sides of the issue, as
is necessary in law.]

The public good is in nothing more essentially interested
than in the protection of every individual's private rights.
        —WILLIAM BLACKSTONE, *Commentaries,* 1765–69

There is no such thing as rights anyhow. It is a question of
whether you can put it over. In any legal sense or practical
sense, whatever is, is "a right."
        —CLARENCE DARROW, debate on
Prohibition, quoted in Kevin Tierney, *Darrow,* 1979

[All men] are endowed by their Creator with certain inalien-
able rights.   —THOMAS JEFFERSON,
        The Declaration of Independence, July 4, 1776
[A full citation is given under AMERICAN HISTORY: MEM-
ORABLE MOMENTS.]

A bill of rights is what the people are entitled to against
every government on earth.
        —THOMAS JEFFERSON, letter to
James Madison, Dec. 20, 1787

Nobody talks more passionately of his rights than he who,
in the depths of his soul, is doubtful about them.
        —FRIEDRICH NIETZSCHE,
        Human, All-Too-Human, 1878

ROME   See CITIES

RUDENESS   See MANNERS; INSULTS & PUT-DOWNS

RUIN   See also POVERTY & HUNGER; TROUBLE;
                WINNING & LOSING, VICTORY & DEFEAT

The road to ruin is always kept in good repair.
                                        —ANONYMOUS

He bears the seed of ruin in himself.
                        —MATTHEW ARNOLD, *Merope*, 1858

How are the mighty fallen in the midst of the battle!
                        —BIBLE, *II Samuel* 1:25

MENE, MENE, TEKEL, UPHARSIN.
                        —BIBLE, *Daniel* 5:25
[The writing on the wall announcing the destruction of Babylon.]

But the children of the kingdom shall be cast out into outer
darkness: there shall be weeping and gnashing of teeth.
                        —BIBLE, *Matthew* 8:12

All men that are ruined are ruined on the side of their
natural propensities.
    —EDMUND BURKE, *Letters on a Regicide Peace*, 1796

Let everyone witness how many different cards fortune has
up her sleeve when she wants to ruin a man.
    —BENVENUTO CELLINI, *Autobiography*, 1558–62,
                        tr. John Addington Symonds, 1888

There is no loneliness greater than the loneliness of failure.
The failure is a stranger in his own house.
    —ERIC HOFFER, *The Passionate State of Mind*, 1954

There is not a fiercer hell than the failure in a great object.
                        —JOHN KEATS, Preface, *Endymion*, 1818

Men fall from great fortune because of the same shortcom-
ings that led to their rise.
                        —LA BRUYÈRE, *Les Caractères*, 1688

From the sublime to the ridiculous there is only one step.
  —NAPOLEON BONAPARTE, remark to the
                Polish ambassador De Pradt after
                the retreat from Moscow, 1812

Men shut their doors against a setting sun.
  —SHAKESPEARE, *Timon of Athens,* I, ii

RULERS   See HIGH POSITION: RULERS & LEADERS

RUMOR

There is a demon who puts wings on certain stories and who
launches them like eagles in the air.
  —ALEXANDRE DUMAS, *La Dame du Monsoreau,* 1849

I know nothing swifter in life than the voice of rumor.
  —PLAUTUS, fragment, c. 200 B.C.

Rumor travels faster, but it don't stay put as long as truth.
  —WILL ROGERS, *The Illiterate Digest,* 1924

Rumor is not always wrong.
  —TACITUS, *Life of Agricola,* c. A.D. 98

RUSSIA   See COMMUNISM; NATIONS

S

SAILING   See NATURE: THE OCEAN; SEAS & SHIPS,
SAILING & BOATING

SAN FRANCISCO   See CITIES

SCOTLAND   See NATIONS

SCIENCE   See also EDUCATION; EVIDENCE;
SCIENCE entries below; UNIVERSE

Enough research will tend to support your theory.
—ANONYMOUS, Murphy's Law of Research, c. 1975

Theory like mist on eyeglasses. Obscure facts.
—EARL DERR BIGGERS, *Charlie Chan in Egypt*, 1935
[Bigger wrote the Chan series of detective stories on which the
movies were based.]

What is now proved was once only imagined.
—WILLIAM BLAKE, *The Marriage
of Heaven and Hell*, 1790–93

It is a capital mistake to theorize before one has data.
—A. CONAN DOYLE, *A Scandal in Bohemia*
in *The Adventures of Sherlock Holmes*, 1894

Most of the fundamental ideas of science are essentially simple, and may, as a rule, be expressed in a language compre-
hensible to everyone.
—ALBERT EINSTEIN (with Leopold Infeld),
The Evolution of Physics, 1938
[See also Einstein at RELIGION for his view of the relation
between science and religion.]

Science must enter into the consciousness of the people.
—ALBERT EINSTEIN, opening day,
World's Fair, Apr. 30, 1939

The whole of science is nothing more than a refinement of everyday thinking.
—ALBERT EINSTEIN, *Out of My Later Years,* 1950
[Similar to an observation by the 19th-century biologist T. H. Huxley: "Science is nothing but trained and organized common sense," *The Method of Zadig.*]

Men love to wonder, and that is the seed of our science.
—RALPH WALDO EMERSON,
Works and Days in *Society and Solitude,* 1870

Science is the knowledge of consequences and the dependence of one fact upon another.
—THOMAS HOBBES, *Leviathan,* 1651

Science says the first word on everything, and the last word on nothing.　　　　　—VICTOR HUGO, d. 1885,
Things of the Infinite: Intellectual Biography

The result, therefore, of our present enquiry is that we find no vestige of a beginning—no prospect of an end.
—JAMES HUTTON, *Theory of the Earth,* 1795
[The last sentence in the original, 1788, version of this work, a sentence called by Stephen Jay Gould "the most famous words ever written by a geologist."]

It is the first duty of a hypothesis to be intelligible.
—T. H. HUXLEY, *Evidence as
to Man's Place in Nature,* 1863

The great tragedy of science—the slaying of a beautiful hypothesis by an ugly fact.
—T. H. HUXLEY, *Biogenesis and Abiogenesis,* 1870

I am sorry to say that there is too much point to the wisecrack that life is extinct on other planets because their scientists were more advanced than ours.
—JOHN F. KENNEDY, speech, Dec. 11, 1959

A first-rate theory predicts; a second-rate theory forbids; a third-rate theory explains after the event.
    —A. I. KITAIGORODSKY, lecture, Amsterdam, Aug. 1975

Science without conscience is but the death of the soul.
        —MONTAIGNE, *Essays*, 1580–88
[Or Rabelais: "Science without conscience is but the ruin of the soul," *Rabelais to the Reader, Gargantua and Pantagruel,* Book I, 1532.]

If I have seen further. . . . it is by standing upon the shoulders of giants.   —ISAAC NEWTON, letter to
Robert Hooke, Feb. 5, 1675/76
[Robert K. Merton's delightful book on this quotation demonstrates that the "shoulders of giants" metaphor was a commonplace of the period. He traces it back to Bernard of Chartres; see under VISION.]

Hypotheses non fingo.
I feign no hypotheses.   —ISAAC NEWTON,
Principia mathematica, scholium, 1687

I know not what I may appear to the world, but to myself I seem to have been only like a boy playing on the seashore, and diverting myself in now and then finding a smoother pebble or a prettier shell than ordinary, whilst the great ocean of truth lay all undiscovered before me.
    —ISAAC NEWTON, d. 1727, quoted in
David Brewster, *Memoirs of Newton,* 1855

Entia non sunt multiplicanda praeter necessitatem.
Entities should not be multiplied unnecessarily.
    —WILLIAM OF OCKHAM, *Quodlibeta,* c. 1320
[This is known as "Ockham's razor." A modern version is the KISS Principle: Keep It Simple, Stupid.]

I am become Death, the shatterer of worlds.
    —J. ROBERT OPPENHEIMER, quoting a
line from the Bhagavad Gita that came to mind
at the test of the first atom bomb, July 16, 1945,
cited in N. P. Davis, *Lawrence and Oppenheimer,* 1969

An important scientific innovation rarely makes its way by gradually winning over and converting its opponents: it rarely happens that Saul becomes Paul. What does happen is that its opponents gradually die out, and that the growing generation is familiarized with the idea from the beginning.
　　　　—MAX PLANCK, *The Philosophy of Physics,* 1936

Science is built of facts the way a house is built of bricks; but an accumulation of facts is no more a science than a pile of bricks is a house.
　　　　—HENRI POINCARÉ, *La Science et l'hypothèse,* 1903

Nature and nature's laws lay hid in night:
God said, "Let Newton be!" and all was light.
　　　　—ALEXANDER POPE, epitaph for
　　　　　　Sir Isaac Newton, d. Mar. 20, 1727

The simplest schoolboy is now familiar with facts for which Archimedes would have sacrificed his life.
　　　　—ERNEST RENAN, *Memories of
　　　　　　Infancy and Youth,* 1883

The work of science is to substitute facts for appearances, and demonstration for impressions.
　　　　—JOHN RUSKIN, *The Stones of Venice,* 1851–53

Even if the open windows of science at first make us shiver . . . in the end, the fresh air brings vigor, and the great spaces have a splendor of their own.
　　　　—BERTRAND RUSSELL, d. 1970, *What I Believe*

Science is always simple and profound. It is only the half truths that are dangerous.
　　　　—GEORGE BERNARD SHAW,
　　　　　　The Doctor's Dilemma, 1906

Science is the great antidote to the poison of enthusiasm and superstition.
　　　　—ADAM SMITH, *Wealth of Nations,* 1776

Religions dissipate like fog, kingdoms vanish, but the works of science remain for all ages.　　　　—ULUGH-BEG, 1529
[Words carved on stone astronomical observatory erected by Ulugh-Beg, Tamerlane's grandson, in Samarkand in 1528–29.]

Science is a cemetery of dead ideas.
—MIGUEL DE UNAMUNO,
The Tragic Sense of Life, 1913

Happy is he who has been able to learn the causes of things.
—VIRGIL, *Georgics,* c. 30 B.C.

Familiar things happen, and mankind does not bother about
them. It requires a very unusual mind to undertake the anal-
ysis of the obvious.   —ALFRED NORTH WHITEHEAD,
Science and the Modern World, 1925

SCIENCE: BIOLOGY

Is man an ape or an angel? Now I am on the side of the
angels.   —BENJAMIN DISRAELI, speech, Nov. 25, 1864

Anatomy is destiny.
—SIGMUND FREUD, *Collected Writings,* Vol. V, 1924

Ex ovo omnia.
Everything from an egg.
—WILLIAM HARVEY, frontispiece,
De generatione animalium, 1651

This survival of the fittest . . . I have here sought to express
in mechanical terms.
—HERBERT SPENCER, *Principles of Biology,* 1864–67
["Survival of the fittest," became identified with Darwinism,
but Darwin himself credited Spencer with having coined it,
noting in his *Origin of the Species* that Spencer's phrase was
"more accurate" than "Natural Selection" and "sometimes
equally convenient," *Origin of the Species,* Book III, 1859.]

SCIENCE: DISCOVERY   See also EFFORT (Tennyson);
   & EXPLORATION   SCIENCE: TECHNOLOGY

Eureka!
I have found it! —ARCHIMEDES, 3rd cent. B.C., quoted in
Vitruvius Polla, *De architectura,*
c. 1st cent. B.C.–1st cent. A.D.
[What he had found is what is now called Archimedes' principle, which relates the density of a body to the quantity of fluid
it will displace. This enabled him to solve a problem posed,

according to tradition, by King Hiero II: was the king's crown pure gold or a gold and silver alloy?]

That's one small step for [a] man, one giant leap for mankind. —NEIL A. ARMSTRONG, disembarking from the
Eagle moon lander, July 20, 1969, mission of Apollo 11 ["A man" is the official version; but he said "for man," according to recordings of the first manned landing on the moon.]

We shall not cease from exploration
And the end of all our exploring
Will be to arrive where we started
And know the place for the first time.
—T. S. ELIOT, *Four Quartets: Little Gidding*, 1940

Then I felt like some watcher of the skies
When a new planet swims into his ken;
Or like stout Cortez, when with eagle eyes
He star'd at the Pacific—and all his men
Looked at each other with a wild surmise—
Silent, upon a peak in Darien.
—JOHN KEATS, *On First Looking
into Chapman's Homer* in *Poems*, 1817

Doctor Livingstone, I presume?
—SIR HENRY MORTON STANLEY,
on finding David Livingstone at Lake Tanganyika,
Nov. 10, 1871; cited in Stanley's book
How I Found Livingstone, 1872

It was wonderful to find America, but it would have been more wonderful to miss it.
—MARK TWAIN, *Pudd'nhead Wilson's
Calendar* in *Pudd'nhead Wilson*, 1894

SCIENCE: MATHEMATICS & STATISTICS

See also UNIVERSE (Galileo)

Multiplication is vexation,
Division is as bad;
The Rule of three doth puzzle me,
And Practice drives me mad.
—ANONYMOUS, c. 16th cent.

Mathematics is the door and the key to the sciences.
—ROGER BACON, *Opus Majus,* 1267–68

Numbers are intellectual witnesses that belong only to mankind.
—HONORÉ DE BALZAC, *Louis Lambert,* 1832–33

Ghosts of departed quantities.
—GEORGE BERKELEY, *The Analyst,* 1734
[Bishop Berkeley was describing Newton's infinitesimals used in the calculus.]

A witty statesman said, you might prove anything by figures.
—THOMAS CARLYLE, *Chartism,* 1839

There are three kinds of lies: lies, damned lies, and statistics.
—BENJAMIN DISRAELI, d. 1881, quoted in
Mark Twain, *Autobiography,* 1924
[Twain's attribution may or may not be correct; no one knows.]

I don't believe in mathematics.
—ALBERT EINSTEIN, d. 1955, quoted in
Carl Seelig, *Albert Einstein,* 1924

It is here [in mathematics] that the artist has the fullest scope of his imagination.
—HAVELOCK ELLIS, *The Dance of Life,* 1923

The mathematician has reached the highest rung on the ladder of human thought.
—*Ibid.*

There is no royal road to geometry.
—EUCLID, 4th cent. B.C., quoted
in Proclus, *Commentaries,* c. A.D. 450

It has been said that figures rule the world. Maybe. But I am sure that figures show us whether it is being run well or badly.
—GOETHE, quoted in Johann Peter Eckermann,
Conversations with Goethe, 1836

Three quarks for Muster Mark!
—JAMES JOYCE, *Finnegans Wake,* 1939
[This is the source of Murray Gell-Mann's term *quark* for a basic, irreducible unit of matter, introduced 1963.]

God made the integers, all the rest is the work of man.
　　　　　—LEOPOLD KRONECKER, d. 1891, *Jahrsberichte
　　　　　　　der Deutsche Mathematiker Vereinigung,* Book 2
[Einstein, however, maintained: "The series of integers is obviously an invention of the human mind, a self-created tool, which simplifies the ordering of certain sensory experiences," cited in *The New York Times,* Feb. 10, 1998.]

I tell them that if they will occupy themselves with the study of mathematics, they will find in it the best remedy against the lusts of the flesh.
　　　　　—THOMAS MANN, *The Magic Mountain,* 1924

To understand God's thoughts, we must study statistics, for these are the measure of his purpose.
　　　　　—FLORENCE NIGHTINGALE, quoted in
　　　　　　　K. Pearson, *Life . . . of Francis Galton,* 1914

Let no one ignorant of geometry enter my door.
　　　　　—PLATO, *The Republic,* 4th cent. B.C.
[Plato's interest, however, had its limits; see below.]

The ludicrous state of solid geometry made me pass over this branch.　　　　　　　　　　　　　　　—*Ibid.*

Order is heaven's first law.
　　　　　—ALEXANDER POPE, *An Essay on Man,* 1733–34

All is number.　—PYTHAGORAS, attributed, 6th cent. B.C.

Mathematics possesses not only truth, but supreme beauty—a beauty cold and austere, like that of sculpture.
　　　　　—BERTRAND RUSSELL, *The Study of
　　　　　　　Mathematics* in *Mysticism and Logic,* 1918

There is divinity in odd numbers.
　　　　　—SHAKESPEARE, *The Merry Wives of Windsor,* V, i

Prayers for the condemned man will be offered on an adding machine. Numbers constitute the only universal language.
　　　　　—NATHANAEL WEST, *Miss Lonelyhearts,* 1933

The science of pure mathematics . . . may claim to be the most original creation of the human spirit.
—ALFRED NORTH WHITEHEAD,
Science and the Modern World, 1925

SCIENCE: PHYSICS & COSMOLOGY
See also CREATION, DIVINE;
NATURE: THE HEAVENS,
THE SKY; UNIVERSE

More is different.   —PHILIP W. ANDERSON, c. 1975,
quoted in *The New York Times,* May 6, 1997
[Anderson, who won the 1977 Nobel Prize in Physics, was commenting here on complex systems.]

Laws of thermodynamics: 1) You cannot win. 2) You cannot break even. 3) You cannot get out of the game.
—ANONYMOUS, cited in Alan L. Mackie, ed.,
The Harvest of a Quiet Eye, 1977
[Similarly, the anonymous Murphy's Law of Thermodynamics is: Things get worse under pressure. For the original Murphy's Law, see Murphy at TROUBLE.]

Give me a firm spot on which to stand, and I will move the earth.   —ARCHIMEDES, 3rd cent. B.C., commenting
on the principle of the lever, quoted in
Pappus of Alexandria, *Collectio,* c. 3rd cent. A.D.

If you aren't confused by quantum physics, then you haven't really understood it.   —NIELS BOHR, d. 1962, saying
[Bohr was the prime creator of quantum theory.]

Nothing exists except atoms and empty space; everything else is opinion.   —DEMOCRITUS, 5th cent. B.C., fragment

Everything existing in the universe is the fruit of chance and necessity.   —DEMOCRITUS, 5th cent. B.C., fragment

$E = mc^2$
Energy equals mass times the speed of light squared.
—ALBERT EINSTEIN, *Ist die Trägheit eines
Körpes von Seinem Energieinhalt Abhängig?*
in *Annalen de Physik,* Vol. XVIII, Series 4, 1905
[The formula as shown above is a slight restatement of the

original formula: $m = L/c^2$ where L equals energy in the form of radiation given off by a body. The sentence expressing the formula was: "If a body gives off the energy L in the form of radiation, its mass diminishes by L/c^2." The title of the paper posed the question: "Is the Inertia of a Body Dependent on Its Energy Content?"]

God does not play dice with the universe.
  —ALBERT EINSTEIN, d. 1955, saying, attributed
[Philip Frank included a qualified version of the quote in *Einstein: His Life and Times* (1947): "I shall never believe that God plays dice with the world." Einstein definitely objected to the random element at the heart of modern quantum physics, especially Werner Heisenberg's uncertainty principle: the energy and position of a subatomic particle cannot both be known simultaneously. Niels Bohr, the father of quantum physics, responded to Einstein's complaint: "Nor is it our business to prescribe to God how He should run the world." See also Stephen Hawking's reaction below, and the Einstein quote at GOD.]

Physical concepts are free creations of the human mind, and are not, however it may seem, uniquely determined by the external world.
  —ALBERT EINSTEIN, *The Evolution of Physics*, 1938

The world we live in is but thickened light.
  —RALPH WALDO EMERSON, *The Scholar*, 1883

God not only plays dice, he also sometimes throws the dice where they cannot be seen.
  —STEPHEN HAWKING, in *Nature* 257, 1975
[A comment on Einstein's famous dice dictum, see above.]

Space isn't remote at all. It's only an hour's drive away if your car could go straight upwards.
  —FRED HOYLE, in the *Observer*, Sept. 9, 1979

I demonstrate by means of philosophy that the earth is round, and is inhabited on all sides; that it is insignificantly small, and is borne through the stars.
  —JOHANNES KEPLER, *Astronomia nova*, 1609

Nothing puzzles me more than time and space; and yet nothing troubles me less as I never think about them.
> CHARLES LAMB, letter to
> Thomas Manning, Jan. 2, 1806

The more important fundamental laws and facts of physical science have all been discovered, and these are now so firmly established that the possibility of their ever being supplanted in consequence of new discoveries is exceedingly remote.
> —ALBERT ABRAHAM MICHELSON,
> dedication ceremony, Ryerson Physical Laboratory,
> University of Chicago, 1894

[The work of Nobel Prize-winner Michelson was a bridge to 20th-century physics.]

Every body continues in its state of rest, or of uniform motion in a right [straight] line, unless it is compelled to change that state by forces impressed upon it.
> —ISAAC NEWTON, first law of motion,
> *Principia mathematica*, 1687

To every action there is always opposed an equal reaction.
> —ISAAC NEWTON, third law of motion, *Ibid.*

We have no right to assume that any physical laws exist, or if they have existed up to now, that they will continue to exist in a similar manner in the future.
> —MAX PLANCK, *The Universe in
> the Light of Modern Physics*, 1931

Astronomy compels the soul to look upwards and leads us from this world to another.
> —PLATO, *The Republic*, 4th cent. B.C.

Natura vacuum abhorret.
Nature abhors a vacuum.
> —RABELAIS, *Gargantua and Pantagruel*, 1532–52

[He is quoting a Latin proverb. Another citation often given is Spinoza, *Ethics* (1677).]

Every cause produces more than one effect.
> —HERBERT SPENCER, *On Progress: Its Law
> and Cause* in *Essays on Education*, 1861

Water is the principle, or the element, of all things. All things are water.
> —THALES OF MILETUS, 7th–6th cent. B.C.,
> quoted in Plutarch, *Placita philosophorum*, c. A.D. 100

There is nothing in the world except empty curved space.
> —JOHN WHEELER, 1957, quoted in
> *New Scientist*, Sept. 26, 1974

SCIENCE: PSYCHOLOGY   See also MADNESS;
SELF-KNOWLEDGE;
SLEEP & DREAMS (Talmud)

Of course "behaviorism" works. So does torture.
> —W. H. AUDEN, *Behaviorism* in *A Certain World*, 1970

The true science and study of man is man.
> —PIERRE CHARRON, Preface, *De Traité
> de la sagesse*, 1601

It might be said of psychoanalysis that if you give it your little finger, it will soon have your whole hand.
> —SIGMUND FREUD,
> *Introductory Lectures on Psychoanalysis*, 1916–17

[It has also been said of psychoanalysis that it is "the treatment of the id by the odd" (author not known). And Viennese writer Karl Kraus called it "the disease of which it purports to be the cure."]

Freud is the father of psychoanalysis. It has no mother.
> —GERMAINE GREER, *The Female Eunuch*, 1970

I am still more frightened by the fearless power in the eyes of my fellow psychiatrists than by the powerless fear in the eyes of their patients.
> —R. D. LAING, *Wisdom, Madness, and Folly:
> The Making of a Psychiatrist*, 1985

Dreams are the true interpreters of our inclinations; but there is art required to sort and understand them.
> —MONTAIGNE, *Essays*, 1580–88

Psychology which explains everything explains nothing, and we are still in doubt.   —MARIANNE MOORE,
> *Marriage* in *Collected Poems*, 1951

MACBETH: Canst thou not minister to a mind diseased,
Pluck from memory a rooted sorrow,
Raze out the written troubles of the brain?
DOCTOR: Therein the patient
Must minister to himself.
—SHAKESPEARE, *Macbeth*, V, iii

If you talk to God, you are praying; if God talks to you, you have schizophrenia.
—THOMAS SZASZ, *Schizophrenia* in *The Second Sin*, 1973

SCIENCE: TECHNOLOGY   See also MEDIA;
RESPONSIBILITY (Tom Lehrer); SCIENCE;
SCIENCE: DISCOVERY & EXPLORATION

Garbage in, garbage out.
—ANONYMOUS, on why computer findings are sometimes unsatisfactory

To err is human, but to really foul things up requires a computer.   —ANONYMOUS

Mr. Watson, come here. I want to see you.
—ALEXANDER GRAHAM BELL, to his assistant, Thomas A. Watson, first telephone communication, Mar. 10, 1876

And was Jerusalem builded here
Among those dark Satanic Mills?
—WILLIAM BLAKE, prefatory poem, *Milton*, 1809

The "control of nature" is a phrase conceived in arrogance, born of the Neanderthal age of biology and the convenience of man.   —RACHEL CARSON, *Silent Spring*, 1962

Machines, from the Maxim gun to the computer, are for the most part means by which a minority can keep free men in subjection.   —SIR KENNETH CLARK, *Civilization*, 1970

Any sufficiently advanced technology is indistinguishable from magic.
—ARTHUR C. CLARKE, *Profiles of the Future*, 1962

If true computer music were ever written, it would only be listened to by other computers.
—MICHAEL CRICHTON, *Electronic Life: How to Think about Computers,* 1983

For a successful technology, reality must take precedence over public relations, for Nature cannot be fooled.
—RICHARD P. FEYNMAN, appendix to presidential commission report, June 9, 1986, on the explosion of the space shuttle *Challenger* following a cold-weather lift-off, Jan. 28, 1986
[Professor Feynman's most famous demonstration of reality vs. public relations came during the televised hearings on the cause of the *Challenger* disaster. Interrupting the ponderous, defensive proceedings, he put a sample of the rubber used for the booster rockets' O-ring seals into a glass of ice water, then clamped the sample, and released it; the rubber had lost its resilience. A month later NASA conceded that joint failure was the most likely cause of the explosion.]

Technology . . . the knack of so arranging the world that we don't have to experience it.
—MAX FRISCH, quoted in Daniel J. Boorstin, *The Image,* 1961

Is it a fact, or have I dreamt it—that, by means of electricity, the world of matter has become a great nerve, vibrating thousands of miles in a breathless point of time?
—NATHANIEL HAWTHORNE, *The House of the Seven Gables,* 1851

Have you heard of the wonderful one-hoss shay,
That was built in such a logical way
It ran a hundred years to a day.
—OLIVER WENDELL HOLMES, SR., *The Deacon's Masterpiece* in *The Autocrat of the Breakfast Table,* 1858

The automobile changed our dress, manners, social customs, vacation habits, the shape of our cities, consumer purchasing patterns, common tastes, and positions in intercourse.
—JOHN KEATS, *The Insolent Chariots,* 1958

Our scientific power has outrun our spiritual power. We have guided missiles and misguided men.
—MARTIN LUTHER KING, JR.,
Strength to Love, 1963

To George F. Babbitt . . . his motor-car was poetry and tragedy, love and heroism.
—SINCLAIR LEWIS, *Babbitt,* 1922

It is critical vision alone which can mitigate the unimpeded operation of the automatic.
—MARSHALL McLUHAN, *The Mechanical Bride,* 1951

The electric age . . . establishes a global network that has much the character of our central nervous system.
—MARSHALL McLUHAN, *Understanding Media,* 1964

The car has become the carapace, the protective and aggressive shell, of urban and suburban man.   *—Ibid.*

What hath God wrought!   —SAMUEL F. B. MORSE, first
electric telegraph message, May 24, 1844
[Morse was quoting the Bible, *Numbers* 23:23; he had asked Annie Ellsworth, daughter of the U.S. Commissioner of Patents, to provide a suitable message for him, and the Biblical text was her suggestion.]

Machines are worshipped because they are beautiful and valued because they confer power; they are hated because they are hideous and loathed because they impose slavery.
—BERTRAND RUSSELL, *Machines and
Emotions* in *Sceptical Essays,* 1928

The machine does not isolate man from the great problems of nature but plunges him more deeply into them.
—ANTOINE DE SAINT-EXUPÉRY,
Wind, Sand, and Stars, 1939

The machine yes the machine
never wastes anybody's time
never watches the foreman
never talks back.
—CARL SANDBURG, *The People, Yes,* 1936

The real problem is not whether machines think, but whether men do.
    —B. F. SKINNER, *Contingencies of Reinforcement*, 1969

Men have become the tools of their tools.
        —HENRY DAVID THOREAU, *Walden*, 1854

Everything in life is somewhere else, and you get there in a car.   —E. B. WHITE, *Fro-Joy* in *One Man's Meat*, 1944
[For E. B. White on television, see under MEDIA.]

In the past, human life was lived in a bullock cart; in the future, it will be lived in an aeroplane; and the change of speed amounts to a difference in quality.
        —ALFRED NORTH WHITEHEAD,
        Science and the Modern World, 1925

SCOTLAND   See NATIONS

SEAS & SHIPS,   See also NATURE: THE OCEAN
SAILING & BOATING

They that go down to the sea in ships, that do business in
    great waters;
These see the works of the Lord, and his wonders in the
    deep.   —BIBLE, *Psalms* 107:23–24

What is a ship but a prison?   —ROBERT BURTON,
        The Anatomy of Melancholy, 1621–51

Water, water, every where,
And all the boards did shrink;
Water, water, every where,
Nor any drop to drink.
        —SAMUEL TAYLOR COLERIDGE,
        The Rime of the Ancient Mariner, 1798

There is nothing more enticing, disenchanting, and enslaving than the life at sea.   —JOSEPH CONRAD, *Lord Jim*, 1900

The life of a sailor is very unhealthy.
        —FRANCIS GALTON, *Inquiries into*
        Human Faculty and Its Development, 1883

There is nothing—absolutely nothing—half so much worth doing as simply messing about in boats.
　　　　　　　　　　　　　　　　—KENNETH GRAHAME,
　　　　　　　　　　　　　　　　The Wind in the Willows, 1908

He that will learn to pray, let him go to sea.
　　　　　　　—GEORGE HERBERT, *Jacula Prudentum*, 1651

His heart was mailed with oak and triple brass who first committed a frail ship to the wild seas.
　　　　　　　　　　　　　　—HORACE, *Odes*, 33–15 B.C.

Ships at a distance have every man's wish on board.
　　　　　　　　　　　　　　　　—ZORA NEALE HURSTON,
　　　　　　　　　　　　　　　　Their Eyes Were Watching God, 1937

Being in a ship is being in jail, with the chance of being drowned.　　　　　　—SAMUEL JOHNSON, Mar. 1759,
　　　　　　　　quoted in James Boswell, *Life of Johnson*, 1791

The Owl and the Pussycat went to sea
In a beautiful pea-green boat,
They took some honey, and plenty of money,
Wrapped up in a five-pound note.
　　　　　　—EDWARD LEAR, *The Owl and the Pussycat*, 1871

There is nothing so desperately monotonous as the sea, and I no longer wonder at the cruelty of pirates.
　　　　　　—JAMES RUSSELL LOWELL, *Fireside Travels*, 1864

I must down to the seas again, to the lonely sea and the sky,
And all I ask is a tall ship and a star to steer her by
And the wheel's kick and the wind's song and the white
　　sail's shaking,
And a grey mist on the sea's face and a grey dawn breaking.
　　　　　　　　　　—JOHN MASEFIELD, *Sea Fever*, 1902

Call me Ishmael.
　　　—HERMAN MELVILLE, opening line, *Moby-Dick*, 1851
[In the Bible, Ishmael is the son of Abraham and the bondservant Hagar, and the older half-brother of Isaac. He was disinherited and sent away, and the name came to stand for an outcast. See FAMILY, the note at Tolstoy, for other first lines.]

There is one knows not what sweet mystery about this sea, whose gently awful stirrings seem to speak of some hidden soul beneath.   —*Ibid.*
[See Melville at TRAVEL for sailing forbidden seas.]

A man who is not afraid of the sea will soon be drowned.
                    —J. M. SYNGE, *The Aran Islands,* 1907

SEASONS IN LIFE   See GENERATIONS; LIFE

SEASONS OF THE YEAR   See NATURE: SEASONS

SECRETS   See RUMOR; SECURITY

SECURITY   See also PRIVACY (Elizabeth I); TALK

Let not thy left hand know what thy right hand doeth.
                              —BIBLE, *Matthew* 6:3
[More at CHARITY: PHILANTHROPY.]

It is good to keep close the secret of a king.
                              —BIBLE, *Tobit* 12:7

In time of war, when truth is so precious, it must be attended by a bodyguard of lies.
          —WINSTON CHURCHILL, remark at Teheran, 1943
["Bodyguard of Lies" was used as the title of Anthony Cave-Brown's 1975 book on deception in World War II.]

What one man can invent another can discover.
              —A. CONAN DOYLE, *The Adventure of the Dancing Men* in *The Return of Sherlock Holmes,* 1905
[The speaker is Sherlock Holmes.]

Three may keep a secret, if two of them are dead.
                              —BENJAMIN FRANKLIN,
                         Poor Richard's Almanac, 1735
[Proverbial.]

Quis custodiet ipsos custodes?
Who will guard the guardians themselves?
                       —JUVENAL, *Satires,* c. A.D. 100
[Juvenal, in this sixth satire, was referring to guards hired by jealous husbands. But the question has usually been applied to

government officials—for example, it is the opening line of the 1987 Tower Commission Report on the so-called Iran-Contra scandal in the administration of Pres. Ronald Reagan.]

Thou wilt not utter what thou dost not know.
                    —SHAKESPEARE, *Henry IV, Part I*, II, iii
[Hotspur is explaining to his wife why he will not tell her his plans for an armed rebellion.]

ALBANY: . . . You may fear too far.
GONERIL: Safer than trust too far.
                    —SHAKESPEARE, *King Lear*, I, iv

SELF   See also HONESTY & SINCERITY;
                        INDIVIDUALITY; PRIDE & VANITY;
                                    SELF entries below

Resolve to be thyself: and know that he
Who finds himself, loses his misery.
                    —MATTHEW ARNOLD, *Self-Dependence*, 1852

The kingdom of God is within you.   —BIBLE, *Luke* 17:21

Angels can fly because they take themselves lightly.
                    —G. K. CHESTERTON, *Orthodoxy*, 1908

The man who masters himself is delivered from the force that binds all creatures.
                    —GOETHE, *Die Geheimnisse*, 1808–32

What other dungeon is so dark as one's own heart! What jailer so inexorable as one's self!
                    —NATHANIEL HAWTHORNE,
                    The House of the Seven Gables, 1851

The least pain in our little finger gives more concern and uneasiness than the destruction of millions of our fellow beings.   —WILLIAM HAZLITT, d. 1830,
                    Dr. Channing in *American Literature*

There is only one corner of the universe you can be certain of improving, and that's your own self.
                    —ALDOUS HUXLEY, *Time Must Have a Stop*, 1945

Self-love is the greatest of all flatterers.
—LA ROCHEFOUCAULD, *Maxims,* 1678

He that would govern others first should be
The master of himself.
—PHILIP MASSINGER, *The Bondman,* 1624

The greatest thing in the world is to know how to belong
to oneself.
—MONTAIGNE, "To the Reader," *Essays,* 1580–88

The self is hateful. —PASCAL, *Pensées,* 1670

The worst of all deceptions is self-deception.
—PLATO, *Cratylus,* 4th cent. B.C.

To understand oneself is the classic form of consolation; to
elude oneself is the romantic.
—GEORGE SANTAYANA, *The Genteel Tradition
in American Philosophy* in *Winds of Doctrine,* 1912

Our remedies oft in ourselves do lie.
—SHAKESPEARE, *All's Well That Ends Well,* I, i

This above all: To thine own self be true,
And it must follow, as the night the day,
Thou canst not then be false to any man.
—SHAKESPEARE, *Hamlet,* I, iii

My closest relation is myself.
—TERENCE, *The Woman of Andros,* 166 B.C.

I celebrate myself, and sing myself.
—WALT WHITMAN, *Song of Myself*
in *Leaves of Grass,* 1855
[For Whitman on self-contradiction, see under CONSISTENCY.]

To love oneself is the beginning of a life-long romance.
—OSCAR WILDE, *An Ideal Husband,* 1895

Men can starve from a lack of self-realization as much as
they can from a lack of bread.
—RICHARD WRIGHT, *Native Son,* 1940

SELF-CONFIDENCE   See also AMBITION;
                                     BOLDNESS & INITIATIVE;
                                     PRIDE & VANITY

Who has self-confidence will lead the rest.
                              —HORACE, *Epistles,* 20–8 B.C.

The bullet that will kill me is not yet cast.
                              —NAPOLEON BONAPARTE,
                                     attributed remark from 1814

I bear a charmed life.   —SHAKESPEARE, *Macbeth,* V, viii

They can do all because they think they can.
                              —VIRGIL, *Aeneid,* c. 19 B.C.

SELF-INTEREST See also CAPITALISM; EXPEDIENCY

Greed is healthy.
                    —IVAN BOESKY, speech at the University
        of California Business School in Berkeley, May 18, 1986
[Financier Boesky was later indicted for fraud and jailed. He
was the model for the Gordon Gekko character in the 1987
movie *Wall Street,* directed and co-authored by Oliver Stone.
Gekko tells stockholders: "Greed, for lack of a better word, is
good. Greed is right. Greed works."]

Cui bono?
To whose profit?   —CICERO, *Pro Milone,* 52 B.C.
[Cicero was quoting the oft-repeated dictum of a famous judge,
L. Cassius Longinus. Lenin posed the same question: "Who
benefits from this?"]

Everyone believes that what suits him is the right thing to
do.   —GOETHE, *Torquato Tasso,* 1790

If I am not for myself, who is for me?
                              —HILLEL "THE ELDER,"
                                Pirqe Aboth, c. 30 B.C.–A.D. 9

It makes a difference whose ox is gored.
                    —MARTIN LUTHER, 16th cent., in *Works,* 1854

SELF-KNOWLEDGE See also SCIENCE: PSYCHOLOGY

Gnóthi seautón.
Know thyself.   —ANONYMOUS, inscription at the
                               temple of Apollo at Delphi
[An axiom of ancient wisdom, repeated often, although chal-
lenged in a fragment from Menander, 4th century B.C.: "This
'Know Yourself' is a silly proverb in some ways; / To know
the man next door is a much more useful rule."]

The questions which one asks oneself begin, at last, to illu-
minate the world, and become one's key to the experience
of others.
        —JAMES BALDWIN, *Nobody Knows My Name*, 1961

O wad some Pow'r the giftie gie us
To see oursels as others see us!
                —ROBERT BURNS, *To a Louse*, 1786

To know oneself, one should assert oneself.
            —ALBERT CAMUS, *Notebooks, 1935–42*, 1962

The humble knowledge of thyself is a surer way to God
than the deepest search after science.
            —THOMAS À KEMPIS, *Imitation of Christ*, c. 1420

Learn what you are and be such.
                        —PINDAR, *Odes*, 5th cent. B.C.

Know then thyself, presume not God to scan;
The proper study of mankind is man.
            —ALEXANDER POPE, *An Essay on Man*, 1733–34

We know what we are, but know not what we may be.
                —SHAKESPEARE, *Hamlet*, IV, v

To know oneself is not necessarily to improve oneself.
                —PAUL VALÉRY, *Choses tuées*, 1930

To enter one's own self, it is necessary to go armed to the
teeth.
        —PAUL VALÉRY, *Quelques pensées de Monsieur Teste*

SELF-PROMOTION   See PUBLICITY &
                                              PUBLIC RELATIONS

SELF-RELIANCE   See also BOLDNESS & INITIATIVE;
           FATE; INDIVIDUALITY; RESPONSIBILITY;
                          WORK & WORKERS

The gods help them that help themselves.
           —AESOP, *Hercules and the Waggoner,* 6th cent. B.C.
[Also in Benjamin Franklin's *Poor Richard's Almanac.*]

If the hill will not come to Mahomet, Mahomet will come
to the hill.
           —FRANCIS BACON, *Of Boldness* in *Essays,* 1625

Put your trust in God, my boys, and keep your powder dry!
           —VALENTINE BLACKER, *Oliver Cromwell's Advice*
                     in Edward Hayes, *Ballads of Ireland,* 1856
[The ballad was based on Cromwell's order to the Roundhead
army prior to the battle of Marston Moor, July 2, 1644, the first
major victory by Parliamentarian forces over the Royalists.]

He was a self-made man who owed his lack of success to
nobody.   —JOSEPH HELLER, *Catch-22,* 1956

I am the master of my fate;
I am the captain of my soul.
           —W. E. HENLEY, *Echoes,* 1888, *Invictus.*
                     In Memoriam R. T. Hamilton Bruce

Never depend on anyone except yourself.
                     —LA FONTAINE, *Fables,* 1668
[And also, "Help yourself and heaven will help you."]

If you want a thing done well, do it yourself.
           —NAPOLEON BONAPARTE, *Maxims,* 1804–15

SELF-RIGHTEOUSNESS   See also VIRTUE

Righteous people terrify me. . . . Virtue is its own
punishment.   —ANEURIN BEVAN, d. 1960, quoted in
                     Michael Foot, *Aneurin Bevan,* 1962

Stand by yourself, come not near me: for I am holier than thou. —BIBLE, *Isaiah* 65:5

God, I thank thee, that I am not as other men are. —BIBLE, *Luke* 18:11

God hates those who praise themselves. —ST. CLEMENT, *First Epistle to the Corinthians,* c.88–A.D. 97

Moral indignation is in most cases two percent moral, forty-eight percent indignation, and fifty percent envy. —VITTORIO DE SICA, quoted in the *Observer,* 1961

The louder he talked of his honor, the faster we counted our spoons. —RALPH WALDO EMERSON, *Worship* in *The Conduct of Life,* 1860

SEX & SENSUALITY   See also HEDONISM; LOVE; LOVE, EXPRESSIONS OF; MARRIAGE; SIN, VICE, & NAUGHTINESS

I made love and was happy. —JOSEPH ADDISON, *The Spectator,* Aug. 27, 1711

Is sex dirty? Only if it's done right. —WOODY ALLEN, screenplay, *Everything You Always Wanted to Know About Sex,* 1972

Post coitum omne animal triste.
After coition every animal is sad. —ANONYMOUS (LATIN SAYING)

Bed is the poor man's opera. —ANONYMOUS (ITALIAN PROVERB), quoted in Aldous Huxley, *Heaven and Hell,* 1956
[See also Baudelaire, below.]

To many, total abstinence is easier than perfect moderation. —ST. AUGUSTINE, *On the Good of Marriages,* A.D. 401
[On the other hand, see Augustine under PRAYERS.]

Sexuality is the lyricism of the masses. —CHARLES BAUDELAIRE, *Mon coeur mis à nu,* 1887

Men make love more intensely at twenty, but make love better, however, at thirty.
> —CATHERINE THE GREAT, letter to Voltaire,
> in Evdokimov, ed., *The Complete
> Works of Catherine II,* 1893

The pleasure is momentary, the position ridiculous, and the expense damnable.   —EARL OF CHESTERFIELD,
> attributed, mid-18th cent.

Those pleasures so lightly called physical.
> —COLETTE, *Mélanges,* 1939

For goodness' sake, if the English hear that Palmerston still has a mistress at eighty, they will make him a dictator!
> —BENJAMIN DISRAELI, reported response
> when advised that his rival, Lord Palmerston,
> might be ruined as a result of a sex scandal, c. 1864

License my roving hands, and let them go,
Before, behind, between, above, below.
> —JOHN DONNE, *To His Mistress
> Going to Bed,* c. 1591–1601

I am the Love that dare not speak its name.
> —ALFRED DOUGLAS, *Two Loves,* 1894

[Lord Alfred was Oscar Wilde's young friend. The poem would have been totally forgotten by now if the prosecution had not introduced it into evidence in Wilde's trial on Apr. 30, 1895. The charge was "gross indecency" (in the words of the relevant statute) with another male. The trial ended with a hung jury but Wilde was convicted on retrial.]

Sex lies at the root of life, and we can never learn to reverence life until we know how to understand sex.
> —HAVELOCK ELLIS,
> *Studies in the Psychology of Sex,* 1897–1928

In your sex life, preserve purity as far as you can before marriage, and if you indulge, take only those privileges that are lawful. However, do not make yourself offensive or censorious to those who do indulge, and do not make frequent mention of the fact that you do not yourself indulge.
> —EPICTETUS, *Discourses,* c. A.D. 100

If your life at night is good, you think you have everything.
—EURIPIDES, *Medea*, 431 B.C.

While a person does not give up on sex, sex does not give up on the person. —GABRIEL GARCÍA MÁRQUEZ, *The New York Times*, Apr. 7, 1985

That nameless charm, with a strong magnetism, which can only be called "It." —ELINOR GLYN, *It*, 1927 [More at CHARM.]

But did thee feel the earth move?
—ERNEST HEMINGWAY, *For Whom the Bell Tolls*, 1940

People will insist . . . on treating the mons Veneris as though it were Mount Everest.
—ALDOUS HUXLEY, *Eyeless in Gaza*, 1936

his heart was going like mad and yes I said yes I will Yes.
—JAMES JOYCE, the ending, *Ulysses*, 1922

A man who has not passed through the inferno of his passions has never overcome them.
—CARL JUNG, *Memories, Dreams, Reflections*, 1962

Most mothers think that to keep young people away from lovemaking it is enough never to speak of it in their presence.
—MARIE MADELEINE DE LA FAYETTE, *La Princesse de Clèves*, 1678

If we resist our passions, it is due more to their weakness than our own strength.
—LA ROCHEFOUCAULD, *Maxims*, 1678

Sex and beauty are inseparable, like life and consciousness.
—D. H. LAWRENCE, *Sex Versus Loneliness*, 1930

You mustn't force sex to do the work of love or love to do the work of sex. —MARY McCARTHY, *The Group*, 1963

Contraceptives should be used on all conceivable occasions.
—SPIKE MILLIGAN, *The Last Goon Show of All*, 1972

The daughter-in-law of Pythagoras said that a woman who goes to bed with a man ought to lay aside her modesty with her skirt, and put it on again with her petticoat.

—MONTAIGNE, *Essays,* 1580–88

Whether a pretty woman grants or withholds her favors, she always likes to be asked for them.

—OVID, *The Art of Love,* c. 2 B.C.

Men seldom make passes
At girls who wear glasses.   —DOROTHY PARKER,
News Item in *Enough Rope,* 1927

Sex Is Never an Emergency.   —ELAINE PIERSON, title of
guide for college students, c. 1970

Civilized people cannot fully satisfy their sexual instinct without love.

—BERTRAND RUSSELL, *Marriage and Morals,* 1929

As I grow older and older
And totter towards the tomb,
I find I care less and less
Who goes to bed with whom.

—DOROTHY SAYERS, *That's Why I Never
Read Modern Novels* in Janet Hitchman,
Such a Strange Lady, 1975

The expense of spirit in a waste of shame
Is lust in action.   —SHAKESPEARE, sonnet 129

Is it not strange that desire should so many years outlive performance.   —SHAKESPEARE, *Henry IV, Part II,* II, iv

She is a woman, therefore may be wooed;
She is a woman, therefore may be won.

—SHAKESPEARE, *Titus Andronicus,* II, i

There are worse occupations in this world than feeling a woman's pulse.

—LAURENCE STERNE, *A Sentimental Journey,* 1768

Sex contains all, bodies, souls,
Meanings, proofs, purities, delicacies, results, promulgations,
All hopes, benefactions, bestowals, all the passions, loves,
   beauties, delights of the earth,
All the governments, judges, gods.
      —WALT WHITMAN, *A Woman Waits for Me,* 1856

Young men want to be faithful, and are not; old men want
to be faithless, and cannot.
      —OSCAR WILDE, *The Picture of Dorian Gray,* 1891

A laugh at sex is a laugh at destiny.
      —THORNTON WILDER, *The Journals
      of Thornton Wilder,* 1939–61

SHIPS   See SEAS & SHIPS, SAILING & BOATING

SICKNESS   See ILLNESS & REMEDIES

SILENCE   See also SECURITY; TALK

The silent dog is the first to bite.
      —ANONYMOUS (GERMAN PROVERB)

Silence is the virtue of fools.
      —FRANCIS BACON, *De Dignatate et
      augmentis scientiarum,* 1623

Drawing on my fine command of language, I said nothing.
  —ROBERT BENCHLEY, *Chips off the Old Benchley,* 1949

Try as we may to make a silence, we cannot.
      —JOHN CAGE, *Silence,* 1961

Speech is of time, silence is of eternity.
      —THOMAS CARLYLE, *Sartor Resartus,* 1833–34
[Similarly, Carlyle wrote, "Silence is deep as eternity; speech is
shallow as time," *Sir Walter Scott* in *Critical and Miscellaneous
Essays,* 1839–57.]

Years of close familiarity rendered silence congenial.
      —COLETTE, *Cheri,* 1920

Blessed is the man who, having nothing to say, abstains from giving in words evidence of the fact.
—GEORGE ELIOT, *Impressions of Theophrastus Such*, 1879

Silence gives consent.
—OLIVER GOLDSMITH, *The Good-Natur'd Man*, 1768

The silence of the mind is the true religious mind, and the silence of the gods is the silence of the earth.
—KRISHNAMURTI, d. 1986, quoted in *The Second Penguin Krishnamurti Reader*, 1991

A sage thing is timely silence, and better than any speech.
—PLUTARCH, *The Education of Children*, c. A.D. 100

I often regret that I have spoken; never that I have been silent. —PUBLILIUS SYRUS, *Moral Sayings*, 1st cent. B.C.

An absolute silence leads to sadness: it is the image of death.
—JEAN JACQUES ROUSSEAU, *Reveries of a Solitary Walker*, 1782

Wise men say nothing in dangerous times.
—JOHN SELDEN, *Wisdom* in *Table Talk*, 1689

The silence often of pure innocence
Persuades when speaking fails.
—SHAKESPEARE, *The Winter's Tale*, II, ii

God is the friend of silence. Trees, flowers, grass grow in silence. See the stars, moon, and sun, how they move in silence.
—MOTHER TERESA, *For the Brotherhood of Man*, 1980

Only silence is great; all else is weakness.
—ALFRED DE VIGNY, *La mort du loup*, 1864

Whereof one cannot speak, thereof one must be silent.
—LUDWIG WITTGENSTEIN, *Tractatus logico-philosophicus*, 1922

[More at PHILOSOPHY.]

SIMPLICITY   See also INNOCENCE (Kipling);
                   THINGS & POSSESSIONS

Less is more.
        —ROBERT BROWNING, *Andrea del Sarto,* 1855
[Also a saying of the architect Mies van der Rohe; see ARTS:
ARCHITECTURE. See also the Mae West quote and note at
EXCESS, and for more on more, see physicist Philip W. An-
derson at SCIENCE: PHYSICS & COSMOLOGY.]

Everything should be made as simple as possible, but not
simpler. —ALBERT EINSTEIN, *Reader's Digest,* Oct. 1977
[This is similar to "Ockham's razor"; see under SCIENCE.]

O sancta simplicitas!
O holy simplicity!   JOHN HUSS, last words before
                           burning at the stake, July 6, 1415

Manifest plainness,
Embrace simplicity,
Reduce selfishness,
Have few desires.
        —LAO-TZU, *Tao Te Ching,* 6th cent. B.C

Simplicity, most rare in our age.
        —OVID, *The Art of Love,* c. 2 B.C.

Beauty of style and harmony and grace and good rhythm
depend on simplicity.
        —PLATO, *The Republic,* 4th cent. B.C.

Simplify, Simplify.   —HENRY DAVID THOREAU,
                           Economy in *Walden,* 1854
[More at DETAILS & OTHER SMALL THINGS.]

The art of art, the glory of expression, and the sunshine of
the light of letters, is simplicity.
        —WALT WHITMAN, Preface, *Leaves of Grass,* 1855

SIN   See EVIL; SIN, VICE, & NAUGHTINESS

SIN, VICE,   See also ALCOHOL & DRINKING;
& NAUGHTINESS   EVIL; EXCESS;
                          HEDONISM; MARRIAGE;
                  SEX & SENSUALITY; TEMPTATION

The vice is not in entering, but in not coming out again.
          —ARISTIPPUS, c. 400 B.C., remark to pupils
             who saw him entering the house of a prostitute,
                           cited in Montaigne, *Essays,* 1580

Never practice two vices at once.
          —TALLULAH BANKHEAD, *Tallulah,* 1952

I'm as pure as the driven slush.
          —TALLULAH BANKHEAD, d. 1968, attributed

I once was a maid, tho' I cannot tell when,
And still my delight is in proper young men:
Some one of a troop of dragoons was my daddie,
No wonder I'm fond of a sodger laddie.
                           —ROBERT BURNS,
          The Jolly Beggars in *Posthumous Pieces,* 1799

It is the function of vice to keep virtue within reasonable
bounds.   —SAMUEL BUTLER, *Notebooks,* 1912

What men call gallantry, and gods adultery,
Is much more common where the climate's sultry.
          —LORD BYRON, *Don Juan,* 1819–24

Pleasure's a sin, and sometimes sin's a pleasure.   *—Ibid.*

Vice is its own reward.
          —QUENTIN CRISP, *The Naked Civil Servant,* 1968

Do you think your mother and I should have lived comfortably so long together if ever we had been married?
                  —JOHN GAY, *The Beggar's Opera,* 1728

The probable fact is that we are descended not only from
monkeys but from monks.
                  —ELBERT HUBBARD, *Roycroft Dictionary
                           and Book of Epigrams,* 1923

Really to sin you have to be serious about it.
—HENRIK IBSEN, *Peer Gynt*, 1867

Adultery is hard on a small town because it can cause sudden population loss, and usually it's the wrong people who get run out. —GARRISON KEILLOR,
The New York Times, Op-Ed article, 1994

We're poor little lambs who've lost our way,
Baa! Baa! Baa!
We're little black sheep who have gone astray,
Baa—aa—aa!
Gentlemen rankers out on the spree,
Damned from here to Eternity,
God ha' mercy on such as we,
Baa! Yah! Baa!

—RUDYARD KIPLING, *Gentlemen
Rankers* in *Barrack-Room Ballads*, 1892
[Known to most Americans as "The Whiffenpoof song," after
the famous Yale University singing group.]

You know, of course, that the Tasmanians, who never committed adultery, are now extinct.
—W. SOMERSET MAUGHAM, *The Bread-Winner*, 1930

Of course heaven forbids certain pleasures, but one finds
means of compromise. —MOLIÈRE, *Tartuffe*, 1664

All fashionable vices pass for virtues.
—MOLIÈRE, *Don Juan or the Stone Guest*, 1665

Men are more easily governed through their vices than
through their virtues.
—NAPOLEON BONAPARTE, *Maxims*, 1804–15

If all the girls attending it [the Yale prom] were laid end to
end—I wouldn't be at all surprised.
—DOROTHY PARKER, quoted in
Alexander Woollcott, *While Rome Burns*, 1934

Enjoyed it! One more drink and I'd have been under the host.
>   —DOROTHY PARKER, on being asked if she enjoyed
>   a cocktail party; quoted in Howard Teichmann,
>   *George S. Kaufman,* 1972

[See also Parker at ALCOHOL & DRINKING.]

When the passions become masters, they are vices.
>   —PASCAL, *Pensées,* 1670

For lawless joys a bitter ending waits.
>   —PINDAR, *Odes,* 5th cent. B.C.

Every vice has its excuse ready.
>   —PUBLILIUS SYRUS, *Moral Sayings,* 1st cent. B.C.

Vices can be learnt even without a teacher.
>   —SENECA, *Natural Questions,* 1st cent. A.D.

Commit
The oldest sins the newest kind of ways.
>   —SHAKESPEARE, *Henry IV, Part II,* IV, v

Let copulation thrive. —SHAKESPEARE, *King Lear,* IV, vi

It's a bawdy planet.
>   —SHAKESPEARE, *The Winter's Tale,* I, ii

Certainly nothing is unnatural that is not physically impossible.   —RICHARD SHERIDAN, *The Critic,* 1779

An improper mind is a perpetual feast.
>   —LOGAN PEARSALL SMITH, *Afterthoughts,* 1931

[On baseball players who break curfew:] It ain't getting it that hurts them, it's staying up all night looking for it. They got to learn that if you don't get it by midnight, you ain't gonna get it, and if you do, it ain't worth it.
>   —CHARLES DILLON "CASEY" STENGEL,
>   quoted in Robert Creamer, *Stengel,* 1984

There is a charm about the forbidden that makes it unspeakably desirable.
>   —MARK TWAIN, d. 1910, Albert B. Paine, ed.,
>   *Mark Twain's Notebook,* 1935

When I'm good I'm very, very good, but when I'm bad I'm better. —MAE WEST, *I'm No Angel*, 1935

Goodness, what beautiful diamonds!
Goodness had nothing to do with it, dearie.
—MAE WEST, *Diamond Lil*, play, 1928;
also in the movie *Night After Night*, 1932
[The line was one of Mae West's favorites, and she titled her autobiography *Goodness Had Nothing to Do With It*, 1959.]

There is nothing in the world like the devotion of a married woman. It's a thing no married man knows anything about.
—OSCAR WILDE, *Lady Windermere's Fan*, 1892

All the things I really like to do are either immoral, illegal, or fattening. —ALEXANDER WOOLLCOTT, quoted in
Howard Teichmann, *George S. Kaufman*, 1972

SINCERITY See HONESTY & SINCERITY

SKEPTICISM See also ATHEISM; FAITH;
PHILOSOPHY; PRAYERS (Renan)

O thou of little faith, wherefore didst thou doubt?
—BIBLE, *Matthew* 14:31

Except I shall see in his hands the print of the nails, and put my finger into the print of the nails, and thrust my hand into his side, I will not believe. —BIBLE, *John* 20:25
["Doubting Thomas" is speaking.]

He that doubteth is damned. —BIBLE, *Romans* 14:23

Mock on, mock on, Voltaire, Rousseau;
Mock on, mock on; 'tis all in vain!
You throw the sand against the wind,
And the wind blows it back again.
—WILLIAM BLAKE, *The Scoffers*, c. 1804

If you would be a real seeker after truth, you must at least once in your life doubt, as far as possible, all things.
—DESCARTES, *Discourse on Method*, 1637

Skepticism is the first step toward truth.
> —DENIS DIDEROT, *Pensées philosophiques*, 1746

Do we, holding that the gods exist, deceive ourselves with unsubstantial dreams and lies, while random careless chance and change alone control the world?
> —EURIPIDES, *Hecuba*, c. 425 B.C.

Ignorance is preferable to error; and he is less remote from the truth who believes nothing, than he who believes what is wrong.
> —THOMAS JEFFERSON, *Notes on the State of Virginia*, 1781–85

Que sais-je?
What do I know?
> —MONTAIGNE, motto, 1576

[Engraved on a medallion with his coat of arms, and referred to in his *Essays* in Book II, 1580. Montaigne reportedly also had carved on a ceiling beam of his study, "The only thing that's certain is that nothing is certain." See also PHILOSOPHY.]

Great intellects are skeptical.
> —FRIEDRICH NIETZSCHE, *The Antichrist*, 1888

Of the gods I know nothing, whether they exist or do not exist, nor what they are like in form. Many things stand in the way of knowledge—the obscurity of the subject, the brevity of human life.
> —PROTAGORAS, 5th cent. B.C., quoted in Diogenes Laërtius, *Lives of Eminent Philosophers*, 3rd cent. A.D.

Modest doubt is called
The beacon of the wise.
> —SHAKESPEARE, *Troilus and Cressida*, II, ii

Life is doubt, and faith without doubt is nothing but death.
> —MIGUEL DE UNAMUNO, *Poesías*, 1907

[See also Unamuno at FAITH.]

One never knows, do one?
> —THOMAS "FATS" WALLER, saying, quoted by Roger Angell, *The New Yorker*, Aug. 5, 1985

SKY   See NATURE: THE HEAVENS, THE SKY

SLEEP & DREAMS   See also SCIENCE: PSYCHOLOGY

The beginning of health is sleep.
                    —ANONYMOUS (IRISH PROVERB)

Dreaming men are haunted men.
  —STEPHEN VINCENT BENÉT, *John Brown's Body*, 1928

He giveth his beloved sleep.   —BIBLE, *Psalms* 127:2

As I walked through the wilderness of this world, I lighted
on a certain place, where was a den; and I laid me down in
that place to sleep: and as I slept I dreamed a dream.
                    —JOHN BUNYAN, *Pilgrim's Progress*, 1678
[The opening line. For other first lines, see Tolstoy at FAMILY.]

Sleep hath its own world,
And a wide realm of wild reality.
                    —LORD BYRON, *The Dream*, 1816

All the things one has forgotten scream for help in dreams.
                    —ELIAS CANETTI, *The Human Province*, 1973

Now blessings light on him that first invented this same
sleep! It covers a man all over, thoughts and all, like a
cloak. . . . 'Tis the current coin that purchases all the pleasures of the world cheap; and the balance that sets the king
and the shepherd, the fool and the wise man even.
                    —CERVANTES, *Don Quixote*, 1605–15

Dreaming permits each and every one of us to be quietly
and safely insane every night of the week.
                    —WILLIAM DEMENT, *Newsweek*, Nov. 30, 1959

A dream is a wish your heart makes.
                    —WALT DISNEY, *Sleeping Beauty*, 1959

Men have conceived a twofold use of sleep: that it is a re-
freshing of the body in this life; that it is a preparing of the
soul for the next.   —JOHN DONNE, *Meditation xv* in
Devotions Upon Emergent Occasions, 1624

Wynken, Blynken, and Nod one night
Sailed off in a wooden shoe
Sailed on a river of crystal light
Into a sea of dew.
>   —EUGENE FIELD, *Wynken, Blynken, and Nod,*
>   c. 1880–95

We are not hypocrites in our sleep.
>   —WILLIAM HAZLITT, *On Dreams*
>   in *The Plain Speaker,* 1826

Sleep is the twin of death.   —HOMER, *Iliad,* 8th cent. B.C.

Preserve me from unseasonable and immoderate sleep.
>   —SAMUEL JOHNSON, 1767, in
>   *Prayers and Meditations,* 1785

In a dream you are never eighty.
>   —ANNE SEXTON, d. 1974, *Old*
[Or, as Sadie Delaney said, at about age 103, "In our dreams,
we are always young," *Having Our Say: The Delaney Sisters'
First 100 Years,* 1993.]

Methought I heard a voice cry "Sleep no more!
Macbeth does murder sleep—the innocent sleep,
Sleep that knits up the ravelled sleeve of care,
The death of each day's life, sore labor's bath,
Balm of hurt minds, great nature's second course,
Chief nourisher in life's feast.
>   —SHAKESPEARE, *Macbeth,* II, ii

[Sleep:] The poor man's wealth, the prisoner's release,
Th' indifferent judge between the high and low.
>   —SIR PHILIP SIDNEY, *Astrophel and Stella,* sonnet, 1591

A dream uninterpreted is like a letter unopened.
>   —TALMUD
[Leo Rosten, in *The Power of Positive Nonsense* (1977), gave
the precise citation as the *Yebamoth* book (118b) of the Baby-
lonian Talmud.]

Sleep my little one, sleep my pretty one, sleep.
>   —ALFRED, LORD TENNYSON, *The Princess,* 1847

Dreams are true while they last, and do we not live in
dreams? —ALFRED, LORD TENNYSON,
The Higher Pantheism, 1869

SMALL THINGS   See DETAILS & OTHER
              SMALL THINGS; THINGS & POSSESSIONS

SNOW   See NATURE: SEASONS;
              NATURE: WIND & WEATHER

SOCIALISM   See also CAPITALISM; COMMUNISM

I am for socialism because I am for humanity.
              —EUGENE V. DEBS, speech, Jan. 1, 1897

We are all socialists nowadays.
              —EDWARD VII, speech, Nov. 5, 1895,
                    when he was Prince of Wales
[Also attributed slightly earlier to Sir William Harcourt, Chancellor of the Exchequer in one of Prime Minister William Gladstone's cabinets, in the form: "We are all socialists now."]

Socialism is . . . not only a way of life, but a certain scientific
approach to social and economic problems.
              —JAWAHARLAL NEHRU, *Credo* in
              The New York Times Magazine, Sept. 7, 1958

All Socialism involves slavery.
              —HERBERT SPENCER, *The Coming Slavery*
                    in *Man Versus the State*, 1884

Any man who is not something of a socialist before he is
forty has no heart. Any man who is still a socialist after he
is forty has no head.
              —WENDELL L. WILLKIE, d. 1944, quoted
              in Richard Norton Smith, *Thomas E. Dewey*, 1982

SOLITUDE   See also INDIVIDUALITY

He who is unable to live in society, or who has no need
because he is sufficient for himself, must be either a beast
or a god.   —ARISTOTLE, *Politics*, 4th cent. B.C.

Woe to him that is alone when he falleth; for he hath not another to help him up.　　　　—BIBLE, *Ecclesiastes* 4:10

'Tis solitude should teach us how to die;
. . . alone—man with his God must strive.
　　　—LORD BYRON, *Childe Harold's Pilgrimage*, 1812–18

We live, as we dream—alone.
　　　—JOSEPH CONRAD, *Heart of Darkness*, 1902

I want to be alone.
　　　—GRETA GARBO, saying, and also one of her lines in
　　　　　　Grand Hotel, 1932, script by William A. Drake
[Her *New York Times* obituary on Apr. 16, 1990, stated that she actually said, "I want to be let alone."]

Full many a flower is born to blush unseen,
And waste its sweetness on the desert air.
　　　　　　—THOMAS GRAY, *Elegy Written*
　　　　　　　in a Country Churchyard, 1750

Pray that your loneliness may spur you into finding something to live for, great enough to die for.
　　　—DAG HAMMARSKJÖLD, *Markings*, tr. 1964

The strongest man in the world is he who stands most alone.
　　　—HENRIK IBSEN, *An Enemy of the People*, 1982

In solitude pride quickly creeps in.
　　　—ST. JEROME, letter to Rusticus, c. A.D. 400

Then on the shore
Of the wide world I stand alone, and think
Till love and fame to nothingness do sink.
　　　　　　—JOHN KEATS, *When I Have Fears*
　　　　　　　That I May Cease to Be, 1818

This delicious Solitude.
　　　—ANDREW MARVELL, *The Garden*, 1650–52

Solitude is the playfield of Satan.
　　　—VLADIMIR NABOKOV, *Pale Fire*, 1962

If you would live innocently, seek solitude.
> —PUBLILIUS SYRUS, *Moral Sayings,* 1st cent. B.C.

To be adult is to be alone.
> —JEAN ROSTAND, *Thoughts of a Biologist,* 1939

I love all waste
And solitary places; where we taste the pleasure of believing
   what we see
Is boundless, as we wish our souls to be.
> —PERCY BYSSHE SHELLEY, *Julian and Maddalo,* 1818

I never found the companion that was so companionable as
solitude.
> —HENRY DAVID THOREAU, *Solitude* in *Walden,* 1854

Only in solitude do we find ourselves.
> —MIGUEL DE UNAMUNO, *Solitude*
> in *Essays and Soliloquies,* 1924

The happiest of all lives is a busy solitude.
> —VOLTAIRE, letter to Frederick the Great, Aug. 1751

She dwelt among the untrodden ways
Beside the springs of Dove,
A maid whom there were none to praise
And very few to love.
> —WILLIAM WORDSWORTH, *She Dwelt*
> *Among the Untrodden Ways,* 1800

Avoid the reeking herd,
Shun the polluted flock,
Live like that stoic bird
The eagle of the rock.
> —ELINOR WYLIE, *The Eagle and the Mole,* 1921

The wind blows out of the gates of the day,
The wind blows over the lonely of heart,
And the lonely of heart is withered away.
> —WILLIAM BUTLER YEATS,
> *The Land of Heart's Desire,* 1894

SORROW, SADNESS, See also DESPAIR, DEPRESSION,
& SUFFERING   & MISERY; EMOTIONS;
                                  RESIGNATION; TROUBLE

Suffering is the sole origin of consciousness.
                              —FEODOR DOSTOEVSKI,
                              Notes from Underground, 1864

Know how sublime a thing it is
To suffer and be strong.
                              —HENRY WADSWORTH LONGFELLOW,
                              The Light of the Stars in *Voices of the Night,* 1839

La chair est triste, hélas! et j'ai lu tous les livres.
The flesh is sad, alas, and I've read all the books.
                              —STÉPHANE MALLARMÉ, *Brise marine,* 1887

It is not true that suffering ennobles the character; happiness
does that sometimes, but suffering, for the most part, makes
men petty and vindictive.   —W. SOMERSET MAUGHAM,
                              The Moon and Sixpence, 1919

No pain, no palm; no thorns, no throne; no gall, no glory;
no cross, no crown.
                              —WILLIAM PENN, *No Cross, No Crown,* 1669

Happiness is beneficial for the body, but it is grief that develops the powers of the mind.
                              —MARCEL PROUST, *Remembrance of
                              Things Past: The Past Recaptured,* 1913–27

When sorrows come, they come not single spies,
But in battalions!   —SHAKESPEARE, *Hamlet,* IV, v

SOUL   See also MIND, THOUGHT,
                              & UNDERSTANDING

What shall it profit a man, if he shall gain the whole world,
and lose his own soul?   —BIBLE, *Mark* 8:36

The human soul develops up to the time of death.
                              —HIPPOCRATES, *Aphorisms,* c. 400 B.C.

The soul is the mirror of an indestructible universe.
—G. W. LEIBNIZ, *The Monadology*, 1714

Dust thou art, to dust returnest,
Was not spoken of the soul.
—HENRY WADSWORTH LONGFELLOW,
A Psalm of Life, 1839
[More at LIFE.]

The wealth of the soul is the only true wealth.
—LUCIAN, *Dialogues*, 2nd cent. A.D.

Every soul is a melody which needs renewing.
—STÉPHANE MALLARMÉ, d. 1898, *Crise de vers*

Those things that nature denied to human sight, she revealed
to the eyes of the soul. —OVID, *Metamorphoses*, c. A.D. 5

A beautiful soul has no other merit than its own existence.
—J.C.F. VON SCHILLER, *On Grace and Dignity*, 1793

The soul alone raises us to nobility.
—SENECA, *Epistles*, 1st cent. A.D.

Throughout this varied and eternal world
Soul is the only element.
—PERCY BYSSHE SHELLEY, *Queen Mab*, 1813

Teach me, like you, to drink creation whole
And casting out my self, become a soul.
—RICHARD WILBUR, *The Aspen and the
Stream* in *Advice to a Prophet and Other Poems*, 1961

SPACE   See NATURE: THE HEAVENS, THE SKY;
SCIENCE: PHYSICS & COSMOLOGY

SPEAKING & SPEECH   See LANGUAGE & WORDS;
TALK

SPEECH, FREE   See FREE SPEECH

SPEED   See HASTE

SPIRIT   See ARTS entries; COURAGE;
                              CULTURE; SOUL

SPIRITS, OTHERWORLDLY   See OCCULT, THE

SPORTS   See also GAMES; PHYSICAL FITNESS;
        WINNING & LOSING, VICTORY & DEFEAT

Float like a butterfly,
Sting like a bee!
Rumble young man! Rumble!
Waaa!
—MUHAMMAD ALI and DREW "BUNDINI" BROWN,
   their "war cry," in Ali, *The Greatest: My Own Story,* 1975

Ave Caesar, morituri te salutant.
Hail Caesar, we who are about to die salute you.
                  —ANONYMOUS, gladiators' salute, quoted in
                     Suetonius, *Life of Claudius,* c. A.D. 121

Say it ain't so, Joe.   —ANONYMOUS, Sept. 1920
[Plea reportedly made by a tearful boy to the great "Shoeless"
Joe Jackson as he emerged from a hearing on charges that he
and seven other Chicago Black Sox players had been bribed
to throw the 1919 World Series to the Cincinnati Reds. All
were banned from baseball for life.]

The game isn't over until the last man is out.
                  —ANONYMOUS, traditional baseball saying
[See also Yogi Berra at ENDINGS.]

In America, it is sport that is the opiate of the masses.
   —RUSSELL BAKER, *The New York Times,* Oct. 3, 1967

Whoever wants to know the heart and mind of America had
better learn baseball.
   —JACQUES BARZUN, *God's Country and Mine,* 1954

Tennis, anyone?   —HUMPHREY BOGART, attributed
[A line that is a proverbial device for getting actors off stage
for a scene transition. Bogart was said to have spoken the line
in a play from the 1920s, but the attribution has not been
pinned down. Bogart, himself, denied ever having posed this
question.]

Honey, I just forgot to duck.
                    —JACK DEMPSEY, Sept. 23, 1926
[Dempsey offered this explanation in a telephone call to his
wife after losing the heavyweight title to Gene Tunney. In 1981,
Pres. Ronald Reagan, after being shot and wounded by a
would-be assassin, made the same comment to his wife, Nancy.]

The bigger they come, the harder they fall.
                    —BOB FITZSIMMONS, remark before
                       losing his fight with Jim Jeffries, 1899
[Also attributed to John L. Sullivan, and probably of ancient
origin.]

There's no crying in baseball.
                    —LOWELL GANZ & BABALOO MANDEL,
                       screenplay, *A League of Their Own,* 1992

[Baseball:] It breaks your heart. It is designed to break your
heart.   —A. BARTLETT GIAMATTI,
                       The Green Fields of the Mind, 1977

We wuz robbed!   —JOE JACOBS, June 21, 1932
[Jacobs managed Max Schmeling, who had just lost the heavyweight title to Jack Sharkey in a controversial split decision.]

In our family, there was no clear line between religion and
fly fishing.
     —NORMAN MACLEAN, *A River Runs Through It,* 1976
[The opening line of this great Montana novel. For other first
lines, see under Tolstoy at FAMILY.]

Because it is there.—GEORGE MALLORY, explaining why
                       he wanted to climb Mt. Everest, 1924
[Mallory, a British schoolteacher, and Andrew Irvine, a Cam-
bridge student, began their final ascent to the peak of Mt.
Everest on June 8, 1924, and were not seen again. Mallory's
body was found on May 1, 1999.]

Take Me Out to the Ball Game.
                    —JACK NORWORTH, song title, 1908

Serious sport has nothing to do with fair play. It is bound up with hatred, jealousy, boastfulness, disregard of all rules, and sadistic pleasure in witnessing violence: in other words, it is war minus the shooting.
—GEORGE ORWELL, *The Sporting Spirit*
in *Shooting an Elephant,* 1950

Win this one for the Gipper.
—KNUTE ROCKNE, exhortation
to the Notre Dame football team
[Rockne seems to have used this line periodically to urge on the team. According to *The Fireside Book of Football,* the first occasion was prior to the Indiana game in 1921, a year after Notre Dame player George Gipp died from a streptococcus infection. In the movie *Knute Rockne, All American,* a thoroughly sanitized Gipp was played by Ronald Reagan. Millions were brought to tears by the character's manly deathbed request: "Some day when things are tough, maybe you can ask the boys to go in there and win just one for the Gipper."]

The race is not always to the swift nor the battle to the strong—but that's the way to bet it.
—DAMON RUNYON, *More Than Somewhat,* 1937

A hit, a very palpable hit. —SHAKESPEARE, *Hamlet,* V, ii

There be some sports are painful.
—SHAKESPEARE, *The Tempest,* III, i

Oh! somewhere in this favored land the sun is shining bright;
The band is playing somewhere; and somewhere hearts are light;
And somewhere men are laughing and somewhere children shout,
But there is no joy in Mudville—mighty Casey has struck out. —ERNEST LAWRENCE THAYER,
Casey at the Bat: A Ballad of the Republic,
Sung in the Year 1888, June 3, 1888

[Golf:] A good walk spoiled. —MARK TWAIN, attributed
[The attribution, although common, may be wrong.]

I love any discourse of rivers, and fish and fishing.
—IZAAK WALTON, *The Compleat Angler,* 1653–55

The English country gentleman galloping after a fox—the unspeakable in full pursuit of the uneatable.
—OSCAR WILDE, *A Woman of No Importance,* 1893

Football combines the two worst features of modern American life: it's violence punctuated by committee meetings.
—GEORGE WILL, in *Baseball,* produced by Ken Burns, PBS television series, 1994

SPRING   See NATURE: SEASONS

SRI LANKA   See NATIONS

STARS   See NATURE: THE HEAVENS, THE SKY; OCCULT, THE; SCIENCE: PHYSICS & COSMOLOGY

STATISTICS   See SCIENCE: MATHEMATICS & STATISTICS

STOICISM   See PATIENCE; RESIGNATION

STORIES   See also ARTS: WRITING; BOOKS & READING

This is the saddest story I ever heard.
—FORD MADOX FORD, *The Good Soldier,* 1915
[The opening sentence. For other first lines, see the list at Tolstoy under FAMILY.]

And thereby hangs a tale.
—SHAKESPEARE, *As You Like It,* II, vii
[Shakespeare used the phrase in four other plays, as well.]

A sad tale's best for winter.
—SHAKESPEARE, *The Winter's Tale,* II, i

STRENGTH   See also POWER; VIOLENCE & FORCE; VIRTUE (Tennyson)

When the going gets tough, the tough get going.
—ANONYMOUS, popularized by John N. Mitchell, Attorney General under Richard M. Nixon, 1969–72

Kraft durch Freude.
Strength through joy.   —ROBERT LEY, slogan for the
German Labor Front, Dec. 2, 1933

If we must choose between them, it is far better to be feared
than loved.   —MACHIAVELLI, *The Prince*, 1532

A nation does not have to be cruel to be tough.
—FRANKLIN D. ROOSEVELT,
radio speech, Oct. 13, 1940

Physical strength can never permanently withstand the im-
pact of spiritual force.
—FRANKLIN D. ROOSEVELT, speech, May 4, 1941

There is a homely adage which runs: "Speak softly and carry
a big stick; you will go far."
—THEODORE ROOSEVELT, speech, Sept. 2, 1901
[Stephen Jay Gould in *Natural History* magazine, May 1985,
traced this adage to an African proverb. Carl Sandburg in *The
Proverbs of a People,* published in *Good Morning America,*
1928, said that it is a Spanish proverb.]

The strongest is never strong enough always to be master,
unless he transforms strength into right, and obedience into
duty.   —JEAN JACQUES ROUSSEAU,
The Social Contract, 1762

O! it is excellent
To have a giant's strength, but it is tyrannous
To use it like a giant.
—SHAKESPEARE, *Measure for Measure,* II, ii

The Gods are on the side of the stronger.
—TACITUS, *Histories,* A.D. 104–09

If you can't stand the heat, get out of the kitchen.
—HARRY S. TRUMAN, saying
[David McCullough wrote in *Truman* (1992) that this is an old
Missouri saying that Truman first heard in the 1930s.]

There is no need to fear the strong. All one needs to know is the method of overcoming them. There is special jujitsu for every strong man.   —YEVGENY YEVTUSHENKO,
A Precocious Autobiography, 1962

STUPIDITY   See FOOLS & STUPIDITY

STYLE   See also APPEARANCES; ARTS: STYLE IN
WRITING & EXPRESSION; FASHION &
CLOTHES; GRACE

Our style betrays us.
   —ANONYMOUS (LATIN PROVERB)

Le style est l'homme même.
The style is the man himself.
   —GEORGES LOUIS DE BUFFON,
Discours sur le style, 1753

Style is character. —JOAN DIDION, *Georgia O'Keeffe,* 1976

To achieve harmony in bad taste is the height of elegance.
   —JEAN GENET, *The Thief's Journal,* 1949

Elegance is refusal.   —DIANA VREELAND, quoted by
   Holly Brubach, *New York Times Magazine,* Jan. 12, 1997
[Vreeland was the editor of *Vogue* from 1962 to 1971.]

In matters of great importance, style, not sincerity, is the vital thing.
   —OSCAR WILDE, *The Importance of Being Earnest,* 1895

SUCCESS & FAME   See also ACCOMPLISHMENT;
GREATNESS; HIGH POSITION:
RULERS & LEADERS; MONEY; POWER

Sic transit gloria mundi.
So passes away the glory of this world.   —ANONYMOUS
[Used in papal coronations since the 15th century but probably of earlier origin. Essentially the same phrase is found in *The Imitation of Christ*; see Thomas à Kempis, below.]

The desire for fame tempts even noble minds.
   —ST. AUGUSTINE, *The City of God,* A.D. 415

Fame is like a river, that beareth up things light and swollen, and drowns things weighty and solid.
— FRANCIS BACON, *Of Praise* in *Essays,* 1625

Fame always brings loneliness. Success is as ice cold and lonely as the North Pole.
— VICKI BAUM, *Grand Hotel,* 1931

Let us now praise famous men. — BIBLE, *Ecclesiasticus* 44:1
[More at GENERATIONS.]

The celebrity is a person who is known for his well-known-ness.
— DANIEL BOORSTIN, *The Image,* 1962

A sign of a celebrity is often that his name is worth more than his services.
— *Ibid.*

Success produces success, just as money produces money.
— SÉBASTIEN R. N. CHAMFORT, *Maximes et pensées,* 1805

That's what fame is: solitude.
— COCO CHANEL, quoted in Marcel Haedrich,
Coco Chanel: Her Life, Her Secrets, 1971

We are all motivated by a keen desire for praise, and the better a man is, the more he is inspired by glory.
— CICERO, *Pro archia,* 62 B.C.

Fame is a bee.
It has a song—
It has a sting—
Ah, too, it has a wing.
— EMILY DICKINSON, poem no. 1763, date unknown

Success is counted sweetest
By those who ne'er succeed.
— EMILY DICKINSON, *Success,* 1878 (written c. 1859)

Nothing succeeds like success.
— ALEXANDRE DUMAS, *Ange pitou,* 1854
[For Oscar Wilde's variation, see EXCESS.]

Along with success comes a reputation for wisdom.
— EURIPIDES, *Hippolytus,* 428 B.C.

Success has ruined many a man.
　　　　　　　　　　—BENJAMIN FRANKLIN,
　　　　　　　　　　Poor Richard's Almanac, 1752

Fame hath sometimes created something of nothing.
　　　　　　　　　　—THOMAS FULLER, *Of Fame*
　　　　　　　　　　in *Holy and Profane State,* 1642

The paths of glory lead but to the grave.
　　　　　　　　　　—THOMAS GRAY, *Elegy Written in*
　　　　　　　　　　a Country Churchyard, 1750

Success has killed more men than bullets.
　　　　　　　　　　—TEXAS GUINAN, saying used
　　　　　　　　　　in nightclub act, c. 1920s

It is better to be envied than pitied.
　　　　　　　　　　—HERODOTUS, *Histories,* 5th cent. B.C.

The moral flabbiness born of the exclusive worship of the
bitch goddess Success. That—with the squalid cash interpretation put on the word success—is our national disease.
　　　　　　　　　　—WILLIAM JAMES, letter to
　　　　　　　　　　H. G. Wells, Sept. 11, 1906

Oh how quickly the world's glory passes away.
　　—THOMAS À KEMPIS, *The Imitation of Christ,* c. 1420
[A variation of the anonymous *Sic transit gloria mundi*; see
above.]

There is no business in the world so troublesome as the
pursuit of fame: life is over before you have hardly begun
your work.　　　　　　—LA BRUYÈRE, *Les Caractères,* 1688

Be nice to people on your way up because you'll need them
on your way down.
　　　　　—WILSON MIZNER, quoted in A. Johnson, *The*
　　　Incredible Mizners [from *New Yorker* profiles, 1942, 1950]
[Also attributed to Jimmy Durante.]

Success is like a liberation or the first phase of a love affair.
　　　　　　　　　　—JEANNE MOREAU, quoted in
　　　　　　　　　　Oriana Fallaci, *The Egoists,* 1963

There is only one success—to be able to spend your life in your own way. —CHRISTOPHER MORLEY, *Where the Blue Begins,* 1922

When men succeed, even their neighbors think them wise. —PINDAR, *Odes,* 5th cent. B.C.

Fame can never make us lie down contentedly on a deathbed. —ALEXANDER POPE, letter to William Trumbell, Mar. 12, 1713

The highest form of vanity is love of fame. —GEORGE SANTAYANA, *The Life of Reason: Reason in Society,* 1905–06

There's hope a great man's memory may outlive his life half a year. —SHAKESPEARE, *Hamlet,* III, ii

There are two tragedies in life. One is to lose your heart's desire. The other is to gain it. —GEORGE BERNARD SHAW, *Man and Superman,* 1903

All you need in this life is ignorance and confidence, and then success is sure. —MARK TWAIN, letter to Mrs. Foote, Dec. 2, 1887

In the future, everyone will be famous for fifteen minutes. —ANDY WARHOL, *Andy Warhol's Exposures,* catalog for exhibition of his photographs, Stockholm, 1968

There is always room at the top. —DANIEL WEBSTER, attributed, c. 1805 [Supposedly this was his reply when advised against becoming a lawyer because the profession was overcrowded, even then.]

What rage for fame attends both great and small! Better be damned than mentioned not at all. —JOHN WOLCOT ("PETER PINDAR"), *To the Royal Academicians,* 1782–85

SUFFERING See SORROW, SADNESS, & SUFFERING; TROUBLE

SUICIDE

As soon as one does not kill oneself, one must keep silent about life. —ALBERT CAMUS, *Notebooks, 1935–1942*, 1962 [For his view of suicide and philosophy, see under PHILOSOPHY.]

When all the blandishments of life are gone,
The coward sneaks to death, the brave live on.
             —MARTIAL, *Epigrams*, 1st cent. A.D.

A suicide kills two people, Maggie, that's what it's for.
             —ARTHUR MILLER, *After the Fall*, 1964

It is always consoling to think of suicide: in that way one gets through many a bad night.
                          —FRIEDRICH NIETZSCHE,
                          Beyond Good and Evil, 1885–86

Razors pain you;
Rivers are damp;
Acids stain you;
And drugs cause cramp;
Guns aren't lawful;
Nooses give;
Gas smells awful;
You might as well live.
     —DOROTHY PARKER, *Résumé* in *Enough Rope*, 1927

Amid the sufferings of life on earth, suicide is God's best gift to man.   —PLINY, *Natural History*, A.D. 77

There is nothing in the world to which every man has a more unassailable title than to his own life and person.
—ARTHUR SCHOPENHAUER, *On Suicide* in *Essays*, 1851

To be, or not to be—that is the question:
Whether 'tis nobler in the mind to suffer
The slings and arrows of outrageous fortune,
Or to take arms against a sea of troubles,
And by opposing end them.
                          —SHAKESPEARE, *Hamlet*, III, i

The man who, in a fit of melancholy, kills himself today, would have wished to live had he waited a week.
—VOLTAIRE, *Cato* in *Philosophical Dictionary,* 1764

SUMMER   See NATURE: SEASONS

SURVIVAL See also APPEASEMENT VS. RESISTANCE;
     CRAFTINESS; PERSEVERANCE & ENDURANCE

He that fights and runs away may live to fight another day.
—ANONYMOUS, in *Musarium deliciae,* 17th cent.

To all the living there is hope; for a living dog is better than a dead lion.   —BIBLE, *Ecclesiastes* 9:4

It isn't important to come out on top. What matters is to be the one who comes out alive.
—BERTOLT BRECHT, *In the Jungle of Cities,* 1924

Happiness in the ordinary sense is not what one needs in life, though one is right to aim at it. The true satisfaction is to come through and see those whom one loves come through.   —E. M. FORSTER, letter, 1922,
in *Selected Letters,* Vol. 11 (1921–1970)

In the clutch of circumstance,
I have not winced or cried aloud;
Under the bludgeoning of chance
My head is bloody but unbowed.
—WILLIAM E. HENLEY, *Echoes,* 1888,
Invictus. In Memoriam R. T. Hamilton Bruce

I bend but do not break.
—LA FONTAINE, *The Oak and the Reed* in *Fables,* 1668

We shall live to fight again and to strike another blow.
—ALFRED, LORD TENNYSON, *The Revenge,* 1880

Endure, and preserve yourselves for better things.
—VIRGIL, *Aeneid,* c. 19 B.C.

SWITZERLAND   See NATIONS

SYMPATHY   See COMPASSION & PITY

T

TALK   See also CONVERSATION;
                                   FOOLS & STUPIDITY;
        LANGUAGE & WORDS; RUMOR; SILENCE

Loose lips sink ships.
                  —ANONYMOUS (World War II poster)
[See also SECURITY.]

Refrain not to speak, when there is occasion to do good.
                        —BIBLE, *Ecclesiasticus* 4:23
[But the same book also advises, "Let thy speech be short,
comprehending much in few words," 32:8.]

Every idle word that men shall speak, they shall give account
thereof in the day of judgment.
    For by thy words thou shalt be justified, and by thy words
thou shalt be condemned.   —BIBLE, *Matthew* 12:36–37

When you're leading, don't talk.
          —THOMAS E. DEWEY, remark in 1948 presidential
     campaign, Richard Norton Smith, *Thomas E. Dewey*, 1982

But far more numerous was the herd of such
Who think too little and who talk too much.
          —JOHN DRYDEN, *Absalom and Achitophel*, 1680

Then words came like a fall of winter snow.
                        —HOMER, *Iliad*, 8th cent. B.C.

They never taste who always drink;
They always talk who never think.
                          —MATTHEW PRIOR, *Upon this
                          Passage in the Scaligerana*, 1697

Speech is a mirror of the soul; as a man speaks so he is.
> —PUBLILIUS SYRUS, *Moral Sayings,* 1st cent. B.C.

Men of few words are the best men.
> —SHAKESPEARE, *Henry V,* III, ii

[Not necessarily Shakespeare's own view, for he also observed that there are those who are "reputed wise for saying nothing," *The Merchant of Venice,* I. i. And in the quote below, it is a murderer who speaks.]

Talkers are no good doers.
> —SHAKESPEARE, *Richard III,* I, iii

Talkativeness is one thing, speaking well another.
> —SOPHOCLES, *Oedipus at Colonus,* 5th cent. B.C.

TAXES   See also AMERICAN HISTORY: MEMORABLE
> MOMENTS (Bush)

Render therefore unto Caesar the things which are Caesar's; and unto God the things that are God's.
> —BIBLE, *Matthew* 22:21

To tax and to please, no more than to love and be wise, is not given to man.   —EDMUND BURKE, *First Speech on Conciliation with America,* Apr. 19, 1774

The art of taxation consists in so plucking the goose as to obtain the largest possible amount of feathers with the least possible amount of hissing.
> —JEAN BAPTISTE COLBERT, attributed

[Colbert was Louis XIV's finance minister, 1665–69.]

In this world, nothing can be said to be certain except death and taxes.   —BENJAMIN FRANKLIN, letter to
> J. B. LeRoy, Nov. 13, 1789

Taxes are what we pay for civilized society.
> —OLIVER WENDELL HOLMES, JR.;
> *Compania General de Tabacos de*
> *Filipines v. Collector of Internal Revenue,* 1904

The wisdom of man never yet contrived a system of taxation that operates with perfect equality.
>—ANDREW JACKSON, *Proclamation to the People of South Carolina,* Dec. 10, 1832

Excise, n. A hateful tax levied upon commodities, and adjudged not by the common judges of property, but by wretches hired by those to whom the excise is paid.
>—SAMUEL JOHNSON, *Dictionary,* 1755

The power to tax involves the power to destroy.
>—JOHN MARSHALL, *McCulloch v. Maryland,* Mar. 6, 1819

Taxation without representation is tyranny.
>—JAMES OTIS, watchword, c. 1761, attributed by John Adams and others

Where there is an income tax, the just man will pay more and the unjust less on the same income.
>—PLATO, *The Republic,* 4th cent. B.C.

The income tax has made more liars out of the American people than golf has.
>—WILL ROGERS, *The Illiterate Digest,* 1924

Taxes, after all, are the dues that we pay for the privileges of membership in an organized society.
>—FRANKLIN D. ROOSEVELT, speech, Oct. 21, 1936

To be a good shepherd is to shear the flock, not skin it!
>—TIBERIUS, favorite proverbial saying, quoted in Suetonius, *Lives of the Caesars,* c. A.D. 121

TECHNOLOGY See SCIENCE: TECHNOLOGY

TELEVISION See MEDIA

TEMPTATION See also SIN, VICE, & NAUGHTINESS

Opportunity can often sway even an honest man.
>—ANONYMOUS (LATIN PROVERB)

Saintliness is also a temptation.
—JEAN ANOUILH, *Becket*, 1959

Lead us not into temptation. —BIBLE, *Matthew* 6:13
[Also *Luke* 11:41.]

Get thee behind me, Satan. —*Ibid.* 16:23

Watch and pray, that ye enter not into temptation: the spirit indeed is willing, but the flesh is weak. —*Ibid.* 26:41

Blessed is the man that endureth temptation.
—BIBLE, *James* 1:12

For to tempt and to be tempted are things very nearly allied, and in spite of the finest maxims of morality impressed upon the mind, whenever feeling has anything to do in the matter, no sooner is it excited than we have already gone vastly farther than we are aware of.
—CATHERINE THE GREAT, d. 1796, *Memoirs*

The last temptation is the greatest treason: To do the right deed for the wrong reason.
—T. S. ELIOT, *Murder in the Cathedral*, 1935

Tempt not a desperate man.
—SHAKESPEARE, *Romeo and Juliet*, V, iii

I never resist temptation, because I have found that the things that are bad for me do not tempt me.
—GEORGE BERNARD SHAW, *The Apple Cart*, 1929

There are several good protections against temptation, but the surest is cowardice.
—MARK TWAIN, *Pudd'nhead Wilson's New Calendar* in *Following the Equator*, 1897

I generally avoid temptation unless I can't resist it.
—MAE WEST, screenplay, *My Little Chickadee*, 1940

I can resist everything except temptation.
—OSCAR WILDE, *Lady Windermere's Fan*, 1892

The only way to get rid of a temptation is to yield to it.
—OSCAR WILDE, *The Picture of Dorian Gray*, 1891

THANKSGIVING

Over the river and through the wood
To grandfather's house we go.
The horse knows the way
To carry the sleigh
Through the white and drifted snow.
> —LYDIA MARIA CHILD, *Thanksgiving Day*
> in *Flowers for Children,* 1844–46

Hurrah for the fun!
Is the pudding done?
Hurrah for the pumpkin pie.   —*Ibid.*
[Child, a prominent reformer and author, did not in fact have
happy memories of family feasts. "Cold, shaded, and uncongenial
was my childhood and youth," she said in 1877.]

'Twas founded by th' Puritans to give thanks f'r bein' presarved fr'm th' Indians, an' . . . we keep it to give thanks
we are presarved fr'm th' Puritans.
> —FINLEY PETER DUNNE,
> *Thanksgiving* in *Mr. Dooley's Opinions,* 1900

What moistens the lip and what brightens the eye?
What calls back the past, like the rich pumpkin pie?
> —JOHN GREENLEAF WHITTIER, *The Pumpkin,* 1844

THEATER   See ARTS: DRAMA & ACTING

THEORY   See SCIENCE

THINGS   See DETAILS & OTHER SMALL THINGS;
         NEW THINGS; OLD THINGS, OLD FRIENDS;
         SIMPLICITY; THINGS & POSSESSIONS

THINGS & POSSESSIONS   See also CAPITALISM;
                NEW THINGS; OLD THINGS,
                OLD FRIENDS; SIMPLICITY

The goal of all inanimate objects is to resist man and ulti-
mately to defeat him.
> —RUSSELL BAKER, *The New York Times,* June 18, 1968

Inanimate objects are classified scientifically into three major categories—those that don't work, those that break down, and those that get lost.
—*Ibid.*

Things have their laws as well as men; things refuse to be trifled with.
—RALPH WALDO EMERSON,
Politics in *Essays: Second Series,* 1844

We are the slaves of objects around us.
—GOETHE, quoted in Johann Peter Eckermann,
Conversations with Goethe, 1836

The generality of mankind are contented to be estimated by what they possess instead of what they are.
—WILLIAM HAZLITT, d. 1830, *On Personal Identity*

Every increased possession loads us with a new weariness.
—JOHN RUSKIN, *The Eagle's Nest,* 1872

An ill-favored thing, sir, but mine own.
—SHAKESPEARE, *As You Like It,* V, iv

A place for everything and everything in its place.
—SAMUEL SMILES, *Thrift,* 1875

How many things I can do without!
—SOCRATES, 5th cent. B.C., in a marketplace,
quoted in Diogenes Laërtius,
Lives of Eminent Philosophers, 3rd cent. A.D.

A coin, sleeve button, or a collar button dropped in a bedroom will hide itself and be hard to find. A handkerchief in bed can't be found.
—MARK TWAIN, d. 1910, Albert B. Paine, ed.,
Mark Twain's Notebook, 1935

THINKING & THOUGHT   See MIND, THOUGHT,
& UNDERSTANDING

TIME   See also FUTURE, THE; PAST, THE;
PRESENT, THE; PROCRASTINATION

Time brings all things to pass.
—AESCHYLUS, *The Libation Bearers,* 5th cent. B.C.

Time and tide wait for no man.
                    —ANONYMOUS (ENGLISH PROVERB)

Vulnerat omnes, ultima necat.
Each hour injures, the last one slays.
                    —ANONYMOUS (LATIN PROVERB)

What then is time? If no one asks me, I know what it is. If I wish to explain it to him who asks, I do not know.
                    —ST. AUGUSTINE, *Confessions,* A.D. 397–401

Time is a great teacher, but unfortunately it kills all its pupils.   —HECTOR BERLIOZ, quoted in
                    Almanach des lettres françaises, 1850

Men talk of killing time, while time quietly kills them.
                    —DION BOUCICAULT, *London Assurance,* 1841
[Herbert Spencer in *Definitions* wrote, "Time: That which man is always trying to kill, but which ends in killing him."]

Time ripens all things. No man's born wise.
                    —CERVANTES, *Don Quixote,* 1605-15

Time is the great physician.
                    —BENJAMIN DISRAELI, *Henrietta Temple,* 1837

Time present and time past
Are both perhaps present in time future,
And time future contained in time past.
                    —T. S. ELIOT, *Burnt Norton* in *Four Quartets,* 1940

The Moving Finger writes; and having writ
Moves on: nor all your Piety nor Wit
Shall lure it back to cancel half a Line,
Nor all your Tears wash out a Word of it.
                    —EDWARD FITZGERALD,
                    The Rubáiyát of Omar Khayyám, 1879

Time is money.   —BENJAMIN FRANKLIN,
                    Advice to a Young Tradesman, 1748

Dost thou love life? Then do not squander time, for that's the stuff life is made of.   —BENJAMIN FRANKLIN,
                    Poor Richard's Almanac, June, 1746

Time flies over us, but leaves its shadow behind.
    —NATHANIEL HAWTHORNE, *The Marble Faun*, 1860

But at my back I always hear
Time's wingèd chariot hurrying near.
    —ANDREW MARVELL, *To His Coy Mistress*, 1650–52
[For more, see under HEDONISM.]

Time wounds all heels.
                            —GROUCHO MARX, d. 1977, attributed

I must govern the clock, not be governed by it.
                            —GOLDA MEIR, quoted in
                        Oriana Fallaci, *L'Europeo*, 1976

Time is the best medicine.   —OVID, *Love's Cure*, c. 1 B.C.

Time is the image of eternity.
                            —PLATO, 4th cent. B.C., quoted in
                    Diogenes Laërtius, *Lives of Eminent Philosophers*,
                                        3rd cent. A.D.

In theory, one is aware that the earth revolves, but in practice one does not perceive it; the ground upon which one
treads seems not to move, and one can live undisturbed. So
it is with time in one's life.
            —MARCEL PROUST, *Remembrance of
        Things Past: Within a Budding Grove*, 1913–27

Everything is a matter of chronology.
            —MARCEL PROUST, *Remembrance of
        Things Past: The Past Recaptured*, 1913–27

Time, which changes people, does not alter the image we
have retained of them.   —*Ibid.*

To realize the unimportance of time is the gate of wisdom.
                            —BERTRAND RUSSELL,
                title essay, *Mysticism and Logic*, 1917

Nothing is ours except time.
                            —SENECA, *Epistles*, 1st cent. A.D.

Ah! the clock is always slow;
It is later than you think.
> —ROBERT W. SERVICE, *It's Later Than
> You Think* in *Ballads of a Bohemian,* 1921

Come what come may,
Time and the hour runs through the roughest day.
> —SHAKESPEARE, *Macbeth,* I, iii

I wasted time, and now doth time waste me.
> —SHAKESPEARE, *Richard II,* V, v

Time eases all things.
> —SOPHOCLES, *Oedipus Rex,* 5th cent. B.C.

[Or, from his *Electra,* "Gentle time will heal our sorrows."]

The butterfly counts not months but moments, and has time
enough. —RABINDRANATH TAGORE, *Fireflies,* 1928

Oh as I was young and easy in the mercy of his means,
Time held me green and dying
Though I sang in my chains like the sea.
> —DYLAN THOMAS, *Fern Hill,* 1946

As if you could kill time without injuring eternity.
> —HENRY DAVID THOREAU,
> *Economy* in *Walden,* 1854

Time is but the stream I go a-fishing in.
> —HENRY DAVID THOREAU.
> *Where I Have Lived and What I Have Lived For* in *Ibid.*

Time bears away all things, even the mind.
> —VIRGIL, *Eclogues,* 37 B.C.

The years like great black oxen tread the world,
And God the herdsman goads them on behind,
And I am broken by their passing feet.
> —WILLIAM BUTLER YEATS,
> *The Countess Cathleen,* 1892

TIMES   See FUTURE, THE; GENERATIONS;
MODERN TIMES; PAST, THE; PRESENT, THE;
TURBULENT TIMES

TIMES OF DAY   See NATURE: TIMES OF DAY

TOBACCO

Tobacco, divine, rare, superexcellent tobacco . . . a sovereign remedy to all diseases. . . . But, as it is commonly abused by most men, which take it as tinkers do ale, 'tis a plague, a mischief, a violent purger of goods, lands, health, hellish, devilish, and damned tobacco, the ruin and overthrow of body and soul.
—ROBERT BURTON, *The Anatomy of Melancholy,* 1621–51

The roots of tobacco plants must go clear through to hell.
—THOMAS EDISON, diary, July 12, 1885

The believing we do something when we do nothing is the first illusion of tobacco.
—RALPH WALDO EMERSON, *Journal,* 1859

A custom [smoking] loathsome to the eye, harmful to the brain, dangerous to the lungs, and in the black stinking fume thereof, nearest resembling the horrible Stygian smoke of the pit that is bottomless.   —JAMES I,
Counterblaste to Tobacco, 1604

A woman is only a woman, but a good cigar is a smoke.
—RUDYARD KIPLING,
The Betrothed in *Departmental Ditties,* 1886

What this country needs is a really good five-cent cigar.
—THOMAS R. MARSHALL, remark 1920
to John Crockett, chief clerk of the Senate,
reported in the *New York Tribune,* Jan. 4, 1920

There's nothing like tobacco; it is the passion of all decent men; a man who lives without tobacco does not deserve to live.   —MOLIÈRE, *Don Juan,* 1665

I have never smoked in my life and look forward to a time when the world will look back in amazement and disgust to a practice so unnatural and offensive.
—GEORGE BERNARD SHAW,
The New York Herald Tribune, Apr. 14, 1946

I have made it a rule never to smoke more than one cigar at a time. I have no other restrictions as regards smoking.
—MARK TWAIN, speech on his
70th birthday, Dec. 5, 1905

TODAY   See MODERN TIMES; PRESENT, THE

TOLERANCE   See also FORGIVENESS & MERCY
& UNDERSTANDING

Live and let live.
—ANONYMOUS (SCOTTISH PROVERB)

Judge not, that ye be not judged.   —BIBLE, *Matthew* 7:1

Why beholdest thou the mote that is in thy brother's eye, but considerest not the beam that is in thine own eye?
—*Ibid.* 7:3

Judge not, and ye shall not be judged: condemn not, and ye shall not be condemned: forgive, and ye shall be forgiven.
—BIBLE, *Luke* 6:37

He that is without sin among you, let him first cast a stone at her.   —BIBLE, *John* 8:7

It is right to hate sin, but not to hate the sinner.
—GIOVANNI GUARESCHI,
The Little World of Don Camillo, 1950

There is so much good in the worst of us.
And so much bad in the best of us,
That it hardly becomes any of us
To talk about the rest of us.
—EDWARD WALLIS HOCH, d. 1925, *Good and Bad*
[Authorship uncertain.]

The highest result of education is tolerance.
—HELEN KELLER, *Optimism,* 1903

No law or ordinance is mightier than understanding.
—PLATO, *Laws,* 4th cent. B.C.

Tout comprendre rend très indulgent.
To understand everything makes one very tolerant.
> —MADAME DE STAËL, *Corinne*, 1807

[Commonly quoted as, *Tout comprendre, c'est tout pardonner,*
"To understand everything is to forgive everything."]

TOMORROW   See FUTURE, THE

TOO MUCH   See EXCESS

TOTALITARIANISM   See TYRANNY &
                                    TOTALITARIANISM

TRAGEDY   See ARTS entries; RUIN

TRAVEL   See also CITIES; ESCAPE; NATIONS

When I am here [Milan], I do not fast on the Sabbath; when
I am at Rome, I do fast on the Sabbath.
> —ST. AMBROSE, *Letters to Augustine*, 4th cent.

[Often rephrased as, "When in Rome do as the Romans do,
when elsewhere live as they live elsewhere." In *Don Quixote*
(1605–15), Cervantes put it, "When thou art at Rome, do as
they do at Rome."]

Travelling is the ruin of all happiness. There's no looking at
a building here after seeing Italy.
> —FANNY BURNEY, *Cecilia*, 1782

Travellers, like poets, are mostly an angry race.
> —SIR RICHARD BURTON,
> *Narrative of a Trip to Harar*, 1855

All places are distant from heaven alike.
> —ROBERT BURTON,
> *The Anatomy of Melancholy*, 1621–51

Why do people so love to wander? I think the civilized parts
of the world will suffice for me in the future.
> —MARY CASSATT, letter to
> Louisine Havermeyer, Feb. 11, 1911

Men travel faster now, but I do not know if they go to better things.　　　　—WILLA CATHER, *Death Comes for the Archbishop*, 1927

Travelling is almost like talking with men of other centuries.
　　　—RENÉ DESCARTES, *Discourse on Method*, 1637

I want to travel in Europe . . . I know that I am only going to a graveyard, but it's a most precious graveyard.
　　　　　　　　—FEODOR DOSTOEVSKI,
　　　　　　　　The Brothers Karamazov, 1879–80

No man should travel until he has learned the language of the country he visits. Otherwise he voluntarily makes himself a great baby,—so helpless and ridiculous.
　　　—RALPH WALDO EMERSON, *Journal*, 1833

Travelling is a fool's paradise.
　　　　　　　　—RALPH WALDO EMERSON,
　　　　　　　　Self-Reliance in *Essays: First Series*, 1841

The woods are lovely, dark and deep,
But I have promises to keep,
And miles to go before I sleep,
And miles to go before I sleep.
　　　　　　　　—ROBERT FROST, *Stopping by Woods on a Snowy Evening*, 1923

He that travels much knows much.
　　　—THOMAS FULLER, *Gnomologia*, 1732

One of the pleasantest things in the world is going a journey; but I like to go by myself.
　　　　　　　　—WILLIAM HAZLITT, *On Going a Journey* in *Table Talk*, 1820–21

There is nothing worse for mortals than a wandering life.
　　　—HOMER, *Odyssey*, 8th cent. B.C.

Those who go overseas find a change of climate, not a change of soul.　　　—HORACE, *Epistles*, Book I, 20 B.C.

He travels fastest who travels alone.
—RUDYARD KIPLING,
The Winners in *Soldiers Three*, 1888

Ship me somewheres east of Suez, where the best is like the
worst,
Where there aren't no Ten Commandments, an' a man can
raise a thirst.   —RUDYARD KIPLING, *Mandalay* in
Barrack-Room Ballads, 1892

I love to sail forbidden seas, and land on barbarous coasts.
—HERMAN MELVILLE, *Moby-Dick*, 1851

Travel is the most private of pleasures. There is no greater
bore than the travel bore. We do not in the least want to
hear what he has seen in Hong Kong.
—VITA SACKVILLE-WEST, *Passenger to Teheran*, 1926

He who would travel happily must travel light.
—ANTOINE DE SAINT-EXUPÉRY,
Wind, Sand, and Stars, 1939

When I was at home, I was in a better place.
—SHAKESPEARE, *As You Like It*, II, iv

Foreigners can always tempt one to abandon any sensible
habit.   —C. P. SNOW, *Strangers and Brothers*,
television broadcast, 1985

A man should know something of his own country, too,
before he goes abroad.
—LAURENCE STERNE, *Tristram Shandy*, 1759–67

I travel not to go anywhere but to go. I travel for travel's
sake. The great affair is to move.
—ROBERT LOUIS STEVENSON,
Travels with a Donkey, 1878

To travel hopefully is better than to arrive.
—ROBERT LOUIS STEVENSON,
El Dorado in *Virginibus Puerisque*, 1881
[More of this is given at WORK & WORKERS.]

Three things are weakening: fear, sin, and travel.
—TALMUD, compiled 6th cent. A.D.

I never travel without my diary. One should always have something sensational to read in the train.
—OSCAR WILDE, *The Importance of Being Earnest,* 1895

TREES See ENVIRONMENT; NATURE: GARDENS, FLOWERS, & TREES

TROUBLE See also CONFLICT; DESPAIR, DEPRESSION, & MISERY; PROBLEMS; RUIN; SORROW, SADNESS, & SUFFERING; TURBULENT TIMES

Who except the gods can live time through forever without any pain?
—AESCHYLUS, *Prometheus Bound,* 5th cent. B.C.

Many are the troubles of mankind.
—AESCHYLUS, *The Suppliant Maidens,* 5th cent. B.C.

In the river, there is the crocodile. On the riverbank, there is the tiger. If you go to the forest, there are the thorns. If you go to the market, there is the policeman.
—ANONYMOUS (CAMBODIAN PROVERB)

If fortune turns against you, even jelly breaks your tooth.
—ANONYMOUS (PERSIAN PROVERB)

You can't have more bedbugs than a blanket-full.
—ANONYMOUS (SPANISH PROVERB)

If you walked into a room and saw everyone's troubles hanging on a wall, you'd head straight to your own.
—ANONYMOUS (JEWISH SAYING)
[Comedienne Joan Rivers calls it a Russian proverb; *New York Times* writer Alex Wichtel says it is Jewish, *The New York Times,* May 1, 1994.]

Prosperity doth best discover vice, but adversity doth best discover virtue.
—FRANCIS BACON, *Of Adversity* in *Essays,* 1625

Man is born unto trouble, as the sparks fly upward.
                                   —BIBLE, *Job* 5:7
[Job accepts his loss of fortune and bitter troubles, saying,
"What? shall we receive good at the hand of God, and shall
we not receive evil?," *Job* 2:10.]

Weeping may endure for a night, but joy cometh in the
morning.   —BIBLE, *Psalms* 30:5

Take us the foxes, the little foxes, that spoil the vines: for
our vines have tender grapes.
                         —BIBLE, *Song of Solomon* 2:15
[In her book *Little Foxes* (1865), Harriet Beecher Stowe explained that by "little foxes" she meant "those unsuspected,
unwatched, insignificant little causes that nibble away domestic
happiness." Lillian Hellman later used this title for a play about
a family thoroughly gnawed by little foxes.]

If it be possible, let this cup pass from me.
                                —BIBLE, *Matthew* 26:39

Whom the Lord loveth he chasteneth.
                                —BIBLE, *Hebrews* 12:6

I am convinced that we have a degree of delight, and that
no small one, in the real misfortunes and pains of, others.
   —EDMUND BURKE, *On the Sublime and Beautiful,* 1756
[The thought has occurred to many, including La Rochefoucauld,
quoted below. The Germans call this delight *Schadenfreude*.]

Adversity is the first path to truth.
                         —LORD BYRON, *Don Juan,* 1819–24

If there were no tribulation, there would be no rest; if there
were no winter, there would be no summer.
      —ST. JOHN CHRYSOSTOM, *Homilie,* c. A.D. 386–98

A *wounded* deer—leaps highest.
                  —EMILY DICKINSON, poem no. 165, c. 1860

Every calamity is a spur and valuable hint.
                              —RALPH WALDO EMERSON,
                         Fate in *The Conduct of Life,* 1860

Everything has two handles: one by which it may be borne, another by which it cannot.
—EPICTETUS, *Encheiridion,* c. A.D. 100

There is no wind that always blows a storm.
—EURIPIDES, *Alcestis,* 438 B.C.
[The classical version of the proverbial, "It's an ill wind that blows no good."]

When written in Chinese, the word *crisis* is composed of two characters. One represents danger and the other represents opportunity.   —JOHN F. KENNEDY, speech, Apr. 12, 1959

In the misfortunes of our best friends, we find something that is not unpleasing.
—LA ROCHEFOUCAULD, *Maxims,* 1678
[Cf. Edmund Burke, above.]

Into each life some rain must fall,
Some days must be dark and dreary.
—HENRY WADSWORTH LONGFELLOW,
The Rainy Day, 1842

And the cares that infest the day
Shall fold their tents like the Arabs,
And as silently steal away.
—HENRY WADSWORTH LONGFELLOW,
The Day Is Done, 1845
[More at ARTS: MUSIC & DANCE.]

Fasten your seat belts. It's going to be a bumpy night.
—JOSEPH L. MANKIEWICZ,
screenplay, *All About Eve,* 1950

If you are distressed by anything external, the pain is not due to the thing itself, but to your own estimate of it; and this you have the power to revoke at any moment.
—MARCUS AURELIUS, *Meditations,* 2nd cent. A.D.

The world is quickly bored by the recital of misfortune, and willingly avoids the sight of distress.
—W. SOMERSET MAUGHAM,
The Moon and Sixpence, 1919

Care
Sat on his faded cheek.
—JOHN MILTON, *Paradise Lost*, 1667

Adversity introduces a man to himself.
—ALONZO MOURNING, quoted in
The New York Times, May 16, 1999
[Mourning was center for the Miami Heat basketball team,
which had just unexpectedly lost a playoff series to their arch-
rivals, the New York Knicks.]

If anything can go wrong, it will.
—EDWARD A. MURPHY, JR., c. 1949
[Recent scholarship has discovered the originator of "Murphy's
law," Capt. Edward A. Murphy, Jr., a development engineer
working on crash research tests at Edwards Air Force Base in
California. Referring to a particular technician, he is said to have
observed, "If there's a way to do it wrong, he will." The law has
inspired numerous variations; see anonymous Murphy's Laws at
SCIENCE (Note) and SCIENCE: PHYSICS & COSMOLOGY.]

That which does not kill me makes me stronger.
—FRIEDRICH NIETZSCHE,
Twilight of the Idols, 1888

I never knew any man in my life who could not bear anoth-
er's misfortunes perfectly like a Christian.
—ALEXANDER POPE,
Thoughts on Various Subjects, 1706

Fire is the test of gold, adversity of strong men.
—SENECA, *On Providence*, 1st cent. A.D.

Sweet are the uses of adversity.
—SHAKESPEARE, *As You Like It*, II, i

The worst is not
So long as we can say, "This is the worst."
—SHAKESPEARE, *King Lear*, IV, i

There's small choice in rotten apples.
—SHAKESPEARE, *The Taming of the Shrew*, I, i

Misery acquaints a man with strange bedfellows.
—SHAKESPEARE, *The Tempest,* II, ii
[For politics and bedfellows, see Warner at POLITICS.]

We have seen better days.
—SHAKESPEARE, *Timon of Athens,* IV, ii

Grief teaches the steadiest minds to waver.
—SOPHOCLES, *Antigone,* 5th cent. B.C.

The greatest griefs are those we cause ourselves.
—SOPHOCLES, *Oedipus Rex,* 5th cent. B.C.

The worst is yet to come.
—ALFRED, LORD TENNYSON, *Sea Dreams,* 1864

Pure and complete sorrow is as impossible as pure and complete joy.   —LEO TOLSTOY, *War and Peace,* 1865–69

Suffering is permanent, obscure, and dark,
And shares the nature of infinity.
—WILLIAM WORDSWORTH, *The Borderers,* 1842

Too long a sacrifice
Can make a stone of the heart.
—WILLIAM BUTLER YEATS, *Easter 1916*
in *Michael Robartes and the Dancer,* 1921

TRUST

Poor Trust is dead; Bad Pay killed him.
—ANONYMOUS (ENGLISH PROVERB)

Trust men and they will be true to you.
—RALPH WALDO EMERSON, *Prudence*
in *Essays: First Series,* 1841
[But still, cut the cards; see the Dunne quote under PRUDENCE & PRACTICAL WISDOM.]

Trust, like the soul, never returns once it is gone.
—PUBLILIUS SYRUS, *Moral Sayings,* 1st cent. B.C.

Love all, trust a few.
—SHAKESPEARE, *All's Well That Ends Well,* I, i

I have always depended on the kindness of strangers.
> —TENNESSEE WILLIAMS,
> *A Streetcar Named Desire,* 1947

[Final words of Blanche DuBois.]

TRUTH   See also FACTS; HONESTY & SINCERITY

"But the emperor has nothing on at all!" said a little child.
> —HANS CHRISTIAN ANDERSEN,
> *The Emperor's New Clothes* in *Fairy Tales,* 1835

All truth is good, but not all truth is good to say.
> —ANONYMOUS (AFRICAN PROVERB)

Truth brings forth hatred.
> —ANONYMOUS (LATIN PROVERB)

Se non è vero, è molto ben trovato.
If it is not true, it is a very good invention.
> —ANONYMOUS (ITALIAN PROVERB)

[Quoted by Giordano Bruno, 1585.]

The truth shall make you free.   —BIBLE, *John* 8:32
[The full verse, "And ye shall know the truth, and the truth shall make you free," is inscribed in the lobby of Central Intelligence Agency headquarters in Langley, Va. Incidentally, the original translation here was by William Tyndale, who was strangled and burned at the stake in 1536 for daring to translate Biblical books from Greek and Hebrew. (Strangulation was considered a mercy, given to those who repented before the fire was lit.) Other Tyndale passages included in the King James version, 1611, include: "Let there be light," *Genesis* 1:4; "Am I my brother's keeper," *Genesis* 4:9; "Love thy neighbor as thyself," *Leviticus,* 19:18; and "Let my people go," *Exodus,* 5:1.]

Pilate saith unto him, What is truth?   —*Ibid.* 18:38

Great is truth and mighty above all things.
> —BIBLE, *I Esdras* 4:41

A truth that's told with bad intent
Beats all the lies you can invent.
>   —WILLIAM BLAKE, *Auguries of Innocence*
>   in *Poems from the Pickering Manuscript,* c. 1805

Truth crushed to earth shall rise again.
>   —WILLIAM CULLEN BRYANT, *The Battle-Field,* 1839

'Tis strange—but true; for truth is always strange;
Stranger than fiction. —LORD BYRON, *Don Juan,* 1819–24

Truth ever lovely—since the world began,
The foe of tyrants and the friend of man.
>   —THOMAS CAMPBELL, *The Pleasures of Hope,* 1799

The aim of the superior man is truth.
>   —CONFUCIUS, *Analects,* 6th–5th cent. B.C.

The truth is always modern, and there never comes a time
when it is safe to give it voice.
>   —CLARENCE DARROW, d. 1938,
>   writing on Voltaire, cited in George Seldes,
>   *The Great Quotations,* 1960

Nature has buried truth at the bottom of the sea.
>   —DEMOCRITUS, 5th cent. B.C., attributed

I can be expected to look for truth, but not to find it.
>   —DENIS DIDEROT, *Pensées philosophiques,* 1746

We swallow greedily any lie that flatters us, but we sip only
little by little at a truth we find bitter.
>   —DENIS DIDEROT, *Rameau's Nephew,* 1762

When you have eliminated the impossible, whatever remains, however improbable, must be the truth.
>   —A. CONAN DOYLE, *The Sign*
>   *of Four, A Demonstration,* 1890

Hell is truth seen too late.
>   —TRYON EDWARDS, *A Dictionary of Thoughts,* 1906
[Probably not original with Edwards. The full line is: "Hell is
truth seen too late—duty neglected in its season."]

God offers to every mind its choice between truth and
repose.   —RALPH WALDO EMERSON, *Intellect*
                            in *Essays: First Series,* 1841

To love the truth is to refuse to let oneself be saddened by
it.   —ANDRÉ GIDE, *Journals,* tr. 1948–51

There are truths which can kill a nation.
                   —JEAN GIRAUDOUX, *Electra,* 1937

Political truth is a libel—religious truth, blasphemy.
                        —WILLIAM HAZLITT, *Commonplaces*
                                in *The Round Table,* 1817

Truth is tough.   —OLIVER WENDELL HOLMES, SR.,
                        The Professor at the Breakfast Table, 1858

It is the customary fate of new truths to begin as heresies
and to end as superstitions.
                   —T. H. HUXLEY, *The Coming of Age of
                        "The Origin of Species,"* 1880

There is not a truth existing which I fear, or would wish
unknown to the whole world.
              —THOMAS JEFFERSON, letter to Henry Lee, 1826

What the imagination seizes as beauty must be truth.
                           —JOHN KEATS, letter to
                            Benjamin Bailey, Nov. 22, 1817
[See Keats also under BEAUTY.]

The exact opposite of what is generally believed is often the
truth.   —LA BRUYÈRE, *Les Caractères,* 1688

Truth is often eclipsed but never extinguished.
                   —LIVY, *History of Rome,* c. A.D. 14

Truth, like gold, is not less so for being newly brought out
of the mine.   —JOHN LOCKE, *An Essay Concerning
                                Human Understanding,* 1690

To love truth is the principal part of human perfection in
this world, and the seed-plot of all other virtues.
              —JOHN LOCKE, letter to Anthony Collins, Oct. 29, 1703

The love of truth has its reward in heaven and even on earth. —FRIEDRICH NIETZSCHE,
Beyond Good and Evil, 1885–86

We arrive at truth, not by reason only, but also by the heart.
—PASCAL, *Pensées*, 1670

Truth is the beginning of every good thing, both in heaven and on earth; and he who would be blessed and happy should be from the first a partaker of truth, for then he can be trusted. —PLATO, *Laws*, 4th cent. B.C.
[See also Plato at PHILOSOPHY.]

Truth is no road to fortune.
—JEAN JACQUES ROUSSEAU,
The Social Contract, 1762

Life is short, but truth works far and lives long; let us speak the truth. —ARTHUR SCHOPENHAUER,
The World as Will and Idea, 1819

How dreadful knowledge of the truth can be when there's no help in truth.
—SOPHOCLES, *Oedipus Rex*, 5th cent. B.C.

Truth is the only safe ground to stand upon.
—ELIZABETH CADY STANTON,
The Woman's Bible, 1895

Rather than love, than money, than fame, give me truth.
—HENRY DAVID THOREAU,
Conclusion, *Walden*, 1854

I never give them hell. I just tell the truth, and they think it's hell. —HARRY S. TRUMAN, saying,
from 1948 presidential campaign

Truth is mighty and will prevail. There is nothing the matter with this, except that it ain't so. —MARK TWAIN, d. 1910,
Albert B. Paine, ed., *Mark Twain's Notebook*, 1935

Truth confronts us, and we can no longer understand anything. —PAUL VALÉRY, *Eupalinos*, 1924

Truth is rarely pure and never simple.
　　—OSCAR WILDE, *The Importance of Being Earnest*, 1895

Truth is on the march; nothing can stop it now.
　　—ÉMILE ZOLA, manifesto, *Le Figaro*, Nov. 25, 1897

TURBULENT TIMES　　See also CONFLICT; DANGER;
　　　　　　　　　DECISION (Anonymous); METHOD;
　　　　　　MODERN TIMES; REVOLUTION; TROUBLE

Lost is our old simplicity of times,
The world abounds with laws, and teems with crimes.
　　　　—ANONYMOUS, *On the Proceedings against America*
　　　　　in the *Pennsylvania Gazette*, Feb. 8, 1775, borrowed
　　　　　from an earlier, unidentified London magazine.

Dictators ride to and fro on tigers from which they dare not
dismount. And the tigers are getting hungry.
　　　—WINSTON CHURCHILL, *While England Slept*, 1936
[Churchill wrote that the observation, "Dictators ride tigers
from which they are afraid to dismount," is a Hindustani proverb. There is a similar proverb among the Chinese: "He who
rides a tiger is afraid to dismount."]

It was the best of times, it was the worst of times, it was
the age of wisdom, it was the age of foolishness, it was the
epoch of belief, it was the epoch of incredulity, it was the season
of Light, it was the season of Darkness, it was the spring of
hope, it was the winter of despair, we had everything before
us, we had nothing before us, we were all going direct to
Heaven, we were all going direct the other way.
　　　　—CHARLES DICKENS, *A Tale of Two Cities*, 1859

The time is out of joint; O cursèd spite,
That ever I was born to set it right!
　　　　　　—SHAKESPEARE, *Hamlet*, I, v

So foul and fair a day I have not seen.
　　　　　　—SHAKESPEARE, *Macbeth*, III, iii

Lechery, lechery; still wars and lechery; nothing else holds
fashion.　　　—SHAKESPEARE, *Troilus and Cressida*, V, ii

TWENTIETH CENTURY　　See MODERN TIMES

**TYRANNY
& TOTALITARIANISM**

See also NECESSITY
(Milton and Pitt);
VIOLENCE & FORCE

Death is preferable—it is a milder fate than tyranny.
—AESCHYLUS, *Agamemnon,* 5th cent. B.C.

Any excuse will serve a tyrant.
—AESOP, *The Wolf and the Lamb,* 6th cent. B.C.

Dictators ride to and fro on tigers from which they dare not dismount.   —ANONYMOUS (HINDUSTANI PROVERB)
[More is given at TURBULENT TIMES under Churchill.]

Government by a tyrant is the worst form of rule.
—ST. THOMAS AQUINAS,
On Princely Government, c. 1252–73

Under conditions of tyranny, it is far easier to act than to think.   —HANNAH ARENDT, quoted in
W. H. Auden, *A Certain World,* 1970

When a nation has allowed itself to fall under a tyrannical regime, it cannot be absolved from the faults due to the guilt of that regime.
—WINSTON CHURCHILL, speech, July 28, 1944

All men would be tyrants if they could.
—DANIEL DEFOE, *The History of
the Kentish Petition,* 1712–13
[See also Abigail Adams at WOMEN & MEN.]

The history of most countries has been that of majorities—mounted majorities, clad in iron, armed with death, treading down the ten-fold more numerous minorities.
—OLIVER WENDELL HOLMES, SR.,
address, Massachusetts Medical Society, May 30, 1860

Rebellion to tyrants is obedience to God.
—THOMAS JEFFERSON, d. 1826, motto on
his seal, sometimes attributed to Benjamin Franklin

Truth forever on the scaffold,
Wrong forever on the throne.
—JAMES RUSSELL LOWELL, *The Present Crisis,* 1844

I am the state—I alone am here the representative of the
people.   —NAPOLEON BONAPARTE,
in the French Senate, 1814
[See also Louis XIV at HIGH POSITION: RULERS &
LEADERS.]

Big Brother is watching you.
—GEORGE ORWELL, *1984,* 1948

Who controls the past controls the future. Who controls the
present controls the past.   —*Ibid.*

Tyranny is always better organized than freedom.
—CHARLES PÉGUY, d. 1914,
War and Peace in *Basic Truths,* tr. 1943

The people always have some champion whom they set over
them and nurse into greatness. . . . This and no other is the
root from which a tyranny springs.
—PLATO, *The Republic,* 4th cent. B.C.

The face of tyranny is always mild at first.
—RACINE, *Britannicus,* 1669

Man was born free, and everywhere he is in chains.
—JEAN JACQUES ROUSSEAU,
The Social Contract, 1762

Why, man, he doth bestride the narrow world
Like a Colossus.   —SHAKESPEARE, *Julius Caesar,* I, ii

They squeeze the orange and throw away the peel.
—VOLTAIRE, describing the court of
Frederick the Great, letter to Mme. Denis, Sept. 9, 1751

The despot, be assured, lives night and day like one condemned to death by the whole of mankind for his
wickedness.   —XENOPHON, *Hiero,* 4th cent. B.C.

U

UNDERSTANDING See MIND, THOUGHT, & UNDERSTANDING; TOLERANCE & UNDERSTANDING; VISION & VISIONARIES; WISDOM

UNHAPPINESS See DESPAIR, DEPRESSION, & MISERY; HAPPINESS; SORROW, SADNESS, & SUFFERING; TROUBLE

UNITED STATES See AMERICA & AMERICANS; AMERICAN HISTORY: MEMORABLE MOMENTS

UNITY & LOYALTY See also CONFLICT; PATRIOTISM

United we stand, divided we fall.
—AESOP, *The Four Oxen and the Lion,* 6th cent. B.C.
[For Benjamin Franklin on hanging together, see AMERICAN HISTORY: MEMORABLE MOMENTS.]

Union gives strength.
—AESOP, *The Bundle of Sticks,* 6th cent. B.C.

Whose bread I eat, his song I sing.
—ANONYMOUS (GERMAN SAYING)

No man can serve two masters. —BIBLE, *Matthew* 6:24

He that is not with me is against me. —*Ibid.*
[Also *Luke* 11:23]

I have kept the faith. —BIBLE, *II Timothy* 4:7
[The full verse is given at ACCOMPLISHMENT.]

When bad men combine, the good must associate; else they will fall, one by one, an unpitied sacrifice in a contemptible struggle.   —EDMUND BURKE, *Thoughts on the Cause of the Present Discontents,* Apr. 23, 1770
[See also the Burke and Martin Luther King, Jr., entries at EVIL.]

All for one, one for all.
    —ALEXANDRE DUMAS, *The Three Musketeers,* 1844

If that plane leaves the ground and you're not with him, you'll regret it. Maybe not today, maybe not tomorrow, but soon and for the rest of your life.
        —JULIUS EPSTEIN, PHILIP EPSTEIN, & HOWARD KOCH, screenplay, *Casablanca,* 1942

Something there is that doesn't love a wall.
    —ROBERT FROST, *Mending Wall,* 1914

There are only two forces that unite men—fear and interest.
    —NAPOLEON BONAPARTE, *Maxims,* 1804–15

He may be a son of a bitch, but he's our son of a bitch.
        —FRANKLIN D. ROOSEVELT, referring to Anastasio Somoza after he assumed the presidency of Nicaragua in 1937

UNIVERSE   See also CREATION, DIVINE; ESCAPE (Cummings); NATURE; QUESTIONS & ANSWERS (Adams); SCIENCE: PHYSICS & COSMOLOGY; WORLD, END OF

The universe . . . is a machine for making deities.
        —HENRI BERGSON, *The Two Sources of Morality and Religion,* 1932

I don't pretend to understand the universe—it's a great deal bigger than I am. . . . People ought to be modester.
    —THOMAS CARLYLE, quoted in D. A. Wilson and D. Wilson McArthur, *Carlyle in Old Age: 1865–81,* 1934

[The universe:] The most exquisite masterpiece ever composed by nobody.
—G. K. CHESTERTON, d. 1936, quoted by Martin Gardner in *New York Review of Books,* June 13, 1985

Law rules throughout existence, a Law which is not intelligent, but Intelligence. —RALPH WALDO EMERSON, *Fate* in *The Conduct of Life,* 1860

Ah Love! Could thou and I with Fate conspire
To grasp this sorry Scheme of Things entire,
Would we not shatter it to bits—and then remold it nearer to the Heart's Desire! —EDWARD FITZGERALD, *The Rubáiyát of Omar Khayyám,* 1879

The book [i.e., the universe] is written in the mathematical language, and the symbols are triangles, circles, and other geometrical figures, without the help of which it is impossible to conceive a single word of it, and without which one wanders in vain through a dark labyrinth.
—GALILEO GALILEI, *Il Saggiatore,* 1623

My own suspicion is that the universe is not only queerer than we suppose but queerer than we *can* suppose.
—J.B.S. HALDANE, *On Being the Right Size* in *Possible Worlds & Other Essays,* 1927

The cosmic process has no sort of relation to moral ends.
—T. H. HUXLEY, *Evolution and Ethics,* 1893

The universe begins to look more like a great thought than like a great machine.
—SIR JAMES JEANS, *The Mysterious Universe,* 1930

All are but parts of one stupendous whole,
Whose body nature is, and God the soul.
—ALEXANDER POPE, *An Essay on Man,* 1733–34

The universe is a spiraling Big Band in a polka-dotted speakeasy, effusively generating new light every one-night stand. —ISHMAEL REED, cited in James A. Haskins, *The Cotton Club,* 1977

Don't let me catch anyone talking about the Universe in my department.   —LORD ERNEST RUTHERFORD, d. 1937, quoted by John Kendrew, BBC broadcast, July 3, 1968

Let the great world spin forever down the ringing grooves of change.
—ALFRED, LORD TENNYSON, *Locksley Hall,* 1842

Thou canst not stir a flower
Without the troubling of a star.
—FRANCIS THOMPSON, *The Mistress of Vision,* 1897

O amazement of things—even the least particle!
—WALT WHITMAN, *Song at Sunset,* 1860

UNREASONABLE PEOPLE   See REASONABLE &
UNREASONABLE PEOPLE

V

VALUE

Neither cast ye your pearls before swine, lest they trample them under their feet, and turn again and rend you.
—BIBLE, *Matthew* 7:6
[T. H. White, in *The Bestiary,* notes that "pearls," written in Latin *margarites,* may be a mistranslation of the Latin *marguerites,* which means "daisies."]

When the well's dry, we know the worth of water.
—BENJAMIN FRANKLIN,
Poor Richard's Almanac, Jan. 1746

Things are only worth what you make them worth.
—MOLIÈRE, *The Precious Damsels,* 1659

Good merchandise, even when hidden, soon finds buyers.
—PLAUTUS, *The Carthaginian,* c. 200 B.C.

[A cynic:] a man who knows the price of everything and the value of nothing.
—OSCAR WILDE, *Lady Windermere's Fan,* 1892

VANITY   See PRIDE & VANITY

VARIETY   See also CHANGE; INDIVIDUALITY;
NEW THINGS

Every fool is different.
—ANONYMOUS (GERMAN PROVERB)

I never saw a Purple Cow,
I never hope to see one;
But I can tell you anyhow,
I'd rather see than be one.
> —GELETT BURGESS, *The Purple Cow*
> in *The Lark* magazine, 1895

[The verse was so wildly popular that Burgess became sick of it, and penned, "Ah, yes! I wrote "The Purple Cow" — / I'm sorry now I wrote it! / But I can tell you anyhow, / I'll kill you if you quote it," *Confessional* in *The Burgess Nonsense Book*, 1914.]

Variety's the very spice of life,
That gives it all its flavor.
> —WILLIAM COWPER, *The Task*, 1785

The great source of pleasure is variety.
> —SAMUEL JOHNSON, *Butler*
> in *Lives of the English Poets*, 1779–81

What is food to one is to another bitter poison.
> —LUCRETIUS, *On the Nature of Things*, c. 57 B.C.

[This is an early version of the English proverb "One man's meat is another man's poison."]

Letting a hundred flowers blossom and a hundred schools of thought contend is the policy.
> —MAO ZEDUNG, speech, May 2, 1956

[Usually shortened to, "Let a hundred flowers blossom."]

No pleasure lasts long unless there is variety in it.
> —PUBLILIUS SYRUS, *Moral Sayings*, 1st cent. B.C.

It were not best that we should all think alike; it is difference of opinion that makes horse races.
> —MARK TWAIN, *Pudd'nhead Wilson's*
> *Calendar* in *Pudd'nhead Wilson*, 1894

VENGEANCE   See REVENGE

VICE See EVIL; EXCESS; SIN; VICE, & NAUGHTINESS

VICTORY   See MILITARY BATTLES; WAR;
WINNING & LOSING, VICTORY & DEFEAT

VIOLENCE & FORCE   See also ANGER;
REVOLUTION; POWER; TYRANNY
& TOTALITARIANISM; WAR

They have sown the wind, and they shall reap the whirlwind.
—BIBLE, *Hosea* 8:7

All they that take the sword shall perish with the sword.
—BIBLE, *Matthew* 26:52
[But see also *Matthew* at REVOLUTION.]

I say violence is necessary. It is as American as cherry pie.
—H. "RAP" BROWN, press conference, July 27, 1967

A whiff of grapeshot.   —THOMAS CARLYLE, *History of
the French Revolution,* 1837

Violence is not a catalyst but a diversion.
—JOSEPH CONRAD, *The Secret Agent,* 1907

God hates violence. He has ordained that all men fairly
possess their property, not seize it.
—EURIPIDES, *Helen,* 412 B.C.

Where wisdom is called for, force is of little use.
—HERODOTUS, *Histories,* 5th cent. B.C.

Force without wisdom falls of its own weight.
—HORACE, *Odes,* 33–15 B.C.

A man may build himself a throne of bayonets, but he cannot sit on it.   —WILLIAM RALPH INGE,
Philosophy of Plotinus, 1923

Force cannot give right.   —THOMAS JEFFERSON,
The Rights of British America, 1774

It is far more convenient to commit an act of violence and
afterwards excuse it, than laboriously to consider convincing
arguments, and lose time listening to objections. This very
boldness itself indicates a sort of conviction of the legitimacy
of the action, and the God of success is afterwards the best
advocate.   —IMMANUEL KANT, appendix,
Perpetual Peace, 1795

Be peaceful, be courteous, obey the law, respect everyone; but if someone puts his hand on you, send him to the cemetery.   —MALCOLM X, *Malcolm X Speaks,* 1965

In violence, we forget who we are.
                    —MARY McCARTHY, *On the Contrary,* 1961

Who overcomes
By force, hath overcome but half his foe.
                    —JOHN MILTON, *Paradise Lost,* 1667

If aggressors are wrong above, they are right here below.
                    —NAPOLEON BONAPARTE, *Maxims,* 1804–15

Violence is good for those who have nothing to lose.
                    —JEAN PAUL SARTRE,
                    The Devil and the Good Lord, 1951

Uncontrolled violence is a fault of youth.
                    —SENECA, *Troades,* 1st Cent. A.D.

Lay on, Macduff,
And damn'd be him that first cries "Hold, enough!"
                    —SHAKESPEARE, *Macbeth,* V, viii

Not believing in force is the same as not believing in gravity.
                    —LEON TROTSKY, *What Next?,* 1932

VIRGIN MARY   See JESUS

VIRTUE   See also COMPASSION & PITY; COURAGE;
                    FORGIVENESS & MERCY; GRACE;
                    HONESTY & SINCERITY; INNOCENCE;
                    SELF-RIGHTEOUSNESS; STRENGTH; WISDOM;
                    WOMEN (Bible); WOMEN & MEN (Otis Skinner)

Virtue is not always amiable.
                    —JOHN ADAMS, *Diary,* Feb. 9, 1779

The happiness of man, as well as his dignity, consists in virtue.   —JOHN ADAMS, *Thoughts on Government,* 1776

No act of kindness, no matter how small, is ever wasted.
                    —AESOP, *The Lion and the Mouse,* 6th cent. B.C.

Kindness effects more than severity.
>—AESOP, *The Wind and the Sun,* 6th cent. B.C.

The eternal *not ourselves* that makes for righteousness.
>—MATTHEW ARNOLD, *Literature and Dogma,* 1873

Let us honor if we can
The vertical man
Though we value none
But the horizontal one.   —W. H. AUDEN, *To Christopher Isherwood,* in *Poems,* 1930

Virtue is like a rich stone, best plain set.
>—FRANCIS BACON, *Of Beauty* in *Essays,* 1625

Righteousness exalteth a nation.   —BIBLE, *Proverbs* 14:34

What doth the Lord require of thee, but to do justly, and to love mercy, and to walk humbly with thy God?
>—BIBLE, *Micah* 6:8

Blessed are the poor in spirit: for theirs is the kingdom of heaven.
Blessed are they that mourn: for they shall be comforted.
Blessed are the meek: for they shall inherit the earth.
Blessed are they which do hunger and thirst after righteousness: for they shall be filled.
Blessed are the merciful: for they shall obtain mercy.
Blessed are the pure in heart: for they shall see God.
Blessed are the peacemakers: for they shall be called the children of God.
Blessed are they which are persecuted for righteousness' sake: for theirs is the kingdom of heaven.
>—BIBLE, *Matthew* 5:3–10, The Sermon on the Mount

Strait is the gate, and narrow is the way, which leadeth unto life, and few there be that find it.   —*Ibid.* 7:14

If thine eye offend thee, pluck it out, and cast it from thee: it is better for thee to enter into life with one eye, rather than having two eyes to be cast into hell fire.   —*Ibid.* 18:9

Unto the pure all things are pure.   —BIBLE, *Titus* 1:15

The souls of the righteous are in the hand of God, and there shall no torment touch them.
—BIBLE, *Wisdom of Solomon* 3:1

My will was to live worthily as long as I lived, and after my life to leave them that should come after, my memory in good works. —BOETHIUS, *The Consolation of Philosophy,* c. A.D. 524, translated by Alfred the Great, 9th cent.

There is no road or ready way to virtue.
—THOMAS BROWNE, *Religio medici,* 1643

The humblest citizen of all the land, when clad in the armor of a righteous cause, is stronger than all the hosts of error.
—WILLIAM JENNINGS BRYAN, speech,
Democratic National Convention, July 8, 1896

The upright, honest-hearted man
Who strives to do the best he can,
Need never fear the church's ban
Or hell's damnation.   —ROBERT BURNS, *Epistle to the Rev. John McMath* in *Posthumous Pieces,* 1799

Absolute virtue is as sure to kill a man as absolute vice is, let alone the dullness of it and the pomposities of it.
—SAMUEL BUTLER, *Notebooks,* 1917

In my experience, good deeds usually do not go unpunished.
—WILLIAM SLOANE COFFIN, speech, Oct. 1984,
in behalf of the Sanctuary Program for protecting refugees
[This bit of sharp cynicism seems to have been around a while in various forms. Clare Boothe Luce, Walter Annenberg, Noel Coward, and others have been credited with the slightly harsher, "No good deed goes unpunished" (or close variations thereof).]

It is a far, far better thing that I do, than I have ever done; it is a far, far better rest that I go to, than I have ever known. —CHARLES DICKENS, *A Tale of Two Cities,* 1859

The essence of greatness is the perception that virtue is enough.   —RALPH WALDO EMERSON,
Heroism in *Essays: First Series,* 1841
[But for Emerson's view of people who talk about their virtue, see SELF-RIGHTEOUSNESS.]

Life is mostly froth and bubble,
Two things stand like stone,
Kindness in another's trouble,
Courage in your own.   —ADAM LINDSAY GORDON,
                                        d. 1870, *Ye Wearie Wayfarer*

I shall pass through this world but once. If therefore there
be any kindness I can show, or any good thing I can do, let
me do it now; let me not defer it or neglect it.
                              —ÉTIENNE DE GRELLET, attributed
[De Grellet was a French Quaker cleric who came to the U.S.
in 1795. He is commonly credited as the author of this prayer.
But the attribution is unproven.]

Be good, sweet maid, and let who will be clever;
Do noble things, not dream them, all day long.
                              —CHARLES KINGSLEY, *A Farewell*, 1856

If you can keep your head when all about you
Are losing theirs and blaming it on you.
If you can trust yourself when all men doubt you
And make allowance for their doubting, too.
    —RUDYARD KIPLING, *If* in *Rewards and Fairies*, 1910
[In *Please Don't Eat the Daisies* (1957), Jean Kerr observed,
"If you can keep your head when all about you are losing
theirs, it is just possible that you haven't grasped the
situation."]

If you can meet with Triumph and Disaster, and treat those
two impostors just the same.   —*Ibid.*

If you can talk with crowds and keep your virtue
Or walk with Kings—nor lose the common touch.   —*Ibid.*

If you can fill the unforgiving minute
With sixty seconds' worth of distance run,
Yours is the earth and everything that's in it,
And—which is more—you'll be a Man, my son!   —*Ibid.*

Very often our virtues are only vices in disguise.
                              —LA ROCHEFOUCAULD, *Maxims*, 1678

Virtue would not go to such lengths if vanity did not keep
her company.   —*Ibid.*

Virtue is harder to be got than knowledge of the world; and, if lost in a young man, is seldom recovered.
—JOHN LOCKE, *Some Thoughts Concerning Education*, 1693

I could not love thee, dear, so much,
Loved I not honor more.
—RICHARD LOVELACE, *To Lucasta, Going to the Wars*, 1649

Virtue may be assailed, but never hurt,
Surprised by unjust force, but not enthralled.
—JOHN MILTON, *Comus*, 1634

I cannot praise a fugitive and cloistered virtue, unexercised and unbreathed, that never sallies out and sees her adversary, but slinks out of the race, where that immortal garland is to be run for, not without dust and heat.
—JOHN MILTON, *Areopagitica*, 1644

I prefer an accommodating vice to an obstinate virtue.
—MOLIÈRE, *Amphitryon*, 1666

Virtue in this world should be malleable.
—MOLIÈRE, *Le Misanthrope*, 1666

There may be guilt when there is too much virtue.
—PASCAL, *Pensées*, 1670

Practice yourself what you preach.
—PLAUTUS, *The Comedy of Asses*, c. 200 B.C.

Do good by stealth, and blush to find it fame.
—ALEXANDER POPE, *Epilogue to the Satires* in *Imitations of Horace*, 1733–38

When men grow virtuous in their old age, they only make a sacrifice to God of the devil's leavings.
—ALEXANDER POPE, *Thoughts on Various Subjects*, 1706

Charms strike the sight, but merit wins the soul.
—ALEXANDER POPE, *The Rape of the Lock*, 1714

Just say no.   —NANCY REAGAN, motto,
                            campaign against drug abuse, 1984

Nature does not bestow virtue, it is an art.
                  —SENECA, *Letters to Lucilius*, 1st cent. A.D.

Hands to work; hearts to God.   —SHAKER motto, c. 1775

Assume a virtue, if you have it not.
                            —SHAKESPEARE, *Hamlet,* III, iv

Virtue is bold, and goodness never fearful.
                  —SHAKESPEARE, *Measure for Measure,* III, i

How far that little candle throws his beams!
So shines a good deed in a naughty world.
                  —SHAKESPEARE, *The Merchant of Venice,* V, i

Mine honor is my life.   —SHAKESPEARE, *Richard II,* I, i

He lives in fame that died in virtue's cause.
                  —SHAKESPEARE, *Titus Andronicus,* I, i

He profits most who serves best.
                  —A. F. SHELDON, motto of International Rotary, 1922

Nothing can harm a good man, either in life or after death.
                  —SOCRATES, quoted in Plato, *Apology,* 5th cent. B.C.

True virtue is life under the direction of reason.
                            —SPINOZA, *Ethics,* 1677

She would rather light candles than curse the darkness, and
her glow has warmed the world.
                            —ADLAI STEVENSON, eulogy for
                  Eleanor Roosevelt, United Nations, Nov. 9, 1962
[Cf. the Christopher Society motto under DOING.]

'Tis only noble to be good.
Kind hearts are more than coronets.
                            —ALFRED, LORD TENNYSON,
                            Lady Clara Vere de Vere, 1833

My strength is as the strength of ten,
Because my heart is pure.
> —ALFRED, LORD TENNYSON, *Sir Galahad*, 1842

Few things are harder to put up with than the annoyance of a good example. —MARK TWAIN, *Pudd'nhead Wilson's Calendar* in *Pudd'nhead Wilson*, 1894

Be good and you will be lonesome.
> —MARK TWAIN, *Pudd'nhead Wilson's New Calendar* in *Following the Equator*, 1897, caption for frontispiece photo of Twain

Always do right. This will gratify some people and astonish the rest. —MARK TWAIN, speech, Greenpoint Presbyterian Church, Brooklyn, N.Y., 1901

Virtue, study, and gaiety are three sisters who should not be separated.
> —VOLTAIRE, letter to Frederick the Great, 1737

That best portion of a good man's life,
His little, nameless, unremembered acts
Of kindness and of love.
> —WILLIAM WORDSWORTH, *Lines Composed a Few Miles Above Tintern Abbey*, 1798

VISION & VISIONARIES   See also IDEAS & IDEALS; MYSTICISM; WISDOM

We are like dwarves upon the shoulders of giants, and so able to see more and farther than the ancients.
> —BERNARD OF CHARTRES, c. 1130, quoted in John of Salisbury, *Metalogicon*, 1159

[For Newton's version, see SCIENCE. Robert K. Merton's *On the Shoulders of Giants* includes many variations on this metaphor. A late one is from Coleridge: "The dwarf sees farther than the giant, when he has the giant's shoulder to mount on," *The Friend*, 1809–10.]

Behold, this dreamer cometh.   —BIBLE, *Genesis* 37:19

Where there is no vision, the people perish.
> —BIBLE, *Proverbs* 29:18

The prophets prophesy lies in my name: I sent them not . . . they prophesy unto you a false vision and . . . the deceit of their own heart. —BIBLE, *Jeremiah* 14:14

Your sons and your daughters shall prophesy, your old men shall dream dreams, your young men shall see visions. —BIBLE, *Joel* 2:28

A prophet is not without honor, save in his own country. —BIBLE, *Matthew* 13:57
[For Matthew on false prophets, see under HYPOCRISY.]

If the blind lead the blind, both shall fall into the ditch. —*Ibid.* 15:14

For now we see through a glass, darkly; but then face to face: now I know in part; but then I shall know even as I am known. —BIBLE, *I Corinthians* 13:11-12

A fool sees not the same tree that a wise man sees. —WILLIAM BLAKE, *The Marriage of Heaven and Hell*, 1790–93

It isn't that they can't see the solution. It is that they can't see the problem. —G. K. CHESTERTON, *The Point of a Pin* in *The Scandal of Father Brown*, 1935

People see only what they are prepared to see. —RALPH WALDO EMERSON, *Journal*, 1863

A danger foreseen is half avoided. —THOMAS FULLER, *Gnomologia*, 1732

Only he who keeps his eye fixed on the far horizon will find his right road. —DAG HAMMARSKJÖLD, d. 1961, *Markings*, 1964

A moment's insight is sometimes worth a life's experience. —OLIVER WENDELL HOLMES, SR., *The Professor of the Breakfast Table*, 1860

You can only predict things after they've happened. —EUGÈNE IONESCO, *Rhinoceros*, 1960

I have a dream.   —MARTIN LUTHER KING, JR.,
                                  theme of his speech in the
                        March on Washington, Aug. 28, 1963
[More at RACES & RACISM.]

Two men look out through the same bars:
One sees the mud, and one the stars.
                        —FREDERICK LANGBRIDGE,
                            Cluster of Quiet Thoughts, 1896

All armed prophets have been victorious, and all unarmed
prophets have been destroyed.
                        —MACHIAVELLI, *The Prince,* 1532

The fellow that can only see a week ahead is always the
popular fellow, for he is looking with the crowd. But the
one that can see years ahead, he has a telescope but he can't
make anybody believe that he has it.   —WILL ROGERS,
                    The Autobiography of Will Rogers, 1949

Nothing happens unless first a dream.
                        —CARL SANDBURG,
                    Washington Monument by Night, 1922
[The preceding line is, "The republic is a dream."]

Vision is the art of seeing things invisible.
                        —JONATHAN SWIFT,
                    Thoughts on Various Subjects, 1711

A dreamer is one who can only find his way by moonlight,
and his punishment is that he sees the dawn before the rest
of the world.   —OSCAR WILDE, *The Critic as Artist,* 1891

W

WAR See also CONFLICT; MILITARY, THE;
MILITARY BATTLES; PEACE; VIOLENCE
& FORCE; WINNING & LOSING, VICTORY & DEFEAT

What Price Glory? —MAXWELL ANDERSON,
title of play about World War I, 1924

To win a war quickly takes long preparation.
—ANONYMOUS (LATIN PROVERB)

The price of pride is high, and paid by the young.
—ANONYMOUS, inscription on the German memorial
at El Alamein, where the British turned back the
German invasion of Egypt in 1942

A bayonet is a weapon with a worker at both ends.
—ANONYMOUS, British pacifist slogan

It takes twenty years or more of peace to make a man; it
takes only twenty seconds of war to destroy him.
—KING BAUDOUIN I of Belgium,
speech in the U.S. Congress, May 12, 1959

It is not merely cruelty that leads men to love war, it is
excitement. —HENRY WARD BEECHER,
Proverbs from Plymouth Pulpit, 1887

This strategy would involve us in the wrong war, at the
wrong place, at the wrong time, and with the wrong enemy.
—OMAR BRADLEY, testimony,
U.S. Senate hearing, May 15, 1951
[General Bradley was referring to confrontation with Communist China.]

War is like love, it always finds a way.
　　　　　　　　　—BERTOLT BRECHT, *Mother Courage
　　　　　　　　　　　　　and Her Children,* 1941

God is ordinarily for the big battalions against the little ones.
　　　　　　　　　—COUNT BUSSY-RABUTIN, letter
　　　　　　　　　　to the Count of Limoges, Oct. 18, 1677
[A thought also voiced by Voltaire, Napoleon, and others.]

In war, whichever side may call itself the victor, there are
no winners but all are losers.
　　　　　　　　　—NEVILLE CHAMBERLAIN, speech, July 3, 1938

The sinews of war, unlimited money.
　　　　　　　　　—CICERO, *Philippic,* V, 44 B.C.

Laws are silent in time of war.
　　　　　　　　　—CICERO, *Pro Milone,* 52 B.C.

All great civilizations, in their early stages, are based on
success in war.　　　　　　—SIR KENNETH CLARK,
　　　　　　　　　　　　　　Civilization, 1970

War is nothing more than the continuation of politics by
other means. —KARL VON CLAUSEWITZ, *On War,* 1833
[This is the traditional translation. In the original German the
quote is longer and slightly different: *"Der Krieg ist nichts als
eine Fortsetzung des politischen Verkehrs mit Einmischung an-
derer Mittel"* ("War is nothing but a continuation of political
intercourse with the intermixing of other means").]

There is nothing that war has ever achieved that we could
not better achieve without it.
　　　　　　—HAVELOCK ELLIS, *The Philosophy of Conflict,* 1919

War educates the senses, calls into action the will, perfects
the physical constitution, brings men into such swift and
close collision in critical moments that man measures man.
　　　　　　　　　—RALPH WALDO EMERSON, d. 1882,
　　　　　　　　　　　　　War in *Miscellanies,* 1884

Men love war because it allows them to look serious. Because it is the one thing that stops women laughing at them.
　　　　　　　　　—JOHN FOWLES, *The Magus,* 1966

There never was a good war or a bad peace.
—BENJAMIN FRANKLIN, letter to
Josiah Quincy, Sept. 11, 1783

Either man is obsolete or war is.
—R. BUCKMINSTER FULLER,
I Seem to Be a Verb, 1970

Guns will make us powerful; butter will only make us fat.
—HERMANN GOERING, radio speech, 1936

It has been a splendid little war.   —JOHN HAY, letter to
Theodore Roosevelt, July 27, 1898
[The Ambassador to Great Britain (he became Secretary of
State two months later) was referring to the war with Spain.
He went on: ". . . begun with the highest motives, carried on
with magnificent intelligence and spirit, favored by the Fortune
which loves the brave."]

War is death's feast.
—GEORGE HERBERT, *Outlandish Proverbs,* 1640

In starting and waging a war, it is not right that matters but
victory.
—ADOLF HITLER, d. 1945, quoted in William L. Shirer,
The Rise and Fall of the Third Reich, 1960
[See also the first MacArthur quote below.]

Older men declare war. But it is youth that must fight and
die.   —HERBERT HOOVER, speech,
Republican National Convention, June 17, 1944

The first casualty when war comes is truth.
—HIRAM JOHNSON,
remark in the U.S. Senate, 1918
[Though generally attributed to Sen. Johnson, the exact citation
has yet to be discovered. *Respectfully Quoted,* published by the
Library of Congress in 1989, notes that an earlier Johnson, Dr.
Samuel, aka the Grand Cham of Literature, reached the same
conclusion, in his own grandly formal fashion: "Among the
calamities of war, may be justly numbered the diminution of
the love of truth, by the falsehoods which interest dictates, and
credulity encourages" (*The Idler,* Nov. 11, 1758).]

If any question why we died,
Tell them, because our fathers lied.
                    —RUDYARD KIPLING, on World War I,
                    Common Form in *The Years Between*, 1919

The slaying of multitudes should be mourned with sorrow.
A victory should be celebrated with the funeral rite.
                    —LAO-TZU, *Tao Te Ching*, 6th cent. B.C.

It is well that war is so terrible, or we should grow too fond
of it.   —ROBERT E. LEE, at Fredericksburg, Va.,
                    Dec. 13, 1862

Make love not war.
    —GERSHON LEGMAN, speech, Ohio University, 1963
[Mr. Legman claimed to be the author of this popular slogan,
as reported in his obituary in the *International Herald Tribune*,
Mar. 15, 1999. We know of no reason to doubt him. His special-
ity was the scholarly study of bawdy jokes, limericks, and
ballads.]

War is the greatest plague that can afflict humanity; it destroys religion, it destroys states, it destroys families. Any
scourge is preferable to it.
                    —MARTIN LUTHER, *Table Talk*, 1569

In war there is no substitute for victory.
                    —DOUGLAS MacARTHUR,
                    address to Congress, Apr. 19, 1951

It is fatal to enter any war without the will to win it.
                    —DOUGLAS MacARTHUR,
                    speech, Republican National Convention, July 7, 1952

War is just when it is necessary; arms are permissible, when
there is no hope except in arms.
                    —MACHIAVELLI, *The Prince*, 1532

To the ashes of the dead, glory comes too late.
                    —MARTIAL, *Epigrams*, 1st cent. A.D.

War will never cease until babies begin to come into the world with larger cerebrums and smaller adrenal glands.
> —H. L. MENCKEN, *Minority Report*
> in *H. L. Mencken's Notebooks,* 1960

For what can war, but endless war still breed?
> —JOHN MILTON, *On the Lord General*
> *Fairfax at the Siege of Colchester,* 1648

There will be no veterans of World War III.
> —WALTER MONDALE, speech, Sept. 5, 1984

An empire founded by war has to maintain itself by war.
> —MONTESQUIEU, *Considérations sur les*
> *causes de la grandeur des Romains et de leur décadence,* 1734

Against war it may be said that it makes the victor stupid and the vanquished revengeful.
> —FRIEDRICH NIETZSCHE,
> *Human, All-Too-Human,* 1878

He who is the author of a war lets loose the whole contagion of hell and opens a vein that bleeds a nation to death.
> —THOMAS PAINE, *The American Crisis,*
> No. V, Mar. 21, 1778

No one won the last war, and no one will win the next.
> —ELEANOR ROOSEVELT,
> letter to Harry S. Truman, Nov. 5, 1948

War is not an adventure. It is a disease.
> —ANTOINE DE SAINT-EXUPÉRY,
> *Flight to Arras,* 1942

Sometime they'll give a war and nobody will come.
> —CARL SANDBURG, *The People, Yes,* 1936

When the rich wage war, it is the poor who die.
> —JEAN-PAUL SARTRE,
> *The Devil and the Good Lord,* 1951

We ask the outcome of a war, not the cause.
> —SENECA, *Mad Hercules,* 1st cent. A.D.

O war, thou son of hell!
> —SHAKESPEARE, *Henry VI, Part II,* V, ii

Cry "Havoc!" and let slip the dogs of war.
> —SHAKESPEARE, *Julius Caesar,* III, i

War is cruelty, and you cannot refine it.
> —WILLIAM TECUMSEH SHERMAN,
> letter to James M. Calhoun, Sept. 12, 1864

War is hell.　　　　　—WILLIAM TECUMSEH SHERMAN,
> attributed, graduation speech,
> Michigan Military Academy, June 19, 1879

[Better known but less well documented than the statement at Columbus, below.]

There is many a boy here today who looks on war as all glory, but, boys, it is all hell.
> —WILLIAM TECUMSEH SHERMAN,
> speech, Columbus, Ohio, Aug. 11, 1880

All warfare is based on deception.
> —SUN TZU, *The Art of War,* 4th cent. B.C.

War is much too serious a thing to be left to military men.
> —CHARLES-MAURICE DE TALLEYRAND,
> d. 1838, attributed

[Also attributed to Clemenceau.]

War is a matter not so much of arms as of expenditure, through which arms may be made of service.
> —THUCYDIDES, *The History of the
> Peloponnesian War,* c. 400 B.C.

War is the unfolding of miscalculations.
> —BARBARA TUCHMAN, *The Guns of August,* 1962

He, therefore, who desires peace should prepare for war. He who aspires to victory should spare no pains to form his soldiers. And he who hopes for success should fight on principle, not chance.　　—VEGETIUS, *De rei militari,* c. A.D. 375

[A favorite quote of George Washington. Used also by Pres. George Bush in 1990 during preparations for the Gulf War.]

WASHINGTON, D.C. See CITIES

WEALTH See HAVES & HAVE-NOTS; MONEY

WEATHER See NATURE: WIND & WEATHER

WICKEDNESS See EVIL; SIN, VICE, & NAUGHTINESS

WILL

"There's no free will," says the philosopher;
"To hang is most unjust."
"There is no free will," assents the officer;
"We hang because we must."
　　　　　　—AMBROSE BIERCE, *Collected Works,* VIII, 1911

Will and wisdom are both mighty leaders. Our times worship
will.　　　　　—CLARENCE DAY, *Humpty-Dumpty and
　　　　　　　　　Adam* in *The Crow's Nest*, 1921

The good or ill of man lies within his own will.
　　　　　　—EPICTETUS, *Discourses,* c. A.D. 100

If you will it, it is no dream.
　　　　　　—THEODOR HERZL, d. 1904, saying
[Herzl was the founder of political Zionism.]

The will to do, the soul to dare.
　　　　　—SIR WALTER SCOTT, *The Lady of the Lake*, 1810

Our wills and fates do so contrary run
That our devices still are overthrown;
Our thoughts are ours, their ends none of our own.
　　　　　　—SHAKESPEARE, *Hamlet*, III, ii

WIND　　　　　See NATURE: WIND & WEATHER

WINE　　　　　See ALCOHOL & DRINKING;
　　　　　　　　FOOD, WINE, & EATING

WINNING & LOSING,   See also EQUALITY
VICTORY & DEFEAT   (Carroll); GAMES;
                    MILITARY BATTLES; RUIN; SPORTS;
                         SUCCESS & FAME; WAR

Victory awaits him who has everything in order—luck people call it. Defeat is certain for him who has neglected to
take the necessary precautions in time—this is called bad
luck.   —ROALD AMUNDSEN, d. 1928,
                  cited in Diana Preston, *A First Rate Tragedy:*
      Robert Falcon Scott and the Race to the South Pole, 1998
[Norwegian explorer Amundsen was the first to reach the
South Pole, Dec. 14, 1911. Scott and his party arrived thirty-
five days later, and perished on the return trip. Seventeen years
later, Amundsen disappeared on a flight in the Arctic while
attempting to rescue a colleague whose dirigible had crashed.]

The laugh is always on the loser.
               —ANONYMOUS (GERMAN PROVERB)
[The Welsh say, "The world laughs at those who fail."]

Victory at all costs, victory in spite of all terror, victory
however long and hard the road may be; for without victory,
there is no survival.
               —WINSTON CHURCHILL, speech, May 13, 1946

The problems of victory are more agreeable than those of
defeat, but they are no less difficult.
               —WINSTON CHURCHILL, speech, Nov. 11, 1942

As always, victory finds a hundred fathers, but defeat is an
orphan.   —COUNT GALEAZZO CIANO, Sept. 9, 1942,
                          The Ciano Diaries: 1939–1943, 1946
[A favorite observation of John F. Kennedy and others, and
used in the 1951 film *The Desert Fox.*]

Victory is by nature insolent and haughty.
                    —CICERO, *Pro Marcello,* 47 B.C.

The race is to the swift;
The battle to the strong.
                    —JOHN DAVIDSON, d. 1909, *War Song*
[For a concurring opinion, see Damon Runyon, under SPORTS;
for the opposing Biblical view, see LUCK.]

Nice guys finish last.　　　　—LEO DUROCHER, attributed
[According to Paul F. Boller, Jr., and John George, authors of
They Never Said It, baseball manager Leo Durocher claimed
to have actually said, of the New York Giants baseball team,
"All nice guys. They'll finish last. Nice guys. Finish last."
Sportswriter Jimmy Cannon used the version we know to sum-
marize Durocher's view of life and Durocher himself entitled
his 1975 autobiography *Nice Guys Finish Last.*]

All is lost save honor.　　—FRANCIS I, letter, Feb. 23, 1525,
　　　　　　　　　　referring to his defeat at Pavia two days before

All victories breed hate.　　　　—BALTASAR GRACIÁN,
　　　　　　　　　　　　The Art of Worldly Wisdom, 1647

If you think you can win, you can win. Faith is necessary to
victory.　　　　　　　—WILLIAM HAZLITT, *On Great and
　　　　　　　　　　Little Things,* in *Literary Remains,* 1836

Lose as if you like it; win as if you were used to it.
　　　　　　　　—TOMMY HITCHCOCK, saying, c. 1935,
　　　　　　　　　　passed on by his father, Jonas Hitchcock
[Tommy Hitchcock excelled at polo.]

Victory often changes her side.
　　　　　　　　　　　　—HOMER, *Iliad,* 8th cent. B.C.

[I feel] somewhat like the boy in Kentucky who stubbed his
toe while running to see his sweetheart. The boy said he
was too big to cry, and far too badly hurt to laugh.
　　　　—ABRAHAM LINCOLN, reply when asked how he felt
　　　　　　about the Democrats winning the N.Y. State elections,
　　　　　　　　quoted in *Leslie's Illustrated Weekly,* Nov. 22, 1862
[Democrat Adlai Stevenson, crediting Lincoln, used this same
anecdote to illustrate his feelings after his loss in the presidential election of 1952.]

Winning isn't everything, it's the only thing.
　　　　　　　　—VINCENT LOMBARDI, d. 1970, attributed
[Widely attributed to Lombardi, the legendary football coach
of the Green Bay Packers (1959–1969), but not original with
him. In *Respectfully Quoted,* published by the Library of Congress, the saying is traced to Red Sanders, football coach of
Vanderbilt University, and dated c. 1948. Lombardi claimed

that what he actually said was something on the lines of: winning isn't everything, but wanting to win (or, making the effort to win) is. But others recollect him taking the harder line.]

Winning is a habit. Unfortunately so is losing.
      —VINCENT LOMBARDI, attributed,
      The New York Times, June 3, 1999

Victory puts us on a level with heaven.
      —LUCRETIUS, *On the Nature of Things,* c. 57 B.C.

To the victor belongs the spoils.
      —WILLIAM LEARNED MARCY, speech,
      U.S. Senate, Jan. 25, 1832
[This is the popular summation of Marcy's comment in the Senate; see under POLITICS.]

There are defeats more triumphant than victories.
      —MONTAIGNE, *Essays,* 1580–88
[On this subject, see King Pyrrhus at MILITARY BATTLES.]

The loser is always suspicious.
      —PUBLILIUS SYRUS, *Moral Sayings,* 1st cent. B.C.

For when the One Great Scorer comes
  To write against your name,
He marks—not that you won or lost—
  But how you played the game.
      —GRANTLAND RICE, *Alumnus Football,* 1930
[See Ralph Kiner's variation at EXCUSES, author Anonymous.]

Show me a good and gracious loser, and I'll show you a failure.   —KNUTE ROCKNE, attributed
[According to *Bartlett's,* the legendary Notre Dame football coach made this remark to Wisconsin basketball coach Walter Meanwell in the 1920s.]

Once you hear the details of a victory, it is hard to distinguish it from a defeat.   —JEAN-PAUL SARTRE,
      The Devil and the Good Lord, 1951

It is best to win without fighting.
      —SUN TZE, *Sun Tze Ping Fa,* 4th cent. B.C.

If you want to have a lot of friends, lose.
> —JOHN THOMPSON,
> *The Wall Street Journal,* May 5, 1997

[The *Journal*'s source was Philip Knight, chairman of the Nike sportswear company, who was making the point that when one is successful, one develops enemies. In this connection, he quoted Thompson, the longtime coach of the Georgetown University basketball team.]

WINTERS   See NATURE: SEASONS

WISDOM   See also MIND, THOUGHT &
UNDERSTANDING; PHILOSOPHY;
PRUDENCE & PRACTICAL WISDOM;
VISION & VISIONARIES

The hours of a wise man are lengthened by his ideas.
> —JOSEPH ADDISON, *The Spectator,* June 18, 1711

Wisdom comes only through suffering.
> —AESCHYLUS, *Agamemnon,* 5th cent. B.C.

Wonder is the beginning of wisdom.
> —ANONYMOUS (GREEK PROVERB)

The fox knows many things, but the hedgehog knows one great thing.
> —ARCHILOCHUS, fragment, early 7th cent. B.C.

[For a slightly different version of this saying see Pigres at CRAFTINESS. Isaiah Berlin titled his classic study of Tolstoy *The Hedgehog and the Fox* (1953). Writers and thinkers can be categorized as foxes or hedgehogs, he said. The latter are inspired by a single organizing principle or world view, and include Dante, Plato, Dostoevski, and Nietzsche. The foxes seize upon a variety of experiences without trying to impose a unitary vision; foxes include Aristotle, Shakespeare, Montaigne, and Balzac. Tolstoy is both fox and hedgehog, according to Berlin.]

The great good is wisdom.
> —ST. AUGUSTINE, *Soliloquies,* c. A.D. 410

The price of wisdom is above rubies.   —BIBLE, *Job* 28:18

The fear of the Lord is the beginning of wisdom.
—BIBLE, *Psalms* 11:10
[Slightly different is *Proverbs* 1:7, "The fear of the Lord is the beginning of knowledge."]

Happy is the man that findeth wisdom, and the man that getteth understanding. —BIBLE, *Proverbs* 3:13

In much wisdom is much grief: and he that increaseth knowledge increaseth sorrow. —BIBLE, *Ecclesiastes* 1:18

The children of this world are in their generation wiser than the children of light. —BIBLE, *Luke* 16:8

Be wiser than other people if you can, but do not tell them so. —EARL OF CHESTERFIELD, letter to his son, Nov. 19, 1745

The function of wisdom is discriminating between good and evil. —CICERO, *De officiis*, 44 B.C.

A sadder and a wiser man
He rose the morrow morn.
—SAMUEL TAYLOR COLERIDGE, *The Ancient Mariner*, 1798

Errors, like straws, upon the surface flow;
He who would search for pearls must dive below.
—JOHN DRYDEN, prologue, *All for Love*, 1678

Those who are held wise among men, and who search for the reason of things, are those who bring the most sorrow on themselves. —EURIPIDES, *Medea*, 431 B.C.

How prone to doubt, how cautious are the wise!
—HOMER, *Odyssey*, 8th cent. B.C.

Wisdom denotes the pursuing of the best ends by the best means. —FRANCIS HUTCHESON, *Inquiry into the Original of Our Ideas of Beauty and Virtue*, 1725

The world is full of people who are not wise enough.
—LA FONTAINE, *Fables*, 1668

The Way of the sage is to act but not to compete.
—LAO-TZU, *Tao Te Ching*, 6th cent. B.C.

To know
That which lies before us in daily life,
Is the prime wisdom.
—JOHN MILTON,
Paradise Lost, 1667

Pure reason avoids extremes, and requires one to be wise in moderation.
—MOLIÈRE, *Le Misanthrope*, 1666

The growth of wisdom may be gauged exactly by the diminution of ill-temper.
—FRIEDRICH NIETZSCHE
The Wanderer and His Shadow, 1880

Wisdom sends us back to our childhood.
—PASCAL, *Pensées*, 1670

No one is wise at all times.
—PLINY, *Natural History*, A.D. 77
[Emerson said it too: "Wise men are not wise at all times," *Wealth*, 1860.]

Nine-tenths of wisdom consists in being wise in time.
—THEODORE ROOSEVELT, speech, June 14, 1917

Wisdom comes by disillusionment.
—GEORGE SANTAYANA, *The Life of Reason:
Reason in Common Sense*, 1905–06

The wise want love; and those who love want wisdom.
—PERCY BYSSHE SHELLEY,
Prometheus Unbound, 1819

Wisdom outweighs any wealth.
—SOPHOCLES, *Antigone*, 5th cent. B.C.

Knowledge comes, but wisdom lingers.
—ALFRED, LORD TENNYSON, *Locksley Hall*, 1842

It is a characteristic of wisdom not to do desperate things.
—HENRY DAVID THOREAU,
Economy in *Walden*, 1854

The highest wisdom has but one science—the science of the whole—the science explaining the whole creation and man's place in it. —LEO TOLSTOY, *War and Peace*, 1865–69

He who is only wise lives a sad life.
—VOLTAIRE, letter to Frederick the Great, 1740

Wisdom is ofttimes nearer when we stoop
Than when we soar.
—WILLIAM WORDSWORTH, *The Excursion*, 1814

Be wise with speed;
A fool at forty is a fool indeed.
—EDWARD YOUNG, *Love of Fame*, 1725–28

WIT   See ARTS: STYLE IN WRITING & EXPRESSION;
HUMOR

WITCHES   See OCCULT, THE

WOMEN   See also HOME; LOVE; MARRIAGE;
PARENTS; WOMEN, BEAUTIFUL &
HOMELY; WOMEN & MEN

An animal that delights in finery.
—JOSEPH ADDISON, *Cato,* 1713

Woman's work is never done.
—ANONYMOUS (ENGLISH PROVERB)
[This dates at least to the 17th century. For a 20th-century update, see Thornton Wilder below.]

Souvent femme varie.
Women are often different.
—ANONYMOUS (FRENCH PROVERB)

A whistling girl and a crowing hen never came to a good end. —ANONYMOUS (IRISH PROVERB)
[Muriel Spark, in *The New Yorker*, Sept. 11, 1989, quoted her grandmother's version: "A whistling woman, a crowing hen / Is neither fit for God nor man."]

Join the union, girls, and together say, "Equal Pay for Equal Work!"
　　—SUSAN B. ANTHONY, in *The Revolution*, Mar. 18, 1869

Woman must not depend upon the protection of man, but must be taught to protect herself.
　　　　　　—SUSAN B. ANTHONY, speech, July 1871

Woman may be said to be an inferior man.
　　　　　　—ARISTOTLE, *Poetics*, c. 322 B.C.

With women, the heart argues, not the mind.
　　　　　　—MATTHEW ARNOLD, *Merope*, 1858

The true worth of a race must be measured by the character of its womanhood.　　—MARY McLEOD BETHUNE,
　　　　　A Century of Progress of Negro Women, June 3, 1933

One is not born a woman, one becomes one.
　　—SIMONE DE BEAUVOIR, *The Second Sex*, 1949–50

Who can find a virtuous woman? for her price is far above rubies.　　　　　　—BIBLE, *Proverbs* 31:10

Let your women keep silence in the churches: for it is not permitted unto them to speak; but they are commanded to be under obedience, as also saith the law.
　　　　　　—BIBLE, *I Corinthians* 14:34

Alas! the love of women! it is known
To be a lovely and a fearful thing.
　　　　　　—LORD BYRON, *Don Juan*, 1819–24
[See Congreve at HATE, "a woman scorned."]

Women never have young minds. They are born three thousand years old.
　　　　　—SHELAGH DELANEY, *A Taste of Honey*, 1958

A woman's hopes are woven of sunbeams; a shadow annihilates them.　　　　—GEORGE ELIOT, *Felix Holt*, 1866

The happiest women, like the happiest nations, have no history.　　—GEORGE ELIOT, *The Mill on the Floss*, 1860

A sufficient measure of civilization is the influence of good women. —RALPH WALDO EMERSON,
Civilization in *Society and Solitude,* 1870

A woman should always challenge our respect, and never move our compassion.
—RALPH WALDO EMERSON, *Journal,* 1836

Woman is woman's natural ally.
—EURIPIDES, *Alope,* fragment, 5th cent. B.C.

Love's all in all to women.
—EURIPIDES, *Andromache,* c. 426 B.C.

Women are but women—tears are their portion.
—EURIPIDES, *Medea,* 431 B.C.

The great question that has never been answered and which I have not been able to answer despite my thirty years of research into the feminine soul, is "What does a woman want?"
—SIGMUND FREUD, d. 1939, quoted in Ernest Jones,
The Life and Works of Sigmund Freud, Vol. 2, 1955

As men become aware that few have had a fair chance, they are inclined to say that no women have had a fair chance.
—MARGARET FULLER, *Woman in
the Nineteenth Century,* 1845

Females have their own agenda.
—PASCAL GAGNEUX, to the press, June 1997
[Primatologist Gagneux was explaining the surprise discovery, in a study of a group of Ivory Coast chimpanzees, that fifty-four percent of the baby chimpanzees were not fathered by any males in the group. Evidently the females were leaving undetected for private trysts.]

I have been a woman for fifty years, and I've never been able to discover precisely what it is I am.
—JEAN GIRAUDOUX, *Tiger at the Gates,* 1935

The eternal female draws us onward.
—GOETHE, last line in *Faust,* Part II, 1832

So few grown women like their lives.
—KATHARINE GRAHAM, quoted by
Jane Howard, *Ms.* magazine, Oct. 1974

Women never reason, and therefore they are (comparatively) seldom wrong.
—WILLIAM HAZLITT, *Characteristics,* 1823

HELMER: First and foremost, you are a wife and mother.
NORA: That I don't believe any more. I believe that first and foremost, I am an individual, just as much as you are.
—HENRIK IBSEN, *A Doll's House,* 1879

There is in every true woman's heart, a spark of heavenly fire, which lies dormant in the broad daylight of prosperity, but which kindles up and beams and blazes in the dark hour of adversity.   —WASHINGTON IRVING, *The Wife* in
The Sketch Book of Geoffrey Crayon, Gent., 1819–20

For the Colonel's lady an' Judy O'Grady
Are sisters under their skins!
—RUDYARD KIPLING, *The Ladies,* 1895

The female of the species is more deadly than the male.
—RUDYARD KIPLING, *The Female of the Species,* 1911

Women run to extremes; they are either better or worse than men.   —LA BRUYÈRE, *Les Caractères,* 1688

A woman's best protection is a little money of her own.
—CLARE BOOTHE LUCE, d. 1987, attributed

Wherever women are honored, there the gods are pleased.
—CODE OF MANU, c. 100 B.C.

Can we today measure devotion to husband and children by our indifference to everything else?
—GOLDA MEIR, *The Plough Woman,* 1930

There is nothing worse than a woman—even a good woman!
—MENANDER, fragment, 4th cent. B.C.
[This pretty well sums up the great majority of traditional quotes on women. See also INSULTS & PUT-DOWNS, Butler and Johnson.]

Women have simple tastes. They can get pleasure out of the conversation of children in arms and men in love.
—H. L. MENCKEN, *Sententiae* in
A Mencken Chrestomathy, 1949

When women kiss, it always reminds me of prize fighters shaking hands. —*Ibid.*

Many women do not recognize themselves as discriminated against; no better proof could be found of the totality of their conditioning. —KATE MILLETT, *Sexual Politics,* 1950

O fairest of creation! last and best
Of all God's works. —JOHN MILTON, *Paradise Lost,* 1667

Women would rather be right than reasonable.
—OGDEN NASH, *Frailty, Thy Name
Is a Misnomer* in *Marriage Lines,* 1964

What one beholds of a woman is the least part of her.
—OVID, *Love's Cure,* c. 1 B.C.

If women are expected to do the same work as men, we must teach them the same things.
—PLATO, *The Republic,* 4th cent. B.C.

Most women have no characters at all.
—ALEXANDER POPE, *To Mrs. M. Blount*
in *Moral Essays,* 1735

A free race cannot be born of slave mothers.
—MARGARET SANGER,
Women and the New Race, 1920

Frailty thy name is woman!
—SHAKESPEARE, *Hamlet,* I, ii

Her voice was ever soft,
Gentle and low, an excellent thing in woman.
—SHAKESPEARE, *King Lear,* V, iii

Woman's virtue is man's greatest invention.
—CORNELIA OTIS SKINNER,
quoted in *Paris '90,* perhaps c. 1960

Silence gives the proper grace to women.
>—SOPHOCLES, *Ajax*, 5th cent. B.C.

By now you will have discovered that women, too, can be militant. —SOPHOCLES, *Electra*, 5th cent. B.C.

Women are always eagerly on the lookout for any emotion.
>—STENDHAL, *On Love*, 1822

The woman is so hard
Upon the woman.
>—ALFRED, LORD TENNYSON, *The Princess*, 1847

If I were asked . . . to what the singular prosperity and growing strength of that people [Americans] ought mainly to be attributed, I should reply: to the superiority of their women. —ALEXIS DE TOCQUEVILLE,
>*Democracy in America*, 1835–39

If the first woman God ever made was strong enough to turn the world upside down all alone, these women together ought to be able to turn it back, and get it right side up again! —SOJOURNER TRUTH, Women's Rights
>Convention, Akron, Ohio, May 29, 1851

The hand that rocks the cradle
Is the hand that rules the world.
>—W. R. WALLACE, *The Hand*
>*That Rules the World*, c. 1865

Whatever women do, they must do it twice as well as men to be thought half as good. Luckily, this is not difficult.
>—CHARLOTTE WHITTON, quoted in
>*Canada Month*, June 1963

[She was mayor of Ottawa.]

A woman's work is seldom done.
>—THORNTON WILDER, *The Skin of Our Teeth*, 1942

Genteel women are, literally speaking, slaves to their bodies.
. . . Taught from their infancy that beauty is woman's scep-
ter, the mind shapes itself to the body, and roaming round
its gilt cage, only seeks to adorn its prison.
> —MARY WOLLSTONECRAFT,
> *A Vindication of the Rights of Woman,* 1792

WOMEN, BEAUTIFUL & HOMELY   See also BEAUTY

She walks in beauty, like the night
Of cloudless climes and starry skies;
And all that's best of dark and bright
Meet in her aspect and her eyes.
> —LORD BYRON, *She Walks in Beauty,* 1815

It was a blonde. A blonde to make a bishop kick a hole in
a stained glass window.
> —RAYMOND CHANDLER, *Farewell, My Lovely,* 1940

Women who are either indisputably beautiful, or indisputably ugly, are best flattered upon the score of their
understandings.   —EARL OF CHESTERFIELD,
> letter to his son, Sept. 5, 1748

She strode like a grenadier, was strong and upright like an
obelisk, had a beautiful face, a candid brow, and not a
thought of her own in her head.
> —JOSEPH CONRAD, *The Return*
> in *Tales of Unrest,* 1898

A beautiful woman is a practical poet.
> —RALPH WALDO EMERSON,
> *Beauty* in *The Conduct of Life,* 1860

I met a lady in the meads
Full beautiful, a faery's child;
Her hair was long, her foot was light,
And her eyes were wild.
> —JOHN KEATS, *La Belle Dame sans Merci,* 1819

[An unfortunate encounter for the protagonist. The poem
opens with a question that sets an ominous scene: "Oh what
can ail thee, wretched wight, / Alone and palely loitering; / The
sedge is withered from the lake, / And no birds sing." A name
is put to the faery's child in stanza ten: "I saw pale kings and

princes too, / Pale warriors, death-pale were they all; / They
cried—'La Belle Dame Sans Merci/ Hath thee in thrall!' "
   La Belle Dame Sans Merci was originally used as a poem
title by the 15th-century French poet Alain Chartier.]

Was this the face that launched a thousand ships?
And burnt the topless towers of Ilium?
Sweet Helen, make me immortal with a kiss!
     —CHRISTOPHER MARLOWE, *Dr. Faustus*, 1604

Oh, thou art fairer than the evening air
Clad in the beauty of a thousand stars.   *—Ibid.*

If the nose of Cleopatra had been a little shorter, the whole
face of the world would have been changed.
     —PASCAL, *Pensées*, 1670

If to her share some female errors fall,
Look on her face, and you'll forget 'em all.
     —ALEXANDER POPE, *The Rape of the Lock*, 1714

Age cannot wither her, nor custom stale
Her infinite variety.
     —SHAKESPEARE, *Antony and Cleopatra*, II, ii

She never yet was foolish that was fair.
     —SHAKESPEARE, *Othello*, II, i

A thoroughly beautiful woman and a thoroughly homely
woman are creations which I love to gaze upon and which
I cannot tire of gazing upon, for each is perfect in her own
line.   —MARK TWAIN, d. 1910, *Autobiography*, 1924

WOMEN & MEN   See also LOVE; MARRIAGE;
                            MEN; WOMEN

Do not put such unlimited power into the hands of husbands. Remember all men would be tyrants if they could.
[We ladies] will not hold ourselves bound by any laws in
which we have no voice, or representation.
     —ABIGAIL ADAMS, letter to
     John Adams, March 31, 1776
[See also Defoe at TYRANNY & TOTALITARIANISM.]

A lady's imagination is very rapid; it jumps from admiration to love, from love to matrimony in a moment.
—JANE AUSTEN, *Pride and Prejudice*, 1813

Women are very pleased when you call them cruel.
—PIERRE-AUGUSTIN DE BEAUMARCHAIS,
The Barber of Seville, 1775

It is not good that the man should be alone; I will make him a help meet for him.   —BIBLE, *Genesis* 2:18

That's the nature of women, not to love when we love them, and to love when we love them not.
—CERVANTES, *Don Quixote*, 1605–15

There's no fury like an ex-wife searching for a new lover.
—CYRIL CONNOLLY, *The Unquiet Grave*, 1945
[For the original comment on woman's fury, see Congreve at HATE.]

I have been faithful to thee, Cynara! in my fashion.
I have forgot much, Cynara, gone with the wind,
Flung vases, roses, riotously, with the throng.
—ERNEST DOWSON, *Non Sum Qualis Eram*, 1896
[Cynara, the daughter of a French café owner in London, was twelve years old when Dowson wrote this poem to her.]

Women fail to understand how much men hate them.
—GERMAINE GREER, *The Female Eunuch*, 1970

The masculine tone is passing out of the world. It's a feminine, a nervous, hysterical, chattering, canting age.
—HENRY JAMES, *The Bostonians*, 1886

The silliest woman can manage a clever man; but it needs a very clever woman to manage a fool.
—RUDYARD KIPLING, *Three and—an
Extra* in *Plain Tales from the Hills*, 1888

Maleness in America is not absolutely defined; it has to be kept and reearned every day, and one essential element in the definition is beating women in every game that both sexes play.   —MARGARET MEAD, *Male and Female*, 1948

For contemplation he and valor formed;
For softness she and sweet attractive grace,
He for God only, she for God in him.
　　　　　　　—JOHN MILTON, *Paradise Lost*, 1667

Disguise our bondage as we will,
'Tis woman, woman, rules us still.
　　　　　　　—THOMAS MOORE, *Sovereign Woman*,
　　　　　　　　　　c. 1820, in *Poetical Works*, 1872

Woman was God's *second* mistake.
　　　　　　　—FRIEDRICH NIETZSCHE, *The Antichrist*, 1888

I can't live either without you or with you.
　　　　　　　—OVID, *Amores*, c. 20 B.C.

Kindness in women, not their beauteous looks,
Shall win my love.
　　　　　　　—SHAKESPEARE, *The Taming of the Shrew*, IV, ii

The queens in history compare favorably with the kings.
　　　　　　　—ELIZABETH CADY STANTON &
　　　　　　　　　　SUSAN B. ANTHONY,
　　　　　　　　　　History of Woman Suffrage, 1881

We hold these truths to be self-evident, that all men and
women are created equal . . .
　　　　　　　—ELIZABETH CADY STANTON,
　　　　　　　　　　Declaration of Sentiment,
　　　　　　　First Woman's Rights Convention, July 19, 1848

Man for the field and woman for the hearth:
Man for the sword and for the needle she:
Man with the head and woman with the heart:
Man to command and woman to obey;
All else confusion.
　　　　　　　—ALFRED, LORD TENNYSON, *The Princess*, 1847

The woman's cause is man's: they rise or sink
Together.　　　　　　　　　　　　　　　　　　*—Ibid.*

'Tis strange what a man may do, and a woman yet think
him an angel.　　　　　　　—WILLIAM THACKERAY,
　　　　　　　　　　The History of Henry Esmond, 1852

Why are women . . . so much more interesting to men than men are to women?
—VIRGINIA WOOLF, *A Room of One's Own,* 1929

Women have served all these centuries as looking-glasses possessing the magic and delicious power of reflecting the figure of man at twice its natural size.   —*Ibid.*

WORDS   See ARTS: STYLE IN WRITING &
EXPRESSION; LANGUAGE & WORDS;
PEOPLE, THE (Herzl)

WORK & WORKERS   See also ACCOMPLISHMENT;
DOING; LEISURE; METHOD;
PERSEVERANCE & ENDURANCE

Work is the curse of the drinking classes. —ANONYMOUS
[Attributed to Oscar Wilde in Hesketh Pearson, *Life of Oscar Wilde,* 1946.]

Work is not the curse, but drudgery is.
—HENRY WARD BEECHER,
Proverbs from Plymouth Pulpit, 1877

What is work? And what is not work? These are questions that perplex the wisest of men.
—BHAGAVAD GITA, c. 250 B.C.–A.D. 250

Go to the ant, thou sluggard; consider her ways, and be wise:
  Which having no guide, overseer, or ruler,
  Provideth her meat in the summer, and gathereth her food in the harvest.   —BIBLE, *Proverbs* 6:6–8

The laborer is worthy of his hire.   —BIBLE, *Luke* 10:7

All composite things decay. Strive diligently.
—BUDDHA, last words, c. 483 B.C.

Be not solitary, be not idle.   —ROBERT BURTON,
The Anatomy of Melancholy, 1621–51
[The closing words.]

Blessed is he who has found his work. Let him ask no other blessedness. —THOMAS CARLYLE, *Past and Present,* 1843

"A fair day's wages for a fair day's work": it is as just a demand as governed men ever made of governing. It is the everlasting right of man. —*Ibid.*

Work is the grand cure of all the maladies and miseries that ever beset mankind.
—THOMAS CARLYLE, speech, Apr. 2, 1886

It is better to wear out than to rust out.
—RICHARD CUMBERLAND, d. 1718, quoted in George Horne, *Sermon on the Duty of Contending for the Truth*

Working people have a lot of bad habits, but the worst of them is work. —CLARENCE DARROW, d. 1938, quoted in Kevin Tierney, *Darrow,* 1979

A lot of fellows nowadays have a B.A., M.D., or Ph.D. Unfortunately, they don't have a J.O.B.
—"FATS" DOMINO, attributed

Originality and a feeling of one's own dignity are achieved only through work and struggle.
—FEODOR DOSTOEVSKI, *A Diary of a Writer,* 1871

There is no substitute for hard work.
—THOMAS ALVA EDISON, d. 1931, *Life,* 1932

The bitter and the sweet come from the outside, the hard from within, from one's own efforts.
—ALBERT EINSTEIN, *Out of My Later Years,* 1950

Farming looks mighty easy when your plow's a pencil and you're a thousand miles from a cornfield.
—DWIGHT D. EISENHOWER, speech, Sept. 25, 1956

To the worker, God himself lends aid.
—EURIPIDES, *Hippolytus,* 428 B.C.

Men for the sake of getting a living forget to live.
—MARGARET FULLER, *Summer on the Lakes,* 1844

All work is empty save when there is love.
—KAHLIL GIBRAN, *The Prophet,* 1923

When work is a pleasure, life is a joy! When work is duty, life is slavery. —MAXIM GORKY, *The Lower Depths,* 1903

It is weariness to keep toiling at the same things so that one becomes ruled by them.
> —HERACLITUS, fragment, c. 500 B.C.

More men are killed by overwork than the importance of the world justifies.
> —RUDYARD KIPLING, *The Phantom Rickshaw,* 1888

I am glad to know that there is a system of labor where the laborer can strike if he wants to! I wish to God that such a system prevailed all over the world.
> —ABRAHAM LINCOLN, speech, Mar. 5, 1860
[By contrast, Calvin Coolidge asserted, "There is no right to strike against the public safety by anybody, anywhere, any time," telegram to Samuel Gompers re the Boston police strike, Sept. 14, 1919.]

Labor is prior to, and independent of, capital. Capital is only the fruit of labor. . . . Labor is the superior of capital, and deserves much the higher consideration.
> —ABRAHAM LINCOLN, first annual
> message to Congress, Dec. 3, 1862
[But see also the continuation of this quote under CAPITALISM.]

Under the spreading chestnut tree
The village smithy stands;
The smith a mighty man is he
With large and sinewy hands.
And the muscles of his brawny arms
Are strong as iron bands.
His brow is wet with honest sweat,
He earns whate'er he can,
And looks the whole world in the face,
For he owes not any man.
> —HENRY WADSWORTH LONGFELLOW,
> *The Village Blacksmith,* 1842

Constant labor of one uniform kind destroys the intensity and flow of a man's animal spirits, which find recreation and delight in mere change of activity.
—KARL MARX, *Capital,* 1867–83

Workers of the world, unite!
—KARL MARX & FRIEDRICH ENGELS,
The Communist Manifesto, 1848
[More at REVOLUTION.]

The average male gets his living by such depressing devices that boredom becomes a sort of natural state to him.
—H. L. MENCKEN, *In Defence of Women,* 1922

No one hates his job so heartily as a farmer.
—H. L. MENCKEN, *What Is Going On in the World Now?* in *American Mercury,* Nov. 1933

Figure it out. Work a lifetime to pay off a house. You finally own it, and there's no one to live in it.
—ARTHUR MILLER, *Death of a Salesman,* 1949

Work expands so as to fill the time available for its completion.
—C. NORTHCOTE PARKINSON, *Parkinson's Law,* 1958

In a hierarchy, every employee tends to rise to his level of incompetence.
—LAURENCE J. PETER, *The Peter Principle,* 1969

When you cease to make a contribution, you begin to die.
—ELEANOR ROOSEVELT, letter
to Mr. Horne, Feb. 19, 1960

Far and away the best prize that life offers is the chance to work hard at work worth doing.
—THEODORE ROOSEVELT,
Labor Day speech, Sept. 7, 1903

Which of us . . . is to do the dirty work for the rest—and for what pay? Who is to do the pleasant and clean work, and for what pay? —JOHN RUSKIN, *Of King's Treasuries* in *Sesame and Lilies,* 1865

If I were a medical man, I should prescribe a holiday to any patient who considered his work important.
                    —BERTRAND RUSSELL, *Autobiography,* 1967

I will have an eternity to rest.
                    —ANDRÉS SEGOVIA, quoted in
                    The New York Times, obituary, 1987
[The great guitarist was explaining why he continued a heavy work schedule into old age.]

Nothing will come of nothing.
                    —SHAKESPEARE, *King Lear,* I, i

My nature is subdued
To what it works in, like the dyer's hand.
                    —SHAKESPEARE, sonnet 3

You may tempt the upper classes
With your villainous demitasses,
But Heaven will protect the working girl.
                    —EDGAR SMITH, *Heaven Will
                    Protect the Working Girl*
[Sung by Marie Dressler in *Tillie's Nightmare,* c. 1914.]

To travel hopefully is a better thing than to arrive, and true success is to labor.   —ROBERT LOUIS STEVENSON,
                    El Dorado in *Virginibus Puerisque,* 1881

Death is the end of life; ah, why
Should life all labor be?   —ALFRED, LORD TENNYSON,
                    The Lotos-Eaters, 1833

Where our work is, there let our joy be.
                    —TERTULLIAN, *Women's Dress,* c. A.D. 200

A small daily task if it be really daily, will beat the labors of a spasmodic Hercules.
                    —ANTHONY TROLLOPE, *An Autobiography,* 1883

Thou, O God, dost sell us all good things at the price of labor.   —LEONARDO DA VINCI, *Notebooks,* 1508–18

Work spares us from three evils: boredom, vice, and need.
                    —VOLTAIRE, *Candide,* 1759

There is as much dignity in tilling a field as in writing a poem. —BOOKER T. WASHINGTON, speech, Sept. 9, 1895

How doth the little busy bee
Improve each shining hour,
And gather honey all the day
From every opening flower.
—ISAAC WATTS, *Against Idleness and Mischief* in *Divine Songs,* 1715

WORKING PEOPLE   See PEOPLE, THE; WORK & WORKERS

WORLD   See CREATION, DIVINE; EPITAPHS (Frost); LIFE; NATURE; REALITY & ILLUSION; UNIVERSE; WORLD, END OF

WORLD, END OF   See also LAST JUDGMENT & THE HEREAFTER

Overhead without any fuss the stars were going out.
—ARTHUR C. CLARKE, final sentence, *The Nine Billion Names of God,* May 1952

This is the way the world ends
Not with a bang but a whimper.
—T. S. ELIOT, *The Hollow Men,* 1925

Some say the world will end in fire,
Some say in ice.
From what I've tasted of desire
I hold with those who favor fire.
But if it had to perish twice
I think I know enough of hate
To say that for destruction ice
Is also great
And would suffice.   —ROBERT FROST, *Fire and Ice,* 1923

When shall the stars be blown about the sky,
Like the sparks blown out of a smithy, and die?
—WILLIAM BUTLER YEATS, *The Secret Rose* in *The Wind Among the Reeds,* 1899

And what rough beast, its hour come round at last,
Slouches towards Bethlehem to be born?
            —WILLIAM BUTLER YEATS, *The Second Coming*
                    in *Michael Robartes and the Dancer*, 1921

WRATH   See ANGER

WRITING   See ARTS: WRITING

XYZ

XANADU See NATIONS (China)

YESTERDAY See PAST, THE

YOUTH See also CHILDREN & CHILDHOOD;
GENERATIONS

The young are permanently in a state resembling intoxication; for youth is sweet and they are growing.
—ARISTOTLE, *Nicomachean Ethics,* 4th cent. B.C.
[See also La Rochefoucauld, below. Aristotle believed that the young are too distractible to benefit from lectures on serious subjects. Shakespeare alluded to this in his reference to "young men," whom Aristotle thought / "Unfit to hear moral philosophy," *Troilus and Cressida,* II, ii.]

Youth is easily deceived because it is quick to hope.
—ARISTOTLE, *Rhetoric,* 4th cent. B.C.

Young men are fitter to invent than to judge, fitter for execution than for counsel, fitter for new projects than settled business.
—FRANCIS BACON, *Of Youth and Age* in *Essays,* 1625

Youth is the pollen
That blows through the sky
And does not ask why. —STEPHEN VINCENT BENÉT,
John Brown's Body, 1928

Rejoice, O young man, in thy youth.
—BIBLE, *Ecclesiastes* 11:9

Youth will be served, every dog has his day, and mine has been a fine one. —GEORGE BORROW, *Lavengro,* 1851

Youth means love.
 —ROBERT BROWNING, *The Ring and the Book,* 1868–69

Youth is like spring, an overpraised season.
 　　　　—SAMUEL BUTLER, *The Way of All Flesh,* 1903

Youth is something very new: twenty years ago, no one mentioned it. 　　　　　　　 —COCO CHANEL, d. 1971, quoted in
 　　　　　　　　　　　Marcel Haedrich, *Coco Chanel,*
 　　　　　　　　　　　Her Life, Her Secrets, 1971

A youth is to be regarded with respect. How do you know that his future will not be equal to our present?
 　　　　—CONFUCIUS, *Analects,* 6th cent. B.C.

Youth is a period of missed opportunities.
 　　　　—CYRIL CONNOLLY, *Journal and Memoir,* 1984

They are not long, the days of wine and roses.
 　　　　—ERNEST DOWSON, *Vitae Summa Brevis*
 　　　　　　Spem Nos Vetat Incohare Longham, 1896
[Dowson died at age 33.]

Youth is the best time to be rich and the best time to be poor. 　　　　 —EURIPIDES, *Heracles,* 422 B.C.

Alas, that Spring should vanish with the Rose!
That Youth's sweet-scented Manuscript should close.
 　　　　—EDWARD FITZGERALD,
 　　　　　The Rubáiyát of Omar Khayyám, 1879

One could do worse than be a swinger of birches.
 　　　　—ROBERT FROST, *Birches,* 1916

Youth's the season made for joys,
Love is then our duty.
 　　　　—JOHN GAY, *The Beggar's Opera,* 1728

Give me back my youth. 　　　—GOETHE, *Faust,* Part I, 1808

No young man believes he shall ever die.
 　　　　—WILLIAM HAZLITT, *On the Feeling of*
 　　　　Immortality in Youth in *Literary Remains,* 1836

Youth is quick in feeling but weak in judgment.
—HOMER, *Iliad,* 8th cent. B.C.

Fugit juventus.
Youth flies. —HORACE, *Epodes,* 30 B.C.

Youth, even in its sorrows, has a brilliance of its own.
—VICTOR HUGO, *Les Misérables,* 1862

Be gentle with the young. —JUVENAL, *Satires,* c. A.D. 100

When all the world is young, lad,
And all the trees are green;
And every goose a swan, lad,
And every lass a queen;
Then hey for boot and horse, lad,
And round the world away:
Young blood must have its course, lad,
And every dog its day.
—CHARLES KINGSLEY, *Water Babies,* 1863

Youth is unending intoxication; it is a fever of the mind.
—LA ROCHEFOUCAULD, *Maxims,* 1678
[He knew his Aristotle; see above.]

A boy's will is the wind's will,
And the thoughts of youth are long, long thoughts.
—HENRY WADSWORTH LONGFELLOW,
My Lost Youth, 1858

It is only an illusion that youth is happy, an illusion of those who have lost it.
—W. SOMERSET MAUGHAM, *Of Human Bondage,* 1915

The American ideal is youth—handsome, empty youth.
—HENRY MILLER, *The Wisdom of the Heart,* 1941

No time to marry, no time to settle down;
I'm a young woman, and I ain't done runnin' around.
—BESSIE SMITH, *Young Woman's Blues,* 1927

Pay attention to the young, and make them just as good as possible. —SOCRATES, 5th cent. B.C.
quoted in Plato, *Euthyphro,* 4th cent. B.C.

Bright youth passes swiftly as a thought.
                              —THEOGNIS, *Elegies,* 6th cent. B.C.

Don't trust anyone over thirty.
    —JACK WEINBERG, interview, *San Francisco Chronicle,*
        c. 1965, cited in the *Washington Post,* Mar. 23, 1970

Bliss it was that dawn to be alive,
But to be young was very heaven!
                              —WILLIAM WORDSWORTH, *The French
                              Revolution as It Appeared to Enthusiasts,* 1809

ZEAL   See ENTHUSIASM, ENERGY, ZEAL

INDEX